Prentice Hall LITERATURE

PENGUIN EDITION

Unit Five
Resources

The American Experience

PEARSON

Upper Saddle River, New Jersey
Boston, Massachusetts
Chandler, Arizona
Glenview, Illinois

Copyright© by Pearson Education, Inc., or its affiliates. All Rights Reserved. Printed in the United States of America. This publication is protected by copyright, and permission should be obtained from the publisher prior to any prohibited reproduction, storage in a retrieval system, or transmission in any form or by any means, electronic, mechanical, photocopying, recording, or likewise. The publisher hereby grants permission to reproduce these pages, in part or in whole, for classroom use only, the number not to exceed the number of students in each class. Notice of copyright must appear on all copies. For information regarding permissions, write to Pearson School Rights & Permissions, One Lake Street, Upper Saddle River, New Jersey 07458.

Pearson® is a trademark, in the U.S. and/or other countries, of Pearson plc or its affiliates.
Prentice Hall® is a trademark, in the U.S. and/or in other countries, of Pearson Education, Inc., or its affiliates.

ISBN-13 978-0-13-366466-9
ISBN-10   0-13-366466-X

3 4 5 6 7 8 9 10 V011 12 11 10

CONTENTS

For information about the Unit Resources, a Pronunciation Guide, and a Form for Analyzing Primary Source Documents, see the opening pages of your Unit One Resources.

from **Hiroshima** by John Hersey

"The Death of the Ball Turret Gunner" by Randall Jarrell

Editorial from the **New York Times, 1943**

Cartoon by Dr. Seuss

Advertisement for Junk Rally or Civil Service

"The Life You Save May Be Your Own" by Flannery O'Connor

"The First Seven Years" by Bernard Malamud

"Constantly Risking Absurdity" by Lawrence Ferlinghetti

"Mirror" by Sylvia Plath

"Courage" by Anne Sexton

"The Rockpile" by James Baldwin

"Life in His Language" by Toni Morrison

Inaugural Address by John F. Kennedy

from Letter From Birmingham City Jail by Dr. Martin Luther King, Jr.

Contemporary Commentary: The Words of Arthur Miller on *The Crucible*

Contemporary Commentary: Arthur Miller Listening and Viewing

The Crucible, *Act I* by Arthur Miller

The Crucible, *Act II* by Arthur Miller

The Crucible, *Act III* by Arthur Miller

The Crucible, *Act IV* by Arthur Miller

from **The Crucible** by Arthur Miller

from **Good Night and Good Luck** by George Clooney and Grant Heslov

Name _____ Starting Date _____ Ending Date _____

Concept Map Unit 5
Prosperity and Protest: Literature of the Post War Era (1945–1970)

Three Essential Questions serve as lenses through which to view the literature—

How does literature shape or reflect society?

Reflected in these selections:

What is the relationship between place and literature?

Reflected in these selections:

What makes American literature American?

Reflected in these selections:

Forms and Movements

- Fiction/Drama
- Lyric Poetry/Voice/Identity
- Essay/Memoir/Anecdote

which are demonstrated in these selections:

Characteristics of the Period and Its Literature

- In the Cold War, political persecution grows and is critiqued in literature.
- The civil and women's rights movements affect every aspect of American life.
- In the 1960s, traditional ideas are questioned, and people rely on the authority of personal experience.

- Writers explore new social realities using familiar techniques.
- As old lifestyles are challenged, writers show the struggle for new meanings.
- Writers address ideas of freedom and oppression, both directly and with irony.
- The lines between high and low art are blurred; writers use language from all walks of life.

which are demonstrated in these selections:

Elements and Techniques

- Foreshadowing/Epiphany
- Grotesque Characters/Static and Dynamic Characters
- Theme/Irony
- Style and Diction/Tone

UNIT 5 STUDENT LOG

VOCABULARY

WRITING & EXTEND YOUR LEARNING

WORKSHOPS

Unit 5 Introduction
Names and Terms to Know

A. DIRECTIONS: *Write a brief sentence explaining each of the following names and terms. You will find all of the information you need in the Unit Introduction in your textbook.*

1. The Cold War: _____

2. The Silent Generation: _____

   _____

3. Sputnik: _____

   _____

4. *The Crucible:* _____

5. John Hersey: _____

6. Martin Luther King, Jr. _____

   _____

B. DIRECTIONS: *Use the hints below to help you answer each question.*

1. Contrast the 1950s and the 1960s. *[Hints: What was the Age of Anxiety, and what caused it? What was the Age of Aquarius, and what caused it?]*

   _____

   _____

   _____

2. What was the effect of suburbia on American life? *[Hints: What brought "suburbia" into existence? What did it replace?]*

   _____

   _____

   _____

3. How did the Civil Rights movement affect American life? *[Hints: What did the Civil Rights movement accomplish? How did these accomplishments affect the lives of African Americans?]*

   _____

   _____

   _____

Name _____ Date _____

Unit 5 Introduction

Essential Question 1: How does literature shape or reflect society?

A. DIRECTIONS: *Answer the questions about the first Essential Question in the Introduction, about the relationship between the writer and society. All the information you need is in the Unit 5 Introduction in your textbook.*

1. *Political and Social Events*

    a. What international conflicts affected life in the 1950s and 1960s? _____
    _____

    b. Two important movements pressing for change in American society were _____
    _____

2. *American Values and Attitudes*

    a. What was the Age of Anxiety, and what did it value? _____
    _____

    b. What was the Age of Aquarius, and what did it value? _____
    _____

3. *These Values and Attitudes in American Literature*

    a. Which writers treated postwar life with irony? _____
    _____

    b. What purposes did writers pursue during this period? _____
    _____

    c. List examples of pop culture favorites in the 1950s and 1960s. _____
    _____

B. DIRECTIONS: *Complete the sentence stems that include the Essential Question Vocabulary words.*

1. Adele's *conformity* to her friends' choices kept her from _____

2. D.B.'s *anxiety* about college acceptance led him to _____

3. Her friends value Jeanie's *idealism* because _____

Name _____ Date _____

Unit 5 Introduction

Essential Question 2: What makes American literature American?

A. DIRECTIONS: *On the lines provided, answer the questions about the second Essential Question in the Introduction, about what makes American literature American. All the information you need is in the Unit 5 Introduction in your textbook.*

1. *Themes Expressed by American Writers*

   a. What questions did writers in the prosperous 1950s raise about the American Dream? _____

   b. How was the rebellion in the 1960s different from that of the American Revolution? _____

   c. How did the issue of race affect the writing of the period? _____
   _____

2. *Roles Played by American Writers*

   a. How did writers assume the role of "Witness" during this period? _____
   _____

   b. How did writers assume the role of "Nonconformist" during this period? _____
   _____

   c. How did writers assume the role of "Standard-Bearer" during this period? _____
   _____

3. *Building on the Past*

   a. Give examples of writers who used events from American history to illuminate the present. _____

   b. Which writers kept earlier forms and styles alive, and how? _____
   _____

   c. Which writers further developed the style of Modernism? _____
   _____

B. DIRECTIONS: *Complete the following sentence stems that include the Essential Question Vocabulary word.*

1. The Bronsons's new *prosperity* allowed them to _____

2. One way to create a new *identity* for yourself is to _____

3. Drew's *alienation* from his friends was caused by _____

4

Unit 5 Introduction

Essential Question 3: What is the relationship between place and literature?

A. DIRECTIONS: *On the lines provided, answer the questions about the third Essential Question in the Introduction, about the relationship between place and literature. All the information you need is in the Unit 5 Introduction in your textbook.*

1. *Wartime Settings*

    a. Which writers wrote about their World War II experiences? _____
_____

    b. How did post–World War II writing differ from the writing that arose after World War I?
_____

2. *Urban Life*

    a. Novels and plays that took place in cities included works by _____
_____

    b. How did the image of the city influence American poetry? _____
_____

3. *Growth of Suburbia and American Literature*

    a. The suburbs offered the middle class _____
_____

    b. What less than rosy view of the American Dream emerged at this time, and which writers expressed this view? _____
_____

B. DIRECTIONS: *Complete the sentence stems based on the Essential Question Vocabulary words.*

    1. In our family, *discord* always arises when _____

    2. The *destruction* of our old town library led to _____

    3. Life in *suburbia* is different from life "out in the country" because _____
_____

Unit 5 Introduction

Following-Through Activities

A. CHECK YOUR COMPREHENSION: *Use this chart to complete the Check Your Comprehension activity in the Unit 5 Introduction. In the middle boxes, fill in two key concepts for each Essential Question. Then in the right box, fill in a key author for each key concept. One key concept for Literature and Society is completed for you.*

Place and Imagination	Key Concept	Key Author
Place and Imagination	1. 2.	1. 2.
American Literature	1. 2.	1. 2.
Literature and Society	1. Individuality and nonconformity 2.	1. Lawrence Ferlinghetti 2.

B. EXTEND YOUR LEARNING: *Use this graphic organizer to plan and conduct your interview for the Extend Your Learning activity. (Q = Question; A = Answer).*

INTERVIEW SUBJECT: _____

Q: *What were your reactions to the assassinations of President John F. Kennedy and Martin Luther King, Jr.?*

A: _____
_____

Q: *What social issues captured your imagination in those years?*

A: _____
_____

Q: *What was school like in the 1960s?*

A: _____
_____

Q: *What songs, movies, and TV shows did you enjoy? What books meant the most to you?*

A: _____
_____
_____

Q: *What public figures did you admire?*

A: _____
_____

Q: *How do you think America has changed since that time?*

A: _____
_____
_____

Vocabulary Warm-up Word Lists

Study these words from the selections. Then, complete the activities.

Word List A

commercial [kuh MER shuhl] *adj.* relating to the buying and selling of goods
There are many shops in this <u>commercial</u> building.

commuting [kuh MYOOT ing] *v.* traveling regularly between places
Dad is <u>commuting</u> by train to work every day.

conjunction [kuhn JUNGK shuhn] *n.* the state of being joined or combined
In <u>conjunction</u> with the hospital, Ms. Ellis is teaching a course on nutrition.

obsessed [uhb SESD] *v.* totally or highly concerned with something; preoccupied greatly
Marcus was <u>obsessed</u> with reaching the highest level of the video game.

proprietor [pruh PRY uh ter] *n.* person who owns and manages a business
As the <u>proprietor</u>, Mr. Green decides when to open and close the store.

reluctantly [ri LUK tuhnt lee] *adv.* unwillingly
Liz <u>reluctantly</u> gave up her seat.

rendezvous [RAHN day voo] *n.* a meeting set up for a specific time or place
We set up a <u>rendezvous</u> with Carla opposite the stationery store.

residential [rez uh DEN shuhl] *adj.* of or relating to dwelling places
No offices are permitted in this <u>residential</u> building.

Word List B

abstinence [AB stuh nuhns] *n.* act of voluntarily doing without
Carl believes that <u>abstinence</u> from smoking contributes to a healthy lifestyle.

burrowing [BER oh ing] *v.* making a hole or tunnel by digging
The rabbits were <u>burrowing</u> under the field.

comprised [kuhm PRYZD] *v.* consisting of; composed of; included
<u>Comprised</u> of two fields, a barn, and a modest house, this is a small farm.

dwindled [DWIN duhld] *v.* became gradually less; diminished
During the winter, the hay supply gradually <u>dwindled</u> to almost nothing.

evacuate [ee VAK yoo ayt] *v.* to withdraw from an area
In the event of a hurricane, you may be asked to <u>evacuate</u> your home.

incessant [in SES uhnt] *adj.* continuing in a way that seems endless
The child's <u>incessant</u> questions wear me out.

prosperous [PRAHS puhr uhs] *adj.* successful; well-off
The <u>prosperous</u> Billings family founded Billings Academy.

restraint [ri STRAYNT] *n.* act of holding back
Melissa exercised <u>restraint</u> in the bakery even though she wanted a cookie.

from **"Hiroshima"** by John Hersey
Vocabulary Warm-up Exercises

Exercise A *Fill in the blanks, using each word from Word List A only once.*

My dad is the [1] _____ of a small business, a delicatessen. Located on the ground floor of a [2] _____ high-rise apartment building, the deli is seldom quiet from morning to night. Customers who are [3] _____ to work buy sandwiches and drinks as early as 5:30 A.M. Later on, the deli serves as a convenient [4] _____ spot, where the neighborhood lunch crowd meets. Last summer, Dad asked me to work at the deli part-time. I agreed only [5] _____, because I thought it would be hard, as the boss's son, to make friends. I was mistaken, though. In [6] _____ with the other employees, I learned a lot about how a small [7] _____ enterprise operates. I understand now why my dad is so [8] _____ with all the details of the business, as everything is important.

Exercise B *Revise each sentence so that the underlined vocabulary word is used in a logical way. Be sure to keep the vocabulary word in your revision.*

Example: Because the offer was so *advantageous*, we declined it firmly.
Because the offer was so <u>advantageous</u>, we eagerly accepted it.

1. Breaking her diet, Janice began a period of <u>abstinence</u> from cheese and ice cream.
   _____

2. Our reports were supposed to be <u>comprised</u> of five sections, so I only included one section.
   _____

3. As sales continued to improve, the company's revenues <u>dwindled</u>.
   _____

4. We obeyed the order to <u>evacuate</u> our house and remained there during the storm.
   _____

5. The noise from the traffic was <u>incessant</u>, making it easy to concentrate on my homework.
   _____

6. To bask in the sun, the dog was <u>burrowing</u> in the ground.
   _____

7. From his ragged suit of clothes, we could tell that he was extremely <u>prosperous</u>.
   _____

8. A basketball player who exercises <u>restraint</u> will commit lots of fouls on the opponents.
   _____

Name _____ Date _____

from "Hiroshima" by John Hersey
Reading Warm-up A

Read the following passage. Then, complete the activities.

In the annals of historic days, the date August 6, 1945, will always be remembered. That morning, the first atomic weapon exploded over the Japanese city of Hiroshima. The atomic bomb was the product of a top-secret program called the Manhattan Project. This program involved scientists working in <u>conjunction</u> with military leaders as a team for three years.

Work on the Manhattan Project was carried out in strict secrecy all over the United States. This work took place in large cities as well as in remote, rural areas. Secret laboratories were built far away from any <u>residential</u> areas where people lived. At the time, a <u>proprietor</u> of a small business in someplace like Tampa or Chicago could be <u>commuting</u> every day, traveling to the store he or she owned, per usual. He or she had no way of knowing that at the same time some of the world's top scientists were researching how to build an atom bomb.

Some of the scientists in the Manhattan Project participated only <u>reluctantly</u>. They had reservations because they knew that the destructive power of an atomic bomb would be immense. During World War II, the peacetime uses and <u>commercial</u> benefits of atomic energy, such as buying and selling nuclear power for energy, were unknown. The race was on to build a bomb for military uses. The U.S. government was <u>obsessed</u> with being the first to do so, before Germany or the Soviet Union, countries also fixated on building an atomic bomb.

Finally, a field test was scheduled for the bomb. The <u>rendezvous</u> point where scientists, engineers, and military leaders met was an air base at Alamogordo, New Mexico. There, at 5:30 A.M. on July 16, 1945—exactly three weeks before Hiroshima—the first atomic bomb was exploded. The Manhattan Project had succeeded in its goals.

1. Circle the words in this sentence that tell who was working in <u>conjunction</u>. What is a synonym for *conjunction*?

2. Circle the words in this sentence that offer a clue to the meaning of <u>residential</u>. What kind of building would you be likely to find in *residential* areas?

3. Underline the words in this sentence that give a clue to the meaning of <u>proprietor</u>. What is a synonym for *proprietor*?

4. Underline the word that gives a clue to the meaning of <u>commuting</u>. What might people use for *commuting*?

5. Underline the words in the next sentence that hint at the meaning of <u>reluctantly</u>. What is a word that means the opposite of *reluctantly*?

6. Circle the words in this sentence that hint at the meaning of <u>commercial</u>. Use the word *commercial* in an original sentence.

7. Tell what the U.S. government was <u>obsessed</u> with being. Name something you are or have been *obsessed* with.

8. Underline the words in this sentence that give a clue to the meaning of <u>rendezvous</u>. Is a *rendezvous* usually planned in advance, or is it spontaneous?

Name _____ Date _____

from **"Hiroshima"** by John Hersey
Reading Warm-up B

Read the following passage. Then, complete the activities.

Because he was dreaming, Peter couldn't know that the destruction all around him was only imaginary. The dream began with a horrific pounding on his door, which soon burst open to reveal a group of soldiers who had come to <u>evacuate</u> him from the burning building.

"Let's go," they said, pulling him up by the wrists and forcing him out of the window to the fire escape.

Outside, the view <u>comprised</u> ruined buildings, smoke, and panicked people running. Bombs kept repeatedly exploding in the distance, making an <u>incessant</u> booming and rumbling. Peter's formerly <u>prosperous</u> street, with its successful shops and popular restaurants, was diminishing before his eyes—it had now <u>dwindled</u> to a row of crumbling bricks and smoke. The enemy had shown no <u>restraint</u> in its efforts to demolish the city, unleashing a seemingly unlimited number of bombs.

The soldiers hurried him down the chaotic street to a bomb shelter they had built, <u>burrowing</u> beneath a movie theater. Inside, more than a hundred people had already occupied the cave-like space. A few wounded lay on cots, but most simply sat on the floor. The lack of chairs and the dimness inside the shelter gave it a strange feeling of unreality.

"What could possibly be worth all this destruction?" said an old man, looking Peter in the eye with a frightening gaze. Then another explosion shook the earth and it felt for a moment as if the shelter's ceiling would collapse on their heads.

That was when Peter woke up from the dream, terrified and covered with sweat. He vowed <u>abstinence</u> from late-night pizza from that day forward, promising himself to stick to a nice warm glass of milk instead.

1. Underline the words in this sentence that tell from what the soldiers would <u>evacuate</u> Peter. What is a synonym for *evacuate*?

2. Circle the words in this sentence that tell what the view <u>comprised</u>. What are two synonyms for *comprised*?

3. Underline the words in this sentence that hint at the meaning of <u>incessant</u>. Give a word that means the opposite of *incessant*

4. Underline the words in this sentence that hint at what made his street <u>prosperous</u>. What are two antonyms of *prosperous*?

5. Circle the word in this sentence that has a similar meaning to <u>dwindled</u>. Use a word meaning the opposite of *dwindled* in a sentence of your own.

6. Circle the words in this sentence telling in what way the enemy had shown no <u>restraint</u>. What is a synonym for *restraint*?

7. Underline the word in this sentence that hints at the meaning of <u>burrowing</u>. Give a word or phrase that means the same as *burrowing*.

8. Circle the words that tell what Peter vowed <u>abstinence</u> from. Give a word that means the opposite of *abstinence*.

from **Hiroshima** by John Hersey
"The Death of the Ball Turret Gunner" by Randall Jarrell
Literary Analysis: Implied Theme

The **theme** is the central idea or message about life that a writer conveys in a literary work. A writer will rarely state a theme outright. Often theme is stated indirectly, or **implied,** through the writer's portrayal of characters and events, use of literary devices, and choice of details.

To understand theme, notice whether or not the narrator presents personal feelings. Your analysis can help you identify the **author's perspective,** the point of view from which a work is written. Works can be objective, subjective, or a mixture of both.

DIRECTIONS: *For each of the following excerpts from* Hiroshima *and "The Death of the Ball Turret Gunner," (a) identify whether the author's perspective is objective or subjective and explain why, and (b) briefly explain what theme is implied in the excerpt.*

from Hiroshima

1. The Reverend Mr. Tanimoto got up at five o'clock that morning. He was alone in the parsonage, because for some time his wife had been commuting with their year-old baby to spend nights with a friend in Ushida, a-suburb to the north. Of all the important cities of Japan, only two, Kyoto and Hiroshima, had not been visited in strength by *B-san,* or Mr. B, as the Japanese, with a mixture of respect and unhappy familiarity, called the B-29; and Mr. Tanimoto, like all his neighbors and friends, was almost sick with anxiety.

   a. Perspective—subjective or objective? Why? _____

   _____

   b. Implied theme: _____

   _____

2. The ceiling dropped suddenly and the wooden floor above collapsed in splinters and the people up there came down and the roof above them gave way; but principally and first of all, the bookcases right behind her swooped forward and the contents threw her down. . . . There, in the tin factory, in the first moment of the atomic age, a human being was crushed by books.

   a. Perspective—subjective or objective? Why? _____

   _____

   b. Implied theme: _____

   _____

"The Death of the Ball Turret Gunner"

3. Six miles from earth, loosed from its dream of life,/I woke to black flak and the nightmare fighters./When I died they washed me out of the turret with a hose.

   a. Perspective—subjective or objective? Why? _____

   _____

   b. Implied theme: _____

   _____

from **Hiroshima** by John Hersey
"The Death of the Ball Turret Gunner" by Randall Jarrell
Reading Strategy: Analyze Political Assumptions

When a writer addresses a historical topic, he or she often brings a clearly stated or implied political viewpoint to the events being recounted. It is therefore useful to **analyze the political assumptions** that each writer makes—in this case, about the nature of war in general and World War II in particular.

DIRECTIONS: *In the following chart, record details, descriptions of characters, and literary devices that strike you as significant and that help to reveal the political ideas of the writer of each selection. Then, summarize the author's political assumptions about war in general and World War II in particular that those details reveal.*

Selection	Details/Events and Characters/Literary Devices	Author's Political Assumptions
from Hiroshima		
"The Death of the Ball Turret Gunner"		

from **Hiroshima** by John Hersey
"The Death of the Ball Turret Gunner" by Randall Jarrell
Vocabulary Builder

Words from Other Languages

A rendezvous was originally a place for assembling of military troops. The word comes from the French words *rendez vous*, meaning "present yourself." Many other words related to the military and warfare have their origins in other languages.

A. DIRECTIONS: *Fill in the blanks with the most appropriate word from the following list of military words that are derived from other languages.*

barricade   blitz   coup   khaki   reconnaissance

1. As our unit approached our objective, we found that we had to climb over an elaborate steel and wooden _____ that had been built by the enemy to thwart our advance.

2. Once our unit was ready to advance again, we sent two soldiers ahead to conduct _____ on the enemy's positions and manpower.

3. To conceal the movements of our troops in the lush vegetation, we wore green camouflage uniforms instead of the usual _____ ones.

4. At all times we surveyed the skies to keep on the lookout for an unexpected _____ by enemy bombers.

5. In an unexpected _____ of good fortune, we found that the enemy troops had abandoned their positions and fled before we reached our objective.

Using the Word List

convivial   evacuated   incessant   rendezvous   volition

B. DIRECTIONS: *For each Word List word, choose the word or phrase that is most* similar *in meaning. Circle the letter of your choice.*

1. evacuated:
   A. departed   B. replenished   C. canceled   D. ended

2. volition:
   A. unwillingness   B. resolution   C. will   D. speed

3. rendezvous:
   A. meeting   B. dance   C. song   D. tradition

4. incessant:
   A. hopeless   B. constant   C. violent   D. clear

5. convivial:
   A. reluctant   B. angry   C. sociable   D. conflicting

from **Hiroshima** by John Hersey
"The Death of the Ball Turret Gunner" by Randall Jarrell
Support for Writing

Both John Hersey and Randall Jarrell present powerful messages about war, but in different ways. Each author has a unique perspective and method for conveying his views and feelings about the experience and consequences of warfare. Write an essay in which you **compare and contrast** each author's views of war and the ways in which they communicate those views. Cite examples from *Hiroshima* and Jarrell's poem to support your analysis.

Before you begin to compare and contrast, review each author's work separately. Try to summarize the basic message about war that each author presents. Then begin your comparison by looking for key similarities and differences. Arrive at a solid overall evaluation before you begin to draft. As an aid in preparing your draft, answer the following questions about the selections.

1. Are the authors' messages about war similar or different? Explain your answer. (This thesis will be the guiding focus for your paper. As you write, refer back to your thesis to be sure you are staying on topic.)

   _____

   _____

   _____

   _____

2. How do the authors' methods of presenting their messages differ? Are the methods the same in any respects?

   _____

   _____

   _____

   _____

3. What are some key quotations from each work that illustrate the author's message about war?
   from *Hiroshima*:

   _____

   _____

   _____

   _____

   "The Death of the Ball Turret Gunner":

   _____

   _____

   _____

   _____

Once you have gathered these details, use them to begin writing a first draft of your comparison-and-contrast essay.

Name _____ Date _____

Enrichment: Ethics of Warfare

In *Hiroshima*, John Hersey writes of a devastating atomic bomb dropped on Hiroshima, Japan, near the end of World War II. The bomb vaporized everything in its immediate vicinity and killed about one hundred thousand people. Three days later, the United States dropped a second bomb in Japan, on the city of Nagasaki. Another one hundred thousand people were killed. As these examples illustrate, war affects not only soldiers but also civilians, who suffer bombings, abuse, and the destruction of their homes. Incidents like these force people to wonder what ethics, or moral standards, should be followed during times of war.

After World War II, the Geneva Conventions—international treaties created in 1864 to protect basic human rights during war—attempted to deal with this issue. The treaties were revised to provide for the ethical treatment of prisoners of war and civilians. According to the new treaty, civilians are protected from torture, violations of human dignity, deportation, group punishments, and discrimination based on race, religion, or nationality.

DIRECTIONS: *Answer each of the following questions.*

1. Why do you think people need to follow certain moral standards during times of war? Why do you think basic human rights are often violated in warfare?

   _____

   _____

2. The United States dropped the two atomic bombs on Japan in an attempt to get Japan to surrender so that World War II would end. The second bomb in Nagasaki did prompt Japan to surrender. Do you think the United States was right or wrong to cause such devastation? Explain your response. Why might reading the selection from *Hiroshima* influence a person's opinion on this issue?

   _____

   _____

   _____

   _____

   _____

   _____

   _____

   _____

   _____

Name _____ Date _____

from **Hiroshima** by John Hersey and
"**The Death of the Ball Turret Gunner**" by Randall Jarrell
Open-Book Test

Short Answer *Write your responses to the questions in this section on the lines provided.*

1. How would you describe the mood of the people in Hiroshima during the time before the bomb drops? Cite evidence from the story to support your answer.

   _____

   _____

   _____

   _____

2. Mr. Tanimoto was 3,500 yards from the center of the explosion. Mrs. Nakamura was 1,350 yards away. Why do you think Hersey specifies so precisely where each person was in relation to the explosion of the bomb that was dropped on Hiroshima?

   _____

   _____

   _____

3. What theme or message is implied in the opening paragraph of *Hiroshima*, with its description of the lives of ordinary people going about their business on a typical working day?

   _____

   _____

   _____

4. *Hiroshima* focuses on the impact of an atomic-bomb explosion on the lives of ordinary people. What kind of political or social observation do you think Hersey is making about the nature of World War II in particular, and modern warfare in general?

   _____

   _____

   _____

5. As a journalist, Hersey spent a great deal of time in East Asia. What effect do you think the time he spent with the people of this region had on his overall political view of the bombing of Hiroshima?

   _____

   _____

   _____

   _____

6. Use the graphic organizer below to help you make inferences about the theme of the excerpt from *Hiroshima*. In the left-hand column of boxes, list details, events, characters, and literary devices that carry importance in Hersey's writing. Then, in the middle column, make inferences about them. Use the inferences to help you state the implied theme.

Details	Inference	Implied Theme
Events	Inference	
Characters	Inference	
Literary Devices	Inference	

7. Hersey was assigned to write articles for news publications, but he wrote *Hiroshima* of his own volition. Does that mean he wrote *Hiroshima* because he was ordered to or because he wanted to? Base your response on the meaning of *volition* as it is used in *Hiroshima*.

_____

_____

8. In your own words, state what happens to the speaker of "The Death of the Ball Turret Gunner."

_____

_____

_____

9. What theme is implied by the fact that Jarrell chose to write about a gunner rather than any other type of soldier in "The Death of the Ball Turret Gunner"?

_____

_____

_____

10. What theme is implied by this line from "The Death of the Ball Turret Gunner"?

When I died they washed me out of the turret with a hose.

_____

_____

Essay

Write an extended response to the question of your choice or to the question or questions your teacher assigns you.

11. In the excerpt from *Hiroshima*, Hersey describes the impact of the explosion several times, each time from the point of view of a different victim of the blast. Why do you think Hersey chose this technique? What effect does it have on the reader? Address these questions in an essay supported by details from the selection.

12. In an essay, discuss what the excerpt from *Hiroshima* directly reveals or implies about John Hersey's attitude toward war in general and the bombing of Hiroshima in particular. Support your answer with details from the story.

13. In an essay, compare and contrast the content and themes of *Hiroshima* and "The Death of the Ball Turret Gunner." In what ways are they similar? In what ways are they different? Develop your thoughts in an essay supported by examples from the selections.

14. **Thinking About the Essential Question: How does literature shape or reflect society?** Both of these selections—the excerpt from Hiroshima and "The Death of the Ball Turret Gunner"—present harsh and unvarnished portraits of the realities of modern war. Do these selections simply reflect the realities of war, or do they also seek to shape the reader's attitude toward war? Develop your answer in an essay supported by details from the selections.

Oral Response

15. Go back to question 2, 3, or 5 or to the question your teacher assigns to you. Take a few minutes to expand your answer and prepare an oral response. Find additional details in *Hiroshima* or "The Death of the Ball Turret Gunner" that support your points. If necessary, make notes to guide your oral response.

from **Hiroshima** by John Hersey
"The Death of the Ball Turret Gunner" by Randall Jarrell
Selection Test A

Critical Reading *Identify the letter of the choice that best answers the question.*

_____ 1. Who are the people described in this selection from *Hiroshima*?
   A. generals and other military planners
   B. ordinary parents and workers
   C. soldiers prepared to die for Japan
   D. the political leaders of Japan

_____ 2. What message is expressed in *Hiroshima's* opening paragraph, which describes the lives of ordinary people going about their day?
   A. Whether one lives or dies in a war is based on chance.
   B. War makes communities pull together to help one another.
   C. No one ever recovers from the effects of war.
   D. Cities at war should prepare for attack at any time.

_____ 3. In *Hiroshima*, who or what is represented by the four ordinary people whose stories are told?
   A. enemies of America
   B. Japanese people
   C. people who were affected by the bombing
   D. the lives of the most important people

_____ 4. Why did many people in Hiroshima believe their city was to be a target, according to *Hiroshima*?
   A. The city was well prepared and defended.
   B. The city had not had a major attack and expected one.
   C. The city was a major center for weapons research.
   D. The city was full of soldiers training to go to war.

_____ 5. What theme is suggested in *Hiroshima*, based on the writer's decision to show what people were doing at 8:15 A.M.?
   A. Hard workers are most likely to survive a terrible catastrophe.
   B. People deal with national tragedy in different ways.
   C. Ordinary life can be shattered by an extraordinary event.
   D. During wartime, people must be ready to leave their homes.

_____ 6. What is the theme of *Hiroshima*, based on this description of each survivor's experience: "he lived a dozen lives and saw more death than he ever thought he would see"?

A. Those who survive have experienced both life and death.

B. Survivors feel guilty and have a hard time going on with life.

C. Doctors see more death than others.

D. Atom bombs have changed the world.

_____ 7. Based on Hersey's focus on the lives of ordinary people in *Hiroshima*, the reader can conclude that Hersey is mainly concerned about the impact of modern warfare on

A. large nations

B. the economy

C. civilians

D. urban life

_____ 8. *Hiroshima* and "The Death of the Ball Turret Gunner" express indignation about which aspect of modern warfare?

A. its huge expense

B. its indifference to individual human life

C. its promotion of mindless patriotism

D. its need to impose economic sacrifices

_____ 9. In "The Death of the Ball Turret Gunner," to what does the gunner in the small, tight space of a bomber compare himself?

A. an animal in its mother's womb

B. a soldier in an open plane

C. a baby sleeping in its crib

D. a warrior flying through the air

_____ 10. What happens to the gunnet in "The Death of the Ball Turret Gunner"?

A. He dies.

B. He parachutes to safety.

C. He climbs out of the turret.

D. He becomes a poet.

Vocabulary

_____ 11. Which word best replaces *incessant* in this sentence: "The sirens would not stop their *incessant* noise"?
   A. hurried
   B. constant
   C. pleasant
   D. friendly

_____ 12. Which word is most nearly OPPOSITE in meaning to *convivial*?
   A. grim
   B. thoughtful
   C. disrespectful
   D. punctual

Essay

13. In *Hiroshima*, why does the writer describe the blast several times, each time from the point of view of a different person? What effect does this have on the reader? Write a brief essay to address these questions.

14. Try to imagine yourself in the situation of the soldier in "The Death of the Ball Turrett Gunner." Expand on the thoughts and feelings expressed indirectly in the poem. What are your surroundings like? Are you afraid? Focused on your task? Thinking about other people in your life? Develop your expanded prose portrait of the ball turret gunner in an essay supported by vivid descriptive details.

15. **Thinking About the Essential Question: How does literature shape or reflect society?** Both of these selections—the excerpt from Hiroshima and "The Death of the Ball Turret Gunner"—present harsh and unvarnished portraits of the realities of modern war. Do these selections simply reflect the realities of war, or do they also seek to shape the reader's attitude toward war? Develop your answer in an essay supported by details from the selections.

from **Hiroshima** by John Hersey
"The Death of the Ball Turret Gunner" by Randall Jarrell
Selection Test B

Critical Reading *Identify the letter of the choice that best completes the statement or answers the question.*

_____ 1. What is the best way to describe how the people in *Hiroshima* are feeling in the days and hours preceding the atomic bomb explosion?
A. calm
B. uneasy
C. riotous
D. hopeful

_____ 2. In *Hiroshima*, what is the main reason John Hersey provides so many details about the activities of people in Hiroshima in the hours before the bomb was dropped?
A. to lengthen his story
B. to give readers insight into their lives, which have been disrupted by the war
C. to entertain readers
D. to show how people in the community interact with one another

_____ 3. What might you infer about the theme of *Hiroshima* from the following passage?
They still wonder why they lived when so many others died. Each of them counts many small items of chance or volition—a step taken in time, a decision to go indoors, catching one streetcar instead of the next—that spared him.

A. The theme deals with the idea that some people are much more fortunate than others.
B. The theme deals with the idea that people are safe only inside their homes.
C. The theme deals with the cruel and random destruction caused by the bomb.
D. The theme deals with the different ways in which people deal with tragedy.

_____ 4. What theme is implied in the following passage from *Hiroshima*?
. . . but undoubtedly she also felt a generalized, community, pity, to say nothing of self-pity. She had not had an easy time. Her husband, Isawa, had gone into the Army just after Myeko was born, and she heard nothing from or of him for a long time, until, on March 5, 1942, she received a seven-word telegram: "Isawa died an honorable death at Singapore."

A. that it is dangerous to be a soldier
B. that war cruelly and coldly destroys the lives of individuals
C. how different people deal with self-pity
D. that fathers should not be soldiers

_____ 5. Who is the speaker in "The Death of the Ball Turret Gunner"?
A. the state
B. the soldier
C. the plane
D. the soldier's family

_____ 6. Which of the following images from *Hiroshima* is ironic?
   A. Dr. Fujii sat down cross-legged in his underwear on the spotless matting of the porch, put on his glasses, and started reading the Osaka *Asahi.*
   B. There, in the tin factory, in the first moment of the atomic age, a human being was crushed by books.
   C. Mrs. Nakamura went back to the kitchen, looked at the rice, and began watching the man next door.
   D. Mr. Tanimoto is a small man, quick to talk, laugh, and cry. He wore his black hair parted in the middle and rather long . . .

_____ 7. In *Hiroshima,* why does Hersey describe over and over the moment of the bomb's explosion, each time from a different person's perspective?
   A. to add a level of suspense to the piece
   B. so that people can understand the terror felt by individuals at that moment
   C. to show how people handle themselves under stress
   D. so that people can see which structures withstood the explosion and which did not

_____ 8. Both *Hiroshima* and "The Death of the Ball Turret Gunner" can be seen as expressing which view of modern warfare?
   A. disgust at the huge, wasteful expense
   B. indignation at the indifference to individual human life
   C. admiration for the efficiency of modern technology
   D. criticism of the abstract ideologies that drive nations to war

_____ 9. Read this line from "The Death of the Ball Turret Gunner." The term "the State" is a symbol for what key aspect of the poem?

   From my mother's sleep I fell into the State. . . .

   A. the soldier
   B. the plane and the whole machinery of war
   C. the ideal of democracy for which the soldier is fighting
   D. the mental confusion the soldier experiences while firing his guns

_____ 10. In "The Death of the Ball Turret Gunner," what woke the speaker when he was six miles from earth?
   A. enemy antiaircraft fire
   B. the sound of a hose
   C. the voice of his pilot
   D. the engine of the plane

_____ 11. In "The Death of the Ball Turret Gunner," to what does the gunner compare the ball turret in which he sits?
   A. a cloud
   B. a dream
   C. a womb
   D. black flak

____ 12. In "The Death of the Ball Turret Gunner," what is thematically significant about the fact that Jarrell chose to write about a gunner rather than any other type of soldier?
   A. The gunner sat in a glass sphere beneath a World War II aircraft.
   B. The gunner's sole function was to shoot at aircraft, so he constantly confronted death.
   C. The gunner fired his gun from an upside-down position.
   D. The gunner constantly thought of his mother.

____ 13. What is implied by this line in "The Death of the Ball Turret Gunner"?
   When I died they washed me out of the turret with a hose.
   A. It is difficult to remove someone from a turret.
   B. People grieved for the gunner.
   C. Treatment of the gunner's body is cold and inhuman.
   D. The gunner died nobly.

Vocabulary

____ 14. Which is the best meaning of *rendezvous* as used in the line ". . . for at that time the B-29s were using Lake Biwa, northeast of Hiroshima, as a rendezvous point . . ."?
   A. resting place
   B. destruction zone
   C. communication
   D. meeting place

____ 15. Which word is most nearly OPPOSITE in meaning to *incessant*?
   A. beautiful
   B. sporadic
   C. confined
   D. efficient

Essay

16. At the end of "The Death of the Ball Turret Gunner," Jarrell writes, "When I died they washed me out of the turret with a hose." In an essay, discuss the theme that is expressed in this line. Support your answer with details from the poem.

17. In an essay, explain John Hersey's attitude toward war and the bombing of Hiroshima. What details provided in the story reveal his attitude?

18. In an essay, compare and contrast the selection from *Hiroshima* and "The Death of the Ball Turret Gunner." What different points of view do the two pieces present? In what ways are they thematically similar?

19. **Thinking About the Essential Question: How does literature shape or reflect society?** Both of these selections—the excerpt from Hiroshima and "The Death of the Ball Turret Gunner"—present harsh and unvarnished portraits of the realities of modern war. Do these selections simply reflect the realities of war, or do they also seek to shape the reader's attitude toward war? Develop your answer in an essay supported by details from the selections.

Name _____ Date _____

Editorial: "Backing the Attack"
Editorial Cartoon: "The Battle of the Easy Chair"
Advertisement Poster: "Junk Rally"
Primary Sources Worksheet

The three selections in this grouping are all concerned with the same topic: winning World War II. Each uses methods unique to its form in order to persuade the reader or viewer to think or act a certain way. These methods include visual elements, verbal elements, and persuasive techniques (logical and emotional appeals).

DIRECTIONS: *Use the table below to identify and compare the methods used in the primary source selections. Some boxes may be blank.*

	Editorial	**Editorial Cartoon**	**Poster**
Thesis (stated or implied main idea)			
Facts and figures			
Visual elements			
Humor			
Quotations			
Catchy phrases			
Appeal to emotion			
Appeal to logic			

Unit 5 Resources: Prosperity and Protest
25

Editorial: "Backing the Attack"
Editorial Cartoon: "The Battle of the Easy Chair"
Advertisement Poster: "Junk Rally"
Vocabulary Builder

Using the Word List

canvass   civilian   collective   estimates

expenditures   license   receipts   undertaking

A. DIRECTIONS: *Answer each questions with an explanation that clarifies the meaning of the word in italics.*

1. If you behaved with *license* at a party, is it likely that you offended someone?

_____

2. Is a serious *undertaking* something a lazy person would welcome?

_____

3. To *canvass* a neighborhood, would one person or a team of five be better?

_____

4. If a hundred people let out a *collective* sigh, would it take longer than one person sighing?

_____

5. What are some *expenditures* you have over the course of a week?

_____

6. Are *estimates* of a home's value usually the precise price it would sell for?

_____

7. Do a company's *receipts* represent its income or its costs?

_____

8. Would a *civilian* be likely to wear a military uniform?

_____

B. DIRECTIONS: *Circle the letter of the word that best completes each analogy.*

1. expenditures : costs : : undertaking :
   A. difficulty   B. endeavor   C. overtaking   D. winning
2. estimates : precise : : license :
   A. wild   B. strict   C. loose   D. expensive
3. civilian : military : : collective :
   A. grouped   B. rich   C. lengthy   D. single
4. receipts : income : : canvass :
   A. solicit   B. run   C. travel   D. oilcloth

Editorial, Cartoon, and Poster: Primary Sources
Selection Test

MULTIPLE CHOICE *Choose the letter of the response that best answers each question.*

_____ 1. What is the main purpose of the newspaper editorial, "Backing the Attack"?

A. to persuade Americans to buy war bonds in order to support the armed forces

B. to inform readers about the time and location of a victory parade

C. to urge the U.S. government to step up its efforts against the enemy

D. to argue that war supplies are too expensive

_____ 2. Which of the following explains why a newspaper editorial like "Backing the Attack" is a primary source?

A. It reflects the opinions of a publication's editor or editorial board.

B. It reflects opinions as they were held at the same time that important historical events occurred.

C. It reflects the opinions of a majority of citizens.

D. It has been classified as a primary source by historians.

_____ 3. In "Backing the Attack," why do you think the authors of the editorial included so many facts and figures?

A. to show that they had reliable sources in the War Department

B. to persuade the public that people could support the war effort on a wide variety of levels

C. to compare and contrast buying a parachute with manufacturing a bomb-sight

D. to impress readers with the amount of money necessary to finance the war

_____ 4. In "Backing the Attack," why do you think the editorial begins with a quotation from President Franklin D. Roosevelt's speech?

A. to report the news of Italy's surrender for the first time

B. to show that President Roosevelt misunderstood General Eisenhower's announcement

C. to hint that war bonds might become increasingly unnecessary

D. to add extra urgency to the persuasive appeal in the main part of the editorial

_____ 5. Which of the following statements is accurate about an editorial cartoon such as "The Battle of the Easy Chair"?

A. It always displays a sarcastic tone.

B. It presents both sides of a controversial or debatable issue.

C. It combines visual and verbal elements.

D. It always has a caption.

Name _____ Date _____

___ 6. In "The Battle of the Easy Chair," what might the flags and buttons pinned to the clothing of the man in the chair symbolize?
   A. a fashion statement
   B. patriotic feeling
   C. a high military rank
   D. membership in the gentlemen's club

___ 7. Which of the following was most likely Dr. Seuss's main purpose in the cartoon, "The Battle of the Easy Chair"?
   A. to persuade large numbers of Americans to buy war bonds
   B. to poke fun of the snobbery that was typical of gentlemen's clubs
   C. to persuade viewers that this was no time to be smug or complacent about the war
   D. to inform viewers that victory parades were a daily fact of life at the time

___ 8. Why is a poster advertisement such as "Junk Rally" a valuable primary source for the World War II period in American life?
   A. The poster shows that most Americans supported the war effort.
   B. The ad shows that scrap metal was a valuable commodity at the time.
   C. The poster provides insight into the practical ways that many Americans felt that they could make a useful contribution to the war effort.
   D. The ad shows the ingenuity of clever slogan writers.

___ 9. In a primary source such as the poster advertisement "Junk Rally," which of the following is the correct term for the words at the bottom, "Let's Jolt them with Junk from Winchester"?
   A. caption
   B. caricature
   C. catchy phrase
   D. statistic

___ 10. Reread the first four lines of the poster, "Junk Rally." What is the main purpose of this part of the poster?
   A. to inform
   B. to entertain
   C. to persuade
   D. to question

Vocabulary Warm-up Word Lists

Study these words from the selection. Then, complete the activities.

Word List A

amble [AM buhl] *n.* leisurely walk; stroll
The children went for a leisurely <u>amble</u> through the woods.

desolate [DES uh lit] *adj.* forlorn; wretched
No one likes to see the <u>desolate</u> wreckage of the old beach boardwalk.

emphasize [EM phuh syz] *v.* to stress; to single out as important
During her speech, Carla used vigorous arm gestures to <u>emphasize</u> her idea.

engulf [en GULF] *v.* to overwhelm, as if by overflowing or enclosing
The fire is so big that it might <u>engulf</u> that row of trees.

gaunt [GAWNT] *adj.* thin and bony
The <u>gaunt</u> old man didn't look healthy.

listed [LIS tuhd] *v.* tilted; inclined to one side
The damaged ship <u>listed</u> dangerously to the right.

ominous [AH mi nuhs] *adj.* threatening; sinister
Those dark clouds certainly look <u>ominous</u>.

uprooted [up ROOT uhd] *v.* pulled up
Karen <u>uprooted</u> the daffodils and moved them to another part of her garden.

Word List B

afflicted [uh FLIK tuhd] *adj.* grievously affected, especially by disease
<u>Afflicted</u> with disease, the trees in this orchard don't produce fruit.

depressed [dee PRESD] *adj.* low in spirits; dejected
Julie feels <u>depressed</u> when it rains so much.

expanse [eks PANS] *n.* wide and open space
The prairie is a remarkable <u>expanse</u> of grassy land.

mechanism [MEK uh nizm] *n.* machine; connected parts inside a machine
The clock stopped because its <u>mechanism</u> is broken.

morose [muh ROHS] *adj.* gloomy; sullen
I can't stand it when Jon gets that <u>morose</u> look on his face.

oppressed [uh PRESD] *v.* kept down by unfair authority
European settlers <u>oppressed</u> many Native American nations.

ravenous [RAV uh nuhs] *adj.* extremely hungry or eager
Judy was <u>ravenous</u> and ate so quickly that she got a stomachache.

sultry [SUL tree] *adj.* very humid and hot
July and August bring <u>sultry</u> days to the towns around Lake Michigan.

"The Life You Save May Be Your Own" by Flannery O'Connor
Vocabulary Warm-up Exercises

Exercise A *Fill in the blanks, using each word from Word List A only once.*

The day after the hurricane, Harry strolled at a slow [1] _____ down
to the harbor. Having spent a sleepless night of anxiety, he looked tired, almost
[2] _____. Although the worst was over now, the sky still looked gray
and [3] _____, as if another storm was on its way. Yesterday, the waves
had been so high that they had threatened to [4] _____ the dockside
shopping area. As Harry walked along Front Street, he thought the harbor looked
forlorn and [5] _____. A hundred yards offshore, a damaged yacht
[6] _____ crazily, as if it had been slapped by a giant. The storm had
[7] _____ some of the pier's pilings, as if to [8] _____
the wind's incredible power. Harry stood awestruck, scarcely believing his eyes.

Exercise B *Revise each sentence so that the underlined vocabulary word is logical. Be sure to
keep the vocabulary word in your revision.*

Example: Because her salary was <u>meager</u>, Lola could afford to purchase a new car.
Because her salary was <u>meager</u>, Lola could not afford to purchase a new car.

1. People are generally relieved if they discover they are <u>afflicted</u> by a disease.

   _____

2. He was so <u>depressed</u> that he decided to write an amusing limerick.

   _____

3. Russia covers a small <u>expanse</u> on the map of Europe and Asia.

   _____

4. The <u>mechanism</u> of a wristwatch is usually visible on the face of the timepiece.

   _____

5. If you are <u>morose</u>, you usually feel upbeat and optimistic.

   _____

6. When you feel <u>oppressed</u> by your employer, you want to work harder willingly.

   _____

7. A person with a <u>ravenous</u> hunger can usually be satisfied with a small bite to eat.

   _____

8. The weather was so delightfully <u>sultry</u> that we decided to linger at the beach.

   _____

"The Life You Save May Be Your Own" by Flannery O'Connor
Reading Warm-up A

Read the following passage. Pay special attention to the underlined words. Then, read it again, and complete the activities. Use a separate sheet of paper for your written answers.

How did Flannery O'Connor develop the unique style of her stories and novels? According to many literary critics, an important influence on O'Connor was the Gothic tradition in fiction. Taking its name from an architectural style in the Middle Ages, this literary tradition began in England in the late 1700s. Gothic novels, many of which were written by women, typically featured lonely, <u>desolate</u> settings in the remote countryside. The plots of these novels often unfold in an isolated, crumbling castle. The castle halls are full of dark shadows that threaten to <u>engulf</u> the characters, swallowing them up. No one ever walks at a leisurely <u>amble</u> in these stories. Instead, the characters skulk, rush, lurch, or sleepwalk down the castle's drafty hallways.

From the very beginning of their stories, writers in the Gothic tradition established an <u>ominous</u> atmosphere. Numerous grim, foreboding details contributed to a suspenseful mood. Some characters struggle to hide fearful secrets. The threat of insanity hangs over others. Still others are typically described as <u>gaunt</u> and desperate-looking from anxiety and sleepless nights. Gothic novelists loved to <u>emphasize</u> the role of the supernatural in their plots. For example, a pale figure who appeared night after night in the castle hallways and who <u>listed</u> crazily to one side would almost certainly turn out to be a ghost.

It may seem strange to compare Flannery O'Connor's tales of the rural American South to stories written in England more than 200 years ago. O'Connor, however, was a remarkably imaginative writer. With skill and sensitivity, she <u>uprooted</u> some of the leading elements of the Gothic tradition and transplanted them effectively to her own cultural context.

1. Underline the words in this sentence that give a clue to the meaning of <u>desolate</u>. Use *desolate* in a sentence of your own.

2. Circle the words in this sentence that give a clue to the meaning of <u>engulf</u>. What is a synonym for *engulf*?

3. Underline the words in this sentence and the next that give a clue to the meaning of <u>amble</u>. Use a word meaning the opposite of *amble* in an original sentence.

4. What is a synonym for <u>ominous</u>? What is an antonym for this word?

5. Circle the words in this sentence that offer a clue to the meaning of <u>gaunt</u>. Write a sentence about someone you would describe as *gaunt*.

6. What is a synonym for <u>emphasize</u>? What is an antonym for this word?

7. Underline the words that give a clue to the meaning of <u>listed</u>. Use *listed* in a sentence of your own, being careful to use it in the same meaning as this context.

8. Underline the words in this sentence that give a clue to the meaning of <u>uprooted</u>. What is a synonym for *uprooted*?

"The Life You Save May Be Your Own" by Flannery O'Connor
Reading Warm-up B

Read the following passage. Pay special attention to the underlined words. Then, read it again, and complete the activities. Use a separate sheet of paper for your written answers.

All that morning, Olivia had felt tired and <u>depressed</u> because she had to be at work waiting tables instead of outside in the sunshine. The restaurant's dim lighting only added to her <u>morose</u> state of mind. Her boss, Vin, would never let her eat anything until she'd finished her shift, and though it was only one o'clock, Olivia was <u>ravenous</u> with hunger, her stomach growling.

"Order up," said Vin, and pounded on a bell to grab her attention. A cheeseburger and fries sat under a heating lamp, an old-fashioned <u>mechanism</u> with a big orange light bulb that kept the food warm. Olivia picked up the scalding plate and brought it over to the customer who had come in fifteen minutes earlier. He wore overalls and a straw hat, an old man <u>afflicted</u> with Parkinson's disease, which made his hands tremble and his voice stutter when he spoke. When Olivia brought him his food, he didn't acknowledge her but just stared down at the table and began to eat.

"This counter is filthy," said Vin. "Get a rag and clean up."

Olivia went back into the kitchen and returned with a gray rag that she ran along the <u>expanse</u> of the vinyl counter. All she could think about was her friends out at Bear Lake, swimming and lying in the sun, enjoying the <u>sultry</u> August heat. While she cleaned the counter, the old man with the cheeseburger started coughing, and the ugly, rasping sound <u>oppressed</u> her even more.

"I know how you feel," said Vin, sighing. "I've been working in this dump for twenty years, slaving behind this grill. At least you know you won't be here forever."

Olivia put down the rag and washed her hands, then helped herself to a bowl of ice cream.

1. Underline the words in this sentence that hint at the meaning of <u>depressed</u>. What are two synonyms for **depressed**?

2. Circle the words in this sentence that hint at the meaning of <u>morose</u>. What is an antonym for **morose**?

3. Underline the words in this sentence that hint at the meaning of <u>ravenous</u>. Use **ravenous** in an original sentence.

4. Underline the words in this sentence that hint at the meaning of <u>mechanism</u>. Why do you think the **mechanism** is described as "old-fashioned" here?

5. Circle the words in this sentence that hint at the meaning of <u>afflicted</u>. What is a synonym for **afflicted**?

6. Circle the words in this sentence that give a good clue to the meaning of <u>expanse</u>. Do you think Olivia ran the rag across the whole counter or just a part of it? Explain.

7. Underline the words in this sentence that hint at the meaning of <u>sultry</u>. Write a sentence using a word that means the opposite of **sultry**.

8. Underline the words in this sentence that hint at the meaning of <u>oppressed</u>. What is an antonym of **oppressed**?

"The Life You Save May Be Your Own" by Flannery O'Connor
Literary Analysis: Grotesque Characters

Flannery O'Connor included in her writing some characters that are **grotesques.** Such characters have a one-track mind; they are controlled by a single emotion, concept, or goal.

On the lines after each of the following passages, identify an emotion, a concept, or a goal that the passage suggests. Then write one or two sentences to explain how the character might act if he or she were a grotesque, controlled by the way of thinking that you have identified.

1. "Is she your baby girl?" he asked.

   "My only," the old woman said, "and she's the sweetest girl in the world. I would give her up for nothing on earth. She's smart too. She can sweep the floor, cook, wash, feed the chickens, and hoe. I wouldn't give her up for a casket of jewels."

   "No," he said kindly, "don't ever let any man take her away from you."

   "Any man come after her," the old woman said, "'ll have to stay around the place."

   _____

   _____

   _____

   _____

2. He had raised the hood and studied the mechanism and he said he could tell that the car had been built in the days when cars were really built. You take now, he said, one man puts in one bolt and another man puts in another bolt and another man puts in another bolt so that it's a man for a bolt. That's why you have to pay so much for a car: you're paying all those men. Now if you didn't have to pay but one man, you could get you a cheaper car and one that had had a personal interest taken in it, and it would be a better car.

   _____

   _____

   _____

3. Mr. Shiftlet felt that the rottenness of the world was about to engulf him. He raised his arm and let it fall again to his breast. "Oh Lord!" he prayed. "Break forth and wash the slime from this earth!"

   _____

   _____

   _____

   _____

Name _____ Date _____

"The Life You Save May Be Your Own" by Flannery O'Connor
Reading Strategy: Draw Conclusions from Details

"The Life You Save May Be Your Own" contains a wealth of revealing details about characters and their motivations, setting, and plot. It can enrich your appreciation of a story if, as you read, you **draw conclusions from details** to evaluate the significance of specific story elements, such as a character's name or a suggestive gesture or action or remark. Attention to such details can often help you to draw conclusions about what characters are likely to do or how the story is likely to turn out.

DIRECTIONS: *On the lines following each excerpt, explain how the details in the excerpt allow you to draw conclusions about what is likely to happen next in the story.*

1. "Although the old woman lived in this desolate spot with only her daughter and she had never seen Mr. Shiftlet before, she could tell, even from a distance, that he was a tramp and no one to be afraid of."

   _____

   _____

2. "The old woman watched from a distance, secretly pleased. She was ravenous for a son-in-law."

   _____

   _____

3. "'Saturday,' the old woman said, 'you and her and me can drive into town and get married.'"

   _____

   _____

4. "'I'm only saying a man's spirit means more to him than anything else. I would have to take my wife off for the weekend without no regards at all for cost. I got to follow where my spirit says to go.'"

   _____

   _____

5. "As they came out of the courthouse, Mr. Shiftlet began twisting his neck in his collar. He looked morose and bitter as if he had been insulted while someone held him."

   _____

   _____

6. "'Give it to her when she wakes up,' Mr. Shiftlet said. 'I'll pay for it now.'"

   _____

   _____

"The Life You Save May Be Your Own" by Flannery O'Connor
Vocabulary Builder

Using the Root -sol-

A. DIRECTIONS: *The root -sol- comes to English from the Latin adjective* solus, *meaning "alone." Use each of the following words in a sentence to demonstrate your understanding of its meaning.*

1. solitary _____

2. sole _____

3. solely _____

4. solitude _____

Using the Word List

desolate   listed   morose   ominous   ravenous

B. DIRECTIONS: *Use one of the Word List words as you write each sentence according to the instructions given. Use the context of the sentence instructions to determine which word to use.*

1. Write a sentence about something that tilts.

   _____

   _____

2. Write a sentence about the isolated setting of a story.

   _____

   _____

3. Write a sentence about someone who is gloomy or sullen.

   _____

   _____

4. Write a sentence about someone who is extremely eager about something.

   _____

   _____

5. Write a sentence about a situation that is threatening or sinister.

   _____

   _____

"The Life You Save May Be Your Own" by Flannery O'Connor

Support for Writing

The title and ending of a story contain essential information that helps you interpret the story's meaning. Write an essay in which you explain the fate of each character in Flannery O'Connor's "The Life You Save May Be Your Own" and interpret the title. Be sure to answer these questions in your essay: What happens to each character at the end of the story? Whose life, if anyone's, is saved?

Use the chart below as in aid in organizing your ideas by reviewing each character's final moments in the story. Try to connect each character's fate with the idea that "the life you save may be your own."

Character	What happens to the character in the end?	How does the character's fate connect to the title?
Mrs. Crater		
Lucynell		
Mr. Shiftlet		

On a separate page, use the ideas and details you have gathered in your chart to begin to draft an introduction in which you present your interpretation of the title. You might begin by writing a one-paragraph sketch about each of the three main characters. Then explain how the final image of each character relates to the key idea of the title. Summarize and extend your analysis in your conclusion. When you are satisfied that your rough draft contains all the ideas and details that are essential to your essay, begin to write your final draft.

"The Life You Save May Be Your Own" by Flannery O'Connor
Enrichment: Human Resources Interview

The management of human resources—the people who do the work—is an important aspect of modern companies. Issues of employee benefits, employee conduct, and job performance are all handled by human resource personnel. At an employment agency, human resource specialists match applicants with appropriate jobs by evaluating each applicant's skills, experience, and personality.

Suppose you are a human resource specialist for an employment agency. Mr. Tom T. Shiftlet is sitting on the other side of your desk. He has stated that he has carpentry skills and would like a job.

The Interview

A. DIRECTIONS: *Part of your job is to assess the applicant's skills, level of knowledge, and personality. Write three questions to find out about Mr. Shiftlet's skills and knowledge. Then write three questions whose answers will reveal information about Mr. Shiftlet's personality. Avoid questions that can be answered with a simple yes or no.*

Skills and Knowledge

1. _____

2. _____

3. _____

Personality

1. _____

2. _____

3. _____

The Evaluation

B. DIRECTIONS: *Imagine that you have finished the interview with Mr. Shiftlet. Write your assessment of his abilities and your recommendation concerning the type of job he can do. Complete the following memorandum. Recommend any job training you think he may need.*

TO: File

RE: Tom T. Shiftlet, applicant

Based on my interview with Mr. Shiftlet, I understand he has the following skills and abilities:

_____

In my judgment, his personality _____

Recommendation

Job Training: _____

Job Opportunities: _____

"The Life You Save May Be Your Own" by Flannery O'Connor
Open-Book Test

Short Answer *Write your responses to the questions in this section on the lines provided.*

1. In the opening scenes of "The Life You Save May Be Your Own," from the way the author describes Mr. Shiftlet's perceptions of the Craters' property, you can conclude that he has stopped at the Craters' house for what reason?

   _____

2. In "The Life You Save May Be Your Own," what grotesque character trait do the old woman and Mr. Shiftlet have in common?

   _____

   _____

   _____

3. What physical element of the grotesque is shared by all three characters in "The Life You Save May Be Your Own"?

   _____

   _____

4. What can the reader conclude from the tone of Shiftlet's remark on the subject of lying in "The Life You Save May Be Your Own"?

   _____

   _____

   _____

5. "The Life You Save May Be Your Own" features characters who are grotesque, twisted, or bizarre in some aspect of their appearance or character. Use the Character Web below to analyze the character traits of Mr. Shiftlet. Then, on the lines below, write a brief description of him as a grotesque character.

Character traits of Mr. Shiftlet.

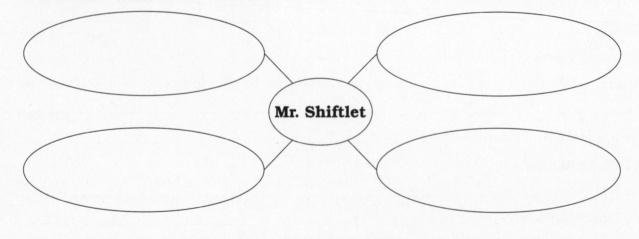

   _____

   _____

38

6. In "The Life You Save May Be Your Own," what aspects of the old woman's character and actions make her a grotesque character? Explain your answer using details from the text.

_____

_____

_____

7. When Mr. Shiftlet finally agrees to marry the younger Lucynell in "The Life You Save May Be Your Own," what aspect of his ensuing line of conversation makes it clear that his motives are suspicious?

_____

_____

_____

8. In view of what "The Life You Save May Be Your Own" reveals about Mr. Shiftlet's character and motives, what is odd or ironic about his statement that he has "a moral intelligence"?

_____

_____

_____

9. When the hitchhiker hears Shiftlet's pious words about his mother near the end of "The Life You Save May Be Your Own," what is so surprising and different about the hitchhiker's reaction, in view of previous events in the story?

_____

_____

_____

10. In an area that had been suffering from the threat of an avalanche, would an ominous weather forecast be one that promised a heavy snowstorm? Why or why not? Base your answer on the meaning of *ominous* as it is used in "The Life You Save May Be Your Own."

_____

_____

Essay

Write an extended response to the question of your choice or to the question or questions your teacher assigns you.

11. All three of the major characters in "The Life You Save May Be Your Own" are physically and/or morally grotesque—bizarre or twisted in some way. What if one or more of the characters had exhibited more "normal" traits? How do you think it would have affected the outcome of the story? Develop your thoughts in a brief essay supported by details from the story.

12. After Mr. Shiftlet is rebuked by the hitchhiker at the end of "The Life You Save May Be Your Own," he becomes very agitated and upset and utters this prayer: "Oh, Lord! . . . Break forth and wash the slime from this earth!" What is odd about his reaction, especially the fact that he is praying? What is the "slime" that he refers to? Develop your thoughts in an essay supported by details from the story.

13. "The Life You Save May Be Your Own" is a story that features grotesque characters. What aspects of Mrs. Crater qualify her for the label "grotesque"? Is it her appearance? Her character? Her surroundings? In an essay, explain why Mrs. Crater is a grotesque character. Support your answer with details from the story.

14. **Thinking About the Essential Question: What is the relationship between place and literature?** Southern literature of the twentieth century developed a tradition of Gothic fiction—a world of eccentrics, oddballs, and misfits who are starkly at odds with the gleaming, self-confident image of twentieth-century America. In an essay, explain the way in which the setting—the sense of place— of Flannery O'Connor's short story "The Life You Save May Be Your Own" places it in this Gothic tradition. Support your answer with details from the story.

Oral Response

15. Go back to question 3, 4, or 9 or to the question your teacher assigns you. Take a few minutes to expand your answer and prepare an oral response. Find additional details in "The Life You Save May Be Your Own" that support your points. If necessary, make notes to guide your oral response.

"The Life You Save May Be Your Own" by Flannery O'Connor
Selection Test A

Critical Reading *Identify the letter of the choice that best answers the question.*

_____ 1. In what way is Mr. Shiftlet grotesque in "The Life You Save May Be Your Own"?
   A. in his view of the world
   B. in the way he talks
   C. in how his farm looks
   D. in how hard he works

_____ 2. In "The Life You Save May Be Your Own," why is Mr. Shiftlet's statement that he has a "moral intelligence" odd?
   A. He does not show any intelligence at all.
   B. The daughter cannot hear him say this.
   C. He shows no morality in the entire story.
   D. The mother sees through his behavior.

_____ 3. What is Mrs. Crater's obsession in "The Life You Save May Be Your Own"?
   A. a worker for her land
   B. a husband for her daughter
   C. a husband for herself
   D. a person to fix the car

_____ 4. What does Mrs. Crater think of Mr. Shiftlet when she first meets him in "The Life You Save May Be Your Own"?
   A. He is a possible hired hand.
   B. He is a traveling salesman.
   C. He is missing an arm.
   D. He is no one to be afraid of.

_____ 5. How does Mr. Shiftlet gain Mrs. Crater's trust in "The Life You Save May Be Your Own"?
   A. by speaking of his background
   B. by admiring the sunset
   C. by buying a new fanbelt for the car
   D. by teaching Lucynell to say "bird"

_____ 6. In "The Life You Save May Be Your Own," what can you conclude about Mrs. Crater's intentions toward Mr. Shiftlet when she asks him, "Are you married or are you single"?

    A. She will try to marry him herself.

    B. She will protect Lucynell from him.

    C. She will try to get him to marry Lucynell.

    D. She will introduce him to her friends.

_____ 7. How are Mrs. Crater and Mr. Shiftlet alike in "The Life You Save May Be Your Own"?

    A. They are both protective of Lucynell.

    B. They are both obsessed with an idea.

    C. They both want the car to work.

    D. They both want to improve the farm.

_____ 8. In "The Life You Save May Be Your Own," what can you conclude about Mr. Shiftlet's intentions based on his statement that a person's spirit is always "on the move"?

    A. He will stay and work on the farm.

    B. He and Lucynell will live in the house.

    C. He will continue to try to fix the car.

    D. He will leave after he fixes the car.

_____ 9. Why is Mrs. Crater upset when she says goodbye to her daughter in "The Life You Save May Be Your Own"?

    A. She knows Mr. Shiftlet will abandon Lucynell.

    B. She fears Lucynell will not like being married.

    C. She has never been apart from her daughter.

    D. She hates to lose Mr. Shiftlet's work on the farm.

_____ 10. How are both Mrs. Crater and Mr. Shiftlet grotesque characters in "The Life You Save May Be Your Own"?

    A. They are both physically ugly.

    B. They are both depressed.

    C. They are both ruled by obsessions.

    D. They are both unpleasant people.

Vocabulary

_____ 11. Which word best replaces *morose* in this sentence: "He was *morose* during the wedding, although he should have been happy"?

    A. eager   C. entertained

    B. unhappy   D. humorous

_____ 12. Which word is most nearly OPPOSITE in meaning to *ominous*?

    A. heartening   **C.** honest

    B. threatening   **D.** devious

_____ 13. If a ship *listed*, what did it do?

    A. tilted   **C.** took on cargo

    B. sounded its hom   **D.** sank

_____ 14. If you were traveling through a *desolate* area, which of the following would you be LEAST likely to see?

    A. an abandoned warehouse

    B. rows of shuttered businesses

    C. lush, green trees and gardens

    D. dense crowds of people on the sidewalks

_____ 15. In "The Life You Save May Be Your Own," O'Connor writes that the old woman was "ravenous for a son-in-law." Based on your knowledge of the word *ravenous*, which of the following words best describes her attitude toward finding a mate for her daughter?

    A. reluctant

    B. indifferent

    C. receptive

    D. eager

Essay

16. In "The Life You Save May Be Your Own," Mrs. Crater is a grotesque character because she is obsessed with getting her daughter married. What does she ignore about Mr. Shiftlet in her focus on him as a husband for her daughter? Write a brief essay and give at least one example from the story to show that she does not see him clearly.

17. At the end of "The Life You Save May Be Your Own," Mr. Shiftlet is upset. He says, "Oh, Lord! . . . Break forth and wash the slime from this earth!" Why is it odd that he is praying? What might you think of as the "slime" he refers to? In a brief essay, respond to these questions. Use details from the story to support your answers.

18. **Thinking About the Essential Question: What is the relationship between place and literature?** Southern literature of the twentieth century developed a tradition of Gothic fiction—a world of eccentrics, oddballs, and misfits who are starkly at odds with the gleaming, self-confident image of twentieth-century America. In an essay, explain the way in which the setting—the sense of place—of Flannery O'Connor's short story "The Life You Save May Be Your Own" places it in this Gothic tradition. Support your answer with details from the story.

"The Life You Save May Be Your Own" by Flannery O'Connor
Selection Test B

Critical Reading *Identify the letter of the choice that best completes the statement or answers the question.*

____ 1. When Mr. Shiftlet meets the old woman and her daughter in "The Life You Save May Be Your Own," the author's description of him conveys the impression that he is most interested in the
   A. chance to teach the daughter.
   B. possibility of a job.
   C. location of the farm.
   D. car in the yard.

____ 2. Mr. Shiftlet's statement in "The Life You Save May Be Your Own" that he has "a moral intelligence" is ironic because
   A. the daughter cannot hear him speak.
   B. he lacks a sense of morality in everything he does in the story.
   C. neither the mother nor the daughter can understand his language.
   D. he shows very little intelligence in the story.

____ 3. Which of the following statements by the old woman in "The Life You Save May Be Your Own" is ironic?
   A. "'One that can't talk,' she continued, 'can't sass you back or use foul language.'"
   B. "'Are you married or are you single?'"
   C. "'And I wouldn't let no man have her but you because I seen you would do right.'"
   D. "'She can sweep the floor, cook, wash, feed the chickens, and hoe.'"

____ 4. How are the old woman and Mr. Shiftlet from "The Life You Save May Be Your Own" similar?
   A. Both are shrewd opportunists.
   B. Both are unconcerned about Lucynell's future.
   C. Both are hypocritical.
   D. Both want to improve the property.

____ 5. In "The Life You Save May Be Your Own," what does Mr. Shiflet do to earn Mrs. Crater's trust?
   A. He makes himself useful and teaches Lucynell a word.
   B. He admires the sunset, and she believes that such a man must be trustworthy.
   C. He expresses a liking for Lucynell.
   D. He speaks of how he was raised, and Mrs. Crater respects his values.

____ 6. In "The Life You Save May Be Your Own," what effect does the wedding have on Mr. Shiflet?
   A. He is momentarily happy.
   B. He admits his mistakes.
   C. He reveals more of his true nature.
   D. He promises to change.

_____ 7. What can a reader reasonably conclude about the old woman's intentions based on the following passage from "The Life You Save May Be Your Own"?

> The old woman watched from a distance, secretly pleased. She was ravenous for a son-in-law.

A. She is falling in love with Mr. Shiflet
B. She has only the best interests of her daughter in mind.
C. She wants Mr. Shiflet to marry her daughter.
D. She wants Lucynell to learn to speak.

_____ 8. Based on the following passage, from "The Life You Save May Be Your Own," what might you conclude will happen next in the story?

> "She [Lucynell] looks like an angel of Gawd," he murmured.

> "Hitchhiker," Mr. Shiftlet explained. "I can't wait. I got to make Tuscaloosa."

A. He will leave Lucynell for good.
B. He will pick up more hitchhikers
C. He will meet Lucynell's mother in Tuscaloosa.
D. He will stay with Lucynell despite his true feelings.

_____ 9. A grotesque character is
A. any physically unattractive character.
B. an unpleasant character.
C. one who acts immorally or unlawfully.
D. one who is dominated by some kind of obsession.

_____ 10. Which of the following statements made by Mr. Shiftlet in "The Life You Save May Be Your Own" reveals that he is a grotesque character?
A. "I'd give a fortune to live where I could see me a sun do that every evening."
B. "Nothing is like it used to be lady. The world is almost rotten."
C. "How you know my name ain't Aaron Sparks, lady . . .?"
D. "Maybe the best I can tell you is, I'm a man . . . ."

_____ 11. In what way is Mrs. Crater in "The Life You Save May Be Your Own" a grotesque character?
A. in the way she is stingy with her money
B. in the way she speaks
C. in the way she dotes on her daughter
D. in the way she keeps her farm

_____ 12. The climax of "The Life You Save May Be Your Own" occurs when Mr. Shiftlet
A. fixes the old car.
B. teaches Lucynell to speak.
C. marries Lucynell.
D. leaves Lucynell in the diner.

_____ 13. At the end of "The Life You Save May Be Your Own," which of the following do you conclude the hitchker is probably doing?
A. running away from home
B. committing a crime
C. hunting for a job
D. visiting his mother

_____ 14. What is the thematic conflict of "The Life You Save May Be Your Own"?
A. innocence versus experience
B. belief versus action
C. wealth versus poverty
D. weakness versus strength

____ 15. What lesson is the author trying to convey in "The Life You Save May Be Your Own"?
   A. Actions speak louder than words.
   B. The meek shall inherit the earth.
   C. Kindness to strangers goes unrewarded.
   D. Life is a gamble.

Vocabulary

____ 16. The old woman's home in "The Life You Save May Be Your Own" is described as *desolate* because
   A. the house is in a small clearing in a forest.
   B. the house and buildings are shabby looking.
   C. it is hard to find.
   D. it suits her and her daughter.

____ 17. The figure walking up the road *listed*, or
   A. counted.
   B. observed shrewdly.
   C. tilted.
   D. strolled.

____ 18. Someone who is *morose* is
   A. gloomy.
   B. eager.
   C. scheming.
   D. seriously ill.

____ 19. If you were to describe your appetite as *ravenous*, it would be reasonable to assume that you
   A. were severely ill with a stomach virus.
   B. had just enjoyed a five-course feast.
   C. had not eaten for a very long time.
   D. had recently consumed a large ice cream sundae.

Essay

20. All three of the characters in "The Life You Save May Be Your Own" story are grotesque in some way. Think carefully about the old woman. Consider her surroundings, her appearance, and her behavior. Then, in an essay, explain how O'Connor reveals the woman as grotesque. Remember to consider anything bizarre about her that might be the result of an obsession of some sort.

21. "The Life You Save May Be Your Own" has a symbolic meaning as well as a literal one. From the moment Mr. Shiftlet's figure forms "a crooked cross," the story contains symbols that add depth. The human heart, the 1928 or '29 Ford, the hitchhiker—these are a few of the elements with symbolic significance. Write an essay in which you point out and interpret at least three of the symbols in this story. You may use the symbols identified here or choose others. Explain clearly your interpretation of the symbols.

22. **Thinking About the Essential Question: What is the relationship between place and literature?** Southern literature of the twentieth century developed a tradition of Gothic fiction—a world of eccentrics, oddballs, and misfits who are starkly at odds with the gleaming, self-confident image of twentieth-century America. In an essay, explain the way in which the setting—the sense of place—of Flannery O'Connor's short story "The Life You Save May Be Your Own" places it in this Gothic tradition. Support your answer with details from the story.

Vocabulary Warm-up Word Lists

Study these words from the selection. Then, complete the activities.

Word List A

anticipating [an TIS uh payt ing] *v.* looking forward to something
  Underline: Anticipating a win, Sal was ready to celebrate before the game even started.

diminished [duh MIN ishd] *v.* lessened; became smaller
  As Greg gained experience, his fear of rock-climbing diminished.

dissatisfied [dis SAT is fyd] *adj.* feeling disappointment
  Frowning, Elsa seemed very dissatisfied with her performance.

grotesquely [groh TESK lee] *adv.* weirdly; in a distorted or bizarre way
  The accident left Mr. Hyde's hand grotesquely twisted and misshapen.

inquired [in KWYRD] *v.* asked about
  When she arrived at the hospital, Ms. Bell inquired about Ben's condition.

inscribed [in SKRYBD] *v.* written, printed, or carved
  Each player's name is inscribed on the trophy.

irritating [IR i tayt ing] *adj.* annoying
  The mother yelled at her daughter, "Please stop that irritating sound!"

probe [PROHB] *v.* to search; to investigate
  Ed wanted to probe for answers and a possible solution to his problem.

Word List B

devious [DEE vee uhs] *adj.* misleading; dishonest
  The devious little boy wouldn't tell his mother where he'd been.

diligence [DIL uh juhns] *n.* constant, careful effort; perseverance
  Hannah's diligence has made her a great artist.

haphazardly [hap HAZ urhd lee] *adv.* in a random manner
  Drivers parked their cars haphazardly during the snowstorm.

illiterate [i LIT uhr it] *adj.* unable to read or write
  Since he's never been to school, the old man is illiterate.

inexplicably [in eks PLIK uh blee] *adv.* difficult to explain
  Inexplicably, the printer stopped working right in the middle of our project.

insight [IN syt] *n.* clear understanding
  Laura asked for insight from coworkers about her new position.

nearsighted [NEER syt id] *adj.* unable to see distant objects clearly
  Because she is nearsighted, Martha needs corrective lenses to drive.

temperamental [tem pruh MEN tuhl] *adj.* extremely sensitive
  The car stalled again because its engine is so temperamental.

Name _____ Date _____

"The First Seven Years" by Bernard Malamud
Vocabulary Warm-up Exercises

Exercise A *Fill in the blanks, using each word from Word List A only once.*

For several weeks, Pia had been eagerly [1] _____ the class field trip.
True, she was suffering from a(n) [2] _____ cold, but her enthusiasm to
see Washington, D.C., for the first time had not [3] _____. Pia knew
several seniors who'd been on the same trip last year, and none of them had been
[4] _____ with the outing. When she had [5] _____ about
the most popular tourist sight, Jeff told her he liked the Lincoln Memorial best of all. As
always, Pia wanted to [6] _____ further, seeking to find out why this particular sight was so appealing. "The seated statue of Lincoln is awesome," Jeff told her,
"and you need to read the quotations from his speeches [7] _____ around
the walls." Some of Pia's classmates reacted [8] _____ to Jeff's enthusiasm, mocking him as a history freak. However, Pia knew she would enjoy visiting the
memorial, as well as the other sights.

Exercise B *Decide whether each statement below is true or false. Circle T or F, and explain
your answer.*

1. Advice from a *devious* person is usually worth taking.
   T / F _____

2. Someone working with *diligence* is often careless.
   T / F _____

3. People driving *haphazardly* are hard to predict and may be dangerous on the road.
   T / F _____

4. If you are *illiterate*, you lack the ability to read and write.
   T / F _____

5. A person behaving *inexplicably* inspires reactions of puzzlement and curiosity.
   T / F _____

6. A truly valuable *insight* into a problem is illuminating and constructive.
   T / F _____

7. If you are *nearsighted*, you probably require glasses to drive.
   T / F _____

8. A *temperamental* performer is always cooperative and patient.
   T / F _____

Unit 5 Resources: Prosperity and Protest

Name _____ Date _____

"The First Seven Years" by Bernard Malamud
Reading Warm-up A

Read the following passage. Pay special attention to the underlined words. Then, read it again, and complete the activities. Use a separate sheet of paper for your written answers.

All that week, Daphne had been eagerly <u>anticipating</u> her date with a boy named John. Her college roommate Amy had assured Daphne that John was just her type: handsome, smart, funny, and athletic. However, when Daphne met John at the coffee shop, he turned out to be <u>grotesquely</u> full of himself, like an exaggerated cartoon of a self-centered movie star. Her enthusiasm had started high. Now, it <u>diminished</u> and all she wanted to do was leave.

"You're five minutes late," John said, before even introducing himself, then produced a business card, on which were <u>inscribed</u> the words, *John—the Greatest.*

Daphne was disappointed. Though she couldn't have been more <u>dissatisfied</u> with John, Daphne believed it would be rude not to at least sit down. John immediately told her that he would buy her a small cup of coffee but that if she wanted anything else she was on her own.

"I keep myself on a strict budget," he said. "I hope you appreciate the importance of spending money wisely."

From his attitude to his way of speaking, everything about John was <u>irritating</u>. Instead of trying to make Daphne feel comfortable, he <u>inquired</u> about her grade point average. When she answered his question, he told her he could not afford to waste his time on someone who wasn't a straight A student.

That night, her friend Amy called to find out how the date had gone. "You must be crazy," Daphne said. "What kind of person do you think I am that you would fix me up with someone like that?"

She kept asking questions, trying to <u>probe</u> Amy for an explanation, but Amy seemed to believe that John was perfect for her. Their friendship was never the same afterwards.

1. Underline the words in this sentence that tell what Daphne was <u>anticipating</u>. Use the word *anticipating* in an original sentence.

2. Circle the words in this sentence that give a clue to the meaning of <u>grotesquely</u>. What is a synonym for *grotesquely*?

3. Underline the words that make a contrast with the meaning of <u>diminished</u>. What is an antonym for *diminished*?

4. Circle the words that offer a clue to the meaning of <u>inscribed</u> here. On what kinds of surfaces might you expect words to be *inscribed*?

5. Circle the word that is a clue to the meaning of <u>dissatisfied</u>. Use a word meaning the opposite of *dissatisfied* in a sentence of your own.

6. Underline the words that tell in which respects John was <u>irritating</u>. What are two antonyms for *irritating*?

7. Circle the word that gives a clue to the meaning of <u>inquired</u>. Use the word *inquired* in an original sentence.

8. Underline the words in this sentence hinting at the meaning of <u>probe</u>. What is a synonym for *probe*?

Name _____ Date _____

"The First Seven Years" by Bernard Malamud
Reading Warm-up B

Read the following passage. Pay special attention to the underlined words. Then, read it again, and complete the activities. Use a separate sheet of paper for your written answers.

One of a writer's most effective techniques is the use of allusion. An allusion is a reference to a well-known event, character, place, or phrase from history or literature.

Good writers, however, do not use allusions casually or <u>haphazardly</u>. Instead, they want the references they employ to add to readers' <u>insight</u> and understanding of the theme or central message of a work. Allusions may pass over the heads of the <u>illiterate</u> or the uneducated, but most readers with the <u>diligence</u> and skill to track down the meaning and context of a writer's allusions will find their efforts repaid.

For example, in the title of his story "The First Seven Years," Bernard Malamud alludes to the Biblical story of Jacob and Laban, found in the Book of Genesis. Jacob, who has fallen in love with Laban's daughter Rachel, agrees to work for her father for seven years. Jacob keeps his part of the bargain, but Laban turns out to be <u>devious</u>. He deceptively substitutes Rachel's sister Leah at the last minute. Jacob's reaction is hard to understand, at least at first: almost <u>inexplicably</u>, he agrees to work for a second period of seven years so that he may gain Rachel, his true love.

With his allusion to this Biblical tale, Malamud clearly wants readers to draw certain conclusions about Sobel, who is really his story's most important character. As Sobel's employer, Feld the shoemaker is portrayed as emotionally <u>nearsighted</u> for most of the story; he does not understand that Sobel has been working for him in the same way as Jacob worked for Laban: to win the love of his life. When he leaves Feld's shop, Sobel may seem <u>temperamental</u> and unpredictable. When he returns, though, he gains the status of a Biblical hero.

1. Underline the word in this sentence that gives a clue to the meaning of <u>haphazardly</u>. Write a sentence of your own using a word that means the opposite of *haphazardly*.

2. Circle the word in this sentence that gives a clue to the meaning of <u>insight</u>. Use the word *insight* in an original sentence.

3. Underline the word in this sentence hinting at the meaning of <u>illiterate</u>. What are two antonyms for *illiterate*?

4. Underline the word in this sentence that gives a clue to the meaning of <u>diligence</u>. What is an antonym for *diligence*?

5. Circle the words in this sentence and the next that give a clue to the meaning of <u>devious</u>. Use a word meaning the opposite of *devious* in a sentence of your own.

6. Underline the words in this sentence that hint at the meaning of <u>inexplicably</u>. What is an antonym for *inexplicably*?

7. Underline the words in this sentence that give a clue to the meaning of <u>nearsighted</u>.

8. Circle the word in this sentence that hints at the meaning of the word <u>temperamental</u>.

"The First Seven Years" by Bernard Malamud
Literary Analysis: Plot and Epiphany

A story follows a sequence of events called a **plot.** The plot reaches a high point of interest or suspense at the **climax.** In this story, Malamud builds toward an **epiphany,** a climax in which a character has a flash of insight that affects the conflict or causes a character to re-examine long-held assumptions.

DIRECTIONS: *On the lines below each of the following quotations, explain why that moment of the plot does or does not represent a true epiphany for Feld, the shoemaker.*

1. Neither the shifting white blur outside, nor the sudden deep remembrance of the snowy Polish village where he had wasted his youth could turn his thoughts from Max the college boy. . . .

   _____

   _____

   _____

   _____

2. An old wish returned to haunt the shoemaker: that he had had a son instead of a daughter. . . .

   _____

   _____

   _____

3. Maybe he could awaken in her a desire to go to college; if not—the shoemaker's mind at last came to grips with the truth—let her marry an educated man and live a better life.

   _____

   _____

   _____

   _____

4. That night the shoemaker discovered that his new assistant had been all the while stealing from him, and he suffered a heart attack.

   _____

   _____

   _____

   _____

5. Feld had a sudden insight. In some devious way, with his books and commentary, Sobel had given Miriam to understand that he loved her.

   _____

   _____

   _____

   _____

Name _____ Date _____

"The First Seven Years" by Bernard Malamud
Reading Strategy: Summarizing

One useful strategy for monitoring your comprehension is **summarizing.** Pause after a significant scene or at a section break and review the events and the developing relationships between the characters. Your summary should state the main points of the scene.

DIRECTIONS: *Use the chart below to summarize Feld's relationship with the three other main characters in "The First Seven Years." In the middle column, write a phrase or short summary of how Feld relates to that character. In the right-hand column, summarize what Feld learns about each of these characters.*

Character	Summary of Relationship with Feld	Summary of What Feld Learns about This Character
Miriam		
Sobel		
Max		

"The First Seven Years" by Bernard Malamud
Vocabulary Builder

Using the Root -litera-

A. DIRECTIONS: *Explain how the meaning of each of the following words is related to the root word -litera- meaning "letter."*

1. literate (*adj.*) _____

_____

_____

2. literature _____

_____

_____

Using the Word List

diligence   discern   illiterate   repugnant   unscrupulous

B. DIRECTIONS: *Answer the following questions to demonstrate your understanding of the Word List words.*

1. Why does Feld think Max has *diligence* and Miriam does not?

_____

_____

2. Why are Sobel and Miriam *not* described as *illiterate*?

_____

_____

3. What might an *unscrupulous* employee have done to Feld?

_____

_____

4. What did Feld think he could *discern* that Miriam could not?

_____

_____

5. Why was the idea of sending Miriam to Sobel's boarding house *repugnant*?

_____

_____

"The First Seven Years" by Bernard Malamud
Support for Writing

Prepare a personality profile for one of the characters in "The First Seven Years" to help persuade a television producer that a show starring this character would be a big hit. Enter information about that character from the story in the graphic organizer below.

Profile of Mr. Feld

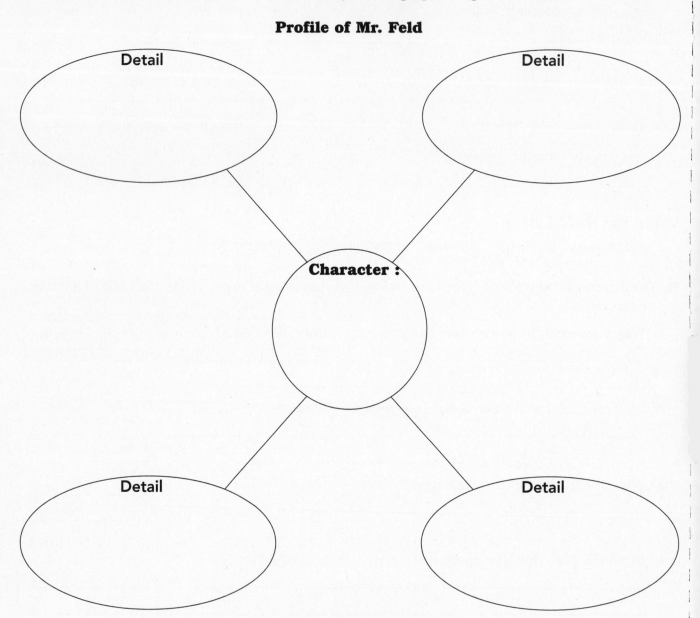

On a separate page, draft your personality profile by introducing the character you have chosen using each detail from your graphic organizer. Expand your profile until you have used all the details. When you revise, compare your cluster diagram with that of one of your classmates who has chosen the same character to see if you (or your classmate) have missed any important details. Then, add those details to your profile.

"The First Seven Years" by Bernard Malamud
Enrichment: Conflict Resolution

Anger can be dealt with in many different ways. In "The First Seven Years," Sobel handled his anger by storming out of the shop. Feld's response was to "let him stew." Are these actions constructive? What more effective ways exist to resolve conflicts?

Workplace conflict is inevitable. The test is to be able to deal with it in a professional manner. Sometimes disagreements help people in the workplace identify problems and make improvements. This is constructive disagreement. Other times disagreements hurt people and get in the way of their work. This, of course, is destructive disagreement.

If disagreements are handled properly, they can almost always be constructive instead of destructive. Here are some tips for dealing with disagreements.

- **Understand the issues.** Make sure you have all the facts before you express disagreement. Furthermore, don't just complain; have a solution ready to propose.
- **Never blame or accuse others in the group.** Don't say, for example, "You've left out part of the data for the September campaign." That accuses the person who made the report. Instead, say, "Let's look more closely at the September campaign data."
- **Disagree with a person's ideas or statements, not with the person.** Don't say, for example, "I disagree with you, Robert." Instead, say, "I disagree with your proposal to lease the new equipment." Then go on to explain why.
- **Communicate honestly but not emotionally.** If you feel yourself getting angry, don't say anything. You probably won't express yourself clearly or effectively. Excuse yourself from the room, if possible. If that is not possible, try organizing your thoughts and writing your ideas down. Then read what you've written and don't allow your emotions to take over.
- **Show goodwill.** Regardless of the outcome, you probably have to continue to work with the same people. Don't keep track of who "wins" or "loses." Learn from each situation and foster strong, stable working relationships.

DIRECTIONS: *Use the information on this page about dealing with conflict in the workplace to answer the following questions.*

1. Suppose that Sobel's anger had been caused by a disagreement about the kind of shoe leather Feld was buying. How should Sobel express his disagreement to Feld?

   _____

   _____

2. Explain how you could have used the Conflict Resolution tips to deal with a specific disagreement in a group or club.

   _____

   _____

   _____

   _____

"The First Seven Years" by Bernard Malamud
Open-Book Test

Short Answer *Write your responses to the questions in this section on the lines provided.*

1. The opening paragraph of "The First Seven Years" describes Feld's admiration for Max, "the college boy." He contrasts Max's ambition for a college education with his own daughter's lack of interest in formal schooling. What key plot development is foreshadowed in this paragraph?

   _____

   _____

   _____

2. In "The First Seven Years," Feld has a complicated relationship with his daughter, Miriam, whose values he does not fully understand. Briefly summarize Feld's relationship with Miriam.

   _____

   _____

   _____

   _____

   _____

3. In "The First Seven Years," Malamud portrays Max and Miriam as having contrasting values. How does this portrayal foreshadow the outcome of Max and Miriam's brief attempt at dating?

   _____

   _____

   _____

4. In "The First Seven Years," Feld recognizes that Sobel is an exceptionally hard-working and trustworthy assistant. How is Sobel different from what another assistant might be like in the same position? What motivates Sobel's exceptional performance?

   _____

   _____

   _____

5. In "The First Seven Years," when Feld first offers Max the opportunity to go out with his daughter, Max first asks to see a picture of her. Then he asks, "And she is sensible—not the flighty kind?" What do Max's questions show about his character?

   _____

   _____

   _____

6. In "The First Seven Years," Feld seems to have mixed feelings about Sobel, depending on whether he is regarding him as an employee or as a potential mate for his daughter. Briefly summarize the relationship between Feld and Sobel.

_____

_____

_____

_____

7. Complete this chart to examine Feld's relationship with the story's three other main characters in "The First Seven Years." In the middle column, write a phrase or short summary of how Feld relates to that character. In the right-hand column, describe what Feld comes to understand about each of these characters.

Character	Relationship with Feld	Realization
Miriam		
Sobel		
Max		

8. What is Sobel's motive in returning to the shoe store at the end of "The First Seven Years"?

_____

_____

_____

9. In "The First Seven Years," why do you think Feld relents and agrees to Sobel's eventual marriage to his daughter? Support your answer with details from the story.

_____

_____

_____

_____

10. If you noticed that someone was applying herself to a task with diligence, would you expect that she would be doing a poor job? Why or why not? Base your answer on the meaning of *diligence* as it used in "The First Seven Years."

_____

_____

_____

Essay

Write an extended response to the question of your choice or to the question or questions your teacher assigns you.

11. In "The First Seven Years," both Feld and Sobel love Miriam, and each believes that he has her best interests at heart, even though they hold conflicting ideas about what is best for her. What does Miriam want? Write a brief essay in the form of a letter from Miriam to her father telling him what she wants. Use details from the story to make the letter emotionally compelling and believable.

12. In "The First Seven Years," Feld is a loving, dutiful husband and father who works hard to protect and advance the interests and happiness of his family. Yet he shows that he can be insensitive to the wishes of other people. In an essay, explain how Feld's insensitivity affects Miriam, Max, and Sobel. Support your answer with details from the story.

13. "The First Seven Years" is a story about conflicting values and ideas about fulfillment and happiness. Each of the four major characters in the story has slightly different sets of values and goals. In an essay, compare and contrast the outlooks and value systems of Feld, Max, Sobel, and Miriam. In what respect do any of them share worldviews? In what respect do they clash? Support your answer with details from the story.

14. **Thinking About the Essential Question: What makes American literature American?** "The First Seven Years" tackles some essentially American themes and conflicts: the desire to move up in the world in a land of opportunity; the pressure to conform to society's materialistic values; and the conflict between the ideals of the spirit and the imperatives of the "real" world of commerce and money. In an essay, explain how each of the story's main characters—Feld, Miriam, and Sobel—represents an aspect of these themes.

Oral Response

15. Go back to question 1, 2, or 4 or to the question your teacher assigns to you. Take a few minutes to expand your answer and prepare an oral response. Find additional details in "The First Seven Years" that support your points. If necessary, make notes to guide your oral response.

"The First Seven Years" by Bernard Malamud
Selection Test A

Critical Reading *Identify the letter of the choice that best answers the question.*

____ 1. Which of the following best summarizes what Miriam might say if she were telling the story "The First Seven Years"?

   A. I wish Max would ask me out on a date.

   B. I wish my father would let me live my own life.

   C. I wish I could learn how to fix shoes.

   D. I wish my father would give me advice about my life.

____ 2. Why does Feld want Max to date Miriam?

   A. Max is a peddler's son.

   B. Miriam has said she likes Max.

   C. Max is a college student.

   D. Max has expressed interest in Miriam.

____ 3. Which choice is the best summary of what Miriam might say when she learns that Feld wants Max to ask her out in "The First Seven Years"?

   A. Why won't Father stop meddling!

   B. Yes, I'd like to go out with Max!

   C. I thought Max would never ask!

   D. I hope Max is rich and handsome!

____ 4. Which word best describes Sobel in "The First Seven Years"?

   A. unintelligent

   B. trustworthy

   C. handsome

   D. charming

____ 5. Why does Feld lie to Miriam, telling her that Sobel has gotten another job in "The First Seven Years"?

   A. He hopes Sobel will find a new job as soon as possible.

   B. He feels guilty that he hasn't asked Sobel to come back.

   C. He doesn't want Miriam to be interested in Sobel.

   D. He wants Miriam to talk more about her date with Max.

_____ 6. Which of these best describes Miriam's character in "The First Seven Years"?

    A. sad

    B. funny

    C. bitter

    D. confident

_____ 7. Why does Miriam reject Max as a possible suitor in "The First Seven Years"?

    A. Max is not rich.

    B. Max is too educated.

    C. Max cares only about things.

    D. Max is not handsome.

_____ 8. After a long time, what is Feld's epiphany, or realization, about Sobel in "The First Seven Years"?

    A. Miriam loves Sobel.

    B. Sobel loves Miriam.

    C. Sobel wants his own business.

    D. Sobel hates working for Feld.

_____ 9. How does the title "The First Seven Years" connect to the epiphany, or realization, that Feld has about Sobel?

    A. Sobel will work for Feld for seven years before he can court Miriam.

    B. Sobel will leave Feld's employment after seven years as his assistant.

    C. Miriam will date Max for seven years and then marry Sobel.

    D. Miriam will work for seven years and then go to college.

_____ 10. What does Feld understand as a result of his epiphany, or realization?

    A. He will have to run the store alone.

    B. He will have to send Miriam to college.

    C. He will have to give up his dreams.

    D. He will have to explain to Max.

Vocabulary

_____ 11. Which word best replaces *repugnant* in this sentence: "Miriam finds Max's interest in money *repugnant,* because she cares more about books and knowledge" from "The First Seven Years"?

    A. attractive

    B. pleasant

    C. disagreeable

    D. frightening

___ **12.** Which word is most nearly OPPOSITE in meaning to *diligence*?

    A. cleanliness

    B. leniency

    C. strength

    D. laziness

___ **13.** If Feld in "The First Seven Years" hired an *unscrupulous* assistant to help with his business, which of the following would be the most likely result?

    A. Feld's profits would increase.

    B. Feld would notice money missing from the cash register.

    C. Feld would consider the assistant a suitable match for his daughter.

    D. Feld would want the assistant to take over the business upon his retirement.

___ **14.** In "The First Seven Years," Feld wants more for Miriam than to meet *illiterate* shipping clerks, or people who are

    A. not wealthy.

    B. uneducated.

    C. unable to read or write.

    D. part of the working class.

Essay

15. In "The First Seven Years," both Feld and Sobel have very strong ideas about what they want for Miriam. What does Miriam want? Write a brief essay in the form of a letter by Miriam to her father. Imagine that Miriam is aware of what Feld has done in her behalf and knows how Sobel feels about her.

16. Despite the fact that Feld is a loving father in "The First Seven Years," he is also very insensitive to the wishes of other people. How is he insensitive, or uncaring, to Miriam? To Max? To Sobel? Write a brief essay in which you choose one of these people and describe how Feld does not take his or her feelings into account.

17. Thinking About the Essential Question: What makes American literature American? "The First Seven Years" tackles some essentially American themes and conflicts: the desire to move up in the world in a land of opportunity; the pressure to conform to society's materialistic values; and the conflict between the ideals of the spirit and the imperatives of the "real" world of commerce and money. In an essay, explain how each of the story's main characters—Feld, Miriam, and Sobel—represents an aspect of these themes.

Name _____ Date _____

Selection Test B

Critical Reading *Identify the letter of the choice that best completes the statement or answers the question.*

_____ 1. Which of the following phrases best summarizes Feld's relationship with his daughter through most of "The First Seven Years"?
   A. proud and boastful of her accomplishments
   B. alienated, but attempting to build a better relationship with her
   C. understanding and appreciative of her uniqueness
   D. loving, but disappointed by her decisions

_____ 2. Which of the following statements illustrates how a reader of "The First Seven Years" might identify with Miriam?
   A. I, too, am devoted to my parents and look to them for guidance.
   B. My parents mean well, but they really need to trust me and let me make my own decisions.
   C. Once I went on a first date and had a really terrific time.
   D. My greatest dream is to attend college and read the classics.

_____ 3. In "The First Seven Years," what happens when Max enters the shop and asks Feld to repair some shoes?
   A. Sobel sees Max, grabs his coat, and storms out.
   B. Max sees Miriam's picture and is immediately taken with her.
   C. Feld trades the repair work for some accounting help.
   D. Feld convinces Max to ask Miriam for a date.

_____ 4. Which of the following does Max represent to Feld in "The First Seven Years"?
   A. a chance to improve his own life
   B. a way to realize a dream
   C. an escape from a life of hard work
   D. a professional with solid values

_____ 5. How does the author characterize Max in "The First Seven Years"?
   A. unattractive, but sensitive
   B. poor, but sincere
   C. unattractive and uninteresting
   D. intelligent and interesting

_____ 6. In "The First Seven Years," how can a reader summarize the way Miriam responds to her father's attempt to match her with Max?
   A. She is resentful toward her father for trying to run her life.
   B. She is willing to experience new things but makes up her own mind.
   C. She is too young and idealistic to know what is good for her.
   D. She is enthusiastic and appreciative of her father's concern for her.

_____ 7. What experience would help a reader identify with Feld and some of his issues with Sobel in "The First Seven Years"?
A. being an employee
B. being a matchmaker
C. being a shoemaker
D. being a small business owner

_____ 8. Which of the following statements best summarizes the relationship between Feld and Sobel in "The First Seven Years"?
A. Feld depends on Sobel but does not regard him highly.
B. Feld feels grateful for Sobel's help but is irritated by his work habits.
C. Sobel works for Feld for very little money because of his gratitude toward Feld.
D. Sobel relies on Feld's good nature to keep his job.

_____ 9. Why is Feld angry when he first realizes that Sobel loves Miriam in "The First Seven Years"?
A. He feels deceived by Sobel.
B. He knows Max doesn't have a chance with Miriam.
C. He feels deceived by Miriam.
D. He is embarrassed by his visit to Sobel's room.

_____ 10. Feld's epiphany in "The First Seven Years" probably leads him to acknowledge that
A. education is not as important as love.
B. Miriam will make her own choices about her life.
C. Sobel and Miriam are more intelligent than he realized.
D. his dreams are based on his own insecurities.

_____ 11. At the end of "The First Seven Years," Feld begins to soften toward Sobel. This occurs because Feld recognizes that
A. he needs Sobel to work for him.
B. Sobel would be a good husband for Miriam.
C. Sobel deeply loves his daughter.
D. Sobel is just like him.

_____ 12. Which of the following lines from "The First Seven Years" hints at how Feld feels following his epiphany?
A. "The room was quiet."
B. "Feld rose and left."
C. "He went slowly down the stairs . . ."
D. ". . . once outside, . . . he walked with a stronger stride."

_____ 13. Based on the information in "The First Seven Years," what can a reader reasonably predict about Miriam?
A. She will probably date Max again.
B. She will probably go to college.
C. She will probably marry Sobel.
D. She will probably lose interest in books.

Name _____ Date _____

_____ 14. What is Sobel doing at the end of "The First Seven Years"?
   A. working out his anger by pounding on the repaired last
   B. working steadily toward the time when he can approach Miriam
   C. returning to Feld's shop because it's the only job he can get
   D. taking pity on Feld because of his poor health

_____ 15. "The First Seven Years" is primarily about
   A. difficulties in communication.
   B. misunderstandings between generations.
   C. the necessity of practical dreams.
   D. the reexamination of cherished values.

Vocabulary

_____ 16. In "The First Seven Years" Feld wants more for Miriam than to meet *illiterate* shipping clerks, people who are
   A. not wealthy. C. unable to read or write.
   B. uneducated. D. part of the working class.

_____ 17. In "The First Seven Years," which quality of Max does Miriam find most *repugnant*?
   A. his physical appearance C. his educational achievements
   B. his materialist values D. his forward manner

Essay

18. In "The First Seven Years," Feld wants his daughter to have a more comfortable life than his own. Miriam, on the other hand, doesn't seem to be complaining. She has chosen "independence," which means she has taken a job instead of committing herself to being supported by her father while she goes to college. In an essay, explain how Miriam's choice gives her independence. What does her choice provide for her that her father's plan does not? What would Feld's plan to send her to college provide for Miriam that her own plan does not? Given that Miriam's father *can* afford to send her to college, do you think she made the best decision?

19. "The First Seven Years" is told from Feld's point of view. This helps readers feel well acquainted with him. In an essay, describe the character of Feld, his hopes and dreams, and how they change. How does the story build to his epiphany? What clues does the story hold to indicate that the answer to his dreams for Miriam may be right in front of him?

20. Everyone has a different idea of what it takes to be happy and successful. In "The First Seven Years," each character has slightly different ideals and goals. In an essay, analyze what is revealed about Feld, Sobel, Max, and Miriam. Explain what each character's actions indicate about that person's notion of what it takes to be happy and successful. With whose notion do you agree most? In your essay, consider attitudes toward love, education, and wealth.

21. **Thinking About the Essential Question: What makes American literature American?** "The First Seven Years" tackles some essentially American themes and conflicts: the desire to move up in the world in a land of opportunity; the pressure to conform to society's materialistic values; and the conflict between the ideals of the spirit and the imperatives of the "real" world of commerce and money. In an essay, explain how each of the story's main characters—Feld, Miriam, and Sobel—represents an aspect of these themes.

Vocabulary Warm-up Word Lists

Study these words from the selections. Then, complete the activities.

Word List A

absurdity [ab SER duh tee] *n.* ridiculousness; nonsense; silliness
   The speech lasted so long that it reached a point of absurdity.

acrobat [AK ruh bat] *n.* an expert performer of gymnastic feats
   He spent years training to be an acrobat in the circus.

balancing [BAL uhns ing] *adj.* achieving a condition of steadiness
   The gymnasts practiced their balancing act by walking on a narrow beam.

death-defying [DETH di FY ing] *adj.* with the risk of being killed; dangerous
   Known for his risk-taking, Mario performed death-defying acts.

existence [eg ZIS tuhns] *n.* life; the state of being
   He knew that he lived a privileged existence in his huge house.

spreadeagled [SPRED ee guhld] *v.* with arms and legs spread out; sprawled
   When I came home, I found her spreadeagled across the bed.

taut [TAWT] *adj.* pulled or stretched tightly
   The wire that formed the railing was pulled taut.

theatrics [thee A triks] *n.* staged or planned effects
   Randi called attention to herself through various theatrics.

Word List B

audience [AW dee uhns] *n.* group of people watching a performance
   The members of the audience clapped a great deal at the end of the concert.

entrechats [AHN truh shahz] *n.* (French) moves in ballet during which a dancer crosses
his legs rapidly while jumping in the air
   That particular dance includes many entrechats for the male dancers to perform.

eternal [ee TER nuhl] *adj.* lasting forever
   Some forms of memorials are said to be eternal.

gravity [GRAV i tee] *n.* seriousness in attitude or behavior
   It was a sad occasion, and everyone behaved with gravity.

leap [LEEP] *n.* long or high jump
   The deer fled through the underbrush and made a giant leap over the cliff.

perceive [per SEEV] *v.* to become aware of; to grasp
   After listening to the speaker for a while, I began to perceive that she didn't know her subject.

realist [REE uh list] *n.* someone who is sensible and practical in their view of life
   Tom was such a realist that he didn't enjoy fantasy novels.

stance [STANS] *n.* a way of standing; posture
   The dog took up an attentive stance once he smelled the treats in my pocket.

"Constantly Risking Absurdity" by Lawrence Ferlinghetti
Vocabulary Warm-up Exercises

Exercise A *Fill in the blanks, using each word from Word List A only once.*

The [1] _____ wire was stretched across the canyon as Evel Knievel prepared to execute one of his [2] _____ stunts. The man took his self-promotion to a new level of [3] _____, risking his very [4] _____ again and again in search of fame and fortune. His sense of the dramatic was so great that even those who normally hated such [5] _____ seemed compelled to watch. [6] _____ his motorcycle wheels on the thinnest of cables, he leapt on the machine with the agility of an [7] _____. And sure enough, he made it across, sprawling [8] _____ on the ground at the finish of his stunt. Once again, he had cheated death and survived to jump again another day.

Exercise B *Decide if each sentence below makes sense. If not, rewrite it so that it does. Be sure to use the underlined vocabulary word in your new sentence.*

1. Fencers have to assume the ready <u>stance</u> before they begin to fight.

   _____

2. He was such a <u>realist</u> that he was always coming up with wild schemes.

   _____

3. The performance was over so quickly that it seemed <u>eternal</u>.

   _____

4. She was so big and clumsy that she could perform fantastic <u>entrechats</u>.

   _____

5. The professor spoke with such <u>gravity</u> that he kept bursting into laughter.

   _____

6. He took a <u>leap</u> off the diving board and made a terrific splash.

   _____

7. If you <u>perceive</u> something, you have no idea what it means.

   _____

8. The <u>audience</u> was so small that the play was sure to make a lot of money.

   _____

"Constantly Risking Absurdity" by Lawrence Ferlinghetti
Reading Warm-up A

Read the following passage. Then, complete the activities.

Sometimes people talk about "running away and joining the circus." For most that's not a very practical idea, but for those who are serious about becoming performers there is an alternative: The San Francisco School of Circus Arts.

In 1773 near London, England, Phillip Astley invented the performance structure that we call a circus. But the techniques of performance and the staged effects that make up a circus, the theatrics that thrill crowds, have been around for thousands of years. They include the skills of acrobatics, tumbling, contortion, juggling, aerial work, and physical comedy or clowning. Balancing acts also thrill crowds with the performer's ability to hold steady while enacting some feat.

Wendy Parkman and Judy Finelli, members of the Pickle Family Circus, began the circus school in 1984. Small at first, it has expanded over the years. At first, a master Chinese acrobat was hired to teach the ancient skills needed to perform gymnastic feats. Those classes formed the core of the school, with other programs added later.

Today, many adults who are seeking circus careers attend the school. It now contains the only year-long clown school in the country, called the Clown Conservatory. People who go there want to learn to harness their own brands of absurdity and become professional clowns, utilizing this silliness. The school also holds children's classes and summer camps.

Some people come to the circus to watch the high-wire act in which risky, death-defying feats are performed on a taut wire, stretched overhead. Others come to laugh at a clown falling spreadeagled on his back, sprawled on the floor. Whatever the reason, people love the circus. This performance form continues to provide entertainment for new generations and a rewarding existence for the performers living and working in the circus.

1. Circle the words that give a clue to <u>theatrics</u>. Use *theatrics* in an original sentence.

2. Describe a <u>balancing</u> act in a circus. Give a word or phrase that means the opposite of *balancing*.

3. Where did the first teacher of <u>acrobats</u> came from? Use the word *acrobat* in a sentence of your own.

4. Does a person who wants to become a clown need a sense of <u>absurdity</u>? Give your own definition of the word *absurdity*.

5. Circle the words that tell where <u>death-defying</u> feats take place. What kind of person engages in *death-defying* behavior?

6. Underline the word that helps explain the meaning of <u>taut</u>. Write an original sentence using the word *taut*.

7. What would a <u>spreadeagled</u> clown look like? Have you ever been *spreadeagled*?

8. Underline the word that tells what kind of <u>existence</u> circus performers have. Give a word that means the same as *existence*.

Name _____ Date _____

"Constantly Risking Absurdity" by Lawrence Ferlinghetti
Reading Warm-up B

Read the following passage. Then, complete the activities.

Rebecca had spent so many years dancing that she had a hard time giving it up. She was moving with her parents to a small town that had no ballet school. Although the <u>realist</u> in her had known from an early age that she would never be good enough to dance at the highest level, the thought of never again performing a <u>leap</u>, of never jumping gracefully through the air, was just too distressing to think about. And what about her specialty, <u>entrechats</u>? She could cross her legs in the air more rapidly than anyone else in her class! She just didn't believe that any other experience could equal the feeling of dancing in front of an <u>audience</u>, even if the people watching were mostly her family and friends, and those of her fellow dancers.

On the other hand, she would be glad to be relieved of the tedious classes and practices. They often went over the correct way to execute a single step so many times that the sessions seemed <u>eternal</u>. Each detail of a <u>stance</u> or step had to be repeated until the posture and step were perfect. The amount of preparation necessary to perform a simple scene in one ballet drove her crazy. There was no time for joking around with the other dancers, as the ballet master treated everything with seriousness and <u>gravity</u>. When the students would <u>perceive</u> his mood worsening, they would stop talking and wait quietly. Should someone not notice his mood and fail to suppress a giggle, a single icy glance silenced her immediately.

After careful consideration, Rebecca decided maybe she wouldn't miss it so much after all. Perhaps she would try writing for the school newspaper—seeing her name in print would be satisfying, too!

1. Underline the words that tell what the <u>realist</u> in her knew. Give a word that means the opposite of *realist*.

2. Circle the word that has a similar meaning to <u>leap</u>. Write your own sentence using the word *leap*.

3. Underline the words in a nearby sentence that give the meaning of <u>entrechats</u>. Do you think it would be hard to do that dance step, and why?

4. Underline the words that tell who is most of the <u>audience</u> for Rebecca's performances. Tell about something for which you have been in the *audience*.

5. Circle the words that explain what made a class seem <u>eternal</u>. Give another word that means the same as *eternal*.

6. Give your own definition of <u>stance</u>. Name another activity that has a special *stance*.

7. Circle the word that has a similar meaning to <u>gravity</u> in this passage. Write an original sentence that uses *gravity* with this meaning of the word.

8. Underline the words that tell what students would <u>perceive</u>. Give another word that means the same as *perceive*.

"Constantly Risking Absurdity" by Lawrence Ferlinghetti
Literary Analysis: Extended Metaphor

In "Constantly Risking Absurdity," Lawrence Ferlinghetti builds the entire poem on a single **extended metaphor**—in this case, a long, sustained comparison between the craft of poetry and the physical skills required of the acrobat. One false step, he implies, and someone could end up flat on the ground—either the acrobat or the poet.

DIRECTIONS: *Use the chart below to identify several examples of the extended metaphor used by Ferlingheti in this poem. In the left-hand column, list an example of the extended metaphor; in the right-hand column, explain how the example contributes to the meaning of the poem.*

Example of Extended Metaphor	How It Adds to the Meaning of the Poem

Name _____ Date _____

"Constantly Risking Absurdity" by Lawrence Ferlinghetti
Reading Strategy: Visualize or Picture the Action

In "Constantly Risking Absurdity," Ferlinghetti uses phrases and line breaks rather than punctuation to signal units of meaning. As you read each line, **visualize or picture the action** being described. If you lose track of the meaning, return to the last line you could clearly picture, and then read from that point forward. Sometimes you will find that an image extends beyond one line—in that case, keep reading until you feel that you have a complete mental picture of the poet's image.

DIRECTIONS: *Use the chart below as in aid in visualizing or picturing the action of various lines from the poem. The left-hand column gives several examples of lines from the poem. In the right-hand column, briefly explain how you picture or visualize the passage from the poem.*

Passage from the Poem	How I Visualize or Picture the Action
1. the poet like an acrobat climbs on rime to a high wire of his own making	
2. performing entrechats and sleight-of-foot tricks	
3. above a sea of faces	
4. little charleychaplin man	

Name _____ Date _____

"Constantly Risking Absurdity" by Lawrence Ferlinghetti
Vocabulary Builder

Word List

absurdity   taut   realist

A. DIRECTIONS: *Think about the meaning of the underlined Word List word in each sentence. Then, answer the question.*

1. During their animated discussion about politics, Juana declared that she thought that Gerald's desire to have a national voter ID card was an <u>absurdity.</u> Was she agreeing with Gerald's position? How do you know?

   _____

   _____

2. The movie critic described the movie's plot as "<u>taut.</u>" Was the critic paying a compliment to the movie? How do you know?

   _____

   _____

3. Tariq said that his proposals for this year's student council would reflect the fact that he considers himself a <u>realist.</u> Do you think that Tariq's program would include any unreasonable demands? How do you know?

   _____

   _____

B. DIRECTIONS: *On each line, write the letter of the word or phrase that is most nearly* opposite *in meaning to the Word List word.*

____ 1. absurdity
   A. caution
   B. seriousness
   C. fragility
   D. sincerity

____ 2. taut
   A. authentic
   B. understood
   C. slack
   D. unsightly

____ 3. realist
   A. idealist
   B. artist
   C. creator
   D. director

"Constantly Risking Absurdity" by Lawrence Ferlinghetti
Support for Writing

Using "Constantly Risking Absurdity" as a model, write a poem using an extended metaphor. In the poem, compare something abstract to a concrete object or a physical activity.

Before you begin, make a list of ways the two things are alike. Use the graphic organizer below as an aid in identifying the abstract idea, the concrete object or physical activity, and the ways in which they are alike.

Abstract idea:

Concrete object or physical activity:

How the abstract idea and object or activity are alike:

1._____

_____

2._____

_____

3._____

_____

4._____

_____

"Constantly Risking Absurdity" by Lawrence Ferlinghetti
Enrichment: Physical Comedy

The poem "Constantly Risking Absurdity" compares the poet/acrobat to "a little charleychaplin man/who may or may not catch" Beauty's "fair eternal form." Charlie Chaplin was one of the greatest entertainers of the twentieth century. A pioneer in the art of cinema early in the century, he catapulted to worldwide fame in a series of silent films featuring his recurring character, "the Tramp"—the "little charleychaplin man" alluded to in the poem.

The Tramp was always attired in worn, faded gentleman's clothes; waddling cheerfully with a twirling cane, he was polite and kind almost to a fault, and always found himself on the receiving end of life's bitter blows and misfortunes. Chaplin's skillful use of facial expressions and acrobatic physical movements helped to pioneer the modern form of physical comedy, which inspired many subsequent movie and TV comedians such as Red Skelton, Jerry Lewis, Lucille Ball, Jim Carrey, and Will Ferrell. In contrast to more verbal comedians such as Jerry Seinfeld or Jay Leno, these comics rely heavily on physical absurdities and a variety of facial expressions to get laughs.

DIRECTIONS: *Answer the questions below to give information and opinions about your favorite physical comedian.*

My favorite physical comedian is: _____

1. Explain why the person you chose is your favorite physical comedian.

   _____

   _____

   _____

2. Name at least two or three major films or TV series in which this comedian has appeared.

   _____

   _____

3. Describe some of the most notable or characteristic routines or highlights of this comedian's physical comedy technique.

   _____

   _____

   _____

4. Explain why the comedian you chose would or would not work as an allusion in place of "little charleychaplin man" in the poem "Constantly Risking Absurdity."

   _____

   _____

   _____

   _____

Name _____ Date _____

"Constantly Risking Absurdity" by Lawrence Ferlinghetti
Open-Book Test

Short Answer *Write your responses to the questions in this section on the lines provided.*

1. In the extended metaphor of "Constantly Risking Absurdity," Ferlinghetti compares the poet to what kind of entertainer?

   _____

   _____

2. "Constantly Risking Absurdity" is built on a single extended metaphor, or long, sustained comparison. This extended metaphor is made up of a series of smaller metaphors or images that work together to create a sustained comparison between the jobs of the poet and the high-wire artist. Using the chart below, list three of these smaller metaphors or images. Then, in the right-hand column, briefly explain what each means in terms of the job of the poet.

Metaphor or Image	Summary of What It Means

3. In "Constantly Risking Absurdity," Ferlinghetti speaks of the poet climbing "to a high wire of his own making." As you try to picture that image, what aspect of the poet's work do you think about?

   _____

   _____

4. In "Constantly Risking Absurdity," when Ferlinghetti speaks of the poet "performing entrechats / and sleight-of-foot tricks," what kind of dancing skills do you visualize? How do such skills relate to the work of the poet? Explain your answer.

_____

_____

_____

_____

5. In "Constantly Risking Absurdity," what does Ferlinghetti imply about the poet's work when he writes that the poet must perform this high-wire act "all without mistaking / any thing/ for what it may not be"? How does this relate to the poem's extended metaphor?

_____

_____

_____

6. In "Constantly Risking Absurdity," Ferlinghetti writes of the poet/acrobat performing "above a sea of faces." As you visualize this image from the poem, what does it say about the attitude of the readers who are the audience for poetry? Explain your answer.

_____

_____

_____

7. Why do you think Ferlinghetti capitalizes the first letter of the word *beauty* in this line from "Constantly Risking Absurdity"?

    where Beauty stands and waits

_____

_____

8. What kind of image do you picture when you think of the "little charleychaplin man" mentioned by Ferlinghetti toward the end of "Constantly Risking Absurdity"? Does this image seem consistent with the image of the high-wire artist portrayed earlier in the poem? Why or why not?

_____

_____

_____

_____

9. Which line of "Constantly Risking Absurdity" most clearly indicates Ferlinghetti's belief that there is a major element of suspense in the act of writing a poem? Explain your answer.

_____

_____

_____

10. If, in a discussion about the problem of global warming, someone characterized your proposal for solving this problem as an "absurdity," would the person be supporting your proposal? Why or why not? Base your answer on the meaning of *absurdity* as it is used in "Constantly Risking Absurdity."

_____

_____

Essay

Write an extended response to the question of your choice or to the question or questions your teacher assigns you.

11. In "Constantly Risking Absurdity," Ferlinghetti characterizes the writing of poetry as a risky business, similar to the dangers of a high-wire act. Do you agree that writing poetry is risky? Why or why not? Explain your answer in an essay that cites details from the poem.

12. In "Constantly Risking Absurdity," Ferlinghetti writes that the poet is "the super realist." Do you agree that the typical poet is a super realist, or a realist of any sort? Why or why not? Explain your answer in an essay that uses clear reasoning and cites details from the poem.

13. In "Constantly Risking Absurdity," Ferlinghetti writes that the poet is "[c]onstantly risking absurdity and death." Does Ferlinghetti believe that the poet is literally risking "death" when he or she writes a poem? In what sense does he think that writing serious poetry is equivalent to putting one's life at stake? Support your answer with details from the poem.

14. **Thinking About the Essential Question: How does literature shape or reflect society?** "Constantly Risking Absurdity" can be read as a portrait of the role of the artist in general—or the poet in particular—in modern society. What personal traits are most important in the artist/poet, according to the poem? What does the importance of these traits say about the society in which the artist poet does his or her work? Develop your answer in an essay supported by details from the poem.

Oral Response

15. Go back to question 1, 3, or 7 or to the question your teacher assigns to you. Take a few minutes to expand your answer and prepare an oral response. Find additional details in "Constantly Risking Absurdity" that support your points. If necessary, make notes to guide your oral response.

Name _____ Date _____

"Constantly Risking Absurdity" by Lawrence Ferlinghetti
Selection Test A

Critical Reading *Identify the letter of the choice that best completes the statement or answers the question.*

_____ 1. As part of the extended metaphor of "Constantly Risking Absurdity," Ferlinghetti compares the poet to a(n)

    A. comedian   C. firefighter

    B. acrobat   D. engineer

_____ 2. In stating that the poet writes on "a high wire of his own making," Ferlinghetti means that the poet

    A. is always original

    B. looks down on his audience

    C. takes risks

    D. must write slowly

_____ 3. The title of "Constantly Risking Absurdity" implies that the poet is always in danger of

    A. physical injury

    B. appearing foolish

    C. offending his audience

    D. making very little money

_____ 4. In "Constantly Risking Absurdity," when Ferlinghetti says that the poet performs "sleight-of-foot tricks," he is comparing the poet to a

    A. singer or musician   C. burglar or other criminal

    B. dancer or acrobat   D. teacher or sage

_____ 5. In "Constantly Risking Absurdity," who makes up the "sea of faces" above which the poet performs?

    A. readers of poetry

    B. the poet's family

    C. the poet's children

    D. other circus performers

_____ 6. In "Constantly Risking Absurdity," as you visualize an acrobat moving across a high wire, balancing on eyebeams, what kind of process does the writing of the poem seem to be?

    A. casual and relaxing   C. quick and breezy

    B. safe and secure   D. slow and careful

_____ 7. Ferlinghetti writes that the poet "climbs on rime." Knowing that *rime* can mean either "tufts of ice" or "rhyme," you can tell that Ferlinghetti is using the word *rime* as a(n)

    A. pun   **C.** symbol

    B. metaphor   **D.** allusion

_____ 8. In "Constantly Risking Absurdity," when Ferlinghetti used the term "high theatrics," you know that he is making a pun because, in this context, *high* can mean both "superior" and

    A. inferior

    B. at a great height

    C. dull

    D. with great passion

_____ 9. In "Constantly Risking Absurdity," when Ferlinghetti writes that the "acrobat" must proceed "without mistaking/any thing/for what it may not be," he means that the poet must

    A. wear a blindfold   **C.** live in a dreamworld

    B. wear a mask   **D.** see the world clearly

_____ 10. In "Constantly Risking Absurdity," when Ferlinghetti calls the poet a "super realist," he means that a poet must always try to find

    A. truth   **C.** money

    B. fame   **D.** power

_____ 11. What activity of the poet in "Constantly Risking Absurdity," would be equivalent to the acrobat's "taking of each stance or step"?

    A. finding a comfortable place to work

    B. deciding how long the poem should be

    C. writing each word

    D. thinking of a subject

_____ 12. In the extended metaphor of "Constantly Risking Absurdity," the poet's "taut truth" is equivalent to the acrobat's

    A. safety net   **C.** partner

    B. high wire   **D.** costume

_____ 13. In "Constantly Risking Absurdity," the poet/acrobat is described as working with what fellow performer?

    A. little charleychaplinman   **C.** taut truth

    B. super realist   **D.** Beauty

_____ 14. In "Constantly Risking Absurdity," the term "eternal form" implies that Beauty is
  A. immortal
  B. fragile
  C. temperamental
  D. unreal

_____ 15. In "Constantly Risking Absurdity," who makes the "death-defying leap" near the end of the poem?
  A. little charleychaplin man
  B. taut truth
  C. super realist
  D. Beauty

Essay

16. In "Constantly Risking Absurdity," Ferlinghetti portrays the poet as someone who takes great risks—just as a high-wire acrobat takes risks. Do you agree that writing poetry involves taking great risks? Why or why not? Explain your answer in an essay supported by clear reasoning and specific examples.

17. In "Constantly Risking Absurdity," Ferlinghetti writes that the poet "must perforce perceive/taut truth/before the taking of each stance or step." How do these lines underscore Ferlinghetti's view of the poet as a "super realist"? Do you agree that the poet is a seeker after truth and reality? Why or why not? Develop your thoughts in an essay supported by details from the poem.

18. In "Constantly Risking Absurdity," Ferlinghetti goes so far as to claim that trying to bring off the high-wire act of writing a poem risks not only absurdity but also death. Do you think that Ferlinghetti believes that the poet is risking his life when he or she writes a poem? If so, in what sense might this be true? Develop your thoughts in an essay supported by details from the selection.

19. **Thinking About the Essential Question: How does literature shape or reflect society?** "Constantly Risking Absurdity" can be read as a portrait of the role of the artist in general—or the poet in particular—in modern society. What personal traits are most important in the artist/poet, according to the poem? What does the importance of these traits say about the society in which the artist poet does his or her work? Develop your answer in an essay supported by details from the poem.

Name _____ Date _____

"Constantly Risking Absurdity" by Lawrence Ferlinghetti
Selection Test B

Critical Reading *Identify the letter of the choice that best completes the statement or answers the question.*

____ 1. In the extended metaphor of "Constantly Risking Absurdity," who is constantly "risking absurdity/and death"?
A. the dancer
B. the audience
C. the poet
D. Beauty

____ 2. In "Constantly Risking Absurdity," the poet is described as performing "above the heads/of his audience." This line can be taken as a pun that means that the poet is performing not only at a great height, but also
A. with jealousy of the audience
B. without concern for the audience
C. with condescension toward the audience
D. beyond the comprehension of the audience

____ 3. Which of the following phrases from "Constantly Risking Absurdity" is an example of a pun?
A. climbs on rime
B. paces his way
C. sea of faces
D. other side of day

____ 4. In "Constantly Risking Absurdity," what is the meaning of the phrase "a high wire of his own making"?
A. The acrobat must also be a skilled craftsman.
B. The acrobat deserves whatever fate might befall him.
C. The poet is to blame for the difficulty of his art.
D. The poet's art is an inherently risky one.

____ 5. In the phrase "performing entrechats," Ferlinghetti likens the poet's craft to that of which performing artist in "Constantly Risking Absurdity"?
A. acrobat
B. actor
C. ballet dancer
D. fire eater

____ 6. In "Constantly Risking Absurdity," the phrase "high theatrics" is a pun because it refers both to the great height at which the acrobat performs and to the
A. exalted nature of his art
B. state of mind of the performer
C. thrills produced in the audience
D. price of admission to the performance

Unit 5 Resources: Prosperity and Protest
© Pearson Education, Inc. All rights reserved.
80

_____ 7. In "Constantly Risking Absurdity," by stating that the acrobat/poet performs "sleight-of-foot tricks," the poet implies that this art form involves an element of
    A. magic
    B. luck
    C. risk
    D. folly

_____ 8. Which phrase from "Constantly Risking Absurdity" contradicts the idea of the poet as a starry-eyed visionary who is out of touch with everyday life?
    A. performing entrechats
    B. super realist
    C. balancing on eyebeams
    D. little charleychaplin man

_____ 9. In "Constantly Risking Absurdity," the phrase "taut truth" implies that truth is
    A. easily found
    B. impossible to achieve
    C. rigorous and demanding
    D. beautiful and abundant

_____ 10. As you visualize the following lines from "Constantly Risking Absurdity," what can you assume about the process of writing poetry?
    For he's the super realist/who must perforce perceive/taut truth /before the taking of each stance or step. . .
    A. It is enriching and gratifying.
    B. It is frustrating and discouraging.
    C. It is slow and exacting.
    D. It is boring and tedious.

_____ 11. Who or what is placed on the highest level in "Constantly Risking Absurdity"?
    A. the poet
    B. death
    C. truth
    D. Beauty

_____ 12. In "Constantly Risking Absurdity," the word *gravity* refers both to Beauty's seriousness and to the fact that it is
    A. so high in the air
    B. about to fall
    C. unattainable
    D. an illusion

_____ 13. From reading the phrase "little charleychaplin man" in "Constantly Risking Absurdity," you are likely to visualize someone who is
    A. nervous and unsure
    B. bold and courageous
    C. bored and indifferent
    D. beautiful and commanding

_____ 14. In "Constantly Risking Absurdity," the phrase "fair eternal form" applies to
   A. the poet
   B. the audience
   C. Beauty
   D. empty air

_____ 15. Which sentence best captures the role of the poet as portrayed in the last ten lines of "Constantly Risking Absurdity"?
   A. He falls to the ground in his futile attempt to capture beauty.
   B. He bravely tries to pluck beauty out of the empty air.
   C. His words only stress the inherent emptiness of existence.
   D. His words appear pathetic and inadequate next to the eternal form of Beauty.

Essay

16. One idea of "Constantly Risking Absurdity" is that the poet takes great risks when composing a poem; like the high-wire artist, he must bring great concentration and skill to a task that involves a high risk of failure before an audience. What other kinds of highly skilled activities involve mastering a difficult skill and performing before an audience with the risk of failure? Are all such activities worthwhile, or are some not worth the risk? Develop your thoughts in an essay supported by clear reasoning and specific examples.

17. "Constantly Risking Absurdity" is an extended metaphor that compares the writing of poetry to the performance of a high-wire act before a circus audience. Do you think that this comparison works? Why or why not? Explain your views in an essay supported by clear reasoning and details from the poem.

18. By the end of "Constantly Risking Absurdity," the reader discovers that the high-wire artist/poet has been using his perception of "taut truth" to advance ever closer to "that still higher perch where Beauty stands and waits." It would appear that Ferlinghetti believes that the poet uses truth—or his perception of truth—as a means of capturing beauty in his poetry. Do you believe that achieving beauty is the highest and most important purpose of the poet? Why or why not? Develop your thoughts in an essay supported by clear reasoning and details from the selection.

19. **Thinking About the Essential Question: How does literature shape or reflect society?** "Constantly Risking Absurdity" can be read as a portrait of the role of the artist in general—or the poet in particular—in modern society. What personal traits are most important in the artist/poet, according to the poem? What does the importance of these traits say about the society in which the artist poet does his or her work? Develop your answer in an essay supported by details from the poem.

Vocabulary Warm-up Word Lists

Study these words from the selections. Then, complete the activities.

Word List A

acid [AS id] *n.* sour liquid
   Vinegar is a common <u>acid</u>.

conclusion [kuhn KLOO zhuhn] *n.* end; final part; outcome
   At the <u>conclusion</u> of the movie, everyone lived happily ever after.

despair [di SPAIR] *n.* deep, sad hopelessness; anguish; despondency
   The <u>despair</u> that had overwhelmed Greta lifted when she saw his face.

fondle [FAHN duhl] *v.* to touch, stroke, or pet affectionately
   We watched our dog, Sadie, <u>fondle</u> her brand new puppies.

kinsman [KINZ muhn] *n.* a relative
   My <u>kinsman</u>, Mark Smith, is related to me through my father's family.

powdered [POW derd] *v.* sprinkled, dabbed, or covered with powder, a dry substance of
fine, dust-like particles
   Sylvia looked into the mirror and <u>powdered</u> her nose.

unmisted [un MISTD] *adj.* not covered over with a thin mist or haze
   Jack had a clear, <u>unmisted</u> view of the situation and knew just what to do.

wallowing [WAH loh ing] *adj.* pitching or rolling back and forth
   The <u>wallowing</u> ship rocked in the waves as it attempted to steer north.

Word List B

agitation [aj uh TAY shuhn] *n.* a disturbance of feelings or actions
   David's <u>agitation</u> resulted from the negative reviews of his book.

awesome [AW suhm] *adj.* remarkable; impressive
   The singer's <u>awesome</u> voice won her performance a standing ovation.

concealed [kuhn SEELD] *v.* hid; covered up
   Isabel's smile <u>concealed</u> her disappointment.

courage [KER ij] *n.* bravely facing difficult, or fearful, tasks or situations
   The man with the artificial leg had the <u>courage</u> to climb the mountain.

flickers [FLIK erz] *v.* burns or shines unsteadily
   The candlelight <u>flickers</u> when a breeze blows across the flame.

meditate [MED uh tayt] *v.* to think deeply and continuously; reflect
   I like reserving thirty minutes out of each day to <u>meditate</u>.

speckles [SPEK uhls] *n.* lots of little dots
   The fur on our dog's nose is sprinkled with cute brown <u>speckles</u>.

wringing [RING ing] *v.* the act of squeezing or twisting
   Juan was <u>wringing</u> the spilled lemonade out of the soaked tablecloth.

"Mirror" by Sylvia Plath and **"Courage"** by Anne Sexton
Vocabulary Warm-up Exercises

Exercise A *Fill in the blanks, using each word from Word List A only once.*

The night Dakota's girlfriend broke up with him, he was feeling such [1]

_____ that he took Fred on a two-hour walk around the neighborhood.

Dakota could not help replaying her last words in his mind: "I finally have a clear, [2]

_____ view of things," Maureen had said, "I realize I will always be second

in your life to Fred. Your spaniel is like a relative, like a [3] _____. Alas,

this certain knowledge is bitter and sour [4] _____ to me. I must refuse to

drink it, release myself, and start over." Dakota realized that Maureen had an exagger-

ated way of speaking that had always irritated him. Perhaps, in [5] _____,

the break-up was all for the best. However, he was so distracted by these thoughts that

he was not paying attention when Fred started [6] _____ in a mud pud-

dle. Back home, Dakota bathed, dried, and [7] _____ Fred with flea pow-

der. Starting to feel better, Dakota decided to watch a movie. Fred hopped up onto the

couch with him, so that Dakota could [8] _____ his ears.

Exercise B *Decide whether each statement below is true or false. Circle T or F, and explain your answer.*

1. A campfire that <u>flickers</u> blazes brightly.
   T / F _____

2. If you buried a treasure, that means you have <u>concealed</u> it.
   T / F _____

3. An <u>awesome</u> performance is ordinary and uninspiring.
   T / F _____

4. A calm, peaceful landscape is a kind of <u>agitation.</u>
   T / F _____

5. If you are <u>wringing</u> a towel, you are wrapping it decoratively around another object.
   T / F _____

6. A painted wall with <u>speckles</u> on it will contain more than one color.
   T / F _____

7. When you <u>meditate</u>, you act without thinking.
   T / F _____

8. If you have <u>courage</u>, you show spunk and daring in the face of obstacles.
   T / F _____

Name _____ Date _____

"Mirror" by Sylvia Plath and **"Courage"** by Anne Sexton
Reading Warm-up A

Read the following passage. Then, complete the activities.

When Brina stayed at Aunt Helen's, she did homework at the dining room table. There was something deeply sad about the room, an atmosphere of <u>despair</u>. After writing up the results of a science experiment one evening, Brina realized why.

She titled her paper *The EGG-speriment*, since she had left three eggs in different liquid solutions: salt water, plain tap water, and vinegar, otherwise known as acetic <u>acid</u>. The boring tap water egg had not changed a smidge. The saltwater egg had floated. The vinegar egg was the most interesting. A chemical reaction had occurred between the calcium carbonate in the shell and the acid in the vinegar. Brina wrote up the <u>conclusion</u> of the experiment, describing the outcome for each egg.

Afterwards, Brina noticed the gloomy family portrait on the wall. She recognized Aunt Helen's father and his <u>kinsman</u>, a cousin named Roddy. The faces of the two boys, appeared to have been <u>powdered</u>, dabbed with some sort of skin powder or fine make-up. In the background of the painting was a pigsty where animals were visible <u>wallowing</u>, rolling back and forth, in what appeared to be mud. In addition, Roddy's hand appeared to <u>fondle</u> the ears of a piglet, petting the pig as though it were a puppy. Why would an artist include these images in a family portrait, Brina wondered? Perhaps the painter had been attempting to create an <u>unmisted</u>, clear view of the earthy experience of growing up on a farm. In any case, Brina realized that it was the picture, not the dining room, which gave her the creeps. For the remainder of her stay at Aunt Helen's, Brina did her homework in the living room, where the only wall decoration was a large mirror.

1. Circle the nearby words that have a meaning similar to <u>despair</u>. Write an antonym for *despair*.

2. Underline the name for a common household item that is a kind of <u>acid</u>. How would you describe the taste of this type of *acid*?

3. Circle the nearby word that is a synonym for <u>conclusion</u>. What happens in the *conclusion* of this story about Brina?

4. Underline the word that is a clue to the meaning of <u>kinsman</u>. Name a person who is your *kinsman* and how he or she is related to you.

5. Underline the words that explain the meaning of <u>powdered</u>. Use the word *powdered* in a sentence.

6. Circle the words that have a meaning similar to <u>wallowing</u>. Use the word *wallowing* in a sentence.

7. Underline the words that describe what Roddy's hand appeared to <u>fondle</u>. Write a synonym for the word *fondle*.

8. Circle the word that has a meaning similar to <u>unmisted</u>. Write an antonym for the word *unmisted*.

"Mirror" by Sylvia Plath and **"Courage"** by Anne Sexton
Reading Warm-up B

Read the following passage. Then, complete the activities.

If you have ever attempted to write a poem, you know that that there is no simple answer to the question: where do poems come from? A poem can recount the awesome, remarkable feats of an epic hero and describe the courage he manifests in order to overcome difficult obstacles and find a way to safety. Or a poem can meditate on a single moment or object, in order to share deep thoughts and keen observations about a particular feeling or experience. From grand and sweeping to tiny and unique, poems fix moments in words.

Some poets discover that what starts them writing is a kind of agitation; a mental or visual disturbance, or an event which is so upsetting, jarring, or moving, that it compels them to write. Others find that writing poetry allows them to release previously covered up, concealed emotions.

But a poet does not require an emotional extreme, such as anguish or euphoria, to start writing. Plenty of poems come from quieter moments and calmer feelings. The light of a star as it flickers and twinkles in the sky might inspire a poem, for example. Or, a poet might write about imagining that the brown ends of cattails in a swamp appear to be small dots, or speckles, to a bird looking down on them from the sky.

If you write a poem, you may feel you are wringing the important essence out of an event or an emotion, to squeeze the truth out of it. Some poems tell stories; others are humorous, documentary, or musical songs. Yet they nearly all share one thing: a quest for meaning. And that quest, some would argue, is what lies at the heart of what it means to be human.

1. Circle the word that has a meaning similar to awesome. Write another synonym for the word *awesome*.

2. Underline the words that give a clue to the meaning of courage. Write an antonym for the word *courage*.

3. Circle the nearby words that give a clue to the meaning of meditate. Describe a situation or activity that you think could help a person to *meditate*.

4. Underline the words that have a meaning similar to agitation. Write a sentence describing something you find to be an *agitation*.

5. Circle the words that have the same meaning as concealed. Give two antonyms for the word *concealed*.

6. Circle the word that has a meaning similar to flickers. Give an example of something else that *flickers*.

7. Underline the words that have a meaning similar to speckles. Use the word *speckles* in a sentence.

8. Circle the nearby words that have a meaning similar to wringing. Use the word *wringing* in a sentence.

"Mirror" by Sylvia Plath
"Courage" by Anne Sexton

Literary Analysis: Figurative Language

To communicate emotions in a vivid, concrete way to the reader, both Sylvia Plath and Anne Sexton use **figurative language,** or language used imaginatively rather than literally. In particular, they use two figures of speech that compare seemingly dissimilar things.

- A **simile** is a comparison that uses a connecting word such as *like* or *as*: "The child's first step,/as awesome as an earthquake."

- A **metaphor** is a comparison that does not use a connecting word. Instead, the comparison is either implied or directly stated: "Now I am a lake."

DIRECTIONS: *Use the chart below to identify four examples of figurative language—metaphors or similes—from either poem. In the middle column, identify which kind of figure of speech it is—metaphor or simile. Then, in the right-hand column, briefly explain the meaning of the figure of speech.*

Example of Figure of Speech	Metaphor or Simile	Meaning of Figure of Speech

"Mirror" by Sylvia Plath
"Courage" by Anne Sexton

Reading Strategy: Interpreting the Connotations of Words

In most poems, the central message is not directly stated. Instead, it is up to you to look for the poem's underlying meaning. Because poets choose every word with great care, you can often gain clues to a poem's meaning by **interpreting the connotations** of individual words. To do this, consider the associations and feelings a word calls to mind, and then try to determine what common thread ties the words together.

For example, in line 14 of "Mirror" the woman in the poem is said to "reward" the mirror "with tears and an agitation of hands." How would the unhappiness shown by tears and agitation be considered a reward? The unusual use of *reward* in this line encourages you to think about the specific connotation of this word in this context and how it adds to the overall impact of the poem.

DIRECTIONS: *Answer the following questions about the connotations of key words in "Mirror" and "Courage."*

1. In line 2 of "Mirror," the mirror states, "Whatever I see I swallow immediately." What is the connotation of *swallow* in this line? How does that connotation contribute to the poem's overall message?

_____

_____

_____

2. In line 12 of "Mirror," the mirror says that the woman "turns to those liars, the candles or the moon." In what sense would candles and the moon be considered liars in the view of the mirror? What does the connotation of *liars* in this line explain about the mirror's view of the world around it?

_____

_____

_____

3. In the third stanza of "Courage," the poet writes, "Later, if you have endured a great despair,/then you did it alone,/getting a transfusion from the fire. . . ." In what sense would one get a "transfusion" from the fire of a "great despair"? How does the unusual connotation of this word in this context contribute to the poet's meaning?

_____

_____

_____

4. In the second stanza of "Courage," the poet writes, "Later, if you faced the death of bombs and bullets/you did not do it with a banner,/you did it with only a hat to/cover your heart." What is the connotation of the word *banner* in this passage? What does it say about what motivates the courage of the person she writes about?

_____

_____

_____

"**Mirror**" by Sylvia Plath
"**Courage**" by Anne Sexton
Vocabulary Builder

Word List

endured   preconceptions   transformed   transfusion

A. DIRECTIONS: *Think about the meaning of the underlined Word List word in each sentence. Then, answer the question.*

1. If your teacher wrote that your essay was filled with underlined preconceptions, does that mean that she thought that you approached your topic with an open mind? How do you know?

   _____

   _____

2. If a book critic wrote that he had "endured" a new science fiction novel, is it likely that he gave it an unfavorable review? How do you know?

   _____

   _____

3. If you were going to the hospital for a transfusion of blood, would you be donating the blood? How do you know?

   _____

   _____

4. If your friend said that the movie she saw last night had left her transformed, does that mean that the movie had a powerful effect on her? How do you know?

   _____

   _____

B. DIRECTIONS: *On each line, write the letter of the word or phrase that is closest in meaning to the Word List word.*

____ 1. preconceptions
     A. prejudices   C. predicaments
     B. predictions   D. preferences

____ 2. endured
     A. withstood   C. investigated
     B. persisted   D. stretched

____ 3. transfusion
     A. judgment   C. transfer
     B. travel   D. creation

____ 4. transformed
     A. understood   C. pretended
     B. altered   D. propelled

"Mirror" by Sylvia Plath
"Courage" by Anne Sexton
Support for Writing

Both "Mirror" and "Courage" address the full sweep of a human life, from youth to adulthood to old age. However, the poets' portrayals of these stages of life are extremely different. Write an **analytical essay** comparing and contrasting how each speaker sees the process or progress of life.

To help you define and organize your thoughts before you begin writing, answer the following questions about the poems:

1. Do the poets have similar or different attitudes toward aging? What words would you use to describe the speaker's attitude toward aging in each poem?

_____

_____

_____

_____

2. How does each poet use language—metaphors, similes, and striking connotations for familiar words—to convey her attitudes and ideas about aging? What are the key images that convey these attitudes and ideas?

_____

_____

_____

_____

3. Which poem's portrayal of old age strikes you as more truthful and more powerful? Or is each equally powerful and truthful in its way? Why?

_____

_____

_____

_____

After you have answered these questions, use the thoughts and ideas you have gathered to begin writing a rough draft of your essay.

"Mirror" by Sylvia Plath

"Courage" by Anne Sexton

Enrichment: Medals for Bravery in Battle

The second stanza of "Courage" evokes the courage of a soldier in battle: "If you faced the death of bombs and bullets/you did not do it with a banner,/you did it with only a hat to/cover your heart." And if the soldier's buddy saved him "and died himself in so doing,/then his courage was not courage, it was love. . . ."

Armed forces around the world have long awarded medals to soldiers for outstanding acts of bravery in battle. The United States military has a long tradition of awarding such medals.

DIRECTIONS: *Use the chart below as a guide in finding out more about the major medals awarded by the United States military for bravery in battle. Fill in each column of the chart.*

Type of Medal	Reason It Is Awarded	Year of Origin
Medal of Honor		
Silver Star		
Legion of Merit		
Distinguished Flying Cross		
Bronze Star		
Purple Heart		

Name _____ Date _____

"**Mirror**" by Sylvia Plath
"**Courage**" by Anne Sexton

Open-Book Test

Short Answer *Write your responses to the questions in this section on the lines provided.*

1. Who is the "I" who speaks in the poem "Mirror"?

   _____

   _____

2. "Mirror" is as much about the woman who peers into the mirror as about the mirror itself. What does the poem reveal about the woman?

   _____

   _____

3. Reread lines 4–5 of "Mirror," below. Identify the metaphor contained in these lines. Does this metaphor tell only about the mirror, or about the woman in the poem who looks into it? Explain your answer.

   > I am not cruel, only truthful—/The eye of a little god, four-cornered.

   _____

   _____

   _____

   _____

4. What is the significance of the following metaphor, which appears in line 10 of "Mirror"?

   > Now I am a lake.

   _____

   _____

5. What connotation is conveyed by the word "rewards" in the context of lines 14–15 of "Mirror"?

   > She rewards me with tears and an agitation of hands./I am important to her.

   _____

   _____

   _____

6. What quality of courage is celebrated in these lines from "Courage" and throughout the poem?

   > Later, / if you faced the death of bombs and bullets / you did not do it with a banner, / you did it with only a hat to / cover your heart.

   _____

   _____

7. What important meaning is conveyed by Sexton's choice of the word "fondle" in these lines from "Courage"?

> You did not fondle the weakness inside you / though it was there.

_____

_____

_____

8. When "Courage" turns to the subject of old age, the speaker says, "your courage will be shown in little ways/each spring will be a sword you'll sharpen." Identify the metaphor contained in these lines, and briefly explain its meaning.

_____

_____

_____

9. "Mirror" and "Courage" make liberal use of figurative language, both similes and metaphors. Use the chart below to identify four metaphors or similes from either poem. In the middle column, identify which kind of figure of speech it is—metaphor or simile. Then, in the right-hand column, briefly explain the meaning of the figure of speech.

Figure of Speech	Metaphor or Simile	Meaning

10. If a film critic began a review by stating that he had just "endured a new romantic comedy," is it likely that the rest of the review will be unfavorable? Why or why not? Base your answer on the meaning of *endured* as it is used in "Courage."

_____

_____

_____

Essay

Write an extended response to the question of your choice or to the question or questions your teacher assigns you.

11. Anne Sexton's poem "Courage" is about the many points in life that require acts of courage. Of the many kinds of courage mentioned in the poem, which do you think is the most important? Or is there a kind of courage not mentioned in the poem that you think is more important than any of those mentioned? Develop your thoughts in an essay supported by clear reasoning and examples from the poem and your own experience.

12. In Sylvia Plath's "Mirror," the mirror repeatedly characterizes itself as an accurate, even godlike reporter of reality: "I am silver and exact"; "I am not cruel, only truthful"; "I see her back, and reflect it faithfully." Does the mirror really tell the whole story of the woman who is peering into it day after day? Why or why not? Develop your thoughts in an essay supported by examples from the poem.

13. Both Sylvia Plath, the author of "Mirror," and Anne Sexton, the author of "Courage," led extremely painful and emotionally turbulent personal lives. Much of that pain is often reflected in their poems. Are both of these poems merely records of personal pain and despair, or does either of them also offer the promise of hope or redemption? Explain your answer in an essay supported by examples from the poems.

14. **Thinking About the Essential Question: How does literature shape or reflect society?** Both of the poems in this section—"Mirror" by Sylvia Plath and "Courage" by Anne Sexton—express deep personal feelings. Can the feelings expressed in either of these poems be seen as reflections of the society that shaped the poet, or do they express only the private feelings of the poet, apart from any social considerations? Explain your answer in an essay supported by details from the poems.

Oral Response

15. Go back to question 1, 3, or 7 or to the question your teacher assigns to you. Take a few minutes to expand your answer and prepare an oral response. Find additional details in "Mirror" or "Courage" that support your points. If necessary, make notes to guide your oral response.

Name _____ Date _____

Critical Reading *Identify the letter of the choice that best answers the question.*

____ 1. In "Mirror," what message is conveyed by the speaker's behavior when she describes the old woman as a "terrible fish"?
   A. the wish for beauty
   B. the fear of aging
   C. the search for truth
   D. the need for happiness

____ 2. Why is the woman upset when she sees the mirror's truthfulness in "Mirror"?
   A. The mirror has been broken.
   B. The candles have gone out.
   C. She does not believe the mirror.
   D. She does not like what she sees.

____ 3. Who is the "I" in this passage from "Mirror"?
   I am silver and exact. I have not preconceptions.
   A. the woman
   B. the poet
   C. the lake
   D. the mirror

____ 4. In line 3 of "Mirror," the word "unmisted" conveys the connotation that the mirror reflects back an image that is
   A. accurate
   B. flattering
   C. puzzling
   D. unreliable

____ 5. Which of the following terms best describes the figure of speech used in this line from "Mirror"?
   The eye of a little god, four-cornered.
   A. simile
   B. metaphor
   C. personification
   D. hyperbole

_____ 6. In the following passage from "Mirror," which phrase is part of a simile?

> In me she has drowned a young girl, and in me an old woman/Rises toward her day after day, like a terrible fish.

A. In me

B. she has drowned

C. Rises toward her day after day

D. like a terrible fish

_____ 7. The following passage from "Courage" contains an example of what figure of speech?

> The child's first step,/as awesome as an earthquake.

A. metaphor

B. simile

C. personification

D. hyperbole

_____ 8. What quality of the courageous person is conveyed by this passage from "Courage"?

> Later,/if you faced the death of bombs and bullets/you did not do it with a banner, . . .

A. sadness

B. modesty

C. recklessness

D. regret

_____ 9. The following passage from "Courage" is an example of which figure of speech?

> Your courage was a small coal/that you kept swallowing.

A. metaphor

B. simile

C. personification

D. hyperbole

_____ 10. The first twelve lines of "Courage" discuss examples of courage during which part of a person's life?

A. childhood

B. adolescence

C. adulthood

D. old age

____ 11. Which choice best captures the meaning of the phrase "and you'll bargain with the calendar," which appears in the part of "Courage" that deals with old age?

A. You will notice time passing more quickly.

B. You will look forward to the coming of spring.

C. You will resign yourself to impending death.

D. You will hope and strive to live a bit longer.

Essay

12. In "Mirror," a woman looks into the mirror, does not like what she sees, and "turns to those liars, the candles or the moon." How might a candle or the moon act like a liar by providing a false image to her? Write an essay to explain why the candle and the moon might act like liars.

13. "Courage" by Anne Sexton examines a series of situations in a person's life that require special acts of courage. Think of a moment from your life—or from the life of someone you know—that required a special act of courage. Why was courage so important at that moment? Was it easy to summon the courage or not? Describe that moment in an essay that uses vivid examples to convey your message to the reader.

14. **Thinking About the Essential Question: How does literature shape or reflect society?** Both of the poems in this section—"Mirror" by Sylvia Plath and "Courage" by Anne Sexton—express deep personal feelings. Can the feelings expressed in either of these poems be seen as reflections of the society that shaped the poet, or do they express only the private feelings of the poet, apart from any social considerations? Explain your answer in an essay supported by details from the poems.

"Mirror" by Sylvia Plath; **"Courage"** by Anne Sexton
Selection Test B

Critical Reading *Identify the letter of the choice that best answers the question.*

_____ 1. Who or what is the speaker of the poem "Mirror"?
   A. the woman
   B. the reader
   C. the lake
   D. the mirror

_____ 2. Which choice best captures the quality of the mirror that is connoted by the poet's use of the word "swallow" in this line from "Mirror"?

   Whatever I see I swallow immediately.

   A. eager
   B. generous
   C. monstrous
   D. courageous

_____ 3. What does Plath reveal about herself in "Mirror"?
   A. She fears her own aging.
   B. She is cruel.
   C. She is vain.
   D. She rejoices in her youth.

_____ 4. In "Mirror," the mirror is important because it
   A. evokes pleasant memories of the poet's childhood
   B. was a favorite object in the poet's room
   C. was given to her by her mother
   D. symbolizes the poet's self-reflection

_____ 5. In "Mirror," the metaphor of a mirror as a lake
   A. emphasizes the smoothness of the mirror's surface
   B. symbolizes the woman's transformation from a young girl into an old woman
   C. echoes the woman's tears as she looks at herself in the mirror
   D. reinforces the objectivity with which the mirror reflects society

_____ 6. In "Mirror," the mirror states, "I see her back, and reflect it faithfully." In this passage, the use of the word "faithfully" connotes that the mirror views itself as a(n)
   A. obedient lover
   B. spiritual guide
   C. loyal servant
   D. kind friend

_____ 7. Which of the following best captures what the mirror implies about the woman's attitude in the following passage from "Mirror"?

   I see her back, and reflect it faithfully./She rewards me with tears and an agitation of hands.

   A. She is weak.
   B. She is delusional.
   C. She is thoughtful.
   D. She is ungrateful.

_____

8. Which of the following passages from "Mirror" is an example of a metaphor?
   A. "I am silver and exact."
   B. "[I am] [t]he eye of a little god, four-cornered."
   C. "A woman bends over me."
   D. "She rewards me with tears and an agitation of hands."

_____ 9. What is significant about the simile contained in these last two lines of "Mirror"?

   In me she has drowned a young girl, and in me an old woman/Rises toward her day after day, like a terrible fish.

   A. It reinforces a sense of the mirrors objectivity in portraying the woman's image.
   B. It evokes the woman's horror of old age.
   C. It shows that the woman has realized that her fears are ridiculous and exaggerated.
   D. It expresses the woman's regrets over the wasted opportunities of her youth.

_____ 10. "Courage" is divided according to what basic organizing principle?
   A. types of personalities   C. stages of life
   B. various parts of the world   D. degrees of courage

_____ 11. Most of "Courage" is written with the poet addressing the reader as "you." The poet most likely does this in order to
   A. create a sense of distance between herself and the reader
   B. create a sense of shared experience with the reader.
   C. impart an accusatory tone to the poem
   D. create the impression that she is talking about no one in particular

_____ 12. In "Courage," when Sexton writes, "You did not fondle the weakness inside you," the use of the word "fondle" connotes that weakness can sometimes be a source of
   A. comfort
   B. fear
   C. confusion
   D. guilt

_____ 13. In "Courage," writing about acts of courage during warfare, Sexton writes, "Your courage was a small coal/that you kept swallowing." This metaphor conveys the message that acts of courage can sometimes be
   A. nourishing
   B. inspiring
   C. regrettable
   D. difficult

_____ 14. Which of the following passages from "Courage" contains a simile?
   A. "wallowing up the sidewalk"
   B. "you drank their acid/and concealed it"
   C. "love as simple as shaving soap"
   D. "getting a transfusion from the fire"

_____ 15. Which of the following best captures Sexton's meaning in these lines from "Courage"?

Later,/if you have endured a great despair,/then you did it alone,/getting a transfusion from the fire, . . .

A. Suffering can make you stronger.

B. Suffering drives you into greater solitude.

C. Suffering can warm the spirit.

D. Suffering lasts longer if you attempt to confront it alone.

_____ 16. Which choice best conveys the connotation of the word "stride" in this passage from "Courage"?

and at the last moment/when death opens the back door/you'll put on your carpet slippers/ and stride out.

A. unsteadiness

B. panic

C. forgetfulness

D. calm

Essay

17. Of the many kinds of courage mentioned in the poem "Courage," which do you think is the most important? Do you think there is a kind of courage not mentioned in the poem that is more important than any of those Sexton writes about? Explain your ideas in an essay supported by clear reasoning and examples from the poem and your own experience.

18. In Sylvia Plath's "Mirror," the mirror is portrayed as having an almost godlike ability to reproduce the details of reality: "I am silver and exact"; "I am not cruel, only truthful—"; "I see her back, and reflect it faithfully." Do you think that the poet shares the mirror's view of itself as an objective reporter of human reality? Do you think the mirror really tells the whole story of the woman who is peering into it day after day? Why or why not? Develop your thoughts in an essay supported by examples from the poem.

19. The background information in this section of your textbook reveals that both Sylvia Plath and Anne Sexton, for all their creative powers and literary renown, led short, unhappy lives, marked by episodes of debilitating despair. Much of that unhappiness is reflected in their poetry. Do you find the two poems in this section—"Mirror" and "Courage"—to be mainly records of inner despair, or do they also sound notes of hope and redemption? Explain your ideas in an essay supported by examples from both poems.

20. **Thinking About the Essential Question: How does literature shape or reflect society?** Both of the poems in this section—"Mirror" by Sylvia Plath and "Courage" by Anne Sexton—express deep personal feelings. Can the feelings expressed in either of these poems be seen as reflections of the society that shaped the poet, or do they express only the private feelings of the poet, apart from any social considerations? Explain your answer in an essay supported by details from the poems.

Vocabulary Warm-up Word Lists

Study these words from the selections. Then, complete the activities.

Word List A

delicate [DEL i kit] *adj.* fragile; easily damaged or broken
That vase is so <u>delicate</u> that I am afraid to use it.

droop [DROOP] *v.* to sag; sink or hang down
Most plants tend to <u>droop</u> when they need water.

grains [GRAYNZ] *n.* small hard seeds
It took her a long time to pick up all the <u>grains</u> of rice that had spilled.

loam [LOHM] *n.* a rich soil mixture that is excellent for growing plants
The dump truck delivered a load of <u>loam</u> for the garden.

nub [NUB] *n.* a small thing that sticks out; a knob or lump
The vet said not to worry about the small <u>nub</u> on the dog's back.

tendrilous [TEN druh uhs] *adj.* like a slim, wispy, curling, or winding part, usually of a climbing plant
A shoot of the <u>tendrilous</u> vine grew through the window into our house.

urge [ERJ] *n.* inclination; impulse to do something
When she had poison ivy, she felt a constant <u>urge</u> to scratch.

wrestle [RES uhl] *v.* to struggle to move something
The box was so large that they had to <u>wrestle</u> it through the doorway.

Word List B

coaxing [KOHKS ing] *v.* inducing or persuading something gently
She spends a lot of time <u>coaxing</u> her cat to come inside.

intricate [IN tri kit] *adj.* containing many details or small parts
That lace has such a beautiful and <u>intricate</u> design.

lopping [LAHP ing] *v.* cutting off, as a branch; severing
Her trees were so overgrown that she spent all day <u>lopping</u> off branches.

nudges [NUJ ez] *v.* pushes or pokes gently
As the jumping frog slows down, his handler <u>nudges</u> it along the course.

seeping [SEEP ing] *v.* leak, drip, or flow slowly through small openings; ooze; trickle
He discovered too late that water was <u>seeping</u> into the foundation of his house.

sprouts [SPROWTS] *n.* buds; new growth
I love spring when the park is covered with <u>sprouts</u>.

struggling [STRUG ling] *v.* trying very hard; working hard
The box was so heavy that he was <u>struggling</u> to carry it.

underground [UN der grownd] *adj.* beneath the surface of the Earth
The tree had a root structure spreading <u>underground</u>.

"Cuttings" and **"Cuttings (later)"** by Theodore Roethke
Vocabulary Warm-up Exercises

Exercise A *Fill in the blanks, using each word from Word List A only once.*

Constructing a pond is not as difficult as it might seem. Once the [1] _____ to hear the soothing sounds of water and to watch the darting motions of [2] _____ fish hits, it's not long from start to finish. The first step is to dig a hole in your backyard or garden [3] _____. The size of the hole is the size of your pond. With luck, you won't have to [4] _____ with any large rocks that have been hidden in the ground. Once the hole is dug, you can place a pond liner in it. A pump is necessary to circulate and aerate the water, ensuring that the fish have enough oxygen to survive. Water plants are easy to grow; they start from a [5] _____ and grow quickly. You never have to worry that they will [6] _____ from lack of moisture! Maintenance is easy as long as you occasionally cut back the [7] _____ plants that tend to spread everywhere. A few [8] _____ of food for the fish should be tossed in occasionally, but they also eat the algae in the pond and the insects that land on its surface.

Exercise B *Decide whether each statement below is true or false. Circle T or F, and explain your answer*

1. People who are <u>struggling</u> have an easy time of it.
   T / F _____

2. If you give someone gentle <u>nudges</u>, you might knock them over.
   T / F _____

3. We found water <u>seeping</u> through a large hole in our pipe.
   T / F _____

4. Tiny green bean <u>sprouts</u> are tender because they are so new.
   T / F _____

5. When he finished <u>lopping</u> off all the branches, the tree looked very bare.
   T / F _____

6. If you are very weak, it is easy to <u>wrestle</u> a heavy object up the stairs.
   T / F _____

7. If you have an <u>urge</u> to do something, it would never occur to you.
   T / F _____

8. If something has an <u>intricate</u> design, it is very finely made.
   T / F _____

Name _____ Date _____

"Cuttings" and "Cuttings (later)" by Theodore Roethke
Reading Warm-up A

Read the following passage. Then, complete the activities.

When I was a child, my mother would have me help her work in the yard and garden. I hated it. I would rather have been inside, reading or watching television or doing just about anything else. Gardening was hot, it was hard work, and mosquitoes found my young flesh too tasty to resist! Sure, I thought that the delicate, fragile flowers she grew were beautiful, but it was just not my thing. I couldn't understand the urge to grow things, the impulse to spend time in the mud with the mosquitoes. Why not just buy things at a flower shop?

However, something happened once I was older, living in my own house on my own piece of earth. Suddenly, I wanted to grow things myself. Adding compost to the soil until it was a dark, rich loam gave me such pleasure. I loved seeing the small nub on the end of a slender tree limb turn into a dark green leaf seemingly overnight. The grains or seeds I planted then produced shoots that seemed to wrestle their way to the surface immediately, fighting through all that soil to reach the sun. The tendrilous vines grew so quickly and thickly that they threatened to climb up and cover everything, house included.

Admittedly, my enthusiasm was stronger in the cool spring and fall than in the scorching summer. Even the hardiest plant tends to droop and sag when the sun beats down on it day after day. But year after year of toiling in the soil and modifying the trees and plants in my yard helped me to make better decisions about plant use and care. These changes have resulted in more beautiful plants and less work for me but I still have much more to learn!

1. Circle the word that tells what was delicate. Name an antonym for *delicate*.

2. Underline the word that has a similar meaning to urge. What is something you have had an *urge* to do?

3. Underline the words that help show the meaning of loam. Use *loam* in a sentence of your own.

4. Underline the words that tell where the nub was located. What did the *nub* turn into?

5. Underline the word that gives a clue to the meaning of grains. Name something else that is in the form of *grains*.

6. Circle the words that tell what seemed to wrestle their way to the surface. Use *wrestle* in a sentence of your own.

7. How do the tendrilous vines grow? Why are vines described as *tendrilous*?

8. What causes a plant to droop? Give some words that mean the same as *droop*.

"Cuttings" and **"Cuttings (later)"** by Theodore Roethke
Reading Warm-up B

Read the following passage. Then, complete the activities.

Xeriscaping is a form of landscape designing that has become increasingly popular in recent years. The term refers to the practice of creating a lawn or garden in a manner that conserves water. Many people think that it requires using a certain type of plant, but that is not the case. Many varieties of flowers, bushes, and trees can be employed, though those native, or natural, to the area are most highly recommended. These native plants are less likely to need <u>coaxing</u> to survive, as they have learned to thrive in the existing conditions and don't need to be persuaded to adapt.

Xeriscapes rarely have an <u>intricate</u> design, like a formal garden. Rather than having many complex parts, they tend to re-create a more natural effect. They employ small pebbles, large stones, and a great deal of organic mulch, which protects new <u>sprouts</u> and prevents evaporation of moisture so the tiny plants have plenty to drink. To further conserve water, often a method of watering called drip irrigation is used. It allows very small amounts of water to continue <u>seeping</u> out of tiny holes in a hose. That way, less is lost to evaporation and more goes <u>underground</u>, where the plants' roots can take it up. Grassy lawns are not a part of xeriscapes, as they are tremendous water-users. Owners often spend the entire summer <u>struggling</u> to provide their lawns with adequate moisture, working hard against the summer sun and heat.

Another advantage of using native plants in a landscape is that they often are resistant to insects. They require little maintenance aside from the occasional <u>lopping</u> of a tree branch or trimming of a spreading plant as it pushes and <u>nudges</u> its way across a walkway. Overall, xeriscapes offer gardeners many advantages.

1. Underline the words that tell what is less likely to need <u>coaxing</u>. Name something that might need *coaxing*.

2. Is a xeriscape design usually <u>intricate</u>? What is a word that means the opposite of *intricate*?

3. Underline the words that tell what protects <u>sprouts</u>. Why would *sprouts* need protection?

4. Underline the words that tell what is <u>seeping</u>. Explain why *seeping* water is good for plants.

5. Circle the words that explain what happens <u>underground</u>. Write your own sentence that uses *underground* in a sentence.

6. Circle the words that tell what people might spend the summer <u>struggling</u> to do. Give some other words or phrases that mean the same as *struggling*.

7. Underline the word that tells what people are <u>lopping</u>. Name a word or words that mean(s) the same as *lopping*.

8. Underline the word that means the same as <u>nudges</u>. Define *nudges* in your own words.

"Cuttings" and "Cuttings (later)" by Theodore Roethke
Literary Analysis: Sound Devices

Roethke's poems often rely on **sound devices** to achieve their impact. Among the sound devices he uses in "Cuttings" and "Cuttings (later)" are the following:

- **Alliteration** is the repetition of a consonant sound at the beginnings of words: "What saint strained so much,/Rose on such lopped limbs to a new life?"

- **Assonance** is the repetition of a vowel sound in stressed syllables with dissimilar consonant sounds: "I quail, lean to beginnings, sheath-wet."

- **Consonance** is the repetition of consonant sounds in stressed syllables in the middle or at the end of words: "The small cells bulge."

DIRECTIONS: *Use the chart below to identify the device used in each of the four examples given (there could be more than one device used in a given example), and underline the letters, words, or syllables involved in the device. Then, in the far-right column, explain how the example highlights or extends the poem's meaning.*

Example	Device	Effect on Meaning
1. This urge, wrestle, resurrection of dry sticks, . . .		
2. What saint strained so much, . . .		
3. I can hear, underground, that sucking and sobbing. . . .		
4. When sprouts break out, . . .		

"**Cuttings**" and "**Cuttings (later)**" by Theodore Roethke

Reading Strategy: Using Background Knowledge

When you read a piece of literature, **using background knowledge** can often help you to gain better understanding of important details and central ideas in the piece. You can gather background information from a variety of sources, including an introduction, footnotes, an author biography, or even from your own experiences.

"Cuttings" and "Cuttings (later)" both use processes of plant growth to explore and evoke basic truths of life. Background knowledge for these poems is provided by the author biography and the background section of your textbook. Think about how this background information helped your understanding as your read these two poems.

DIRECTIONS: *Answer the following questions, based on background information provided in your textbook about this selection.*

1. Where did Theodore Roethke's grandparents immigrate from? Where did they settle? What business did they go into after they settled in the United States?

   _____

   _____

2. What business did Roethke's father and uncle go into? How did they end up in that business? How did they do in their business?

   _____

   _____

3. Where did Roethke spend countless hours of his childhood, and what did he learn there?

   _____

   _____

4. What is a cutting?

   _____

   _____

5. What role does diffusion play in the creation of new plants from a cutting?

   _____

   _____

6. What role does water pressure play in the growth of new cells, stems, and leaves?

   _____

   _____

"Cuttings" and "Cuttings (*later*)" by Theodore Roethke
Vocabulary Builder

Word List

intricate   seeping   quail

A. DIRECTIONS: *Think about the meaning of the underlined Word List word in each sentence. Then, answer the question.*

1. The professor proposed an <u>intricate</u> method of solving the equation. Was his solution a simple one? How do you know?

   _____

   _____

2. I noticed that water was <u>seeping</u> from the bottom of the pitcher. Was the water leaking quickly? How do you know?

   _____

   _____

3. I started to <u>quail</u> during the climactic scene of the movie. Was the movie scary? How do you know?

   _____

   _____

B. DIRECTIONS: *On each line, write the letter of the word or phrase that is most nearly* opposite *in meaning to the Word List word.*

____ 1. seeping
   A. plodding
   B. glaring
   C. gushing
   D. laughing

____ 2. intricate
   A. delicate
   B. unsightly
   C. safe
   D. simple

____ 3. quail
   A. pretend
   B. confront
   C. deny
   D. limit

"Cuttings" and "Cuttings (later)" by Theodore Roethke
Support for Writing

Your assignment is to write an essay in which you compare and contrast the information in a science text with the depiction of plant growth in Roethke's poems, evaluating the merits of each type of writing. Use the chart below to help you to organize your basic information and ideas for the essay.

Source	Type of Language Used	Author's Purposes	Author's Perspectives
Roethke's poems			
Science text			

Then, answer this question: In your view, which presentation of plant growth is more engaging and effective? Why?

_____

_____

_____

On a separate piece of paper, write a rough draft of your essay based on the information and ideas you have gathered on this page.

Name _____ Date _____

"Cuttings" and **"Cuttings (*later*)"** by Theodore Roethke
Enrichment: Family History

In the background section of this selection, we learn about Theodore Roethke's family history: when his grandparents came to this country, where they immigrated from, how they earned their living, what kind of business they passed on to their children, and so on. We learn how his family's business helped to inspire the interest in plant growth that is evident in these two poems.

How much do you know about your own family history? Interview your family members to gain as much information as you can about your own family history. Use the questions below as a guide to uncovering key facts about your family history, and then fill in the answers.

1. Where are my grandparents from? On my mother's side? On my father's side? What kind of work did they do?

   _____

   _____

   _____

2. What kind of town or towns did my parents grow up in? What kinds of schools and/or college did they attend?

   _____

   _____

   _____

3. Did my grandparents and parents live mostly in one place, or did they move around a lot? If so, why did they move from place to place?

   _____

   _____

   _____

4. Did my parents have any special interests or talents growing up? If so, what were they?

   _____

   _____

   _____

5. In what important ways did my grandparents influence my parents?

   _____

   _____

   _____

6. In what ways have I been influenced by my grandparents and parents?

   _____

   _____

   _____

"Cuttings" and "Cuttings (later)" by Theodore Roethke
Open-Book Test

Short Answer *Write your responses to the questions in this section on the lines provided.*

1. Both "Cuttings" and "Cuttings (later)" are poems that focus on what basic processes of nature?

   _____

   _____

   _____

2. In reading both "Cuttings" and "Cuttings (later)," it is useful to know about what key aspect of the author's upbringing?

   _____

   _____

   _____

3. The following line from "Cuttings" is an example of which two poetic sound devices? Explain your answer.

   The small cells bulge; . . .

   _____

   _____

   _____

4. Sound devices are often used to underscore various meanings that the poet is trying to convey. Where does alliteration occur in this line from "Cuttings"? How does the use of alliteration in this line emphasize the meaning the poet is trying to convey?

   Sticks-in-a-drowse droop over sugary loam, . . .

   _____

   _____

   _____

5. Alliteration can occur across lines as well as within lines in a poem. Identify the alliteration in these two lines from "Cuttings," and explain how the alliteration underscores a key meaning that the poet is trying to convey.

   One nub of growth / Nudges a sand crumb loose, . . .

   _____

   _____

   _____

   _____

6. What is the most important piece of background knowledge a reader could have to help him or her understand the meaning of "Cuttings" and "Cuttings (later)"?

_____

_____

_____

_____

7. Although both "Cuttings" and "Cuttings (later)" describe processes of plant growth, there is an important difference in emphasis and tone between the two poems. Briefly explain this basic difference. Cite examples from the poems to support your answer.

_____

_____

_____

_____

8. Although "Cuttings" and "Cuttings (later)" cover similar topics, each carries a distinct message. What is the essential meaning of "Cuttings (later)"? Summarize the basic theme or message of the poem in one sentence.

_____

_____

9. Both "Cuttings" and "Cuttings (later)" make frequent and effective use of sound devices—alliteration, assonance, and consonance—to convey their meanings. Use the chart below to identify the device used in each of the four examples given (there could be more than one device used in a given example), and underline the letters, words, or syllables involved in the device. Then, in the right-hand column, explain how the example highlights or extends the poem's meaning.

Example	Device	Effect on Meaning
1. This urge, wrestle, resurrection of dry sticks, . . .		
2. What saint strained so much, . . .		
3. I can hear, underground, that sucking and sobbing. . . .		
4. When sprouts break out, . . .		

10. If the climactic moment of a movie made you quail, would you most likely be watching a horror film or a love story? Explain your answer, basing it on the meaning of *quail* as it is used in "Cuttings (later)."

_____

_____

Essay

Write an extended response to the question of your choice or to the question or questions your teacher assigns you.

11. Much of the wonderment at growth and new life that Theodore Roethke expresses in his observations of plants in "Cuttings" and "Cuttings (later)" can be traced to his childhood experiences in his father's and uncle's large commercial greenhouses. In an essay, describe a childhood experience of nature—a hike, a park, a plant, a tree, and so on—that left a strong impression on you and affected your outlook on life in some way. Was your experience similar to the feelings that Roethke expresses in his poems? Support your essay with vivid, concrete details and images.

12. Both "Cuttings" and "Cuttings (later)" describe and reflect on barely perceptible aspects of plant growth and renewal. Compare and contrast the overall processes described in the two poems. Which poem affected you more strongly? Why? Explain your reactions in an essay supported by details from the poems.

13. The last line of "Cuttings (later)" suggests that the processes of plant renewal and growth described in the two poems might suggest important aspects of human experience: "I quail, lean to beginnings, sheath-wet." Why does the narrator "quail" at the sight of sprouts breaking out? What does this reaction suggest about the relationship between the natural processes described in the poem and the inner growth—emotional and intellectual—of human beings? Develop your thoughts in an essay supported by examples from the poems.

14. **Thinking About the Essential Question: What is the relationship between place and literature?** Theodore Roethke grew up surrounded by plants in his father's commercial greenhouse. His memories of that environment inspired many of the images of growth expressed in "Cuttings" and "Cuttings (later)." In an essay, explain how an especially vivid or important environment from your childhood has shaped your perceptions of the world. Use concrete, vivid images and descriptions to convey your childhood environment to your reader and to help to explain how it has shaped your view of the world.

Oral Response

15. Go back to question 2, 3, or 8 or to the question your teacher assigns to you. Take a few minutes to expand your answer and prepare an oral response. Find additional details in "Cuttings" and "Cuttings (later)" that support your points. If necessary, make notes to guide your oral response.

"**Cuttings**" and "**Cuttings (later)**" by Theodore Roethke

Selection Test A

Critical Reading *Identify the letter of the choice that best answers the question.*

_____ 1. Both "Cuttings" and "Cuttings (*later*)" deal with what kind of process in the natural world?

   A. animal growth

   B. human development

   C. death and decay of organic matter

   D. plant growth

_____ 2. What sound device is evident in this line from "Cuttings"?

   Sticks-in-a-drowse-droop over sugary loam, . . .

   A. alliteration

   B. assonance

   C. consonance

   D. rhyme

_____ 3. Which phrase from "Cuttings" contains an example of consonance?

   A. "Sticks-in-a-drowse-droop"

   B. "intricate stem-fur dries"

   C. "delicate slips keep coaxing up water"

   D. "small cells bulge"

_____ 4. Which piece of background knowledge would be most useful in understanding the meaning of this line from "Cuttings"?

   Their intricate stem-fur dries; . . .

   A. Theodore Roethke's father owned a commercial greenhouse.

   B. Theodore Roethke won a Pulitzer Prize for poetry.

   C. Stem fur helps to prevent water loss.

   D. Energy in nature is converted but never lost.

_____ 5. The phrase "One nub of growth" tells you that the process of growth being described in "Cuttings" is

   A. sudden and rapid

   B. slow and gradual

   C. nonexistent

   D. not confined to plants alone

_____ 6. The phrase "but still" in this line from "Cuttings" encourages the reader to feel what about the growth process being described?

> Their intricate stem-fur dries;/But still the delicate slips keep coaxing up water; . . ."

A. It is entirely predictable and routine

B. It is invisible to the naked eye.

C. It is common in all forms of plant life.

D. It is difficult, even miraculous.

_____ 7. The words "urge" and "wrestle" in the first line of "Cuttings (*later*)" signal that, compared to the slow, delicate growth described in "Cuttings," the growth being described in this poem is

A. slower

B. less noisy

C. more turbulent

D. quieter

_____ 8. What sound device is evident in this line from "Cuttings (*later*)"?

> I quail, lean to beginnings, sheath-wet.

A. alliteration

B. assonance

C. consonance

D. rhyme

_____ 9. In "Cuttings (*later*)," Roethke describes the process of new plant growth in these words: "What saint strained so much." With these words, Roethke is conveying the idea that new plant growth from cut stems is

A. a struggle

B. easy

C. a delight

D. instantaneous

_____ 10. Which of the following contains an alliterative phrase from "Cuttings (*later*)" that evokes the desperate quality of the plant's growth?

A. "urge, wrestle"

B. "put down feet"

C. "what saint strained so much"

D. "The tight grains parting at last"

_____ 11. Which line from "Cuttings (*later*)" shows that the narrator emotionally identifies with the new plant's struggle to come to life?

A. "This, urge wrestle, this resurrection of dry sticks, . . ."

B. "In my veins, in my bones I feel it,—"

C. "The small waters seeping upward, . . ."

D. "The tight grains parting at last."

____ 12. Which of the following identifies a key way in which "Cuttings (*later*)" differs from "Cuttings"?

  A. It is about plant growth.

  B. It it better understood with some backgound knowledge about botany.

  C. It uses sound devices.

  D. It features a speaker who refers to himself.

____ 13. Which word in this line from "Cuttings (*later*)" implies that the growth of a new plant from a cutting carries the religious overtones of a miracle?

   This urge, wrestle, resurrection of dry sticks, . . .

  A. urge

  B. wrestle

  C. resurrection

  D. dry

Essay

14. In "Cuttings (*later*)" Theodore Roethke focuses on dramatic spurts of growth that bring a new plant to life from a cut stem. He implies that there can be such moments in the emotional growth of a human being. Think about an experience from your own life that spurred you to a sudden spurt of emotional growth. In an essay, explain what you learned from that experience and how it caused you to grow emotionally. Support your answer with specific examples and details.

15. In "Cuttings" and "Cuttings (*later*)" Theodore Roethke dwells on some key aspects of plant growth that fascinate him even though he is not a botanist or scientist of any kind. Think of some aspect of the plant or animal world that you find especially interesting. If you had a chance to study it in detail to write a poem about it, which area would it be? Why? Explain your choice in an essay that is supported by specific examples and details.

16. **Thinking About the Essential Question: What is the relationship between place and literature?** Theodore Roethke grew up surrounded by plants in his father's commercial greenhouse. His memories of that environment inspired many of the images of growth expressed in "Cuttings" and "Cuttings (later)." In an essay, explain how an especially vivid or important environment from your childhood has shaped your perceptions of the world. Use concrete, vivid images and descriptions to convey your childhood environment to your reader and to help to explain how it has shaped your view of the world.

"Cuttings" and "Cuttings (later)" by Theodore Roethke
Selection Test B

Critical Reading *Identify the letter of the choice that best answers the question.*

_____ 1. Which piece of background information about Theodore Roethke, the author of "Cuttings" and "Cuttings (*later*)," would be most useful to a reader of these poems?

A. He studied at Harvard.

B. He won the Pulitzer Prize for poetry in 1953.

C. He is of German descent.

D. His father owned commercial greenhouses.

_____ 2. What quality of new plant growth is conveyed by the alliteration in this line from "Cuttings"?

Sticks-in-a-drowse droop over sugary loam, . . .

A. slowness   C. robustness

B. noisiness   D. urgency

_____ 3. If you knew that stem fur helps to prevent water loss, then you would know that the following line from "Cuttings" indicates what about the state of the plant?

Their intricate stem-fur dries; . . ."

A. The plant is in some kind of crisis.

B. The plant is in robust health.

C. The plant is completely doomed.

D. The plant is getting just the right amount of water.

_____ 4. Which of the following lines from "Cuttings" contains an example of alliteration?

A. "Their intricate stem-fur dries; . . ."

B. "But still the delicate slips keep coaxing up water; . . ."

C. "One nub of growth . . ."

D. "Pokes through a musty sheath . . ."

_____ 5. Which line of "Cuttings" uses both alliteration and consonance?

A. "Sticks-in-a-drowse droop over sugary loam, . . ."

B. "But still the delicate slips keep coaxing up water; . . ."

C. "The small cells bulge; . . ."

D. "Its pale tendrilous horn."

_____ 6. Which quality of the growth process is underscored by the alliterative association of the words *nub* and *nudges* in the following lines from "Cuttings"?

One nub of growth/Nudges a sand-crumb loose, . . .

A. mysteriousness   C. certainty

B. strength   D. gradualness

_____ 7. The last line of "Cuttings" speaks of a "pale, tendrilous horn." This phrase implies that the new growth is

A. colorful   C. delicate

B. routine   D. stillborn

_____ 8. Which of the following professions would arm the reader with the background knowledge best suited to understanding the processes described in "Cuttings" and "Cuttings (*later*)"?

A. poet   B. critic   C. botanist   D. chemist

_____ 9. In "Cuttings (*later*)," the speaker compares the turbulent growth process of the new plant to the struggles of what kind of religious figure?

A. saint   B. priest   C. angel   D. deity

_____ 10. Which line from "Cuttings (*later*)" uses both alliteration and assonance?

A. "This urge, wrestle, resurrection of dry sticks, . . ."

B. "What saint strained so much, . . ."

C. "Rose on such lopped limbs to a new life?"

D. "I can hear, underground, that sucking and sobbing, . . ."

_____ 11. What is a major difference in technique between "Cuttings" and "Cuttings (*later*)"?

A. "Cuttings (*later*)" uses alliteration.

B. "Cuttings" uses assonance.

C. In "Cuttings (*later*)" the speaker describes microscopic processes of growth.

D. In "Cuttings (*later*) the speaker refers to himself in the first person.

_____ 12. When the speaker of "Cuttings (*later*)" speaks of hearing "sucking and sobbing," he means that the universal urge to life is one that involves

A. struggle and suffering   C. vast consumption of water

B. inevitable decay and death   D. joyous triumph over all obstacles

_____ 13. In which lines of "Cuttings (*later*)" does the speaker make it clear that he personally identifies with the plant's struggle to assert new life?

A. "This urge, wrestle, resurrection of dry sticks, . . ."

B. "Cut stems struggling to put down feet, . . ."

C. "In my veins, in my bones I feel it, —"

D. "The tight grains parting at last."

_____ 14. In "Cuttings (*later*)," Roethke uses the assonance in the phrase "sprouts break out" to help emphasize

    A. the suddenness of the emergence of new life

    B. the randomness of the processes of growth

    C. the subtle noises made by an emerging new plant

    D. his feelings of identification with the new sprout

_____ 15. When the speaker in "Cuttings (*later*)" states of the plant's growth process, "I can hear, underground, that sucking and sobbing,/In my veins, in my bones I feel it,—" he is relying primarily on his

    A. sense of hearing   C. imagination

    B. sense of touch   D. powers of inference

Essay

16. "Cuttings" and "Cuttings (*later*)" are based in part of Roethke's childhood memories of his father's commerical greenhouses in Michigan. These memories obviously left a powerful impression on the mind and imagination of the poet. In an essay, discuss a childhood experience that had a powerful effect on you—for better or for worse—and helped to shape your view of life. Support you answer with concrete examples.

17. Both "Cuttings" and "Cuttings (*later*)" are based to a large extent on Roethke's personal identification with the processes of growth and renewal he observed among plants. Some people have been known to talk to their plants and even believe that the plants in some sense understand what they are saying. To what extent do you identify with plants—what qualities and features do they seem to share with humans, and in what ways do they strike you as alien or different? Develop your thoughts in an essay supported by clear reasoning and specific examples.

18. In "Cuttings (*later*)," the speaker compares the plant's struggles to achieve renewal and growth to the struggles of a saint: "What saint strained so much,/Rose on such lopped limbs to a new life?" Do you find this comparison compelling or instructive? Why or why not? Explain your answer in an essay that is supported by details from the poem.

19. **Thinking About the Essential Question: What is the relationship between place and literature?** Theodore Roethke grew up surrounded by plants in his father's commercial greenhouse. His memories of that environment inspired many of the images of growth expressed in "Cuttings" and "Cuttings (later)." In an essay, explain how an especially vivid or important environment from your childhood has shaped your perceptions of the world. Use concrete, vivid images and descriptions to convey your childhood environment to your reader and to help to explain how it has shaped your view of the world.

Vocabulary Warm-up Word Lists

Study these words from the selections. Then, complete the activities.

Word List A

alien [AYL ee uhn] *adj.* strange; foreign
The stark, rocky landscape seemed uninviting, almost <u>alien</u>.

exiled [eg ZYLD] *v.* banished; forced to leave a community or homeland
Dante wrote his masterpiece after being <u>exiled</u> from the city of Florence.

fleshing [FLESH ing] *v.* to fill in an idea or project with details and make it full
The architect was <u>fleshing</u> out plans to add trees around the new building.

liberty [LIB er tee] *n.* freedom; release from captivity
The prison inmate regained his <u>liberty</u> after serving his jail sentence.

rhetoric [RET er ik] *n.* showy, elaborate language that contains little relevant substance
Jason's <u>rhetoric</u> masked the fact that he had no clear idea what to do.

vague [VAYG] *adj.* imprecisely sensed or expressed; unclear
His <u>vague</u> answers left her confused about what had happened.

Word List B

din [DIN] *n.* loud noise
The <u>din</u> of sirens was so loud that we could scarcely hear each other.

frayed [FRAYD] *adj.* worn or ragged
The jacket he had owned since childhood was worn and <u>frayed</u>.

gaudy [GAW dee] *adj.* flashy or showy, but lacking in good taste
Everyone noticed and talked about her <u>gaudy</u>, brightly-colored costume.

instinct [IN stingkt] *n.* a natural, in-born ability, tendency or reaction
An adult bird has a natural <u>instinct</u> to protect its young chicks from harm.

reflex [REE fleks] *adj.* reacting automatically to a stimulus
When Emma saw the boy fall, her <u>reflex</u> action was to rush and help.

spiraling [SPY ruhl ing] *v.* rising or falling while circling around a central point
We watched autumn leaves <u>spiraling</u> through the air to the ground.

Name _____ Date _____

"The Explorer" by Gwendolyn Brooks and **"Frederick Douglass"** by Robert Hayden
Vocabulary Warm-up Exercises

Exercise A *Fill in the blanks, using each word from Word List A only once.*

When Madeline arrived for the first time at her new college, it seemed a strange and
[1] _____ place. The college official who checked her in and handed her a
room key had carried on and one with a lot of [2] _____ about all the
rules and regulations. Then Madeline discovered that the dorm she had been assigned
to was half a mile away from campus, which made her feel as if she had been
[3] _____ to a different country. She had only a [4] _____
idea of how to walk back from there, through the city, to the main campus area. Thank-
fully, her apprehensions melted away as soon as her new roommate showed up. Trisha
was an upbeat person who told Madeline they were lucky to have been assigned to this
dorm because it was the most comfortable. As the two young women were [5]
_____ out the best route to take to reach their classes, Madeline realized
she had never before had so much [6] _____ to plan her day and make
decisions about her own schedule.

Exercise B *Decide whether each statement below is true or false. Circle T or F, and explain your answer*

1. A jacket that is <u>frayed</u> is usually brand new.
   T / F _____

2. Battlefields often resound with the <u>din</u> of gunfire and other explosives.
   T / F _____

3. If you never had to read a book or watch a cooking show to be a great chef, then cooking is probably something you have figured out by <u>instinct</u>.
   T / F _____

4. A person who gives lengthy, eloquent speeches where a few words might do is skilled at <u>rhetoric</u>.
   T / F _____

5. <u>Vague</u> instructions will give you a clear and detailed explanation.
   T / F _____

6. A <u>reflex</u> is the result of deliberation and planning.
   T / F _____

"The Explorer" by Gwendolyn Brooks and **"Frederick Douglass"** by Robert Hayden

Reading Warm-up A

Read the following passage. Then, complete the activities.

Frederick Douglass was born into slavery and grew up with only <u>vague</u> information about the date of his birth. He never knew who his father was. He saw his mother only a handful of times before she died, when he was probably around seven. Her comments led Douglass to believe he was born in 1817. However, historians who spent time <u>fleshing</u> out the details of Douglass's early life discovered records stating that he was born in Maryland in February 1818.

Slaves were not allowed to be educated when Douglass was growing up, yet the wife of one of his masters taught him the alphabet. Reading fueled Douglass's desire for <u>liberty</u>.

Douglass escaped to freedom in 1838 by disguising himself as a sailor and traveling north from his home in Baltimore to New York City. He settled in New Bedford, Massachusetts, and married a free woman.

Douglass became known as a substantive, important abolitionist speaker. His speeches were not full of <u>rhetoric</u> and empty flowery language, because he could testify in detail to the horrific experience of slavery. In 1845, he published his famous autobiography, *Narrative of the Life of Frederick Douglass, An American Slave.*

The book was so successful that friends suggested he travel abroad to avoid being pursued by the slave owner from whom he had escaped. Douglass essentially <u>exiled</u> himself for two years in England and Ireland, banishing himself from the United States for his protection. Even in this <u>alien</u>, foreign culture, people appreciated his speeches about equal rights for all races and for women.

During his time, Douglass became the most famous and influential African American in the United States. Upon his return to the country, he published newspapers, worked with President Lincoln, and held important political positions. He continued writing, speaking, and traveling until his death in 1895.

1. Circle the phrase that tells what was <u>vague</u>. Write an antonym for *vague*.

2. Underline the phrase that explains what historians spent time <u>fleshing</u>. Write your own definition for *fleshing*.

3. Circle the word in a nearby sentence that has a meaning similar to <u>liberty</u>. Why do you think reading books and magazines fueled Douglass' desire for *liberty*?

4. Circle the words that have a meaning similar to <u>rhetoric</u>. Underline the phrase that describes what made Douglass' speeches the opposite of *rhetoric*.

5. Circle the words that tell where Douglass temporarily <u>exiled</u> himself. Use the word *exiled* in a sentence.

6. Circle the word that <u>alien</u> describes. Write an antonym for *alien*.

"The Explorer" by Gwendolyn Brooks and **"Frederick Douglass"** by Robert Hayden

Reading Warm-up B

Read the following passage. Then, complete the activities.

Aaron and his extended family celebrated most of their holiday gatherings at his grandmother's century-old house on Ivy Street. The house had some gaudy flourishes, inside and out, including three staircases, and crystal chandeliers everywhere, even in the kitchen and bathrooms. The front exterior was decorated with a lacy, iron balcony, a tower with a pointed roof, and scarlet, climbing rosebushes. Above the front door, set into brick, was a carved, stone mural depicting ten figures dancing with spiraling, circling ribbons.

However grand it might once have been, the building had become worn and rundown. Every item of upholstered furniture had frayed fabric, and each chandelier was missing crystal pieces. The roof lacked tiles, and the balcony sagged. Aaron thought that even the stone dancers above the front door looked fatigued, after holding up those ribbons for so long.

His instinct told him to be sad when he saw things that were broken, disintegrating, and decaying, for his natural reaction was to think that they were dying. Yet sadness was not the prevailing emotion when Aaron's family congregated here. Though his grandmother was aging, like her home, she spread joy to those around her. She had eight children and when they brought their families home for meals and celebrations, happiness was almost a reflex action, a natural part of their time together. There was an enormous din of talk, laughter, jokes, and conversation. No matter what this house looked like, Aaron realized, everyone in the family automatically reacted to it, and to his grandmother, with feelings of gladness.

1. Underline the phrases that describe the gaudy flourishes. Write a synonym for *gaudy*.

2. Circle the word that has a meaning similar to spiraling. Name something else that you might see *spiraling* in the air.

3. Underline the nearby words that have a meaning similar to frayed. Use the word *frayed* in a sentence.

4. Circle the words that have a meaning similar to instinct. Write a sentence describing something you know by *instinct*.

5. Underline the phrase that tells when happiness was almost a reflex action in Aaron's family. Use the word *reflex* in a sentence.

6. Circle the words that explain what made the din. Write an antonym for *din*.

"The Explorer" by Gwendolyn Brooks
"Frederick Douglass" by Robert Hayden

Literary Analysis: Repetition and Parallelism

Two common rhetorical devices that are prominent in these two poems are **repetition** and **parallelism**.

- Repetition is the repeating of key words or concepts: "<u>this man,</u> this Douglass . . . <u>this man,</u> superb in love and logic, <u>this man</u> / shall be remembered. . . ."

- Parallelism is the repetition of a grammatical structure: "<u>There were</u> no bourns. / <u>There were</u> no quiet rooms."

Rhetorical devices emphasize a message or excite an emotion.

Directions: *For each poem in this grouping, provide one example of repetition and parallelism. In each case, state whether the basic purpose of the device is to emphasize a message, excite an emotion, or both.*

"The Explorer"

1. **Example of repetition:** _____

_____

_____

Purpose: _____

2. **Example of parallelism:** _____

_____

_____

Purpose: _____

"Frederick Douglass"

1. **Example of repetition:** _____

_____

_____

Purpose: _____

2. **Example of parallelism:** _____

_____

_____

Purpose: _____

"The Explorer" by Gwendolyn Brooks
"Frederick Douglass" by Robert Hayden

Reading Strategy: Read the Poems Aloud

When poets use repeated or parallel words or phrases, they are often trying to emphasize a point or give added intensity to an emotion. When we read a text silently, though, we sometimes fail to grasp the full impact of these repetitions or parallel phrasings—they often convey their full impact only if read aloud. To enhance your appreciation of the author's message, **read the poems aloud.** When you encounter a repetition or parallel structure, slow down and emphasize it. What message becomes clear? What emotions do you feel?

DIRECTIONS: *Use the chart below to write a passage that you read aloud in each of the poems in this grouping. For each passage, identify the main technique used—parallelism or repetition—and then, in the final column briefly state how reading the passage aloud enhanced your understanding of the meaning of the poem.*

"The Explorer"

Passage I Read Aloud	Technique Used in Passage	How Reading Aloud Enhanced Meaning

"Frederick Douglass"

Passage I Read Aloud	Technique Used in Passage	How Reading Aloud Enhanced Meaning

"The Explorer" by Gwendolyn Brooks
"Frederick Douglass" by Robert Hayden

Vocabulary Builder

Word/Phrase Relationships

The meaning of a descriptive word can change when it is connected to other words in a phrase. For example, the adjective *smooth* means "having a continuous surface" if applied to an object you are touching, but it means "serene" or "suave" if you are talking about someone's manner or disposition.

A. DIRECTIONS: *Read each pair of sentences below. Then, explain how the meaning of the word differs in the context of each underlined phrase.*

1. a. My blanket was so <u>frayed</u> that it had begun to fall into pieces.
   b. My patience was <u>frayed</u> by my inability to solve the math problem after countless attempts.

Difference in meaning between *a and b*: _____

_____

_____

2. a. The hotel was comfortable, but we were put off by the <u>gaudy</u> decor of the lobby.
   b. The speaker made a <u>gaudy</u> recitation of his credentials in the area of political science.

Difference in meaning between *a and b*: _____

_____

_____

Using the Word List

    frayed   wily   gaudy

B. DIRECTIONS: *For each Word List word, chose the word or phrase that is most clearly opposite in meaning. Circle the letter of your choice.*

1. frayed
   A. cooked   B. typical   C. intact   D. peaceful

2. wily
   A. stupid   B. large   C. sad   D. respectful

3. gaudy
   A. dark   B. patient   C. tasteful   D. unique

"**The Explorer**" by Gwendolyn Brooks
"**Frederick Douglass**" by Robert Hayden
Support for Writing
"The Explorer" and "Frederick Douglass" can be read in two different ways: (a) from a **social perspective,** as a reflection of the struggles of African Americans during the mid-twentieth century and (b) from an **archetypal perspective,** as an expression of universal human longings. Prepare to write an essay in which you examine both poems from each of these perspectives. Use the questions below to help you begin to gather information and organize your thoughts in preparation for your first draft.

"The Explorer"

1. **Connections between details in the poem and events or issues in mid-1900s America:**

_____

_____

_____

_____

_____

2. **How the poem expresses universal human problems and longings:**

_____

_____

_____

_____

_____

"Frederick Douglass"

1. **Connections between details in the poem and events or issues in mid-1900s America:**

_____

_____

_____

_____

_____

2. **How the poem expresses universal human problems and longings:**

_____

_____

_____

_____

_____

On a separate page, gather your information and thoughts together in a first draft of your essay. Identify points in your draft at which you make important general statements about the poem. Strengthen your analysis by adding accurate quotations from the poem to support your interpretation.

"The Explorer" by Gwendolyn Brooks
"Frederick Douglass" by Robert Hayden
Enrichment: Poetry of Protest

There are many ways in which to express social criticism or to support causes and movements that are important to you. Some people give speeches, write essays, or organize marches to express their concerns about problems in society. Poets often express social criticism through their poetry. The two poems you have read are examples of protest poetry, and they reflect concerns about specific societal values, attitudes, and prejudices.

DIRECTIONS: *Answer each of the following questions.*

1. Many of Gwendolyn Brooks's poems focus on the problems faced by people, particularly African Americans, living in urban tenements in which they are looked on as second-class citizens. According to the poem "The Explorer," what problems exist in this environment? How might a person's environment, and the way in which he or she is treated by society, hurt his or her ability to take advantage confidently of choices and opportunities?

_____

_____

_____

_____

_____

_____

_____

_____

_____

2. What specific historical issue is addressed by Robert Hayden in his poem "Frederick Douglass"? How does Hayden feel about the effect the beliefs of Frederick Douglass have had, or not had, on modern society?

_____

_____

_____

_____

_____

_____

_____

_____

Name _____ Date _____

"The Explorer" by Gwendolyn Brooks and
"Frederick Douglass" by Robert Hayden
Open-Book Test

Short Answer *Write your responses to the questions in this section on the lines provided.*

1. In "The Explorer," Brooks repeats the word *frayed* in line 2, writing of "frayed inner want" and "frayed hope." What meaning does this repetition help to convey?

   _____

   _____

2. In "The Explorer," what does the "still spot in the noise" (line 1) represent for the subject of the poem?

   _____

   _____

3. In "The Explorer," Brooks repeats the word "somewhere" in lines 4 and 5. What aspect of the subject's state of mind is emphasized by the repetition of this word?

   _____

   _____

   _____

4. In "The Explorer," what does the line "A room of wily hush somewhere within" (line 5) suggest about the setting of the search that is taking place in the poem?

   _____

   _____

   _____

5. What is the parallel structure of the last two lines of "The Explorer" (lines 13 and 14)? Explain briefly how the parallel structure of these lines underscores a key message or theme of the poem.

   _____

   _____

   _____

   _____

6. In "Frederick Douglass," what is the effect of the parallel repetition of the phrase "when it" throughout the first six lines of the poem?

   _____

   _____

   _____

7. How might the impact of line 4 of "Frederick Douglass" be enhanced by reading it aloud—especially the last two words: "diastole, systole"?

_____

_____

_____

_____

8. If you were reading aloud lines 11 and 12 of "Frederick Douglass," which repeated word would you emphasize vocally to enhance the meaning of the lines?

_____

9. The poem "Frederick Douglass" makes use of the technique of parallelism, the repetition of phrases with the same grammatical structure. Each parallelism enhances the meaning or message of the poem in a distinctive way. Use the chart below to identify three examples of parallelism in the poem. Then, in the right-hand column, briefly explain how that instance of parallelism enhances or underscores the poem's message or theme.

Example of Parallelism	How It Enhances Message of Poem
a.	
b.	
c.	
d.	

10. If an architecture critic wrote that she found the lobby of a new hotel to be gaudy, would she be finding fault with the design of the lobby? Why or why not? Base your answer on the meaning of the word *gaudy* as it is used in "Frederick Douglass."

_____

_____

_____

_____

Essay

Write an extended response to the question of your choice or to the question or questions your teacher assigns you.

11. In "Frederick Douglass," Robert Hayden vividly evokes the ways in which Frederick Douglass's life still serves as an example and inspiration. Choose a person from history or your personal experience who has been especially inspiring to you. In an essay, explain how and why that person's life has served as an inspiration and example to you. Do you admire your inspirational person for the same reasons Hayden admires Douglass? Support your answer with specific examples and clear reasoning.

12. In "The Explorer," Gwendolyn Brooks implies that peace of mind is difficult to achieve because of the great variety of choices that life presents. Do you agree with this view? Why or why not? Develop your thoughts in an essay supported by examples from the poem and your own experience.

13. "The Explorer" and "Frederick Douglass" both deal with the subject of freedom, but in different ways. "The Explorer" portrays the potential problems involved in freedom of choice. "Frederick Douglass" seems to present a more positive overall portrait of freedom as a major goal in life. In an essay, compare and contrast the way these two poems portray the subject of freedom. Which poem's treatment of freedom was more persuasive and appealing to you? Support your answer with examples from the poems.

14. **Thinking About the Essential Question: How does literature shape or reflect society?** Both of the poems in this section—"The Explorer" and "Frederick Douglass" express longings for a different way of life. Such poems can tell the reader a great deal about the society about which—and in which—the poet expresses him/herself. In an essay, explain which poem is more a reflection of society, and which poem seeks to shape society. Support you answer with details from the poems.

Oral Response

15. Go back to question 3, 5, or 8 or to the question your teacher assigns to you. Take a few minutes to expand your answer and prepare an oral response. Find additional details in "The Explorer" or "Frederick Douglass" that support your points. If necessary, make notes to guide your oral response.

Name _____ Date _____

Selection Test A

Critical Reading *Identify the letter of the choice that best answers the question.*

_____ 1. What is the explorer searching for in "The Explorer"?
   A. a specific room in the house
   B. a path to follow in life
   C. a new place to live
   D. a giant office building

_____ 2. What blocks the explorer's personal growth in "The Explorer"?
   A. There are no open doors.
   B. There are too many choices.
   C. There is too much noise.
   D. There are places to fall.

_____ 3. In describing the explorer's search for peace in the first stanza of "The Explorer," Brooks repeats the word "somewhere." This repetition implies that the explorer's search is
   A. unfulfilled
   B. successful
   C. exciting
   D. misdirected

_____ 4. In the first stanza of "The Explorer," Brooks describes the explorer's "frayed inner want" and "frayed hope." Which choice best describes the quality of the explorer's search that is emphasized by the repetition of the word "frayed"?
   A. victorious
   B. confusing
   C. wearing
   D. instructive

_____ 5. If you were reading aloud the following lines from "The Explorer," your repetition of the word "griefs" would emphasize what part of the poem's message?

   There were behind/Only spiraling, high human voices,/The scream of nervous affairs,/Wee griefs,/Grand griefs. And choices.

   A. the great size of the building
   B. the unhappiness of the human condition
   C. the problems of poverty
   D. the heroic qualities of everyday people

_____ 6. What is the overall message of "Frederick Douglass"?

  A. Freedom can be won only by people like Douglass.

  B. Heroes are remembered by their families.

  C. Heroes deserve statues, legends, and poems.

  D. A hero leaves a legacy that lives on in others.

_____ 7. What does the poet call for in "Frederick Douglass," when he refers to liberty that will someday be part of everyone's "instinct"?

  A. a time when Frederick Douglass will be remembered

  B. a time when poets will be more important than politicians

  C. a time when freedom will be as automatic as breathing

  D. a time when slavery will be outlawed

_____ 8. Which rhetorical device is exemplified in the following passage from "Frederick Douglass"?

  . . . when it belongs at last to all, when it is truly instinct, . . .; when it is finally won . . .

  A. repetition

  B. parallelism

  C. exclamation

  D. metaphor

_____ 9. What message of "Frederick Douglass" is emphasized by the repetition of the phrase "the lives" in these lines from the poem?

  this man shall be remembered. . . / with the lives grown out of his life, the lives/fleshing his dream of the beautiful, needful thing.

  A. Human beings cannot live without a dream.

  B. Human beings need beauty to make life bearable.

  C. Frederick Douglass's ideals will live on in the lives of others

  D. Frederick Douglass was a beautiful human being.

_____ 10. A key message of "Frederick Douglass" is that all human beings have a need for

  A. love   C. instinct

  B. logic   D. freedom

Vocabulary

_____ 11. If you noticed that your friend's T-shirt was _frayed_, you could reasonably conclude that

  A. he had just bought it

  B. it was made of all cotton

  C. it was of very high quality

  D. it was very old and worn

_____ **12.** Which word is CLOSEST in meaning to *wily*?

    A. sly

    B. mean

    C. charming

    D. dishonest

_____ **13.** Which word is most nearly OPPOSITE in meaning to *gaudy*?

    A. tasteful

    B. showy

    C. passionate

    D. indifferent

Essay

14. Normally, we think it is a good thing to have as many choices as possible. In "The Explorer," Gwendolyn Brooks presents the idea that having a lot of choices can be frustrating, even disorienting. Do you agree? Why or why not? Explain your views in an essay that draws on examples from the poem and your own experience.

15. In "Frederick Douglass," Robert Hayden characterizes freedom as both "beautiful" and "terrible." In an essay, discuss these two sides of freedom: what is beautiful about it, and what is potentially terrible about it? Support your answer with examples from the poem and/or your own knowledge and experience.

16. **Thinking About the Essential Question: How does literature shape or reflect society?** Both of the poems in this section—"The Explorer" and "Frederick Douglass"—express longings for a different way of life. Such poems can tell the reader a great deal about the society about which—and in which—the poet expresses him/herself. In an essay, explain which poem is more a reflection of society, and which poem seeks to shape society. Support you answer with details from the poems.

"The Explorer" by Gwendolyn Brooks;
"Frederick Douglass" by Robert Hayden
Selection Test B

Critical Reading *Identify the letter of the choice that best answers the question.*

_____ 1. In "The Explorer," the explorer's main goal is to
   A. talk to his neighbors.
   B. deal with his grief.
   C. escape from poverty.
   D. find a quiet place.

_____ 2. If you were to interpret the details in the "Explorer," what might you reasonably conclude about the surroundings?
   A. The apartment building is dirty.
   B. The apartment building is burning.
   C. Neighbors are trying to keep the explorer out of their homes.
   D. The explorer is at ease in his surroundings.

_____ 3. In the first stanza of "The Explorer," the word "somehow," is echoed by the repetition of "somewhere." These words together help to evoke an atmosphere of
   A. enlightenment   C. uncertainty
   B. peace   D. anger

_____ 4. Which word that is repeated in "The Explorer" most clearly suggests the man's frustration?
   A. room   C. he
   B. frayed   D. there

_____ 5. What does the phrase "throbbing knobs" in the following passage from "The Explorer" suggest about the man's state of mind?
   So tipping down the scrambled halls he set / Vague hands on throbbing knobs. . . .
   A. listlessness   C. satisfaction
   B. enchantment   D. agitation

_____ 6. Which of these words best describes the man's attitude toward choice as described in "The Explorer"?
   A. dread   C. relief
   B. delight   D. curiosity

_____ 7. In "The Explorer," the quiet room so desperately sought by the man represents which of the following?

    A. a place where there are only pleasant choices to be considered

    B. a spot where he can get some badly needed sleep

    C. a refuge from the chaos of an evil world

    D. an escape from the burdens of choice

_____ 8. According to "Frederick Douglass," how will Douglass be remembered?

    A. by the words carved on a statue

    B. by the lives of free people

    C. by bronze statues

    D. by poetic tributes

_____ 9. In "Frederick Douglass," which repeated word or phrase creates a question about the future?

    A. this   C. when it

    B. not   D. the lives

_____ 10. Throughout "Frederick Douglass," freedom is portrayed mainly as

    A. a terrible burden from which humans instinctively flee in terror

    B. the hypocritical plaything of politicians

    C. a deep-seated need of all humans

    D. a luxury afforded only to a lucky few

_____ 11. In "Frederick Douglass," the poet expresses his hope

    A. for a time when liberty will automatically be assumed for all.

    B. for a formal tribute to the work of Frederick Douglass.

    C. that politicians will legislate freedom for all.

    D. that his freedom to hunt will continue.

_____ 12. Which of the following best describes the portrait of Douglass that emerges from "Frederick Douglass"?

    A. tormented slave   C. shrewd politician

    B. gifted orator   D. courageous idealist

_____ 13. If you were reading "Frederick Douglass" aloud, the repetition of the word "none" in this passage would help you to emphasize which of the following?

    . . . visioning a world where none is lonely, none hunted, alien . . .

    A. the futility of the ideals that Douglass believed in

    B. the complete end of the conditions that Douglass fought against

    C. the conditions under slavery that have been long since reformed

    D. the conditions that exist in many overseas countries

_____ 14. In "Frederick Douglass," the poet implies that, as forms of tribute to Frederick Douglass, statues, legends, poems, and wreaths of bronze are

A. insulting

C. insufficient

B. welcome

D. excessive

Vocabulary

_____ 15. Which word is CLOSEST in meaning to *frayed*?

A. tattered

C. impatient

B. crooked

D. overheated

_____ 16. Which word is most nearly OPPOSITE in meaning to *wily*?

A. cunning

C. uncontrollable

B. stupid

D. docile

_____ 17. If you were staying in a *gaudy* hotel, you would probably find the decor in the lobby and rooms to be

A. restrained and dull

C. strikingly original

B. old-fashioned

D. tacky and overdone

Essay

18. "Frederick Douglass" shows how the stirring example of a dedicated idealist like Douglass can inspire the lives of people for many generations. In an essay, write about a person from history or your personal experience who has served as an inspiration to you in some way. Support your answer with specific examples and clear reasoning.

19. In "The Explorer," Gwendolyn Brooks presents a picture of a troubled soul tormented by all the many choices that life presents to him. Do you agree that having an abundance of choices can be a source of anxiety and frustration rather than satisfaction? Why or why not? Develop your thoughts in an essay supported by examples from the poem and your own experience.

20. Both "The Explorer" and "Frederick Douglass" have something to say about freedom, but in very different ways. "The Explorer" shows how freedom of choice can be as much of a burden as a blessing, whereas "Frederick Douglass" portrays freedom as an essential human need. Which poem's treatment of freedom was more persuasive and appealing to you? Develop your thoughts in an essay supported by details from the poems.

21. **Thinking About the Essential Question: How does literature shape or reflect society?** Both of the poems in this section—"The Explorer" and "Frederick Douglass" express longings for a different way of life. Such poems can tell the reader a great deal about the society about which—and in which—the poet expresses him/herself. In an essay, explain which poem is more a reflection of society, and which poem seeks to shape society. Support you answer with details from the poems.

Name _____ Date _____

Benchmark Test 9

MULTIPLE CHOICE

Literary Analysis and Reading Skills

Read the poem titled "Dead Men Tell No Tales." Then, answer the questions that follow.

Dead Men Tell No Tales

THEY say that dead men tell no tales!   1

Except of barges with red sails
And sailors mad for nightingales;

Except of jongleurs stretched at ease
Beside old highways through the trees;   5

Except of dying moons that break
The hearts of lads who lie awake;

Except of fortresses in shade,
And heroes crumbled and betrayed.

But dead men tell no tales, they say!   10

Except old tales that burn away
The stifling tapestries of day:

Old tales of life, of love and hate,
Of time and space, and will, and fate.

—Haniel Long

1. What relationship does the title have to the theme of the poem?
   A. The title expresses the theme.
   B. The title contradicts the theme.
   C. The title is unrelated to the theme.
   D. The title illuminates an aspect of the theme.

2. Lines 2, 4, 6, and 8 illustrate which of the following?
   A. alliteration
   B. metaphor
   C. oxymoron
   D. parallelism

3. Which of these would be the most helpful in visualizing lines 4 and 5?
   A. reading other poems by Haniel Long
   B. seeing photos of old highways
   C. learning more about Haniel Long's life
   D. knowing that *jongleur* means "a wandering minstrel"

Read the introduction and the passage. Then, answer the questions that follow.

In this excerpt from *Winesburg, Ohio* by Sherwood Anderson, an elderly writer has had a "dream that was not a dream," in which grotesque figures appear before his eyes. As he attempts to write about certain truths connected to the figures, the people begin to snatch up the truths.

(1) It was the truths that made the people grotesques. (2) The old man had quite an elaborate theory concerning the matter. (3) It was his notion that the moment one of the people took one of the truths to himself, called it his truth, and tried to live his life by it, he became a grotesque and the truth he embraced became a falsehood. (4) You can see for yourself how the old man, who had spent all of his life writing and was filled with words, would write hundreds of pages concerning this matter. (5) The subject would become so big in his mind that he himself would be in danger of becoming a grotesque.

4. What is a grotesque character in a literary work?
   A. a character who is in conflict with the main character
   B. a character who is the object of ridicule or scorn
   C. a character who has become ludicrous due to an obsession with an idea
   D. a character who is misshapen and has disgusting habits

5. Why might you predict that the old man will have an epiphany?
   A. He appears to be in conflict with the figures and their truths.
   B. A sudden new insight would reveal to him what effect his theory is having on him.
   C. His dream shows that he is probably unstable.
   D. This episode is early in the story, which is usually where the epiphany occurs.

6. Which sentence from the passage is an example of foreshadowing?
   A. sentence 1
   B. sentence 2
   C. sentence 4
   D. sentence 5

Read the passage. Then, answer the questions that follow.

(1) Our assignment in the science lab was to develop a glue that would permanently hold pieces of paper together, regardless of stress or water damage. (2) Our usual procedure was to mix up a batch of glue, use it to adhere two papers together, leave it overnight, and check our results the following morning. (3) We were trying our fourth formula, and as usual, left it to dry overnight. (4) In the morning we examined our greatest failure yet. (5) True, the papers we had glued were stuck together. (6) However, when we pulled on one sheet, it peeled free from the other. (7) Then, we had an idea. (8) Would this glue formula work as a temporary glue? (9) Could it be used on memos and bookmarks that would stick in place and could also be easily removed? (10) That idea elicited a surprising "Well done!" from our teacher. (11) We had accidentally re-invented the self-stick notes used in offices everywhere.

7. Which of the following plot elements appear in sentences 1 and 2?
   A. the exposition
   B. the climax
   C. the conflict
   D. the resolution

8. Which sentence states the denouement?
   A. sentence 4
   B. sentence 6
   C. sentence 10
   D. sentence 11

Read the passage. Then, answer the questions that follow.

(1) Unlike most land masses, New Zealand has no native mammals. (2) The first mammals arrived long ago, when visitors and settlers arrived from Europe and Asia with their pet cats, dogs, and weasels. (3) Before their arrival, many species of flightless birds, such as the dodo, the moa, the takahe, the kakapo, and the kiwi thrived in New Zealand. (4) Their natural enemies were other birds, such as eagles and hawks that hunted by sight. (5) Therefore, the flightless birds could protect themselves by standing very still and blending in with their surroundings. (6) However, mammals hunt primarily by scent. (7) Therefore, the protection of camouflage was not enough to save the flightless birds. (8) Many, including the dodo and the moa, became extinct. (9) Others, like the takahe and the kakapo, are now seriously endangered.

9. Which is the best summary of this passage?
   A. Most birds hunt by sight, but most mammals hunt by scent. New Zealand's flightless birds could not depend on camouflage to protect them against their new predators. Therefore, many of them became either extinct or endangered.
   B. New Zealand has native birds that fly and birds that do not fly. Some birds that fly, such as eagles and hawks, hunted the flightless birds, using their sense of sight. The flightless birds protected themselves by blending in with their surroundings. This form of protection didn't work once dogs came to New Zealand.
   C. Examples of New Zealand's flightless birds include the dodo, the moa, the takahe, the kakapo, and the kiwi. Examples of their natural predators include eagles and hawks. New settlers introduced cats, dogs, and weasels. These mammals soon joined the eagles and hawks as predators of the flightless birds.
   D. Before settlers brought mammals to New Zealand, the native flightless birds used camouflage to protect themselves against birds that hunted by sight. However, camouflage could not protect them from the imported dogs and other mammals, who hunted by scent. Therefore, many flightless birds became either extinct or endangered.

10. What background knowledge might help you predict the fate of the takahe and the kakapo?
    A. migratory patterns of the dodo and moa
    B. a history of New Zealand's native mammals
    C. environmental legislation in New Zealand
    D. a physical description of their camouflage

11. The synonyms *bold* and *courageous* have different connotations. Which of the following explains this connotation?
   A. *Bold* is a shorter word, with fewer syllables, than *courageous*.
   B. *Bold* suggests more surprise and risk than *courageous*.
   C. *Bold* comes from an Old German word, while *courageous* comes from Old French.
   D. *Bold* has more meanings than *courageous*; it can also refer to a style of printing.

Read the stanza from the poem. Then, answer the questions that follow.

> Thus, some tall tree that long hath stood
> The glory of its native wood,
> By storms destroyed, or length of years,
> Demands the tribute of our tears.
> —from "On the Death of Dr. Benjamin Franklin" by Philip Morin Freneau

12. What conclusion can you draw about the speaker's feelings toward Benjamin Franklin?
   A. The speaker admires and loves Franklin.
   B. The speaker is indifferent toward Franklin.
   C. The speaker thinks that Franklin helped his country.
   D. The speaker feels as though Franklin was a member of the family.

13. Both "tall tree" and "tribute of our tears" are examples of which of the following?
   A. assonance
   B. alliteration
   C. consonance
   D. personification

Answer the following questions.

14. Which of these can most directly reveal the implied theme of a literary work?
   A. an author's collective works
   B. critical reviews of the work
   C. characters' comments and actions
   D. the author's background

15. Which of these helps the author develop a distinct voice?
   A. foreshadowing
   B. theme
   C. diction
   D. epiphany

16. What is a character's sudden revelation or flash of insight called?
   A. aphorism
   B. climax
   C. epiphany
   D. resolution

17. When encountering repetition in a poem that you are reading aloud, which of these should you do?
   A. speed up and gloss over it
   B. do not change the pace
   C. ignore any punctuation marks
   D. slow down and emphasize it

18. Which of these is the presentation of similar ideas using the same grammatical structure?
    A. parallelism   C. apostrophe
    B. alliteration   D. hyperbole

19. For which of the following selections would it be most important to analyze political assumptions?
    A. a movie review   C. an essay about mountain climbing
    B. a poem about war   D. a story about a family in crisis

20. Which is the best description of an extended metaphor?
    A. sustained comparison   C. overused comparison
    B. illogical comparison   D. direct comparison

21. The title of Walt Whitman's poem, "O Captain! My Captain!", makes use of which literary device?
    A. personification   C. imagery
    B. repetition   D. irony

22. Throughout the poem "O Captain! My Captain!", Walt Whitman compares President Abraham Lincoln to the captain of a ship. What is this an example of?
    A. mixed metaphor   C. simple metaphor
    B. dead metaphor   D. extended metaphor

23. Which of these is the repetition of vowel sounds in conjunction with dissimilar consonant sounds?
    A. consonance   C. assonance
    B. alliteration   D. scansion

24. What is the most likely use of a pun?
    A. humor   C. drama
    B. suspense   D. tragedy

25. Which of the following is an example of a pun?
    A. She could not stand the deafening silence in the room.
    B. He was egged on by his friends at the food fight.
    C. This steak is tougher than an old shoe.
    D. Fear gripped his heart.

26. What is a major reason for a poet to use repetition?
    A. for humor   C. for atmosphere
    B. for irony   D. for emphasis

Vocabulary

27. The word *blitz* comes from German meaning "lightning." Use this information to choose the definition of *blitz*.
    A. a spectacular and entertaining event   C. a sudden, destructive attack
    B. a tranquil experience   D. an obstacle to overcome

28. Based on your knowledge of the root *-sol-*, choose the person who would most likely enjoy solitude.

- **A.** a farmer
- **B.** an athlete
- **C.** a hermit
- **D.** a politician

29. Based on your knowledge of the root *-litera-*, choose the meaning of *literate* as it is used in the following sentence.

Most villagers became <u>literate</u> after a year of Eduardo's instruction.

- **A.** dependent on others
- **B.** full of generosity
- **C.** more intelligent
- **D.** able to read and write

30. What is the meaning of the word *rigid* in the following sentence?

Once he has made up his mind, nobody can sway him from his <u>rigid</u> opinions.

- **A.** stiff and hard
- **B.** firmly fixed
- **C.** strict and harsh
- **D.** having a framework

ESSAY

31. Think about two movies or television shows about war that you have seen. What essential messages were conveyed? Write an essay to compare and contract the themes expressed in your chosen works. Include references to each work to support your points.

32. Think of a memorable character from literature, movies, or television. Write a personality profile of that character. Concentrate on the character's personality traits and how they are illustrated in the work.

33. Write a poem on the theme of friendship. Use an extended metaphor in your poem in which you compare friendship to a concrete object or a physical activity.

Vocabulary Warm-up Word Lists

Study these words from the selections. Then, complete the activities.

Word List A

disaster [di ZAS ter] *n.* great misfortune
   If Reggie doesn't show up, the concert will be a <u>disaster</u>.

disturbing [di STERB ing] *adj.* causing worry or concern
   She saw some very <u>disturbing</u> sights when she visited the animal shelter.

fluster [FLUS ter] *n.* nervous or agitated state
   When she was in a <u>fluster</u> it was hard for her to concentrate.

high-strung [HY STRUNG] *adj.* having a nervous or easily upset nature
   Antoinette is so <u>high-strung</u> that she gets upset easily.

hirsute [HER soot] *adj.* hairy
   I had never realized that orangutans are so <u>hirsute</u>.

intent [in TENT] *n.* a plan or purpose
   It was his <u>intent</u> to continue his education once he had earned enough money to pay for it.

master [MAS ter] *v.* to become highly skilled or competent at something
   It took Marilyn only a week to <u>master</u> the new computer program.

realms [RELMZ] *n.* empires or kingdoms
   I love reading because it lets me visit magical <u>realms</u> in my imagination.

Word List B

begonia [bi GOHN yuh] *n.* an ornamental tropical plant with bright blooms
   My teacher told me that her favorite plant is the <u>begonia</u>.

crochet [kroh SHAY] *n.* needlework formed with interlocking loops on a single needle
   The type of <u>crochet</u> that we learned in class focused on making pillows and blankets.

embroidered [em BROY derd] *v.* decorated with stitching that forms a pattern or picture
   I am so lucky to have a collection of pillowcases <u>embroidered</u> by my grandmother.

evident [EV uh duhnt] *adj.* obvious; clear
   It was <u>evident</u> from the beginning of the movie that the bad guy would be caught.

marguerites [mahr guh REETS] *n.* types of daisies
   Her garden was full of blooming <u>marguerites</u> and other flowers.

saucy [SAW see] *adj.* amusingly forward and flippant
   Her <u>saucy</u> answer made everyone in the audience burst into laughter.

vaster [VAS ter] *adj.* larger; more enormous
   The arena was far <u>vaster</u> than I had realized from seeing it on television.

wickerwork [WIK er werk] *n.* something made of woven twigs or branches
   The front porch of the old house was furnished with a set of <u>wickerwork</u> furniture.

"One Art" and **"Filling Station"** by Elizabeth Bishop
Vocabulary Warm-up Exercises

Exercise A *Fill in the blanks, using each word from Word List A only once.*

From the beginning, it looked as though the trip to the zoo would be a [1]
_____. It was a holiday tradition in my family to visit the animals. However,
this time my mother was in a [2] _____ about the dinner preparations and
declared she couldn't possibly go. My [3] _____ young cousin was involved
with his video game, in which he was attempting to [4] _____ many levels
and rule many [5] _____. It was my [6] _____, however, to
make sure that the outing took place, as I find it [7] _____ to abandon
tradition. And once everyone got there, they enjoyed viewing the [8] _____
monkeys and the scaly snakes, the chattering birds and the slow-moving bears.

Exercise B *Revise each sentence so that the underlined vocabulary word is used in a
logical way. Be sure to keep the vocabulary word in your revision.*

Example: Because the offer was so *advantageous*, we declined it firmly.
Because the offer was so <u>advantageous</u>, we eagerly accepted it

1. The weather was so cold and dry that the <u>begonia</u> was thriving.
   _____

2. The dusty and worn <u>wickerwork</u> furniture looked brand new.
   _____

3. My tiny cubicle is far <u>vaster</u> than the large office I worked in before.
   _____

4. Most teachers love students who make <u>saucy</u> comments in class.
   _____

5. When I was little, I loved to watch my grandmother decorate dinner with <u>crochet</u>.
   _____

6. In the summer, I love wearing peasant blouses <u>embroidered</u> with snowflakes.
   _____

7. From his ragged suit of clothes, it was <u>evident</u> that he was extremely prosperous.
   _____

8. There is nothing so ugly in the springtime as a field of <u>marguerites</u>.
   _____

Name _____ Date _____

Reading Warm-up A

Read the following passage. Then, complete the activities.

I'm not sure how I ended up working in the lost and found at the mall for over twenty years. It certainly was never my goal or intent to make a career of dealing with the misplaced objects of other people's lives. Some people come looking for the most trivial items and get into quite a fluster if they aren't here. Other people lose things that are truly valuable and it must not bother them at all because they never come looking for them. However, I keep track of everything, no matter what its value.

Somehow, this little part of the mall has become my kingdom. It's not the most beautiful of realms, yet it's one over which I reign supreme. It's a little unsettling or disturbing when someone else comes to work here. Last month I caught the flu and was unable to crawl out of bed for two days. When I returned, I found a disaster of disorganization awaiting me, my temporary replacement having wreaked havoc in my workspace. I have developed my own system of organization, and although it is perfectly logical to me, others seem to find it difficult to master. The person who had taken over during my temporary absence had made quite a mess of things, and I even noted something that looked like a hirsute peppermint candy crushed beneath the desk. I was not pleased at having to clean up hairy candy!

Some people call me high-strung because I get so upset and agitated when things are not done my way. They seem to think I'm crazy to care so much about a job, but that's just the way I am

1. Underline the word that helps explain the meaning of intent. Give another word that means the same as *intent*.

2. Circle the words that tell what people get in a fluster about. Give a word or phrase that means the same as *fluster*.

3. Underline the word that gives a clue to the meaning of realms. Use the word *realms* in a sentence.

4. Underline the word that gives a hint to the meaning of disturbing. Give another word that means the same as *disturbing*.

5. Circle the word that tells what kind of disaster was awaiting the narrator. What kinds of things can be referred to as a *disaster*?

6. Circle the words that tell what other people found difficult to master. Tell something you have found it difficult to *master*.

7. Underline the words that tell what was hirsute. Use *hirsute* in a sentence.

8. Underline the words in the sentence that help explain what high-strung means. Give an antonym for *high-strung*.

145

Name _____ Date _____

Read the following passage. Then, complete the activities.

Many cities and towns host flea markets. They are places that are usually open a few days a week where people rent tables or booths to sell things. Some are held in small halls or lots, and others in far <u>vaster</u> spaces, like giant parking lots or open fields. The origin of the name is generally accepted to be a translation from French, *marché aux puces*. That term, literally "market of the fleas," was applied to a market outside of Paris that specialized in used furniture. Some <u>saucy</u> and witty person thought that the merchandise was likely to be infested with fleas. The colorful name stuck, and it came to be applied to large markets where many different people sell a hodge-podge of items.

After a quick glance at the merchandise at most flea markets, it is quite <u>evident</u> from the obvious lack of new items that used goods are what people most commonly offer for sale. It is not unusual to spot a set of charming old <u>wickerwork</u> porch furniture, the woven wood having become worn with age. Nearby might be an example of the arts of knitting or <u>crochet</u> or a tea towel <u>embroidered</u> with lovely old-fashioned designs.

Other vendors might specialize in plants. You are likely to see a booth spilling over with pots holding everything from a tropical, furry-leafed <u>begonia</u> to yellow and white <u>marguerites</u>, their cheery blooms bringing smiles to passers-by. Some people sell homemade baked goods. Others might offer vintage postcards or military souvenirs.

Flea markets are the perfect venue to demonstrate that one person's junk may be another person's treasure. A flea market is unlike a standard store, where you know what you will find inside. It is fun to go to a flea market for the very reason that you never know what you might stumble across!

1. Underline the words that give a hint to the meaning of <u>vaster</u>. Give a word or phrase that means the opposite of *vaster*.

2. Circle the word that suggests the meaning of <u>saucy</u>. Name an antonym for *saucy*.

3. Underline the words that tell what is <u>evident</u>. Define *evident* in your own words.

4. Circle the word that tells what is described as <u>wickerwork</u>. Use *wickerwork* in a sentence of your own.

5. Circle the word that gives a hint to the meaning of <u>crochet</u>. Do you know anyone who knows the art of *crochet*?

6. Underline the words that give a clue to the meaning of <u>embroidered</u>. Use *embroidered* in a sentence of your own.

7. Underline the word that gives a clue to <u>begonia</u>. Name a type of plant that you like.

8. Circle the words that give a clue to what <u>marguerites</u> are. Give a word that is also a name for the white and yellow flowers known as *marguerites*

Name _____ Date _____

"One Art" and "Filling Station" by Elizabeth Bishop
Literary Analysis: Diction

Elizabeth Bishop carefully crafts her poems to create a sense of intimacy with and connection to the reader. A major formal element that she uses to connect with the reader is **diction,** or word choice. Consider the rhyming words in the following lines from "One Art":

The art of losing isn't hard to <u>master</u>;
so many things seem filled with the intent
to be lost that their loss is not <u>disaster</u>.

The words *master* and *disaster* are common, everyday words, yet the way in which she places and repeats them throughout the poem gives them fresh meaning. In "Filling Station," Bishop creates a strong sense of place through the skillful diction with which she describes key details of the filling station and the people who work and live there.

DIRECTIONS: *Use the graphic organizer below to list four examples of vivid words or phrases in "Filling Station" that vividly evoke the reality of this place for the reader.*

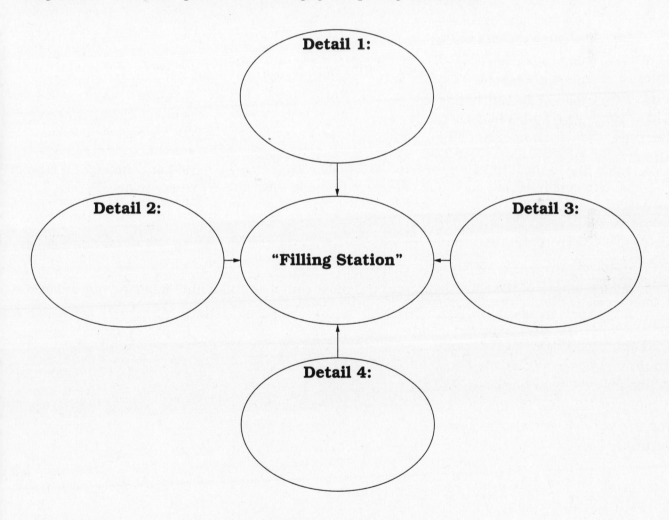

"One Art" and **"Filling Station"** by Elizabeth Bishop

Reading Strategy: Read According to Punctuation

Many poems—including "One Art" and "Filling Station"—are written in sentences and use the same punctuation marks that you find in prose. To better understand the meaning of a poem, **read according to punctuation.** Instead of pausing at line breaks, pause only when you encounter a comma, a colon, a semicolon, a dash, or an end mark.

DIRECTIONS: *Write your answer to the following questions on the lines provided.*

1. The first line of "Filling Station" ends with an exclamation point ("Oh, but it is dirty!"). How does this punctuation affect the impact and meaning of that line?

   _____

   _____

2. How many sentences or complete thoughts are expressed in the following lines from "Filling Station"?

   > Some comic books provide
   > the only note of color—
   > of certain color. They lie
   > upon a big dim doily
   > draping a taboret
   > (part of the set), beside
   > a big hirsute begonia.

   _____

3. Each line of the fifth stanza of "One Art" ends with a stop—a period or comma. Is it reasonable to conclude that each line expresses a single thought? Why or why not?

   _____

   _____

   _____

4. Which stanza of "One Art" expresses the most complete thoughts? Explain your answer.

   _____

   _____

"One Art" and **"Filling Station"** by Elizabeth Bishop
Vocabulary Builder

Using the Root -*extra*-

A. DIRECTIONS: *The root -extra- means "additional," "outside," or "beyond." Tell what the meaning of each of these words has to do with these meanings.*

1. extraterrestrial _____

2. extrapolate _____

3. extralegal _____

4. extramarital _____

Using the Word List

extraneous   intent   master   permeated

B. DIRECTIONS: *Circle the letter of the answer that is closest in meaning to the Word List word.*

1. MASTER
   A. learn   B. judge   C. rule   D. define

2. INTENT
   A. goal   B. concentration   C. analysis   D. force

3. PERMEATED
   A. diluted   B. requested   C. spread   D. founded

4. EXTRANEOUS
   A. diverting   B. inessential   C. complicated   D. courteous

Name _____ Date _____

"One Art" and **"Filling Station"** by Elizabeth Bishop
Support for Writing

Use the following chart to help get started in creating a multigenre response to either "One Art" or "Filling Station." First, illustrate the poem with drawings, paintings, or photographs of your own, or with a collage of images you find in other sources. Next, write an explanation of your choices. Finally, combine the images with the written text to create a poetry display. Post your display in the classroom, if possible.

Use the chart below as an aid in generating ideas for your project.

Type of Drawing, Painting, or Photograph	Is Image Realistic or Symbolic?	Why I Chose This Image

"One Art" and **"Filling Station"** by Elizabeth Bishop

Enrichment: Alternative Fuels

"Filling Station" paints a vivid word portrait of one of the most common features of American life: the corner service station, where we fill up our cars with gasoline. For decades, petroleum-based gasoline has provided an affordable and reliable way to fuel Americans' automobiles—and hence their ability to travel to school, work, stores, and to leisure destinations. Now, however, with increasing concerns about air pollution and global warming, scientists and government officials are searching for alternatives to fossil fuels such as petroleum to meet the world's automotive needs.

Use the chart below to explain briefly the potential advantages and disadvantages of various fuels as alternatives to gasoline for keeping the world's automobiles on the road without endangering the environment.

Alternative Fuel	Source	Advantages	Disadvantages
Ethanol			
Hydrogen			
Electric battery (and hybrid)			
Biodiesel			
Natural gas			
Solar			

"One Art" and **"Filling Station"** by Elizabeth Bishop
Open-Book Test

Short Answer *Write your responses to the questions in this section on the lines provided.*

1. If you read lines 4–5 of "One Art" aloud and followed the punctuation, at what two points would you come to a full stop? Explain your answer.

   _____

   _____

2. In "One Art," Elizabeth Bishop makes use of varied rhetorical devices. Beginning with lines 4–5, she shifts from declarative to imperative sentences. Why do you think she makes this change at this point in the poem? Explain your answer.

   _____

   _____

   _____

3. In "One Art," what do you notice about the scale of the items the speaker loses as the poem progresses?

   _____

   _____

4. In "One Art," what is the effect of inserting an exclamation into the middle of these lines (10–11)?

   > I lost my mother's watch. And look! my last, or / next-to-last, of three loved houses went.

   _____

   _____

5. The last line of "One Art" contains a combined imperative/exclamation: "(*Write* it!)." What is unique about this exclamation? How does it reinforce the poem's final message about the meaning of loss?

   _____

   _____

   _____

6. Why do you think Bishop begins "Filling Station" with an exclamation?

   > Oh, but it is dirty!

   _____

   _____

7. Bishop sprinkles "Filling Station" with several questions, especially in the fifth stanza, which begins with three questions. What do these questions convey about the speaker's state of mind as she takes in the details of the filling station?

   _____

   _____

8. Based on the kinds of details that the speaker associates with the "somebody" of the last two stanzas of "Filling Station," who do you think "somebody" is? Briefly explain your answer.

_____

_____

_____

_____

9. In "Filling Station," Bishop creates a strong sense of place through the skillful diction, or word choice, with which she describes key details of the filling station and the people who work and live there. Use the graphic organizer below to list four examples of vivid words or phrases in the poem that vividly evoke the reality of this place for the reader.

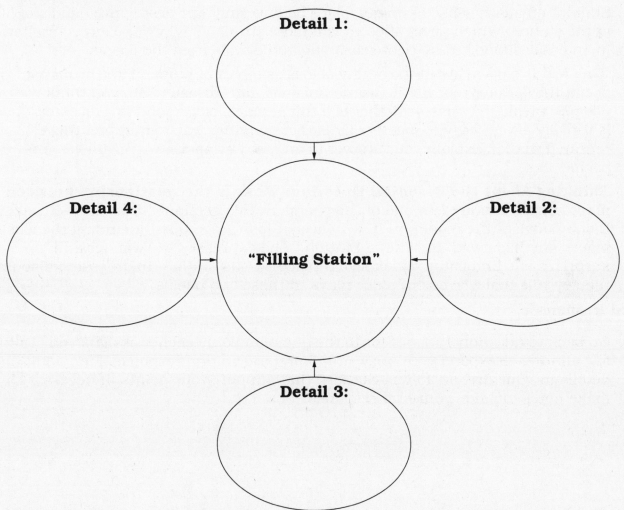

Detail 1:

Detail 4:

"Filling Station"

Detail 2:

Detail 3:

10. If your teacher commented that an essay that you wrote contained extraneous details, would those details be relevant to the topic you were writing about? Why or why not? Base your answer on the meaning of *extraneous* as it is used in "Filling Station."

_____

_____

Essay

Write an extended response to the question of your choice or to the question or questions your teacher assigns you.

11. In "Filling Station," the speaker wonders who the "somebody" is behind all of the details she observes on the cement porch. Based on the details the speaker provides, who do you think this "somebody" is? In an essay, write a detailed character sketch of this somebody, using your imagination supported by details from the poem. Include concrete, vivid details such as what the person looks like, what his/her function is at the filling station, what his/her personality is like, what his/her relationship is to the father and sons who work there, and so on.

12. The two poems by Elizabeth Bishop, "One Art" and "Filling Station," deal with very different subjects. "One Art" reflects on loss and how humans cope with it. "Filling Station" creates a sense of unique place by lingering over descriptive details of life at the station. Which poem affected you more strongly? Why? Explain your answer in an essay supported by clear reasoning and details from the poems.

13. "One Art" is a poem about the reality of loss as a part of human life. Throughout the poem, the speaker repeats the words "master" and "disaster." Do you think the poem is saying that loss—whether of a thing, place, or person—is a disaster? If so, is it really always easy to master? Or is there another way to interpret those repeated words? Explain your answer in an essay supported by examples from the poem.

14. **Thinking About the Essential Question: What is the relationship between place and literature?** In one of the poems in this section—"One Art"—Elizabeth Bishop advises the reader on how to accept loss gracefully—including the loss of places one has loved. In "Filling Station," she expresses the wonder and surprises she finds at an unexpected place—a gas station. In an essay, discuss the key role that a sense of place plays in these two poems.

Oral Response

15. Go back to question 1, 3, or 5 or to the question your teacher assigns you. Take a few minutes to expand your answer and prepare an oral response. Find additional details in "One Art" or "Filling Station" that support your points. If necessary, make notes to guide your oral response.

"One Art" and **"Filling Station"** by Elizabeth Bishop
Selection Test A

Critical Reading *Identify the letter of the choice that best answers the question.*

____ 1. What rhetorical device does Bishop use in the following line from "One Art":

Lose something every day.

A. imperative

B. exclamation

C. statement

D. exaggeration

____ 2. In "One Art," what does Bishop mean when she writes, "so many things seem filled with the intent / to be lost . . ."?

A. Inanimate objects have a will of their own.

B. People actually intend to lose things but do not realize it.

C. It is good to lose a certain number of things.

D. Losing things is a common occurrence.

____ 3. Which word in the following line from "One Art" points to Bishop's idea that losing is an art that one needs to work at?

Then practice losing farther, losing faster: . . .

A. practice

B. losing

C. farther

D. faster

____ 4. The brief sentence "And look!" in "One Art" employs which *two* rhetorical devices?

A. imperative and exclamation

B. exclamation and question

C. question and imperative

D. statement and question

____ 5. If you were reading aloud these lines from "One Art," at what point would you make your first full stop?

Lose something everyday. Accept the fluster of lost door keys, the hour badly spent.

A. after "everyday"

B. after "fluster"

C. after "keys"

D. after "spent"

___ 6. In reading aloud this line from "One Art," why would you come to a full stop after "ones"?

I lost two cities, lovely ones.

A. because of the sound of the word

B. because of the meaning of the word

C. because of the punctuation that follows it

D. because of the words that come after it

___ 7. To whom is the exclamation addressed in the following passage from "One Art"?

It's evident / the art of losing's not too hard to master / though it may look like (*Write* it!) like disaster.

A. to the reader

B. to the person lost

C. the speaker herself

D. to an unnamed third party

___ 8. Which words from "Filling Station" most forcefully convey the speaker's overall impression of the filling station?

A. "Oh, but it is dirty!"

B. "this little filling station"

C. "black translucency"

D. "Be careful with that match!"

___ 9. In "Filling Station," what is the substance that makes everything "dirty" at the filling station, according to the speaker?

A. mud

B. soot

C. oil

D. debris

___ 10. Why does Bishop employ the rhetorical device of three consecutive questions— "Why the extraneous plant? / Why the taboret? / Why, oh why, the doily?"—in "Filling Station"?

A. to create a smooth sense of rhythm

B. to convey the urgency of her curiosity about the life of this family

C. to convey her mounting disgust at the overall dirtiness of the place

D. to introduce new descriptive details

_____ 11. Who might Bishop feel is the "somebody" she mentions in these lines from "Filling Station"?

> Somebody embroidered the doily. / Somebody waters the plant, / or oils it, maybe.

A. the father and his sons

B. a person who cares about the place and the family.

C. an unknown visitor to the filling station

D. a person who is hired to attend to these household details

Essay

12. In "Filling Station," it appears that the filling station is a place where people both work and live. In the Internet age, more and more people work from home. Does home still feel like "home" in these situations? How does working at home affect people's motivation to work? Examine the example of the filling station or any others that you are familiar with. Address these points in an essay supported by clear reasoning and specific examples.

13. "One Art" is a reflection on the impact of loss on human life. At the beginning of the poem, while discussing minor losses, the speaker asserts that loss is easy to master. As she progresses to ever more serious losses throughout the poem—ending with the loss of a person—she finally and reluctantly admits that losing is indeed a disaster. Think of something or someplace you have lost in your life. Was the loss easy for you to master, or was it a disaster? Express your thoughts in an essay supported by specific details.

14. In "Filling Station," Elizabeth Bishop asks herself a series of questions about the people who live and/or work at the filling station. In an essay, use your imagination to write character portraits of these people—the father, his two sons, and whoever you imagine "someone" to be. Describe both their physical characteristics and personalities, and whether or not you think they lead happy, fulfilling lives. Support your essay with vivid descriptive details, both from the poem and your imagination.

15. **Thinking About the Essential Question: What is the relationship between place and literature?** In one of the poems in this section—"One Art"—Elizabeth Bishop advises the reader on how to accept the loss gracefully—including the loss of places one has loved. In "Filling Station," she expresses the wonder and surprises she finds at an unexpected place—a gas station. In an essay, discuss the key role that a sense of place plays in these two poems.

"One Art" and **"Filling Station"** by Elizabeth Bishop
Selection Test B

Critical Reading *Identify the letter of the choice that best answers the question.*

_____ 1. In "One Art," Bishop instructs the reader to "Lose something every day" in order to
  A. become better at finding things
  B. become accustomed to the reality of loss
  C. distract oneself from more serious matters
  D. realize that material possessions are not important

_____ 2. In "One Art," Bishop's notion that losing is an "art" is supported by her notion that, like other art forms, it requires
  A. money   B. time   C. practice   D. patience

_____ 3. In which of these lines from "One Art" would you pause twice in the middle of the line if you were reading it aloud?
  A. "The art of losing isn't hard to master;"
  B. "Lose something every day. Accept the fluster"
  C. "I lost my mother's watch. And look! my last, or"
  D. "though it may look like (Write it!) like disaster."

_____ 4. In "One Art," Bishop writes, "Accept the fluster / of lost door keys, the hour badly spent." Her use of the word "fluster" in these lines indicates that she believes that a lost door key or a wasted hour is an example of a(n)
  A. minor annoyance   C. life-changing experience
  B. major disaster   D. paralyzing misfortune

_____ 5. In these lines from "One Art," Bishop's use of the exclamation "And look!" signals the reader that she is moving in what direction in her list of things lost?
    I lost my mother's watch. And look! my last, or / next-to-last, of three loved houses went.
  A. She is moving from small objects to large objects.
  B. She is moving to items of increasing monetary value.
  C. She is moving to emotionally more trying losses.
  D. She is moving toward gains instead of losses.

_____ 6. Which of the following from "One Art" is an example of the use of the imperative?
  A. "The art of losing isn't hard to master."
  B. "None of these will bring disaster."
  C. "Then practice losing farther, losing faster. . . ."
  D. "I miss them, but it wasn't a disaster."

_____ 7. Which choice best captures the meaning of the word "owned" as it is used in the following passage from "One Art"?

> I lost two cities, lovely ones. And, vaster, / some realms I owned, two rivers, a continent.

A. bought and paid for   C. was the only resident of

B. ruled over politically   D. felt strongly attached to

_____ 8. In the last four lines of "One Art," the poem shifts from things that were lost to a person who was lost. Why does the speaker have to force herself to write the final word "disaster" with the imperative "(*Write* it)"?

A. The loss really is a disaster that is hard to acknowledge.

B. She is weary of writing this long list of losses.

C. The memory of this person is unpleasant to the speaker.

D. She feels she has already made the point that loss is not a disaster.

_____ 9. Which word does Bishop repeat four times in "Filling Station" to describe the station, its surroundings, the men's clothing, even the family dog, and to convey her overall impression of the place?

A. black   B. translucency   C. saucy   D. dirty

_____ 10. What is the likeliest reason that the following line from "Filling Station" is phrased in question form?

> Do they live in the station?

A. to show that the speaker has reached a conclusion

B. to get the reader to share the speaker's thoughts

C. to show the speaker's curiosity and uncertainty

D. to invite the reader to give a clear answer to the issue posed

_____ 11. In "Filling Station," which of the following best describes the attitude of the speaker toward the workers and/or inhabitants of the filling station?

A. open disdain   B. engaged curiosity   C. outright ridicule   D. humble admiration

_____ 12. If you were reading the following words from "Filling Station" aloud, after which word would you come to the first FULL stop?

> . . . Somebody / arranges the rows of cans so that they softly say: / ESSO-SO-SO / to high-strung automobiles.

A. Somebody   B. say: C. SO   D. automobiles

_____ 13. "Filling Station" includes three consecutive questions: "Why the extraneous plant? / Why the taboret? / Why, oh why, the doily?" To whom are these questions addressed?

A. the father   C. the speaker herself

B. the "somebody" mentioned in the poem   D. the reader

___ 14. In "Filling Station," why is the speaker so vexed with curiosity about the presence of an "extraneous" plant, a taboret, and a doily?

  A. She finds all of these items to be ugly.

  B. These are items that seem weirdly out of place at a filling station.

  C. She is amazed at how well these items blend in with the rest of the atmosphere of the filling station.

  D. These items seem to distract the father and his sons from their duties.

___ 15. In "Filling Station," the "somebody" of the poem is a person who contributes what to the life of the filling station?

  A. manual labor on a par with the father and sons

  B. small touches of beauty and caring

  C. cooking and cleaning and household errands

  D. management duties

Essay

16. In "Filling Station," the speaker spends a good deal of time wondering about the lives of the people who work and live there. She finds the station "dirty," right down to the workers' clothes and the dog on the porch. Do you think that the father and the sons find their surroundings "dirty"? Do you think they are happy with their lives working and living at the filling station? Why or why not? Express your opinions in an essay supported by details from the poem.

17. In "One Art," Elizabeth Bishop reflects on the reality of loss and how people cope with it. Is there a discernible trend to the kinds of losses she discusses, and the order in which she discusses them? Why or why not? If so, what is the significance of that order? Explain your answer in an essay supported by examples from the poem.

18. In both of the poems in this grouping, Elizabeth Bishop makes liberal use of rhetorical devices to set the poem's tone and convey its message: mainly imperatives (or combined imperatives/exclamations) in "One Art," and mainly questions in "Filling Station." In an essay, explain why imperatives/exclamations are more appropriate to a poem about how to deal with loss, and why questions are appropriate to a poem that inquires into the lives of the family at the filling station. Support your answer with details from the poems.

19. **Thinking About the Essential Question: What is the relationship between place and literature?** In one of the poems in this section—"One Art"—Elizabeth Bishop advises the reader on how to accept loss gracefully—including the loss of places one has loved. In "Filling Station," she expresses the wonder and surprises she finds at an unexpected place—a gas station. In an essay, discuss the key role that a sense of place plays in these two poems.

Vocabulary Warm-up Word Lists

Study these words from the selection. Then, complete the activities.

Word List A

acquire [uh KWYR] *v.* to get; to gain possession of
   Leon has enrolled in a computer class and hopes to <u>acquire</u> new skills.

apprehension [ap ree HEN shuhn] *n.* fearful anticipation of the future
   Sandra feels <u>apprehension</u> about going to a new school in the fall.

clambering [KLAM ber ing] *v.* climbing with difficulty
   <u>Clambering</u> over the old picket fence, Mark and Sam took a shortcut.

confirmation [kahn fir MAY shuhn] *n.* verification of the truth
   Nodding his head, Dad gave Gina the <u>confirmation</u> she wanted.

fidget [FIJ uht] *v.* to fuss; to behave restlessly
   If the baby begins to <u>fidget</u>, please give her a bottle.

intimidated [in TIM uh dayt uhd] *adj.* frightened
   Chelsea is too <u>intimidated</u> to sail the boat by herself.

jagged [JAG uhd] *adj.* rough and irregular
   The river traces a <u>jagged</u> path through the national park.

reckless [REK lis] *adj.* careless; acting in a risky way
   John is a <u>reckless</u> driver, so it's no surprise he's been in two accidents.

Word List B

benevolent [buh NEV uh luhnt] *adj.* kindly; charitable
   The <u>benevolent</u> old woman donated her antique collection to the museum.

decorously [DEK uhr uhs lee] *adv.* in a way that shows good taste or decorum
   The polite audience applauded <u>decorously</u> after Martin's speech.

engrossed [en GROHSD] *v.* absorbed; wholly occupied
   Su was so <u>engrossed</u> in the TV show that she didn't hear the phone ringing.

exasperated [eg ZAS per ayt uhd] *adj.* annoyed; impatient
   Bart looks <u>exasperated</u> because he's been waiting for three hours.

fascination [fas uh NAY shuhn] *n.* intense interest
   Scott's <u>fascination</u> with alligators inspired his trip to Florida.

intriguing [in TREEG ing] *adj.* interesting or curious
   Alice is traveling to Arizona because she finds the desert <u>intriguing</u>.

recoiled [ree KOYLD] *v.* shrank or pulled pack, as if with fear
   Arthur's hand <u>recoiled</u> when he touched the hot surface.

superficial [soo per FISH uhl] *adj.* shallow; not thorough
   That book review was extremely <u>superficial</u>; it offered very little analysis.

Name _____ Date _____

"The Rockpile" by James Baldwin
Vocabulary Warm-up Exercises

Exercise A *Fill in the blanks, using each word from Word List A only once.*

Last summer, Sal discovered bird-watching. His first step was to
[1] _____ a good pair of binoculars, a notebook, and a field guide. He
knew he might be [2] _____ over some rough terrain, so he also pur-
chased a stout pair of boots. He soon became so wrapped up in his hobby that he would
[3] _____ impatiently if bad weather kept him indoors. The challenge of
long walking tours did not fill him with doubt or [4] _____. On the contrary, he would climb over the most difficult and [5] _____ parts of the
mountain gorges in order to obtain with certainty the [6] _____ of a rare
species sighting. Sal didn't think he was [7] _____ or prone to taking
unnecessary risks. Instead, the hiking challenges he faced made him feel confident,
rather than [8] _____.

Exercise B *Decide whether each statement below is true or false. Circle T or F, and explain your answer.*

1. A <u>benevolent</u> person can usually be trusted to have your best interests at heart.
   T / F _____

2. If you are acting <u>decorously</u>, you can expect that quite a few people will be shocked.
   T / F _____

3. A person watching TV with an <u>engrossed</u> look is usually bored with the program.
   T / F _____

4. Smiles and jokes are typically signs of <u>exasperated</u> reactions or emotions.
   T / F _____

5. <u>Fascination</u> with a hobby often leads a person to spend hours on it every day.
   T / F _____

6. Someone who finds a subject <u>intriguing</u> will normally spend little time on it.
   T / F _____

7. When she dropped the tray of glassware, she instinctively <u>recoiled</u>.
   T / F _____

8. A person with <u>superficial</u> knowledge about a topic can rightly claim to be an expert.
   T / F _____

"The Rockpile" by James Baldwin
Reading Warm-up A

Read the following passage. Pay special attention to the underlined words. Then, read it again, and complete the activities. Use a separate sheet of paper for your written answers.

When people looked at Brian now, they saw a muscular kid who played starting quarterback for the high school team. They didn't realize how much work he had done to <u>acquire</u> such toughness.

It started in fifth grade, when an older kid, Gary, kept taunting Brian in a game during lunch recess. Back then, Brian's small size made him fearful since he was <u>intimidated</u> by the physical power of the other boys. He watched as they were <u>clambering</u> on top of each other for a fumbled ball, and all he could do was back away.

"What are you—a fraidy-cat?" asked Gary.

Brian was so stunned by the attack that he couldn't respond. It hadn't occurred to him that everyone could see his <u>apprehension</u>, the fearful way he was playing. It got even worse on the next play, when Brian dropped a pass thrown right to him—a <u>confirmation</u> that he was too weak to play the game.

"Get off the field, you loser," said Gary.

With everyone laughing at him, Brian desperately wanted to redeem himself. Gary continued to mock him, but Brian steeled himself and did not even <u>fidget</u> or act nervously as the insults came. On defense, he rushed over to tackle whatever opponent had the ball. He got more and more <u>reckless</u>, diving for interceptions, until finally he had the chance to tackle Gary. Both of them fell to the ground, and Brian landed on a sharp, <u>jagged</u> stone, which injured his right arm. The pain was agonizing, but after that Gary never taunted him again.

1. Underline the words that explain how Brian was able to <u>acquire</u> toughness. Use the word **acquire** in an original sentence.

2. Circle the words in this sentence that give a clue to the meaning of <u>intimidated</u>. What is a synonym for **intimidated**?

3. Underline the words that give a clue to the meaning of <u>clambering</u>. Write a definition of **clambering** in your own words.

4. Circle the words that offer a clue to the meaning of <u>apprehension</u>. What are two antonyms for **apprehension**?

5. Circle the words in this sentence that describe the <u>confirmation</u> of Brian's fear. What is an antonym for **confirmation**?

6. Underline the word in this sentence that gives a clue to the meaning of <u>jagged</u>. What are two synonyms for **jagged**?

7. Circle the phrase that gives a clue to the meaning of <u>fidget</u>. Use the word **fidget** in an original sentence.

8. Underline the words in this and the previous sentence that hint at the meaning of <u>reckless</u>. What is an antonym for **reckless**?

Name _____ Date _____

"The Rockpile" by James Baldwin
Reading Warm-up B

Read the following passage. Pay special attention to the underlined words. Then, read it again, and complete the activities. Use a separate sheet of paper for your written answers.

One of the most important and inspiring influences on the young James Baldwin was the writer Richard Wright. Born in Mississippi in 1908, Wright was sixteen years older than Baldwin. He can be considered the younger man's <u>benevolent</u> mentor. Wright was the grandchild of slaves and grew up in poverty. As a young man, he worked as an unskilled laborer in Memphis and then Chicago. Thanks to the Federal Writers' Project in the early 1930s, Wright was able to explore his <u>fascination</u> with writing, first as a journalist and then as an author of fiction. <u>Engrossed</u> and totally absorbed by a single, over-arching theme, Wright focused in his initial stories on how a black man could live in a country that denied his humanity.

With the publication of his novel *Native Son* in 1940, Wright's literary reputation took a huge step forward. Reviewers had received his early stories quietly and <u>decorously</u>, but the attention paid to *Native Son* made the book a best-seller. The <u>intriguing</u> character of Bigger Thomas, the book's appealing and complex hero, inspired producers to sponsor stage and film adaptations.

Four years later, in 1944, Wright scored a repeat success with an autobiography, *Black Boy.* This book recorded the author's extreme poverty, as well as the ways in which he <u>recoiled</u> in shock from racial prejudice.

After World War II, an <u>exasperated</u> Wright made the decision to forsake his homeland and settle in Paris, France. One can only assume that he felt, like James Baldwin later, that life abroad would be more meaningful, less <u>superficial</u>, for a black man in France. It was in Paris that Wright died in 1960, at the age of fifty-two.

1. Underline the words in a previous sentence that give a clue to the meaning of <u>benevolent</u>. Write a sentence of your own using this word.

2. Circle the words in this sentence that give a clue to the meaning of <u>fascination</u>. Write a definition for *fascination* in your own words.

3. Underline the words that help explain the meaning of <u>engrossed</u>. What is a synonym for *engrossed*?

4. Underline the word in this sentence that gives a clue to the meaning of <u>decorously</u>. What are two antonyms for *decorously*?

5. Circle the words in this sentence that give a clue to the meaning of <u>intriguing</u>. Use a word meaning the opposite of *intriguing* in a sentence.

6. Underline the words in this sentence that hint at the meaning of <u>recoiled</u>. What is a synonym for *recoiled*?

7. Circle the words in this sentence that hint at the meaning of <u>exasperated</u>. Why might Wright have felt *exasperated*?

8. Circle the words in this sentence that hint at the meaning of the word <u>superficial</u>. What is a synonym for *superficial*?

Name _____ Date _____

"The Rockpile" by James Baldwin
Literary Analysis: Setting

Every story has a **setting,** a particular time and place in which it occurs. The setting of a story affects how the characters feel and how they behave. Setting encompasses details that fall into several categories, such as location, weather, geography, time of day, season, and atmosphere. The social and economic conditions that prevail in a story are also an important aspect of its setting.

A specific story setting might also be a **symbol,** which is a person, place, or object that has a meaning in itself but also suggests a larger meaning. For example, in this story, the rockpile represents both failure in the community and conflict in the family.

A. DIRECTIONS: *Each of the following passages from the selection reflects or symbolizes a particular category of setting. Review the categories listed below. On the line before each passage, write the letter of the category (or the letters of the categories) that best applies to the passage. You will not use every category.*

A. location	B. geography	C. weather	D. time of day
E. social and economic conditions		F. season	G. atmosphere

____ 1. "At the end of the street nearest their house was the bridge which spanned the Harlem River . . ."

____ 2. ". . . John and Roy sat on the fire escape and watched the forbidden street below."

____ 3. "Dozens of boys fought each other in the harsh sun . . ."

____ 4. "One Saturday, an hour before his father would be coming home, Roy was wounded on the rockpile and brought screaming upstairs."

____ 5. "They filled the air, too, with flying weapons: stones, sticks, tin cans, garbage, whatever could be picked up and thrown."

B. DIRECTIONS: *In each of the sentences in Part A, at least one word is related to a particular category (or categories) of setting. Change the setting of each sentence by replacing the word or words with your own. On the lines below, rewrite each sentence with your new words. Your new sentences can make the setting imaginative and fun.*

_____

_____

_____

_____

_____

_____

_____

_____

_____

Name _____ Date _____

Reading Strategy: Identify Cause and Effect

When you **identify cause and effect** relationships in fiction, you can take several approaches. You might figure out what causes characters to behave as they do. You might note the effects that one character's words or actions have on other characters. Identifying cause and effect in fiction can help you understand a story's action and meaning.

DIRECTIONS: *Complete the following flow charts to identify cause and effect in "The Rockpile."*

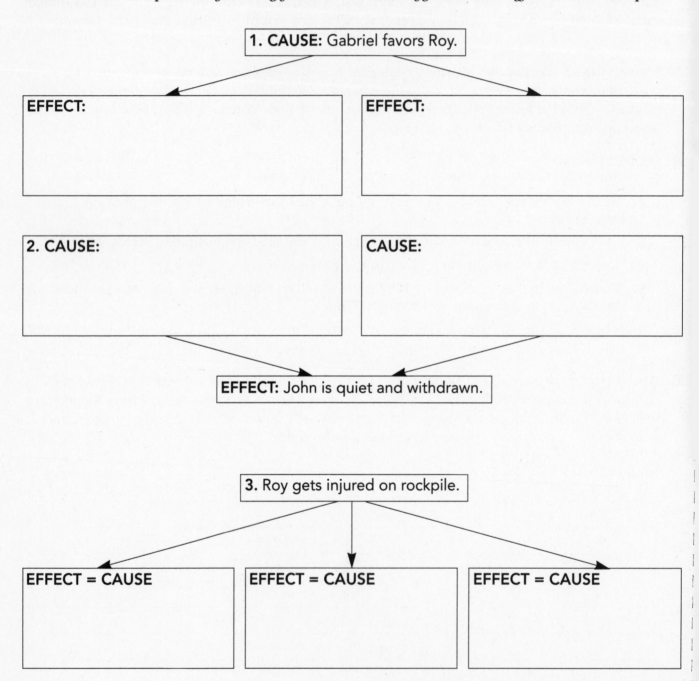

1. **CAUSE:** Gabriel favors Roy.

EFFECT:

EFFECT:

2. CAUSE:

CAUSE:

EFFECT: John is quiet and withdrawn.

3. Roy gets injured on rockpile.

EFFECT = CAUSE

EFFECT = CAUSE

EFFECT = CAUSE

"**The Rockpile**" by James Baldwin
Vocabulary Builder

Using the Latin Prefix *super-*

A. DIRECTIONS: *The prefix* super- *means "over, above, beyond." For each word or phrase that follows, write a synonym that contains the prefix* super-.

1. of higher rank or quality _____

2. naughty or snobby _____

3. displace or supplant _____

4. boss or manager _____

Using the Word List

benevolent   engrossed   jubilant   latent   perdition

B. DIRECTIONS: *Choose the word or phrase that is most nearly* opposite *in meaning to the word in the Word List. Circle the letter of your choice.*

1. benevolent:
   A. unaware
   B. stingy
   C. careless
   D. saintly

2. latent:
   A. dormant
   B. tardy
   C. invisible
   D. evident

3. engrossed:
   A. forgetful
   B. preoccupied
   C. uninterested
   D. serene

4. jubilant:
   A. happy
   B. sad
   C. skillful
   D. jumpy

5. perdition:
   A. relief
   B. intuition
   C. salvation
   D. focus

"The Rockpile" by James Baldwin
Grammar and Style: Avoiding Shifts in Verb Tense

A **verb** has different forms, called **tenses,** to show the time of the action. Generally, use the same tense. When your verbs **shift** unnecessarily from one tense to another, it's difficult to follow your meaning. Here's an example of consistent use of verb tenses:

When I *finished* this story, I *knew* more about life in Harlem in the 1930s

However, you can shift tenses if you want to show a change in time:

"The Rockpile" *was* so interesting that I *am* now eager to read more of Baldwin's work.

Here is an example of an inconsistent shift in verb tense of the kind you should avoid:

I *sit* on the couch while I *did* my homework.

The present-tense action of *sit* conflicts with the past-tense shift to *did*. The unnecessary shift in verb tense is corrected in the examples below:

I *sit* on the couch while I *do* my homework.

I *sat* on the couch while I *did* my homework.

DIRECTIONS: *Rewrite each sentence below to correct any unnecessary shift in verb tense. If the sentence is correct, write correct on the line.*

1. I _____ ll the guests when I got home.

   _____

2. There are lots of exciting music acts at the concert I attended.

   _____

3. It is the duty of all citizens to help all those who were in need.

   _____

4. Last year's basketball team had a losing record despite the high hopes we have for it.

   _____

5. The movie we are watching now is not as interesting as the one we saw last week.

   _____

"The Rockpile" by James Baldwin
Support for Writing

A radio drama can capture the sounds and emotions of a story, while allowing the listeners to imagine for themselves what the characters and settings look like. Work with a group of classmates to prepare an adaptation of "The Rockpile" as a **radio play.** Answer the questions below as an aid in organizing the details and tasks you will have to consider in putting on your radio play. Sketch your answers on the lines below or on a separate sheet of paper.

1. Who should draft the script for the play? Should it be one person or a group? Which would work better? If it's one person, who should that be; if it's a group, who should be in the group?

   _____

   _____

   _____

   _____

2. How many scenes will there be in the play, and where in the plot will each scene begin and end?

   _____

   _____

   _____

   _____

   _____

3. Make a list of characters, and think about what the characters are thinking and feeling in each scene.

   _____

   _____

   _____

   _____

   _____

4. Make a list of appropriate sound effects and music to give the audience a feeling for the time and place of the story.

   _____

   _____

   _____

   _____

   _____

Once you have prepared a draft of the script of the play and have gathered your sound effects and music, rehearse the play until you are satisfied with the results. Then present the play to the rest of your classmates. If other groups in the class have prepared different versions of a radio play of "The Rockpile," compare your adaptation with those of other groups.

"The Rockpile" by James Baldwin
Enrichment: Emergency Services

In "The Rockpile," Roy receives a nasty cut above his eye. Even though it produces a lot of blood, the cut is merely a "superficial scar." However, more serious accidents such as Richard's drowning occurred in the community at other times. What resources can a community access in such crisis situations?

In the 1960's, the Emergency Medical Services system was introduced in the United States. In nearly half the country, people in need of immediate medical services can dial 9-1-1 and be connected with a trained dispatcher. The dispatcher fields the call and, if necessary, sends an ambulance to the scene. When the emergency medical technicians, or EMTs, arrive they administer first aid (or if the team contains paramedics, more advanced life support) and take the victim to the nearest hospital. If the injury is severe or life-threatening, the victim may be taken to a trauma center, which treats only the most severe cases of injury or illness.

Communities must pool their human and financial resources to get the best performance from emergency services. For example, EMTs and paramedics must be trained to determine which cases should be sent to trauma centers. Because trauma centers require specialized equipment, facilities, and personnel, special funding is needed. Most trauma centers are located in urban areas; however, victims from rural areas might be flown in by emergency helicopters or airplanes.

DIRECTIONS: *Write your answers to the following questions. If necessary, use a telephone book.*

1. What number would you dial to access the Emergency Medical Services system in your community?

   _____

2. What types of emergency treatment might Roy and Richard have received had such services been available in 1930's Harlem? Explain your answer.

   _____

   _____

3. How might socioeconomic issues affect the availability of emergency services to a community?

   _____

   _____

   _____

   _____

   _____

   _____

   _____

   _____

   _____

   _____

Name _____ Date _____

"The Rockpile" by James Baldwin
Open-Book Test

Short Answer *Write your responses to the questions in this section on the lines provided.*

1. The setting is an especially significant part of "The Rockpile." Briefly describe the setting, using details and images from the story.

   _____

   _____

2. Why do John and Roy sit on the fire escape and look out longingly at the activities taking place on the rockpile? What do the rockpile and its associated activities symbolize to them?

   _____

   _____

   _____

3. What does the accidental drowning death of Richard, a neighborhood boy, symbolize to Elizabeth in "The Rockpile"? Support your answer with at least one detail from the story.

   _____

   _____

   _____

4. What is the immediate cause of Roy's decision to run downstairs to play on the rockpile?

   _____

   _____

   _____

5. In "The Rockpile," after she brings Roy up from the street to tend to his wound, Elizabeth "looked with apprehension toward the clock." What is she concerned about as she eyes the clock?

   _____

   _____

   _____

6. In "The Rockpile," Gabriel confronts John about allowing Roy to go out into the street without telling his mother. Elizabeth takes a protective attitude toward John. What is a major cause of her protectiveness toward John?

   _____

   _____

   _____

Name _____ Date _____

7. Often it is helpful to pause to check your comprehension of key facts and details in a story. A key element of "The Rockpile" is the contrast between the personalities and backgrounds of John and Roy. Monitor your comprehension of this key element by filling in the details of the chart below. Then, on the lines below, write a brief summary of the similarities and differences between the two characters.

	John	**Roy**
Personality Traits		
Reputation in the Family		
Feelings About the Rockpile		
Relationship with Parents		
Feelings About Each Other		

_____

_____

8. In "The Rockpile," during the family confrontation that follows Gabriel's return from work, everyone is upset about Roy's injury. However, Elizabeth and Gabriel are arguing about far more than Roy's accident. At a deeper level, what are they really arguing about? Provide details from the story to support your answer.

_____

_____

_____

9. Near the end of "The Rockpile," Gabriel's fury at Elizabeth softens at the last minute. What causes this softening of his anger toward Elizabeth?

_____

_____

10. If you were engrossed in reading a novel, would you be easily distracted? Explain your answer, basing it on the meaning of *engrossed* as it is used in "The Rockpile."

_____

_____

Essay

Write an extended response to the question of your choice or to the question or questions your teacher assigns you.

11. In "The Rockpile," all of the children in the household except John are Gabriel's biological children. What effects does John's having a different biological father have on the story and the characters in it? Develop your thoughts in an essay supported by details from the story.

12. In "The Rockpile," Roy's injury leads to a painful family argument. In an essay, explain what you feel are the immediate and deeper causes of this argument. Do you think the issues that arise are unique to this family, or are they typical of families in general? Support your answer with details from the story.

13. The setting of 1930s Harlem plays a major role in "The Rockpile." What dangers and influences of that setting are real? Which are symbolic? In an essay, explain how this story's setting influences the characters' beliefs and behavior.

14. **Thinking About the Essential Question: How does literature shape or reflect society?** In "The Rockpile," James Baldwin paints a vivid portrait of the busy, sometimes menacing urban street life of Harlem in the 1930s and the ways in which that environment affects the life of an African American family. In an essay, discuss ways in which Baldwin's portrayal of those city streets in general—and the rockpile in particular—shapes the life of the family portrayed in the story.

Oral Response

15. Go back to question 3, 4, or 8 or to the question your teacher assigns you. Take a few minutes to expand your answer and prepare an oral response. Find additional details in "The Rockpile" that support your points. If necessary, make notes to guide your oral response.

Name _____ Date _____

"**The Rockpile**" by James Baldwin
Selection Test A

Critical Reading *Identify the letter of the choice that best answers the question.*

_____ 1. In "The Rockpile," what is the most important part of the setting?
   A. the apartment
   B. the rockpile
   C. the river
   D. the fire escape

_____ 2. In "The Rockpile," when do the children feel most free?
   A. when they are eating dinner
   B. when they think about the rockpile
   C. when Gabriel is away from home
   D. when they walk along the river

_____ 3. What does the rockpile represent to the children in "The Rockpile"?
   A. the remains of an old building
   B. a place of danger and excitement
   C. a place for boys to compete
   D. a place to support subway cars

_____ 4. What is the meaning of the story of the boy who drowned in "The Rockpile"?
   A. The boy had never liked the river.
   B. The drowned boy was John's friend.
   C. The neighborhood is feared by Elizabeth.
   D. The neighborhood is a place of danger.

_____ 5. Why does Gabriel treat John more harshly than the other children in "The Rockpile"?
   A. John is not his biological child.
   B. John needs to be taught to be careful.
   C. John is older than the others.
   D. John disobeys more than the others.

_____ 6. What feeling do the children mostly have about Gabriel in "The Rockpile"?
   A. fear
   B. anger
   C. joy
   D. curiosity

_____ 7. Why does Roy take a chance and sneak outside in "The Rockpile"?

  A. Everyone else has fallen asleep.

  B. He knows John will not tell on him.

  C. He knows his father is not home.

  D. The other boys challenge him.

_____ 8. Which character is especially hard on John in "The Rockpile"?

  A. Sister McCandless

  B. his sister

  C. his brother

  D. his mother

_____ 9. According to his mother, who is to blame for spoiling Roy too much in "The Rockpile"?

  A. John

  B. Aunt Florence

  C. herself

  D. his father

_____ 10. Why might readers be concerned about Gabriel's reaction to Elizabeth after her outburst in "The Rockpile"?

  A. He looks like he will be kind to her.

  B. He looks like he might hate her.

  C. He looks like he might leave the house.

  D. He looks like he is feeling sad and hurt.

Vocabulary and Grammar

_____ 11. Which word is CLOSEST in meaning to *perdition*?

  A. refund

  B. triumph

  C. loss

  D. disgust

_____ 12. Which word is most nearly OPPOSITE in meaning to *superficial*?

  A. lighthearted

  B. profound

  C. practical

  D. similar

___ **13.** If you found yourself deeply absorbed in a book, you would be

    A. engrossed

    B. superficial

    C. latent

    D. jubilant

___ **14.** Which sentence contains an improper shift in verb tense?

    A. If I had known how crowded it would be, I would have stayed home.

    B. They walked us to the door and waved good-bye.

    C. I have seen that happen so many times that I am no longer surprised by it.

    D. As I make my way through this book I found the plot rather dull.

Essay

15. In "The Rockpile," John is the only one of four children who is not Gabriel's biological son. What effect does this situation have on the story and the characters in it? In a brief essay, offer your opinions about how this information affects people in the story.

16. In "The Rockpile," Roy knows that he is favored over John. How does this information affect how Roy behaves? Write a brief essay to address this question.

17. Thinking About the Essential Question: How does literature shape or reflect society? In "The Rockpile," James Baldwin paints a vivid portrait of the busy, sometimes menacing urban street life of Harlem in the 1930s and the ways in which that environment affects the life of an African American family. In an essay, discuss ways in which Baldwin's portrayal of those city streets in general—and the rockpile in particular—shapes the life of the family portrayed in the story.

"The Rockpile" by James Baldwin
Selection Test B

Critical Reading *Identify the letter of the choice that best completes the statement or answers the question.*

_____ 1. Why were the boys in "The Rockpile" forbidden to play on the rockpile?
   A. The other boys who played there were not nice.
   B. It was too dangerous.
   C. Their mother couldn't watch them while they played there.
   D. Their father thought it was evil.

_____ 2. In the story "The Rockpile," John is different from the boys on the rockpile because he is _____.
   A. younger   C. more timid
   B. less studious   D. less responsible

_____ 3. What does the rockpile symbolize in the story "The Rockpile"?
   A. carefree youth   C. forbidden joys
   B. evil and danger   D. blind obedience

_____ 4. In "The Rockpile" the episode of the boy who drowned is presented to
   A. explain why Elizabeth wouldn't let the boys play on the rockpile.
   B. convey the evils of the neighborhood.
   C. introduce important characters in the story.
   D. make the reader believe that another character will die.

_____ 5. What is the most immediate effect of Roy's injury in "The Rockpile"?
   A. Gabriel demands an explanation.
   B. John anticipates his father's anger.
   C. Roy lies silent on the sofa.
   D. Elizabeth begins to worry.

_____ 6. Which is a cause of Elizabeth's protectiveness toward John in the story "The Rockpile"?
   A. John is not Gabriel's child.
   B. The other children tease him.
   C. John often gets into trouble.
   D. Gabriel favors him.

_____ 7. Which phrase best describes the kind of mother Elizabeth is in the story "The Rockpile"?
   A. devoted and supportive   C. neglectful and cold
   B. attentive but uncaring   D. harsh but concerned

_____ 8. What makes John's relationship with Gabriel different from that of other children in "The Rockpile"?
   A. He is the oldest.
   B. He looks like Gabriel.
   C. He is not Gabriel's biological son.
   D. He frequently disobeys Gabriel.

_____ 9. Which word or phrase best describes the kind of father Gabriel is to John in "The Rockpile"?
A. lenient
B. uncaring
C. stern but loving
D. strict and unforgiving

_____ 10. Which of the following sentences from "The Rockpile" demonstrates the effect of the setting on the characters?
A. "The sun fell across them and across the fire escape with a high, benevolent indifference . . ."
B. "In the summertime boys swam in the river, diving off the wooden dock, or wading in from the garbage-heavy bank."
C. "Then someone screamed or shouted; boys began to run away, down the street, toward the bridge."
D. "John stood near the window, holding the newspaper advertisement and the drawing he had done."

_____ 11. In Elizabeth's view, who is responsible for Roy's accident in "The Rockpile"?
A. Elizabeth   C. John
B. Roy   D. Gabriel

_____ 12. In "The Rockpile" what causes Gabriel to soften his hatred toward Elizabeth?
A. John agrees to pick up his lunchbox.
B. He remembers his love for Roy.
C. He remembers that Elizabeth is his wife and the mother of his children.
D. Roy stops crying.

_____ 13. The theme of "The Rockpile" is best described as a tension between
A. urban and suburban environments.
B. father and son.
C. anger and compassion.
D. religion and society.

_____ 14. What kind of mood is created by the phrase "bending his dark head near the toe of his father's heavy shoe" from "The Rockpile"?
A. ominous
B. intimate
C. playful
D. tedious

Vocabulary and Grammar

_____ 15. In "The Rockpile" John was _____ in his drawing when he was startled by the sounds of shouting from the rockpile.
A. engrossed
B. superficial
C. latent
D. jubilant

_____ 16. Which word is most nearly OPPOSITE in meaning to *jubilant*?
   A. frivolous
   B. irritable
   C. depressed
   D. trusting

_____ 17. If you gave "The Rockpile" a *superficial* reading, your retention and understanding of details from the story would probably be
   A. excellent
   B. very good
   C. better than average
   D. poor

_____ 18. Which sentence contains an improper shift in verb tense?
   A. When the going gets tough, the tough get going.
   B. There were many beautiful shells among those I will find on the seashore.
   C. If the package is going to arrive early, I will not be home to receive it.
   D. I am standing right in the middle of the station, and I still do not see the big clock.

Essay

19. "The Rockpile" reveals many cause-and-effect relationships. In a brief essay, identify one cause-and effect relationship, and explain how identifying cause and effect helps you understand the characters' attitudes and behavior.

20. How does the 1930s Harlem setting affect the characters in "The Rockpile"? Which dangers or influences are real? Which are symbolic? Write an essay in which you explain how the setting influences the characters' beliefs and behavior.

21. The conflicts that create dramatic tension in a story may arise from internal struggle within one person, struggle among humans, or struggle between humans and nature. In an essay, describe which of these categories you think best fits the conflict present in "The Rockpile." Support your conclusions with evidence from the story.

22. **Thinking About the Essential Question: How does literature shape or reflect society?**
In "The Rockpile," James Baldwin paints a vivid portrait of the busy, sometimes menacing urban street life of Harlem in the 1930s and the ways in which that environment affects the life of an African American family. In an essay, discuss ways in which Baldwin's portrayal of those city streets in general—and the rockpile in particular—shapes the life of the family portrayed in the story.

Vocabulary Warm-up Word Lists

Study these words from the selections. Then, complete the activities.

Word List A

compatriots [kuhm PAY tree uhts] *n.* companions; colleagues
   She and her <u>compatriots</u> bonded because of the stress of medical school.

exposed [ik SPOHZD] *v.* allowed to be seen; revealed; displayed
   The detective soon <u>exposed</u> the guilty person.

fathom [FATH uhm] *v.* come to understand
   Often it is difficult to <u>fathom</u> the behavior of another person.

forbidden [fawr BID uhn] *adj.* not permitted or allowed
   My parents have made it very clear what activities are <u>forbidden.</u>

innocence [IN uh suhns] *n.* simplicity; lack of cunning
   Her <u>innocence</u> means that she often doesn't understand the plots of others.

international [in ter NASH uh nuhl] *adj.* reaching beyond national boundaries
   Basketball now has an <u>international</u> following.

intimacy [IN tuh muh see] *n.* familiarity; close association
   After traveling together all summer, our friendship had achieved a deeper level of <u>intimacy</u>.

unassailable [uhn uh SAYL uh buhl] *adj.* not open to doubt or question
   After breaking the record, his credentials as a top-ranked runner are <u>unassailable</u>.

Word List B

astonishing [uh STAHN ish ing] *adj.* surprising; amazing
   When she began to sing we realized that her voice is <u>astonishing</u>.

clarity [KLAIR uh tee] *n.* clearness
   Juan expresses himself with such <u>clarity</u> that everyone understands what he means.

contemplation [kahn tuhm PLAY shuhn] *n.* deep thought
   Often she is so lost in <u>contemplation</u> that she doesn't know what is going on.

hypocrisy [hi PAHK ruh see] *n.* pretending to believe something you do not
   It is the height of <u>hypocrisy</u> for her to pretend to be interested in sports.

inhabited [in HAB it id] *v.* occupied in any manner or form; lived in
   He was so creative that imaginary creatures often <u>inhabited</u> his head!

insistent [in SIS tuhnt] *adj.* compelling the attention
   The sound was so <u>insistent</u> that I couldn't concentrate.

profound [proh FOWND] *adj.* characterized by intense feeling
   His <u>profound</u> thanks made me happy I had taken the trouble to help.

rebel [REB uhl] *n.* one who is disobedient or refuses to obey authority
   Even in high school, Jeremy was a <u>rebel</u> who liked to break rules.

"Life in His Language" by Toni Morrison
Vocabulary Warm-up Exercises

Exercise A *Fill in the blanks, using each word from Word List A only once.*

Pirates are real, not just characters in movies! They operate in [1] _____

waters and recognize no [2] _____ other than their shipmates. The cama-

raderie and [3] _____ that develop during months at sea enable them to

work as a team. Their activities are illegal and [4] _____ since they violate

laws. Honest ship captains might cross the paths of pirates. While a ship might have an

[5] _____ right to operate on the open sea, [6] _____ is no

protection again pirates! It is hard to [7] _____ that criminals would

attack any boat that is [8] _____ to them, but they have no regard for the

rights of others. Operating outside of the law, pirates live only to prey on others.

Exercise B *Decide whether each statement below is true or false. Circle T or F, and explain your answer.*

1. If something is <u>astonishing</u> then everyone expects it to happen.
   T / F _____

2. Rachael was a <u>rebel</u>, so she always followed the rules.
   T / F _____

3. He expressed himself with such <u>clarity</u> that no one understood him.
   T / F _____

4. She was lost in <u>contemplation</u> and so she didn't hear him come in.
   T / F _____

5. If someone has <u>profound</u> feelings, their feelings are deep and serious.
   T / F _____

6. If you are <u>insistent</u> about doing something, you don't care about it.
   T / F _____

7. If you engage in <u>hypocrisy</u>, you are honest about your beliefs.
   T / F _____

8. The actor <u>inhabited</u> the role and so he gave a great performance.
   T / F _____

"Life in His Language" by Toni Morrison
Reading Warm-up A

Read the following passage. Then, complete the activities.

When she was growing up in Ohio, Chloe Anthony Wofford worked hard and was a good student. Her parents had moved north to escape the racism of the south. Chloe had benefited by attending a school where her schoolmates and compatriots were of multiple races and ethnicities. She went to college at Howard University. There, Chloe began calling herself Toni, a variant of her middle name. And then, after she married Harold Morrison, she became known as Toni Morrison. It is under this name that she garnered international fame for her novels, whose popularity spread around the world.

Morrison had a long career as a book editor and then a university professor. She is also the mother of two sons. She published her first novel, *The Bluest Eye*, in 1970. It told the story of a young black girl who, in her simplicity and innocence, thinks her extremely difficult life would be better if she had blue eyes. Morrison's next novel, *Sula*, explored the relationship between two black women. It and subsequent books won major literary prizes. But it was her novel *Beloved* that catapulted Morrison into certain and unassailable membership in the ranks of great writers. It won the prestigious Pulitzer Prize for fiction in 1988.

In her novels, Toni Morrison often dealt with controversial and forbidden topics, telling stories that were sometimes difficult to read because of the truths they exposed. Yet by writing of special types of closeness and intimacy between people as well as cruelties that are initially difficult to fathom, she led readers to a deeper understanding. Morrison's body of work was recognized in 1993 with the Nobel Prize for Literature, a sign of the esteem in which she is held around the world. She was the first African-American woman to be awarded this honor.

1. Underline the word that helps explain the meaning of compatriots. Name some people who are your **compatriots**.

2. Circle the word that tells for what Morrison gained international fame. Give a word that means the opposite of *international*.

3. Underline the word that gives a clue to the meaning of innocence. Name a word that means the same as *innocence*.

4. Underline the word that gives a hint to the meaning of unassailable. What event made Morrison's status as a great writer *unassailable*?

5. Circle the word that helps explain the meaning of forbidden. Why might a topic be regarded as *forbidden*?

6. Circle the words that tell what was exposed. Give a word or phrase that means the same as *exposed*.

7. Underline the words that give a hint about the meaning of intimacy. Tell about someone with whom you share a feeling of *intimacy*.

8. Underline the word that tells what was hard to fathom. Give a synonym for *fathom*

"Life in His Language" by Toni Morrison
Reading Warm-up B

Read the following passage. Then, complete the activities.

Hall Montana narrates one of James Baldwin's novels, *Just Above My Head*. One of two sons in a middle-class black family, Hall <u>inhabited</u> the calm center of the complex world the family occupied. The book's focus is on Hall's brother, Arthur, who became a famous gospel singer, and Julia, a child preacher whose life takes unexpected and <u>astonishing</u> turns in the course of the book.

Many critics believe Hall's tendency towards deep thought and <u>contemplation</u> reflect Baldwin's own qualities. In his books, Baldwin often portrayed the outsider and the <u>rebel</u>. Yet he was also able to bring <u>clarity</u> to his portrayal of the mind of a middle-class, conventional man, living with the effects of racism, illuminating the subject for all to understand. The previously forbidden or generally avoided topics of race, class, and sexuality were often the subjects of Baldwin's work. He refused to engage in the <u>hypocrisy</u> and dishonesty that characterized much of the writing of black and white writers alike. He felt that it was important to deal with all issues confronting society, no matter how controversial.

While this quality caused many younger black writers to idolize him, Baldwin also had his detractors. Some militants were <u>insistent</u> that he should deal only with racism, firmly asserting that he should focus on the ongoing oppression of black people. Baldwin—and his supporters—felt that he should write about those deep and <u>profound</u> topics that affect all people, regardless of race. In this way, Baldwin worked to overcome the narrow-mindedness that is a source of racism.

Baldwin contributed many memorable characters, like Hall, to modern literature. Modern writers continue to draw inspiration from Baldwin, like Toni Morrison, who quotes Hall in her tribute.

1. Underline the words that tell what the family <u>inhabited</u>. Give a word or phrase that means the same as *inhabited*.

2. Circle the word that suggests the meaning of <u>astonishing</u>. Name an antonym for *astonishing*.

3. Underline the words that hint at the meaning of <u>contemplation</u>. Define *contemplation* in your own words.

4. Circle the word that gives a hint at the meaning of <u>rebel</u>. Use *rebel* in a sentence of your own.

5. Circle the words that tell to what Baldwin brought <u>clarity</u>. Give a word that means the same as *clarity*.

6. Underline the word that gives a clue to the meaning of <u>hypocrisy</u>. Use *hypocrisy* in a sentence of your own.

7. Underline what people were <u>insistent</u> that Baldwin should do. Tell something that someone has been *insistent* that you do.

8. Circle the word that gives a clue to what <u>profound</u> means. Give a word that means the opposite of *profound*.

Name _____ Date _____

"**Life in His Language**" by Toni Morrison
Literary Analysis: Eulogy and Mood

A **eulogy** is a speech or essay written to pay tribute to someone who has died, to honor his or her life and accomplishments. An effective eulogy can help an audience understand the subject's personality and unique contributions.

Because most eulogies are written shortly after the subject's death, they focus on that person's strengths and positive features and are thus usually written in a respectful tone. **Mood** is the feeling created in the reader by a literary work. Elements that can influence the mood of a work include word choice, tone, and rhythm. Even though all eulogies are respectful, they do not all have the same mood: some might be somber, while others are celebratory or angry.

DIRECTIONS: *Use the graphic organizer below to help you identify the basic overall mood of Morrison's eulogy "Life in His Language." Once you have identified the basic mood, provide four examples of language from the eulogy that expresses that mood.*

Example 1:

_____
_____
_____

Example 2:

_____
_____
_____

Mood of "Life in His Language":

_____
_____

Example 3:

_____
_____
_____

Example 4:

_____
_____
_____

Name _____ Date _____

"Life in His Language" by Toni Morrison
Reading Strategy: Analyze Syntax and Patterns of Organization

Syntax is the order of words and their relationships. **Analyzing syntax and patterns of organization**—looking at grammar and placement of words and phrases—can be a useful tool in understanding an essay.

Patterns of organization reveal the structure of ideas in an essay. In this essay, Morrison's discussion of the "three gifts" that Baldwin shared with others is a key example of such a pattern.

DIRECTIONS: *Use the chart below to analyze each of Baldwin's "three gifts." In the first column, identify each gift. In the second column, briefly explain the significance and meaning of the gift.*

GIFT	Significance and Meaning of Gift
1.	
2.	
3.	

Name _____ Date _____

"**Life in His Language**" by Toni Morrison
Vocabulary Builder

Word List

appropriate   platitudes   scenario   summation

A. DIRECTIONS: *Write whether each statement is true or false. Then, explain your answer using the meaning of the word in italics.*

1. Jury members can expect to hear the *summation* of a lawyer's argument at the beginning of his remarks.

   _____

2. A chief executive who wants to make the right decision will ask his assistants to present him with the consequences of every conceivable *scenario*.

   _____

3. An essay that is notable for its originality will not rely on *platitudes*.

   _____

4. A writer who tends to *appropriate* the ideas of other authors is usually very careful about citing and acknowledging his sources.

   _____

B. DIRECTIONS: *Circle the letter of the word that is closest in meaning to the word in CAPITAL LETTERS.*

1. SUMMATION
   A. peak
   B. interval
   C. trial
   D. conclusion

2. SCENARIO
   A. sensation
   B. pace
   C. situation
   D. enclosure

3. PLATITUDES
   A. investigations
   B. feelings
   C. crowds
   D. cliches

4. APPROPRIATE
   A. receive
   B. prepare
   C. accuse
   D. steal

"Life in His Language" by Toni Morrison
Support for Writing

"Life in His Language" is Toni Morrison's moving account of the ways in which James Baldwin influenced and inspired her work and those of other African American writers and activists. Write an **essay of tribute** to honor someone who has inspired you. Your subject might be someone you know or someone whose work affected you. Organize your essay using a clear pattern of three—start out by sketching three key ways in which your subject's life and/or work has inspired and influenced you, using Morrison's description of Baldwin's "three gifts" as your model.

Answer the questions below as an aid in organizing your thoughts for this essay:

1. Who is the person who has had the greatest impact on me?

_____

2. Briefly summarize the life and key accomplishments, personal or professional, of the person you have chosen.

_____
_____
_____
_____

3. What are three major ways in which that person has influenced and/or inspired me?

A. _____
_____
_____

B. _____
_____
_____

C. _____
_____
_____

Using the material you have gathered in your answers to these questions, write a first draft of your essay. Include the following:

- an introduction that identifies your subject and focus

- one paragraph for each of the three features or elements you will discuss

- a conclusion that summarizes and extends your view of this person

"Life in His Language" by Toni Morrison
Enrichment: African American Novelists

In "Life in His Language," Toni Morrison offers a moving tribute to James Baldwin and explains the many ways in which he influenced and inspired her and other African American writers and activists. During the twentieth century, many African American writers emerged as major voices in American literature in general and in the novel in particular. Each generation influenced the next—just as Baldwin had a major impact on Morrison, so Baldwin often cites the novelist Richard Wright as his most important influence.

DIRECTIONS: *The chart below lists six of the many important African American novelists who became major figures in American literature during the twentieth century. For each writer listed in the left-hand column, fill in the information specified in the remaining columns. Use Internet or library resources to find the information that you need.*

Name of Novelist	Dates (birth-[death])	Titles and Dates of Major Novel(s)	Literary Awards
Richard Wright			
Ralph Ellison			
James Baldwin			
Zora Neale Hurston			
Toni Morrison			
Alice Walker			

Name _____   Date _____

"Life in His Language" by Toni Morrison
Open-Book Test

Short Answer *Write your responses to the questions in this section on the lines provided.*

1. Toni Morrison addresses "Life in His Language" to "Jimmy." What kind of mood does this opening create?

   _____

   _____

2. "Life in His Language" is a tribute to James Baldwin, written shortly after his death in 1987. Morrison begins her tribute by writing, "The difficulty is your life refuses summation—it always did—and invites contemplation instead." Briefly summarize Morrison's meaning.

   _____

   _____

   _____

3. In "Life in His Language" Morrison writes of Baldwin, "the season was always Christmas with you there." What kind of mood does this statement establish for the rest of the eulogy?

   _____

   _____

4. What are the two most important achievements of James Baldwin in transforming American English, according to Toni Morrison in "Life in His Language"? Give examples from the essay to support your answer.

   _____

   _____

   _____

   _____

   _____

5. In "Life in His Language," Morrison writes that one of the three major gifts that Baldwin left to his readers was the example of his courage. Morrison's tribute to Baldwin's courage is organized around a discussion of two characteristics that combined to create the unique quality of Baldwin's courage. What were those characteristics?

   _____

   _____

6. In "Life in His Language," Morrison pays tribute to Baldwin's discovery that "this world (meaning history) is white no longer and it never will be again." Briefly explain the meaning of this statement by Baldwin.

   _____

   _____

   _____

7. In "Life in His Language," Morrison cites these words from Baldwin: "the world is before [me] and [I] need not take it or leave it as it was when [I] came in." Briefly explain what this statement implies about the role of the writer in society.

_____

_____

_____

8. In "Life in His Language," Morrison pays tribute to Baldwin by discussing his third major "gift": his personal tenderness. Morrison writes that this gift "was hard to fathom and even harder to accept." Why does she feel that this gift was hard to accept?

_____

_____

_____

9. A eulogy is always written in a respectful tone. That respect can be expressed in a variety of moods: somber, angry, mournful, or celebratory. Use the graphic organizer below to help you identify the basic overall mood of Morrison's eulogy "Life in His Language." Once you have identified the basic mood, provide three examples of language from the eulogy that express that mood.

Example of mood:

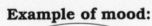

Example of mood: **Mood of "Life in His Language":**   **Example of mood:**

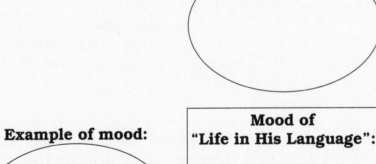

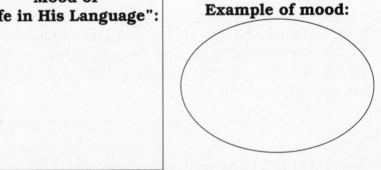

10. If a political commentator wrote that a candidate's speech was "full of platitudes," would she be criticizing the speech for a lack of originality? Why or why not? Base your answer on the meaning of *platitudes* as it is used in "Life in His Language."

_____

_____

Essay

Write an extended response to the question of your choice or to the question or questions your teacher assigns you.

11. After reading Toni Morrison's impassioned tribute to the life and work of James Baldwin in "Life in His Language," do you find yourself wanting to read more of his work or to know more about his life? Why or why not? Explain your answer in an essay supported by examples from the selection.

12. In "Life in His Language," Toni Morrison talks about the many ways that James Baldwin inspired her as a person and as a writer. Is there someone in the arts—a writer, a director, an actor, a singer, songwriter, composer, hip-hop artist, painter, or sculptor—who has had a similar influence on your life? In an essay, discuss the influence of a person in the arts on your life. How has this person inspired you? How is this inspiration similar to or different from what Morrison expressed in how she was inspired by Baldwin? Support your essay with specific examples from the artist's life and work.

13. In "Life in His Language," Morrison cites the following words from Baldwin as being especially inspiring to her as a person and as a writer: "the world is before [me] and [I] need not take it or leave it as it was when [I] came in." Do you agree that the writer has an obligation to help to change the world through his/her work and/or personal example? Why or why not? Explain your answer in an essay supported by examples from the selection.

14. **Thinking About the Essential Question: How does literature shape or reflect society?** Based on "Life in His Language," what does Morrison seem to believe about the effects a writer can have on people's lives and on society as a whole? Address this question in an essay that uses Morrison's quotations and examples about James Baldwin to support her general beliefs about the role of a writer in society.

Oral Response

15. Go back to question 3, 4, or 5 or to the question your teacher assigns to you. Take a few minutes to expand your answer and prepare an oral response. Find additional details in "Life in His Language" that support your points. If necessary, make notes to guide your oral response.

"Life in His Language" by Toni Morrison
Selection Test A

Critical Reading *Identify the letter of the choice that best answers the question.*

_____ 1. In "Life in His Language," Toni Morrison begins her eulogy with the word "Jimmy." This opening word establishes a tone of
   A. grief
   B. formality
   C. reflectiveness
   D. familiarity

_____ 2. In using "you" in "Life in His Language," Morrison is directing her remarks to
   A. the audience
   B. James Baldwin
   C. African Americans
   D. literary critics

_____ 3. In "Life in His Language," when Toni Morrison praises James Baldwin for "the astonishing gift of your art and your friendship," she is fulfilling what function of a eulogy?
   A. voicing regret
   B. looking to the future
   C. paying tribute
   D. expressing grief

_____ 4. In "Life in His Language," Morrison writes "the season was always Christmas with you there. . . ." This statement about Baldwin reflects which kind of tone common to a eulogy?
   A. mournful
   B. celebratory
   C. solemn
   D. distant

_____ 5. In "Life in His Language," Morrison writes, "Like many of us left here I thought I knew you. Now I discover that in your company it is myself I know." In this statement Morrison implies that Baldwin was a great
   A. writer
   B. activist
   C. teacher
   D. friend

_____ 6. In "Life in His Language," when Morrison remarks that Baldwin "did not neglect to bring at least three gifts," she is announcing which of the following?
   A. the mood of the eulogy
   B. Baldwin's key talents as a writer
   C. Baldwin's main strengths as a person
   D. the organizing principle of the eulogy

_____ 7. In "Life in His Language," the first gift from Baldwin that Morrison discusses is
   A. language
   B. friendship
   C. courage
   D. wisdom

_____ 8. In "Life in His Language," Morrison implies that James Baldwin's writing helped to make American writing
   A. more sophisticated
   B. more popular
   C. less false
   D. less frivolous

_____ 9. In "Life in His Language," Morrison writes that Baldwin helped to make American English more accessible to
   A. all readers
   B. poor people
   C. immigrants
   D. African Americans

_____ 10. In "Life in His Language," Morrison asserts that Baldwin's ability to stand against the status quo of society was mainly a kind of
   A. anger
   B. creativity
   C. intelligence
   D. courage

_____ 11. In "Life in His Language," Morrison writes that "I was always a bit better behaved around you, smarter, more capable." She is implying that for her Baldwin was a
   A. friendly companion
   B. role model
   C. harsh taskmaster
   D. superb artist

Essay

12. In "Life in His Language," Morrison makes it clear that James Baldwin considered it part of the writer's role to speak out and act against social problems and injustices. If you were an influential writer today, what social or political issue would move you to speak out and act? Explain your choice in an essay that is based on clear reasoning and specific examples.

13. In "Life in His Language," Morrison singles out James Baldwin for the courage he showed as an African American writer taking on controversial issues in his day. Reflect on the character trait of courage. In an essay, discuss a time in your life—or the life of someone you know—when courage played a key role in helping you to overcome an obstacle or to achieve a goal. Use specific, vivid details and examples to support your answer.

14. **Thinking About the Essential Question: How does literature shape or reflect society?** Consider what "Life in His Language" suggests about James Baldwin's significance and achievement. What does Morrison seem to believe about the effects a good writer can have on people's lives and on society as a whole? Answer this question in an essay that uses Morrison's example about James Baldwin to support her ideas about the role of writers in general.

"Life in His Language" by Toni Morrison
Selection Test B

Critical Reading *Identify the letter of the choice that best answers the question.*

_____ 1. Which choice best clarifies these lines from "Life in His Language"?

The difficulty is your life refuses summation—it always did—and invites contemplation instead.

A. You always invited people to think about your life rather than to summarize it.
B. You always refused those who wanted to write about your life.
C. Your life was rich and complex.
D. Your life was too complicated to think about.

_____ 2. In which passage from "Life in His Language" does Morrison make clear that she was influenced by Baldwin both as a writer and as a person?
A. "There is too much to think about you, and too much to feel."
B. "Like many of us left here I thought I knew you."
C. "That is the astonishing gift of your art and your friendship."
D. "In your hands language was handsome again."

_____ 3. In which sentence from "Life in His Language" does Morrison state the basic organizing principle of her eulogy?
A. ". . . you did not neglect to bring at least three gifts."
B. "I have been seeing the world through your eyes for so long."
C. "You made American English honest—genuinely international."
D. "In your hands language was handsome again."

_____ 4. In writing about Baldwin's contributions to shaping American English, Morrison writes that Baldwin "went into that forbidden territory and decolonized it. . . ." To whom does she mean that "territory" of literary English is forbidden?
A. young people
B. poor people
C. African Americans
D. immigrants

_____ 5. Morrison writes of Baldwin, "In your hands language was handsome again. In your hands we saw how it was meant to be. . . ." The repetition of the phrase "in your hands" contributes to the mood of the eulogy by creating
A. rhythm
B. intimacy
C. celebration
D. syntax

_____ 6. In "Life in His Language," Morrison cites these words from Baldwin: "the world is before [me] and [I] need not take it or leave it as it was when [I] came in." According to this quotation, Baldwin believed that the writer can and should
   A. understand the world
   B. change the world
   C. amuse readers
   D. record events

_____ 7. Given Baldwin's pioneering role as an African American literary figure of the twentieth century, what is the likeliest meaning of "village" in the following sentence from "Life in His Language"?

   "the courage of one who could go as a stranger in the village and transform the distances between people into intimacy with the whole world. . . ."

   A. African villages
   B. European civilization
   C. the entire literary world
   D. the African American community

_____ 8. Which of the following passages from "Life in His Language" is a tribute to Baldwin's personal sense of authenticity?
   A. "You gave me a language to dwell in. . ."
   B. "Yours was the courage to live life in and from its belly as well as beyond its edges,. . . ."
   C. "Because our joy and our laughter were not only all right, they were necessary."
   D. "This then is no calamity. No. This is jubilee."

_____ 9. Of all the virtues of Baldwin's prose that Morrison cites in "Life in His Language," the one she prizes most highly is its
   A. beauty
   B. truthfulness
   C. sophistication
   D. simplicity

_____ 10. In "Life in His Language," Morrison quotes these words from Baldwin: "A person does not lightly elect to oppose his society." In this sentence, Baldwin is reflecting on the difficulties experienced by the writer who is also a(n)
   A. businessman
   B. philosopher
   C. social activist
   D. journalist

_____ 11. In "Life in His Language," Morrison states that of all of Baldwin's gifts, the one that she found hardest to understand and to accept was his
   A. language
   B. courage
   C. tenderness
   D. morality

____ 12. In which of the following passages from "Life in His Language" does Morrison use an unusual word order to establish a rhythm and capture the reader's attention?
   A. "I never heard a single command from you. . . ."
   B. "It is a courage that came from a ruthless intelligence. . . ."
   C. "The third gift was hard to fathom and even harder to accept."
   D. "I thought it could not last, but last it did and envelop me it did. . . ."

____ 13. Which passage from "Life in His Language" most clearly conveys a celebratory tone?
   A. "This then is no calamity. No. This is jubilee."
   B. "You gave us ourselves to think about, to cherish."
   C. "Because our joy and our laughter were not only all right, they were necessary."
   D. "You knew, didn't you, how I loved your love?"

____ 14. In the following passage from "Life in His Language," Morrison repeats a key pairing of ideas, each time with slightly different wording: "mind/heart" and "intellect/passion." What is the main purpose of this repetition?

   When that unassailable combination of mind and heart, of intellect and passion was on display it guided us though treacherous landscape. . . ."

   A. clarification   C. emphasis
   B. rhythm   D. reconsideration

____ 15. Which of the following best summarizes the portrait of James Baldwin that emerges from Morrison's eulogy in "Life in His Language"?
   A. world-class novelist   C. world-weary sophisticate
   B. demanding taskmaster   D. seeker of truth and justice

Essay

16. "Life in His Language" is Toni Morrison's eulogy to her friend James Baldwin, one of America's leading African American writers and social critics. Think of a figure from history or fiction that you admire and, in a brief essay, write a eulogy about that person. You can adopt Morrison's style of writing in the second person (addressing the deceased person as "you"), or you can write in a style and tone of your own.

17. What impression of James Baldwin as a person did you get from reading "Life in His Language"? Is he someone you would have wanted to know or have as a friend? Why or why not? Explain your answer in an essay supported by details from the selection.

18. In "Life in His Language," Toni Morrison cites the three great gifts James Baldwin left to her and others: language, or a new way of expressing their thoughts, feelings, and aspirations; courage, or the strength to speak clearly about and stand up to social injustice; and tenderness, or the ability to show loving concern for others on a personal level. Which of these gifts do you think is the most important? Why? Express your opinion in an essay supported by clear reasoning and specific examples.

19. **Thinking About the Essential Question: How does literature shape or reflect society?**
Based on "Life in His Language," what does Morrison seem to believe about the effects a writer can have on people's lives and on society as a whole? Address this question in an essay that uses Morrison's quotations and examples about James Baldwin to support her general beliefs about the role of a writer in society.

Unit 5 Resources: Prosperity and Protest
197

Vocabulary Warm-up Word Lists

Study these words from the selections. Then, complete the activities.

Word List A

attain [uh TAYN] *v.* to gain or achieve
Mel will <u>attain</u> his college diploma after four years of hard work.

brutal [BROOT uhl] *adj.* extremely harsh or cruel
The <u>brutal</u> treatment of animals is illegal.

foe [FOH] *n.* enemy
Deborah is too popular to have a <u>foe</u>.

loyalty [LOY uhl tee] *n.* sense of being devoted or affectionate
A good dog shows <u>loyalty</u> to its master.

pledge [PLEJ] *n.* promise to do, give, or refrain from doing something
In his campaign, the mayoral candidate gave a <u>pledge</u> to improve city parks.

preserve [pree ZERV] *v.* to protect or keep from harm
Ralph wants to <u>preserve</u> his family's traditions.

renewal [ree NOO uhl] *n.* act of making new again
In recent years, there has been a <u>renewal</u> of interest in ballroom dancing.

segregation [seg ruh GAY shuhn] *n.* policy of separating people based on race or class
During the 1950s, <u>segregation</u> was common throughout the Southern states.

Word List B

adversary [AD ver sayr ee] *n.* opponent; enemy
The chemical company is an <u>adversary</u> of those trying to keep rivers clean.

civility [si VIL uh tee] *n.* polite behavior
People who work together must show one another <u>civility</u>.

embodied [em BAHD eed] *v.* represented in bodily or material form
The stuffed animal <u>embodied</u> the child that Philip used to be.

inexpressible [in eks PRES uh buhl] *adj.* impossible to express
The grief of losing a loved one is often <u>inexpressible</u>.

precise [pree SYS] *adj.* exact; clearly expressed; definite
Jen gave the boutique owner a <u>precise</u> description of the dress she wanted.

profoundly [proh FOUND lee] *adv.* deeply; of the greatest degree
Toni is <u>profoundly</u> deaf, but she communicates well by using sign language.

testimony [TES ti moh nee] *n.* evidence; proof
That Sam calls his mother every day is <u>testimony</u> of his love for her.

vitality [vy TAL uh tee] *n.* life force; power to endure or survive
A rare snowstorm in spring caused the cherry trees to lose their <u>vitality</u>.

Selections by John F. Kennedy and Martin Luther King, Jr.
Vocabulary Warm-up Exercises

Exercise A *Fill in the blanks, using each word from Word List A only once.*

Seeking to [1] _____ social justice and equal rights for people of color,
the civil rights movement reached a peak in the 1950s and 1960s. Leaders like
Dr. Martin Luther King, Jr., regarded the practice of [2] _____ as
a(n) [3] _____ [4] _____. They called for a vigorous
[5] _____ of the American commitment to equality and opportunity
recorded in such founding national documents as the Declaration of Independence.
[6] _____ to American traditions, the civil rights leaders affirmed,
demanded that the government issue a(n) [7] _____ to right the wrongs
of the past: in education, in jobs, and in public accommodations. A half a century later,
Americans [8] _____ the memory and courageous example of these
heroic leaders in behalf of civil rights.

Exercise B *Revise each sentence so that the underlined vocabulary word is logical. Be sure to keep the vocabulary word in your revision.*

Example: Because the movie was so <u>suspenseful</u>, we quickly lost interest.
Because the movie was so <u>suspenseful</u>, we were on the edge of our seats.

1. When we had our first sight of the <u>adversary</u>, we were overjoyed.
   _____

2. His rude remarks were a sign of his <u>civility</u>.
   _____

3. Since Prof. Adams had influenced her so little, Mary's thesis <u>embodied</u> his philosophy.
   _____

4. We could easily explain the <u>inexpressible</u> emotions that we experienced that day.
   _____

5. Teresa's conclusions were <u>precise</u>, and she had great trouble in communicating them.
   _____

6. I was <u>profoundly</u> affected by the story and forgot it soon after I first heard it.
   _____

7. The convincing <u>testimony</u> of the witness did not influence the jury.
   _____

8. The sluggish behavior of the dogs was proof of their <u>vitality</u>.
   _____

Selections by John F. Kennedy and Martin Luther King, Jr.

Reading Warm-up A

Read the following passage. Pay special attention to the underlined words. Then, read it again, and complete the activities. Use a separate sheet of paper for your written answers.

In his inaugural address and his public speeches as president, John F. Kennedy displayed verbal wit and considerable grace under pressure. He seemed to have a rare talent for memorable phrases. The president was quick on his feet with a witty comment. As a result, Kennedy was not slow to <u>attain</u> the admiration of journalists who covered the White House.

The Kennedy years were a time of challenge. This was also an era of <u>renewal</u>, though. A younger generation took the reins of power in Washington. Abroad, the nation faced a formidable <u>foe</u> in the Cold War: the Soviet Union and its allies. At home, the civil rights struggle continued to protest the <u>brutal</u> injustices of racial <u>segregation</u>. Kennedy made no secret of his <u>loyalty</u> to a code of self-sacrifice and dedication. He challenged Americans to ask what they could do for their country, not what their country could do for them.

Despite the serious issues during his administration, Kennedy was quick with a quip when the occasion warranted it. At such times, he would usually <u>preserve</u> the dry, deadpan face of a skilled comedian. He once joked about the First Lady's popularity in France, for example. He introduced himself as "the man who accompanied Mrs. Kennedy to Paris." When a formal dinner and reception was held at the White House honoring Nobel Prize winners, the president gave a witty <u>pledge</u> of his esteem. "I think," he said, "this is the most extraordinary collection of talent, of human knowledge, that has ever been gathered together at the White House, with the possible exception of when Thomas Jefferson dined alone."

1. Underline the words that give a clue to the meaning of <u>attain</u>. Use the word *attain* in a sentence of your own.

2. Circle the words in this and the previous sentence that give a clue to the meaning of <u>renewal</u>. Use a word that means the opposite of *renewal* in a sentence of your own.

3. Underline the words in this sentence that give a clue to the meaning of <u>foe</u>. Use a word meaning the opposite of *foe* in an original sentence.

4. What is a synonym for <u>brutal</u>? What is an antonym for this word?

5. Circle the words in this sentence that offer a clue to the meaning of <u>segregation</u>. Use *segregation* in a sentence of your own.

6. Underline the words in this sentence that hint at the meaning of <u>loyalty</u>. What are two synonyms for *loyalty*?

7. Circle the words in this sentence that hint at the meaning of <u>preserve</u>. What is a synonym for *preserve*?

8. Underline the words in this sentence that give a clue to the meaning of <u>pledge</u>. What is a synonym for *pledge*?

Selections by John F. Kennedy and Martin Luther King, Jr.

Reading Warm-up B

Read the following passage. Pay special attention to the underlined words. Then, read it again, and complete the activities. Use a separate sheet of paper for your written answers.

Most historians now agree that Jacqueline Kennedy <u>profoundly</u> affected the office of First Lady. Jackie left this position permanently changed. The youngest first lady in nearly 80 years, she moved into the White House with President Kennedy when she was only thirty-one years old. She was determined to make the White House a showcase for American <u>vitality</u> in the arts. Therefore, she began to invite musicians, artists, actors, and intellectuals—including Nobel Prize winners—to the executive mansion. She believed that such individuals were <u>testimony</u> to American achievement and creativity.

Jackie was one of the most popular first ladies in history. She <u>embodied</u> for many Americans an ideal of feminine beauty and a sense of style and fashion. She was also admired for the <u>civility</u> and charming good manners with which she easily conversed with foreign leaders in their own languages. Even a political opponent or <u>adversary</u> of the administration would have to admit that Jacqueline was an asset to the nation.

The first lady's most lasting contribution was to organize and carry out a large-scale restoration of the White House to its original elegance. Aided by experts, she oversaw <u>precise</u> historical studies that painstakingly researched paintings, antique furniture, and interior design in the White House. It is hard to exaggerate the impact that Jacqueline had on the White House in less than three years of residence there. Historians now agree that the outcome of her support was an <u>inexpressible</u> improvement in the White House, which, during the Kennedy years, became truly worthy of the status of a national museum.

1. Underline the words in this sentence and the next that hint at the meaning of <u>profoundly</u>. What are two antonyms for *profoundly*?

2. Circle the words in this sentence that hint at the meaning of <u>vitality</u>. What is a synonym for *vitality*?

3. Underline the words in this sentence that hint at the meaning of <u>testimony</u>. Use *testimony* in an original sentence.

4. Underline the words in this sentence that hint at the meaning of <u>embodied</u>. Use *embodied* in a sentence of your own.

5. Circle the words in this sentence that hint at the meaning of <u>civility</u>. Use a word meaning the opposite of *civility* in a sentence of your own.

6. Circle the word in this sentence that gives a good clue to the meaning of <u>adversary</u>. What is an antonym for *adversary*?

7. Underline the words in this sentence that hint at the meaning of <u>precise</u>. What is a synonym for *precise*?

8. What is a synonym for <u>inexpressible</u>?

Name _____ Date _____

"Inaugural Address" by John F. Kennedy;
from **"Letter from Birmingham City Jail"** by Martin Luther King, Jr.
Literary Analysis: Persuasion

Persuasion is writing or speech meant to get a reader or listener to think or act in a particular way. To make their words persuasive, both Kennedy and King use a variety of **rhetorical devices.** Some of the rhetorical devices that are prominent in Kennedy's speech and King's letter are as follows:

- **Parallellism** is the repetition of grammatical structures to express similar ideas: "born in this century, tempered by war, disciplined by a hard and bitter peace. . . ."

- **Antithesis** is a form of parallelism in which strongly contrasting words, phrases, clauses, or sentences are repeated: "not as a call to battle, . . but as a call to bear the burden of a long twilight struggle. . . ."

Use the chart below to give another example of each of these rhetorical devices from either selection. Then, in the right-hand column, explain briefly how the use of the device helps to make the work more persuasive.

Example of Rhetorical Device	**How It Makes the Work More Persuasive**
Parallellism:	
Antithesis:	

"Inaugural Address" by John F. Kennedy;
from **"Letter from Birmingham City Jail"** by Martin Luther King, Jr.

Reading Strategy: Identify Main Ideas and Supporting Details

The **main ideas** in a selection are the key points that the writer or speaker wants to express. The **supporting details** are the facts, examples, or reasons that explain or justify those main ideas. For example, when Martin Luther King, Jr., writes of African Americans, "Our destiny is tied up with the destiny of America," he supports this main idea with the following historical facts:

• Before the Pilgrims landed at Plymouth, we were here.

• Before the pen of Jefferson etched across the pages of history the majestic words of the Declaration of Independence, we were here.

• For more than two centuries our foreparents labored in this country without wages; they made cotton king; and they built the homes of their masters in the midst of brutal injustice and shameful humilation.

On the graphic organizer below, identify a main idea from each of the two selections and the details that support the main idea.

Selection:		
Main Idea:		
Supporting Detail	**Supporting Detail**	**Supporting Detail**

Selection:		
Main Idea:		
Supporting Detail	**Supporting Detail**	**Supporting Detail**

Inaugural Address by John F. Kennedy
from **"Letter from Birmingham City Jail"** by Martin Luther King, Jr.

Vocabulary Builder

Using the Latin Root *-vert-* or *-vers-*

The Latin root *-vert-* or *-vers-* means "to turn." For example, the word *reverse* means "to turn completely around in direction."

A. DIRECTIONS: *Complete the following sentences by circling the word containing the root -vert- or -vers- that best fits the meaning of the sentence. Use a dictionary if necessary.*

1. When Stephanie lost control of her motorcycle, I quickly (averted/converted) my eyes for fear of what I might see.

2. The police immediately began (conversing/diverting) traffic away from the accident.

3. The medical helicopter that took Stephanie to the hospital flew (vertically/inversely) before heading to the northeast.

4. While Stephanie had suffered a few scrapes and bruises, she mostly complained about (vertigo/conversion).

5. She said that while she loved the thrill of riding on two wheels, she might (reverse/convert) to four-wheel transportation in the near future.

Word List

adversary   alliance   eradicate   flagrant   invective   profundity

B. DIRECTIONS: *Show that you understand the meaning of the italicized words from the Word List by briefly answering the following questions.*

1. Why might countries form an *alliance*?

   _____

2. Why might one country be the *adversary* of another?

   _____

3. What kind of substance might I wish to *eradicate* from my carpet?

   _____

4. Why might a philosopher speak with *profundity* about life?

   _____

5. Why might a politician appear shocked if another politician shouted an *invective* at her or him?

   _____

6. How was segregation *flagrant* in its lack of obedience to the nation's law?

   _____

"Inaugural Address" by John F. Kennedy;
from **"Letter from Birmingham City Jail"** by Martin Luther King, Jr.

Grammar and Style: Use Active, Not Passive, Voice

A verb is in the **active voice** when the subject of the sentence performs the action. A verb is in the **passive voice** when the subject of the sentence receives the action. The passive voice uses a form of *to be* together with a past participle.

Active Voice: King emphasized the importance of using moral means to achieve moral ends.

Passive Voice: The importance of using moral means to achieve moral ends was emphasized by King.

Use the active voice whenever possible. It is livelier and more direct than the passive voice. Use the passive voice only if the person or thing performing the action is unknown or unimportant.

A. PRACTICE: *Read each sentence and write* A *above any verbs or verb phrases in the active voice and* P *above any in the passive voice.*

1. When the influence of Gandhi's philosophy on King was posed by the questioner, the lecturer affirmed that King considered himself a disciple of Gandhi's philosophy of nonviolence.

2. Many presidents have delivered forgettable or undistinguished inaugural addresses; Kennedy's address, by contrast, is considered among the finest and most memorable by many historians.

3. Ask not what your country can do for you.

4. . . . we were carrying our whole nation back to those great wells of democracy which were dug deep by the Founding Fathers. . . .

B. Writing Application: *Rewrite the following sentences, changing all verbs in the passive to the active voice.*

1. All this will not be finished by us in the first 100 days.

   _____

2. Only a few generations have been granted the role of defending freedom in its hour of maximum danger.

   _____

   _____

3. Let us hope that the deep fog of misunderstanding will be lifted from our fear-drenched communities.

   _____

   _____

4. Dr. Martin Luther King, Jr., has been honored throughout the country in the many communities that have named schools and streets after him.

   _____

   _____

"Inaugural Address" by John F. Kennedy;
from **"Letter from Birmingham City Jail"** by Martin Luther King, Jr.

Support for Writing

To prepare to write a letter to the editor on an issue about which you feel strongly, first enter information into the chart below.

Letter from [_____: your name] about [_____: issue]

Issue:
Opinion Statement:
Persuasive Support

Logical:	Emotional:	Ethical:

On a separate page, draft your letter. Begin by presenting your main idea about the issue in the form of an opinion statement. In your draft, support your main idea with details, using logical, emotional, and ethical appeals. Use parallel structure as a device. As you revise, be sure you have supported your opinion statement with enough persuasive evidence.

"Inaugural Address" by John F. Kennedy
from **Letter from Birmingham City Jail** by Dr. Martin Luther King, Jr.
Enrichment: Social Studies

The 1960s were difficult times in America. The Bay of Pigs invasion and the Cuban missile crisis were followed by the assassination of President John F. Kennedy. Vice President Lyndon B. Johnson took over the presidency, and his administration soon escalated the war in Vietnam.

Although Johnson helped pass civil rights laws during his term in office, Americans soon witnessed the assassination of Martin Luther King, Jr., and Senator Robert F. Kennedy, the former president's brother. In addition, thousands of young American soldiers were killed or injured in Vietnam. For many people, it seemed as if America had lost her way, but there were words of hope even throughout these times of tremendous national difficulty.

DIRECTIONS: *Find another speech delivered by John F. Kennedy, Martin Luther King, Jr., Robert F. Kennedy, Lyndon B. Johnson, or another leader during the 1960s. On a separate page, summarize the main ideas of the speech. Include several of the most memorable or convincing details—those that really stand out in your mind. Finally, compare the strengths and weaknesses of the speech with either* "Inaugural Address" *or* "Letter from Birmingham City Jail."

"Inaugural Address" by John F. Kennedy and
from **"Letter from Birmingham City Jail"** by Martin Luther King, Jr.
Open-Book Test

Short Answer *Write your responses to the questions in this section on the lines provided.*

1. This passage from Kennedy's "Inaugural Address" is an example of which rhetorical device? Explain your answer.

   we shall pay any price, bear any burden, meet any hardship

   _____
   _____
   _____

2. In his "Inaugural Address," when Kennedy states that "the rights of man come not from the generosity of the state, but from the hand of God," what rhetorical device is he using? Why is it effective in this context? Explain your answer.

   _____
   _____
   _____
   _____

3. In "Inaugural Address," what is the element of antithesis in the following passage? What purpose does it serve?

   Let the word go forth from this time and place, to friend and foe alike, that the torch has been passed to a new generation of Americans. . . .

   _____
   _____
   _____

4. In "Inaugural Address," Kennedy states, "those who foolishly sought power by riding the back of a tiger ended up inside." What does he mean by this statement?

   _____
   _____
   _____

5. In the middle of "Inaugural Address," a series of paragraphs begin with the repeated phrase "Let both sides. . . ." What major argument is Kennedy advancing through the emphasis of parallel structure in these paragraphs? Whom is he appealing to, and why?

   _____
   _____
   _____

6. In "Letter from Birmingham City Jail," who is the "we" that Martin Luther King, Jr., speaks about in the opening paragraph?

_____

_____

_____

7. In the opening paragraph of "Letter from Birmingham City Jail," Dr. King makes use of the following parallel structure in successive sentences: "Before . . . we were there." What key argument does Dr. King underscore through parallelism in these sentences?

_____

_____

_____

_____

8. In "Letter from Birmingham City Jail," who is Dr. King's intended audience? What is it about them that makes Dr. King hopeful that they will be receptive to his arguments in favor of brotherhood and equality?

_____

_____

_____

_____

9. What aspect of Dr. King's philosophy of social and political activism is reflected in the following passage from "Letter from Birmingham City Jail"? Explain your answer.

> So I have tried to make it clear that it is wrong to use immoral means to attain moral ends.

_____

_____

_____

_____

10. If, in commenting on your term paper, your English teacher wrote of the "profundity" of your ideas, would she be paying you a compliment? Why or why not? Base your answer on the meaning of *profundity* as it is used in "Letter from Birmingham City Jail."

_____

_____

_____

_____

Essay

Write an extended response to the question of your choice or to the question or questions your teacher assigns you.

11. "Ask not what your country can do for you—ask what you can do for your country." This line from Kennedy's "Inaugural Address" is one of the best-known passages in all American speeches. In an essay, explain how this idea expresses the overall message of Kennedy's speech. Discuss whether you think this idea remains relevant in today's United States.

12. In his "Letter from Birmingham City Jail," Dr. King argues that "if the inexpressible cruelties of slavery could not stop" African Americans from trying to gain their freedom, the practice of racism would also fail. Do you consider this an effective argument? Why or why not? Explain your response in an essay supported by details from the selection.

13. Indian activist Mohandas K. Gandhi heavily influenced Martin Luther King, Jr., with his philosophy of nonviolent struggle. Gandhi's influence on Dr. King is reflected in the following passage from "Letter from Birmingham City Jail": "I have consistently preached that nonviolence demands that the means we use must be as pure as the ends we seek." In an essay, explain what King means by this remark. Support your answer with clear reasoning and specific examples.

14. **Thinking About the Essential Question: What makes American literature American?** Each of the two selections in this section—"Inaugural Address" by John F. Kennedy and "Letter from Birmingham City Jail" by Martin Luther King Jr.—addresses key concerns and hopes of American democracy—in Kennedy's case, from the peak of power, the presidency, and in King's case, from the margins of society, as an outsider seeking equality and justice. In an essay, explain the way in which each essay expresses important concerns and hopes for American democracy from these two very different standpoints.

Oral Response

15. Go back to question 1, 3, or 9 or to the question your teacher assigns to you. Take a few minutes to expand your answer and prepare an oral response. Find additional details in "Inaugural Address" or "Letter from Birmingham City Jail" that support your points. If necessary, make notes to guide your oral response.

Inaugural Address by John F. Kennedy
from **Letter from Birmingham City Jail** by Dr. Martin Luther King, Jr.
Selection Test A

Critical Reading *Identify the letter of the choice that best answers the question.*

_____ 1. Which of these passages from "Inaugural Address" is an example of a structure that is parallel in how the phrases are arranged?
   A. "We dare not forget today."
   B. "All this will not be finished in the first one hundred days."
   C. "We shall not always expect to find them supporting our view."
   D. "North and South, East and West"

_____ 2. In "Inaugural Address," what power does Kennedy say humans have for helping others in today's world?
   A. the power to agree on all matters
   B. the power to eliminate poverty
   C. the power to explore space
   D. the power to end all war

_____ 3. What argument does Kennedy use in "Inaugural Address" to invite opposing nations to work with the U.S.?
   A. If they work with the U.S., they will become wealthy nations.
   B. If they work with the U.S., they will never have to go to war.
   C. If they work with the U.S., there is a better chance for peace.
   D. If they work with the U.S., they will have better education.

_____ 4. What is Kennedy asking of Americans in this passage from "Inaugural Address": "And so, my fellow Americans, ask not what your country can do for you; ask what you can do for your country"?
   A. to join the armed forces
   B. to put country before oneself
   C. to put America before others
   D. to apply for government jobs

_____ 5. What is the main idea in this paragraph from "Inaugural Address"?

   All this will not be finished in the first one hundred days . . . nor even perhaps in our lifetime on this planet. But let us begin.

   A. We must start soon in order to complete our project within our lifetime.
   B. Our job can be completed during this administration if we begin now.
   C. We must start now because our goal will take a long time to accomplish.
   D. Our job will take less time if we get started immediately.

Name _____ Date _____

_____ 6. Which of these passages from *Letter from Birmingham City Jail* is an example of parallel construction?

    A. "I wish you had commended the Negro sit-inners and demonstrators of Birmingham for their sublime courage."

    B. "We will win our freedom because the sacred heritage of our nation and the eternal will of God are embodied in our echoing demands."

    C. "Before the Pilgrims landed at Plymouth we were here. Before the pen of Jefferson etched . . . the majestic words of the Declaration of Independence, we were here."

    D. "I also hope that circumstances will soon make it possible for me to meet each of you. . . as a fellow clergyman."

_____ 7. In *Letter from Birmingham City Jail,* what does King describe as the problem that he and the protesters have been fighting against?

    A. justice

    B. segregation

    C. freedom

    D. nonviolence

_____ 8. What details from *Letter from Birmingham City Jail* support the main idea that the Birmingham police department was undeserving of praise?

    A. They pushed, cursed, and used violent dogs against African Americans.

    B. They were successful at keeping order while African Americans protested.

    C. They fought African Americans who were using violence to protest.

    D. They assumed that African Americans did not want to work with whites.

_____ 9. Which of the following statements from *Letter from Birmingham City Jail* serves as part of a parallel construction that begins: "I have no despair about the future"?

    A. I have no fear about the outcome of our struggle.

    B. Before the Pilgrims landed, we were here.

    C. I'm sorry I can't join you in your praise.

    D. One day the South will recognize its real heroes.

_____ 10. In *Letter from Birmingham City Jail,* why is King hopeful that his readers will agree with the need for brotherhood and equality among people?

    A. They are all businessmen.

    B. They are all from Alabama.

    C. They are all lawyers.

    D. They are all clergymen.

Vocabulary and Grammar

____ 11. Which word is CLOSEST in meaning to *invective*?
   A. roundabout   C. tirade
   B. retreat   D. denial

____ 12. "Inaugural Address" states that the presidents of the five countries decided that they could achieve their goals more effectively if they formed a(n)
   A. invective
   B. profundity
   C. alliance
   D. adversary

____ 13. If someone told you that she wanted to *eradicate* poverty, she would be expressing a desire to _____ it.
   A. eliminate   C. ignore
   B. limit   D. analyze

____ 14. Which sentence is written in the active voice?
   A. Juanita was elected class president.
   B. Idaho is known for its potatoes.
   C. The room was painted in a light shade of pink.
   D. I was eating my dessert when the phone rang.

Essay

15. In "Inaugural Address," Kennedy says that "a few generations have been granted the role of defending freedom in its hour of maximum danger." What do you think would have been the "maximum danger" to all people in 1963? What other times can you think of that would call for the defense of freedom? Write a brief essay to discuss these questions.

16. In "Letter from Birmingham City Jail," Dr. King notes that if the "inexpressible cruelties of slavery could not stop" African Americans from trying to gain their freedom, the practice of racism would also fail. Why is his argument so powerful? Write a brief essay to respond.

17. **Thinking About the Essential Question: What makes American literature American?** Each of the two selections in this section—"Inaugural Address" by John F. Kennedy and "Letter from Birmingham City Jail" by Martin Luther King Jr.—addresses key concerns and hopes of American democracy—in Kennedy's case, from the peak of power, the presidency, and in King's case, from the margins of society, as an outsider seeking equality and justice. In an essay, explain the way in which each essay expresses important concerns and hopes for American democracy from these two very different standpoints.

Inaugural Address by John F. Kennedy
from **"Letter from Birmingham City Jail"** by Martin Luther King, Jr.
Selection Test B

Critical Reading *Identify the letter of the choice that best completes the statement or answers the question.*

____ 1. In his "Inaugural Address," John F. Kennedy describes how humans still fight for the same goals as their ancestors. Which goal does he see as most important?
   A. education
   B. freedom
   C. war
   D. change

____ 2. When Kennedy says in his "Inaugural Address" that humans have "the power to abolish all forms of human life," to what is he referring?
   A. Humans have nuclear weapons.
   B. Humans understand how life is created.
   C. Humans can cure all diseases.
   D. Humans do not have to put up with people they do not like.

____ 3. Which quotation from the "Inaugural Address" contains an example of parallel structure?
   A. "our forbears prescribed nearly a century and three quarters ago"
   B. "the belief that the rights of man come not from the generosity of the state"
   C. "let the word go forth from this time and place"
   D. "we shall pay any price, bear any burden, meet any hardship"

____ 4. In the opening part of his "Inaugural Address," Kennedy expresses the main idea that the United States will go to any length to defend an important value. What is this value?
   A. ending the military
   B. honoring history
   C. protecting liberty
   D. maintaining friendship

____ 5. In his "Inaugural Address," Kennedy describes people "who foolishly sought power by riding the back of a tiger," saying that they "ended up inside" the tiger. What message is he offering to his listeners?
   A. Those who seek power through violence are usually overthrown by violence.
   B. Those who seek power are no different from an animal tamer in a circus.
   C. Those who can carefully keep their balance will never end up inside.
   D. Those foolish enough to seek power know that things will end badly.

____ 6. In his "Inaugural Address," Kennedy expresses the belief that the rights of man come not from the state but from
   A. God.
   B. communism.
   C. liberty.
   D. democracy.

____ 7. Which of the following expressions from the "Inaugural Address" avoids the use of parallelism?
   A. "not because the communists may be doing it, not because we seek their votes"
   B. "to convert our good words into good deeds"
   C. "let all our neighbors know that we shall join with them"
   D. "the instruments of war have far outpaced the instruments of peace"

____ 8. In the "Inaugural Address," what request does Kennedy make of the enemies of the United States?
   A. He asks that they give advance notice of a nuclear strike.
   B. He asks that they try to divide the hemispheres of the world.
   C. He asks that they're either with us or against us.
   D. He asks that both sides work toward a peace settlement.

____ 9. In the "Inaugural Address," what main idea does Kennedy express about the United Nations?
   A. It is an organization that has no power.
   B. The United States fully supports the U.N.
   C. Nuclear weapons must be controlled by the U.N.
   D. The U.N. has to become more up-to-date.

____ 10. In his "Inaugural Address," Kennedy's willingness to come to the aid of other countries is referred to as
   A. a treaty.   C. a sacrifice.
   B. an offer.   D. a pledge.

____ 11. Which of the following details from the "Inaugural Address" supports Kennedy's ideas for the relationship between the United States and other nations in North and South America?
   A. The United States will work to support economic progress in North and South America.
   B. The United States will plan the inspection and control of arms in North and South America.
   C. The United States will create new scientific inventions that will benefit North and South America.
   D. The United States will send soldiers and other military support to all of North and South America.

____ 12. Read this line from the "Inaugural Address": "Together let us explore the stars, conquer the deserts, eradicate disease, tap the ocean depths, and encourage the arts." Which phrase has less parallelism than the other phrases below?
   A. explore the stars   C. eradicate disease
   B. conquer the deserts   D. encourage the arts

____ 13. In *Letter from Birmingham City Jail*, who is the "we" that Martin Luther King, Jr., speaks about in the opening paragraph?
   A. African Americans   C. liberal Democrats
   B. Birmingham City Police   D. Baptist Church

____ 14. In "Letter from Birmingham City Jail," King says that even when police acted nonviolently in dealing with protestors, they were doing something wrong. According to King, what was wrong about the actions of these police officers?

A. King does not truly believe that there can be peace among the races.

B. They were using nonviolence to protect the injustice of racial discrimination.

C. There was evidence confirming that police did use force.

D. Nobody knows what really happened while protestors were in custody.

Vocabulary and Grammar

____ 15. Which of the following words is most nearly OPPOSITE in meaning to *adversary*?

A. ally

B. willingness

C. slight

D. subordinate

____ 16. Which word is CLOSEST in meaning to *profundity*?

A. clarity

B. harmony

C. depth

D. zeal

____ 17. If a player in a basketball game commits a *flagrant* foul, you can assume that the resulting penalty will be

A. standard

B. optional

C. more lenient

D. more severe

____ 18. Which answer best describes the meaning of *eradicate* in this sentence: "It is the goal of this presidency to *eradicate* poverty in all parts of the nation"?

A. to defeat in war

B. to criticize strongly

C. to wipe out completely

D. to make big changes

____ 19. Which of the following sentences is written in the passive voice?

A. There was the aroma of autumn in the air.

B. The rain was so heavy that we had to pull to the side of the road.

C. We were surprised by the ending of the movie.

D. I was in favor of the motion.

Essay

20. One of the most famous lines from all American speeches is Kennedy's "Ask not what your country can do for you—ask what you can do for your country." Write an essay describing how this idea fits into the overall message of Kennedy's "Inaugural Address." In addition, discuss how you see this idea at work in the United States today.

21. Martin Luther King, Jr., was a well-known advocate of nonviolent protest. He says in *Letter from a Birmingham City Jail:* "I have consistently preached that nonviolence demands that the means we use must be as pure as the ends we seek." Write an essay explaining what King means by this remark. Do you agree with him? Explain why or why not.

22. **Thinking About the Essential Question: What makes American literature American?** Each of the two selections in this section—"Inaugural Address" by John F. Kennedy and "Letter from Birmingham City Jail" by Martin Luther King Jr.—addresses key concerns and hopes of American democracy—in Kennedy's case, from the peak of power, the presidency, and in King's case, from the margins of society, as an outsider seeking equality and justice. In an essay, explain the way in which each essay expresses important concerns and hopes for American democracy from these two very different standpoints.

Name _____ Date _____

Contemporary Commentary
Arthur Miller on *The Crucible*

DIRECTIONS: *Use the space provided to answer the questions.*

1. Briefly identify the "correspondence" Arthur Miller says he perceived in two widely separated periods of American history as he started to write *The Crucible*.

_____

_____

_____

2. How does Miller connect the Salem witch hunt with poetry?

_____

_____

3. What specific similarities does Miller identify between the prosecutions and the confessions of the accused?

_____

_____

_____

_____

4. According to Miller, why has *The Crucible* become his most-produced play?

_____

_____

5. What questions for further research or investigation does this commentary leave you with? Identify at least two issues you would like to pursue as you read the play.

_____

_____

_____

_____

_____

_____

Arthur Miller
Listening and Viewing

Segment 1: Meet Arthur Miller
• What are the titles of Arthur Miller's most famous plays?
• How do you think growing up during the Depression influenced Arthur Miller's writing?

_____

_____

_____

_____

Segment 2: *The Crucible*
• How is Senator Joseph McCarthy historically significant?
• How does *The Crucible* reflect what was going on in America in the 1950s?

_____

_____

_____

_____

Segment 3: The Writing Process
• According to Arthur Miller, why is theater a "changeable art"?
• Why do you think dramas written long ago are still relevant today?

_____

_____

_____

_____

Segment 4: The Rewards of Writing
• How does Arthur Miller's writing reflect his political concerns?
• What do you think is Arthur Miller's greatest contribution to American society and literature?

_____

_____

_____

_____

Vocabulary Warm-up Word Lists

Study these words from the selection. Then, complete the activities.

Word List A

autocratic [aw toh KRA tik] *adj.* dictatorial
In an <u>autocratic</u> system of government, the people have little or no power.

faction [FAK shuhn] *n.* party or interest group
A <u>faction</u> on the student council is unhappy with the class president.

homage [HAH mij] *n.* respectful attention
The flag flew at half mast in <u>homage</u> to a local firefighter who died recently.

hypocrisy [hi PAHK ruh see] *n.* pretending to believe something you do not
If you say one thing and do another, you may be guilty of <u>hypocrisy</u>.

paradox [PAR uh dahks] *n.* apparent contradiction
Philosophers think that every <u>paradox</u> is an illusion.

somber [SAHM buhr] *adj.* serious; solemn
Joe's <u>somber</u> expression as he entered was a clue that he had bad news.

villainous [VIL uh nuhs] *adj.* evil
The court punished the criminal's <u>villainous</u> behavior.

vindictive [vin DIK tiv] *adj.* vengeful
Glenda felt <u>vindictive</u> and decided to get revenge on her tattle-tale brother.

Word List B

anarchy [AN ahr kee] *n.* state of chaos
For some years after the revolution, that country was in a state of <u>anarchy</u>.

blatantly [BLAY tuhnt lee] *adv.* very openly; brazenly
Terence <u>blatantly</u> crossed the street against the light.

defamation [def uh MAY shuhn] *n.* slander
The star sued the tabloid publication for <u>defamation</u> when it published a scandalous story.

drastic [DRAS tik] *adj.* severe; harsh; extreme
If a tornado is forecast, we will have to take <u>drastic</u> action.

parochial [puh ROH kee uhl] *adj.* narrow-minded
Some people who have lived all their lives in small towns have a <u>parochial</u> outlook.

propriety [proh PRY uh tee] *n.* conformity with what is proper or fitting
Sandra is never unconventional and always behaves with complete <u>propriety</u>.

rankle [RAN kuhl] *v.* irritate; anger
Study hard, because if you get a low grade on the test it will surely <u>rankle</u>.

squabble [SKWAH buhl] *n.* small quarrel
The children became involved in a foolish <u>squabble</u> over some glass marbles.

Name _____ Date _____

The Crucible, *Act I* by Arthur Miller
Vocabulary Warm-up Exercises

Exercise A *Fill in the blanks, using each word from Word List A only once.*

Throughout history and all across the world, a long series of [1] _____ leaders have tried to seize absolute power. This collection of dictators has included some of the most [2] _____ evildoers known to humanity. There can be few people unaware of the [3] _____, even frightening, details of the dictatorships of Adolf Hitler in Germany and Josef Stalin in Russia. It is a(n) [4] _____ that, even as these rulers thoroughly oppressed their people, they insisted on total [5] _____ and praise from their subjects. When faced by any resistance group or opposing [6] _____, these dictators invariably became [7] _____ and took revenge on their opponents. For many who lived under such dictatorships, the necessity to survive led to a type of [8] _____, in which they said one thing publicly and believed another in private.

Exercise B *Revise each sentence so that the underlined vocabulary word is logical. Be sure to keep the vocabulary word in your revision.*

Example: Her behavior was <u>consistent</u>, so her actions were hard to predict.
Her behavior was <u>consistent</u>, so her actions were easy to predict.

1. That nation's government was fair and just, so a state of <u>anarchy</u> prevailed.
   _____

2. They defied the law so <u>blatantly</u> that the police didn't even observe them.
   _____

3. Inez was delighted when she heard about Joseph's <u>defamation</u> of her.
   _____

4. Our decision was <u>drastic</u>, so we changed course only slightly.
   _____

5. Because of his <u>parochial</u> mentality, he took note of a wide range of different views.
   _____

6. When you act with <u>propriety</u>, most people are surprised and shocked.
   _____

7. The team's win <u>rankled</u> John, who had played his heart out as captain.
   _____

8. The <u>squabble</u> between the children over toys was a source of pleasure to their mother.
   _____

Name _____ Date _____

The Crucible, *Act I* by Arthur Miller
Reading Warm-up A

Read the following passage. Pay special attention to the underlined words. Then, read it again, and complete the activities. Use a separate sheet of paper for your written answers.

To appreciate Arthur Miller's play *The Crucible*, it is helpful to understand the historical background of the Massachusetts Bay Colony, which included Salem. In the seventeenth century, Massachusetts had a special kind of <u>autocratic</u>, dictatorial government, called a *theocracy*. In this government, there was no separation of church and state. Only church members in good standing could vote. The Puritan authorities demanded citizens' complete loyalty and also their <u>homage</u>. They met any party or <u>faction</u> that opposed or criticized them with <u>vindictive</u>, even ruthless, opposition.

In England, the Puritans had been victims of persecution. This sad, even <u>somber</u>, part of their history was an important reason for their decision to emigrate. They first traveled to Holland and then to America in search of religious freedom. Once in America, however, the Puritans' unwillingness to tolerate dissent presents us with a <u>paradox</u>, or apparent contradiction.

Consider the case of Anne Hutchinson, who was hounded out of Massachusetts in 1637 as a <u>villainous</u> threat to society. Hutchinson was a religious liberal. She founded a woman's group in Boston to discuss religious views and recent sermons by ministers. She criticized the Puritan clergy, saying they were guilty of <u>hypocrisy</u>. The clergy, Hutchinson said, emphasized narrowly legalistic concepts of morality but ignored the individual's ability to choose ethical behavior.

Hutchinson's opposition to the Puritan establishment soon led to the powerful opposition of John Winthrop, the most influential clergyman in Massachusetts. She was tried on the charge of "betraying the ministers" and then sentenced to banishment. With some of her followers, she then established a settlement in what is now Rhode Island.

1. Underline the word that gives a clue to the meaning of <u>autocratic</u>. Use a word meaning the opposite of *autocratic* in a sentence of your own.

2. Circle the words in this sentence that give a clue to the meaning of <u>homage</u>. What is a synonym for *homage*?

3. Underline the words in this sentence that give a clue to the meaning of <u>faction</u>. Use the word *faction* in an original sentence.

4. What is a synonym for <u>vindictive</u>? What is an antonym for *vindictive*?

5. Circle the words in this and the previous sentence that offer a clue to the meaning of <u>somber</u>. Write a sentence about something or someone that you feel is *somber*.

6. Underline the words in this sentence that give a clue to the meaning of <u>paradox</u>. In your own words, restate the *paradox* identified in this and the preceding sentences.

7. What is a synonym for <u>villainous</u>? What is an antonym for the word *villainous*?

8. Underline the words in the next sentence that give a clue to the meaning of <u>hypocrisy</u>. What is a synonym for *hypocrisy*?

Name _____ Date _____

The Crucible, *Act I* by Arthur Miller
Reading Warm-up B

Read the following passage. Pay special attention to the underlined words. Then, read it again, and complete the activities. Use a separate sheet of paper for your written answers.

An important character in Act I of Arthur Miller's play is the slave Tituba, who was brought to Massachusetts from the Caribbean island of Barbados. The English first established a colony on Barbados in 1627. The colonists' early years there were marked by disorder, even underline{anarchy}, because of their troubles in obtaining supplies. Another problem was the frequent quarrels or underline{squabbles} between colonial leaders, who often disagreed about land claims. In addition, many of the leaders had narrow-minded, underline{parochial} views on what exact relationship should exist between the colony, the British Parliament, and the King.

Other problems in early Barbados stemmed from the search for a profitable export crop. In the 1640s, however, the colonists agreed on a underline{drastic}, thoroughgoing shift from tobacco to sugar. This decision had important consequences. Sugar needed a large labor force, so landowners turned openly and underline{blatantly} to the importation of African slaves. Small farms were combined into much larger plantations. This is a trend that must surely have underline{rankled} the less prosperous colonists. Large landowners, however, reaped huge profits, because sugar was in high demand in European markets. Such landowners settled comfortably into political power as a planter aristocracy, leading life with elegant underline{propriety} and enjoying the privileges of an elite class. Other colonists, as well as slaves, understood for the most part that criticism of the planter slaveholders would be interpreted as underline{defamation}, and would be severely punished as a slander on the island's leadership.

In 1834, slavery was abolished; the Barbados sugar trade, however, continued on. Even today, most farmland is planted with sugarcane, although the island's chief source of revenue is tourism. In 1966, Barbados won independence from Great Britain.

1. Underline the words in this sentence that hint at the meaning of underline{anarchy}. What are two antonyms for **anarchy**?

2. Circle the words that hint at the meaning of underline{squabbles}. Are **squabbles** usually about important issues, or about small ones?

3. Underline the word in this sentence that hints at the meaning of underline{parochial}. Use a word meaning the opposite of **parochial** in a sentence.

4. Underline the words in this sentence that hint at the meaning of underline{drastic}. What are two synonyms for **drastic**?

5. Circle the words in this sentence that hint at the meaning of underline{blatantly}. Use a word meaning the opposite of **blatantly** in a sentence of your own.

6. Circle the words in this and the previous sentence that give a good clue to the meaning of underline{rankled}. What is an antonym for **rankled**?

7. Underline the words in this sentence that hint at the meaning of underline{propriety}. What is a synonym for **propriety**?

8. Underline the words in this sentence that hint at the meaning of underline{defamation}. Use the word **defamation** in an original sentence.

The Crucible, *Act I*, by Arthur Miller
Biography: Arthur Miller

DIRECTIONS: *Fill in the time line with important events from playwright Arthur Miller's life.*

1932:

1947:

1949:

1953:

1956:

1956:

Name _____ Date _____

The Crucible, *Act I,* by Arthur Miller

Literary Analysis: Plot and Dramatic Exposition

Arthur Miller's *The Crucible* is a **political drama** because it is both a historical narrative about the Salem witch hunts of the 1600s and a commentary on American politics during the "Red Scare" of the 1950s, when Senator Joseph McCarthy ran "witch hunts" to expose communists and communist sympathizers in the United States. The **plot,** or series of events, of *The Crucible* can be interpreted as a metaphor for the events of the Red Scare and the political climate it created. In Act I, Miller uses **dramatic exposition,** or the revealing of background information through stage directions and dialogue, to set up this extended metaphor.

DIRECTIONS: *Refer to Act I of* The Crucible *as you answer the following questions.*

1. Miller uses lengthy prose commentaries for much of his dramatic exposition in Act I. What kind of information does he reveal in these commentaries?

   _____

   _____

2. Why do you think Miller uses this unusual expository strategy for his drama?

   _____

   _____

3. How would the experience of reading the play be different without this type of dramatic exposition?

   _____

   _____

4. At what point does the rising action begin?

   _____

   _____

5. What conflict prompts the beginning of the rising action?

   _____

   _____

6. What do you feel is the most important piece of information revealed in Act I? Why?

   _____

   _____

Name _____ Date _____

Reading Strategy: Dialogue and Stage Directions

Arthur Miller's **stage directions** in *The Crucible* are extensive, detailed, and full of historical information. They provide the setting, background on the situation, and information about characters' backgrounds, motives, and personalities. A reader of the play benefits from Miller's background information by gaining an understanding of the characters as people and why they act the way they do.

Still, *The Crucible* is a play. As in all plays, the **dialogue** carries the burden of communicating to the audience. From the dialogue a reader or an audience member learns how the characters think, how they express themselves, and how they feel about one another and about the situation at hand. It is only through the dialogue that the plot develops.

DIRECTIONS: *Refer to dialogue, stage directions, and background information in Act I as you fill in the chart.*

Question	Answer	Where You Found the Information
1. What do you learn about Reverend Parris's relationship with the community in Act I?		
2. What are Abigail's circumstances? What led her to reside with her uncle?		
3. What relationship exists between Abigail and Proctor?		
4. What kind of person is Goody Putnam? What makes her this way?		
5. Why is Mary Warren embarrassed and fearful when John Proctor enters the room?		

The Crucible, *Act I,* by Arthur Miller
Vocabulary Builder

Using the Root *-grat-*

A. DIRECTIONS: *The root -grat- means "pleasing" or "grateful." Explain how the meaning of the word root -grat- contributes to the meaning of each of the following words.*

1. gratitude _____

_____

_____

2. gratuitous _____

_____

_____

Using the Word List

calumny	evade	dissembling	inculcation
ingratiating	predilection	propitiation	

B. DIRECTIONS: *Match each word in the left column with its definition in the right column. Write the letter of the definition on the line next to the word it defines.*

___ 1. predilection   **A.** charming

___ 2. calumny   **B.** slander

___ 3. propitiation   **C.** escape

___ 4. evade   **D.** instilling

___ 5. ingratiating (adj.)   **E.** appeasement

___ 6. inculcation   **F.** lying

___ 7. dissembling   **G.** preference

The Crucible, *Act I*, by Arthur Miller
Support for Writing: Newspaper Article

DIRECTIONS: *Fill in the chart below to help you write your newspaper article reporting Betty's sudden illness and the accusations of witchcraft in Salem that followed. Collect your information from Act I of The Crucible. You may use your imagination to fill in more details, but remember that your article should be made up of objective facts rather than your personal opinions.*

Who (is involved)?	
What (happened)?	
When (did it happen)?	
Where (did it happen)?	
Why (did it happen)?	
How (did it happen)?	

The Crucible, *Act I,* by Arthur Miller

Enrichment: Social Studies

The climate of fear and false charges about which Arthur Miller writes in *The Crucible* reflect the climate of suspicion he lived through in the 1940s: the period of McCarthyism. The word *McCarthyism* came from the name of Joseph R. McCarthy, a Wisconsin senator who made numerous charges—usually with little evidence—that certain officials and individuals were communists or cooperated with communists.

McCarthyism developed during the Cold War, an era of great hostility between the communist and noncommunist nations of the world. In the late 1940s and early 1950s, communists took over Czechoslavakia and China, the Soviet Union exploded its first atomic bomb, and the Soviet Union equipped the North Korean communist forces that invaded South Korea. Because of these and other events, many in the United States government deeply feared communism and began to investigate its influence, sometimes using questionable methods.

In 1947, the House Committee on Un-American Activities (HUAC) investigated claims that Hollywood was full of those who advocated the overthrow of the United States. Many writers refused to testify before the committee, and some were blacklisted by the industry and could no longer work. HUAC expanded its investigations. In the early 1950s, Senator McCarthy accused so many people of being communists that the whole era became known as the "McCarthy Era." His dubious evidence, brutal tactics, and unfair questioning eventually led to his being discredited, but the fear of being labeled a communist caused some people to name others as suspects merely to prove their own loyalty.

Called by HUAC in 1956, Arthur Miller refused to name individuals he had seen ten years earlier at a meeting at which communists were allegedly present. He was convicted of contempt. The conviction was later overturned. In 1957 the first film of *The Crucible* was made in France, because American companies feared to produce it. It took decades for paranoia to subside, and using techniques of unproven charges, guilt by association, and sensational accusation in the media is still known as *McCarthyism.*

Write answers to the questions in the space provided.

1. Why did some Americans fear communism so much?

   _____

   _____

   _____

2. What similarities do you see between the McCarthy era and the time of *The Crucible*?

   _____

   _____

   _____

   _____

   _____

Name _____ Date _____

The Crucible, *Act I* by Arthur Miller
Open-Book Test

Short Answer *Write your responses to the questions in this section on the lines provided.*

1. In Act I of *The Crucible*, what is wrong with Betty? Describe Abigail's and Tituba's reactions to Betty's condition.

   _____

   _____

   _____

2. In Act I of *The Crucible*, it is apparent that rumors have been flying through the town about incidents of witchcraft. Why are Abigail and Parris especially concerned about such rumors?

   _____

   _____

   _____

3. The girls' activities in the woods arouse Parris's suspicions and help to generate rumors of witchcraft. Explain how Parris's suspicions and the gathering rumors advance the dramatic exposition of Act I of *The Crucible*.

   _____

   _____

   _____

4. Review the stage directions concerning the characters of Thomas Putnam and John Proctor in Act I of *The Crucible*. Then briefly explain how those stage directions help to portray the personality of each character.

   _____

   _____

   _____

5. How would you describe the relationship between Abigail and the Proctors in Act I of *The Crucible*? Give one example from the play that sheds light on their relationship.

   _____

   _____

   _____

6. What motivates Tituba to begin naming names to the Reverend Hale toward the end of Act I of *The Crucible*? How does her naming of names advance an important part of the drama of the play?

_____

_____

_____

7. Abigail Williams plays a significant role in advancing the action of Act I of *The Crucible*. How would you describe her character?

_____

_____

8. In Act I of *The Crucible*, there's a scene in which the girls are alone conversing with one another. What can you infer about Abigail's influence over the other girls from this scene? Where does her influence come from?

_____

_____

9. Reread the stage directions from Act I of *The Crucible* that appear below. From these stage directions, what can you conclude about Tituba's cooperative behavior toward the Reverend Hale at the end of Act I?

> TITUBA: *terrified, falls to her knees*
> TITUBA: *frightened by the coming process*

_____

_____

_____

10. If the judge at a trial told a witness that he thought he was dissembling in his testimony, would the judge be complimenting or criticizing the witness? Explain your response, basing it on the meaning of *dissembling* as it is used in Act I of *The Crucible*.

_____

_____

Essay

Write an extended response to the question of your choice or to the question or questions your teacher assigns you.

11. The plot developments come quickly in Act I of *The Crucible*. Much of the gathering hysteria over witchcraft arises from the episode in the woods involving Abigail, Tituba, and the other girls. In an essay, recount this key plot development: what the girls were doing in the woods, what Parris saw when he came across them, and why their activity has stirred up such suspicion and disapproval.

12. Reverend Parris plays a key role in the unfolding plot developments in Act I of *The Crucible*. What does the reader learn about Reverend Parris's personality in Act I? How do Parris's character and background affect his reactions to the issues that arise during the act? Answer these questions in an essay supported by examples from Act I of the play.

13. As part of his dramatic exposition in Act I of *The Crucible*, Miller provides extensive background information about the dynamics and personalities of Salem. In an essay, describe the dynamics of the community and the interactions of its key citizens in Act I. Base your response on the plot developments of Act I as well as Miller's prose expositions. How does the information that Miller provides enhance the meaning of the events of Act I?

14. **Thinking About the Essential Question: How does literature shape or reflect society?** Arthur Miller had a specific, critical agenda in mind in writing *The Crucible*—to show the damage that can result from widespread suspicion, paranoia, and repression in a society. What kind of picture of the sixteenth-century Puritan society of Salem does Miller convey in Act I of *The Crucible*? Develop your answer in an essay supported by details from Act I of the play.

Oral Response

15. Go back to question 1, 7, or 9 or to the question your teacher assigns to you. Take a few minutes to expand your answer and prepare an oral response. Find additional details in Act I of *The Crucible* that support your points. If necessary, make notes to guide your oral response.

The Crucible, *Act I,* by Arthur Miller
Selection Test A

Critical Reading *Identify the letter of the choice that best answers the question.*

____ 1. What does the dramatic exposition that describes arguments about deeds and boundaries in *The Crucible, Act I,* prepare you for?
   A. Reverend Parris's anger over not being given firewood
   B. the real story about what went on with the girls in the woods
   C. John Procter's attempt to deny his lust for Abigail
   D. Putnam's and Procter's disagreement over a piece of land

____ 2. Based on the background exposition from *The Crucible, Act I* that describes children who had to "walk straight, eyes slightly lowered . . . mouths shut until bidden to speak," what kind of life do you think children in Salem had?
   A. joyful
   B. wild
   C. joyless
   D. educated

____ 3. What is the setting of *The Crucible*?
   A. Salem, Massachusetts, today
   B. England today
   C. England in the 1600s
   D. Salem, Massachusetts, in the 1600s

____ 4. In *The Crucible, Act I,* Reverend Parris acts concerned about his daughter. What is the real reason for his concern?
   A. fear that she will lose her soul
   B. fear for his reputation
   C. fear that she will die
   D. fear that he will become ill

____ 5. According to *The Crucible, Act I,* what did Puritans believe about slaves?
   A. They believed slaves would fight for freedom.
   B. They believed slaves should be freed.
   C. They believed slaves were uncivilized.
   D. They believed slaves were their equals.

_____ 6. In *The Crucible, Act I,* what frightening reason drives Mrs. Putnam to hunt for witches?

A. anger at Reverend Parris

B. curiosity about the woods

C. the deaths of her children

D. sympathy for the ill children

_____ 7. In *The Crucible, Act I,* which of the young women has the most influence over the others?

A. Mercy

B. Tituba

C. Abigail

D. Mary

_____ 8. In *The Crucible, Act I,* what can the reader infer about Salem, based on the fact that Reverend Hale asks Giles why his wife is hiding books and reading them?

A. Salem residents were well educated.

B. Reading books was a suspicious activity.

C. More women read books than men.

D. Women and men read books together.

_____ 9. Based on *The Crucible, Act I,* what seems to motivate Abigail's actions?

A. her wish to protect her uncle

B. her wish to help Betty

C. her wish to leave Salem

D. her wish to have power

_____ 10. In *The Crucible, Act I,* why is John Proctor guilty about Abigail?

A. He has refused to hire her.

B. He has seduced and abandoned her.

C. He has accused her of witchcraft.

D. He has thrown her out of the church.

Vocabulary

_____ 11. Which word best replaces *ingratiating* in this sentence: "The child was *ingratiating* at first, but people then learned she was really not so nice"?

A. skilled

B. charming

C. fearful

D. annoying

___ 12. Which word is CLOSEST in meaning to *inculcation*?

    A. curse

    B. intimidation

    C. warning

    D. teaching

___ 13. If your friend has a *predilection* for contact sports, he would most likely tune in to which of the following sporting events on TV?

    A. tennis

    B. golf

    C. football

    D. sailing

___ 14. Someone would most likely be trying to *evade* the authorities if he

    A. had just witnessed a crime.

    B. had just robbed a bank.

    C. wanted to run for political office.

    D. had just been mugged on the street.

___ 15. Which of the following is most nearly OPPOSITE in meaning to *dissembling*?

    A. revealing

    B. concealing

    C. tempting

    D. unappetizing

Essay

16. As you read *The Crucible*, you learn how much importance Abigail Williams has in the events that occur. After Elizabeth Proctor tells her to leave their house, Abigail tells John Proctor, "You loved me then and you do now!" What do these words tell you about Abigail and how she might behave during the rest of the play? Write a brief essay to respond.

17. In the first act of *The Crucible*, numerous accusations of witchcraft are made by various characters. What do you learn in Act I that helps account for such an outbreak of hysterical accusations? Write a brief essay to explain the characters' need to accuse each other.

18. **Thinking About the Essential Question: How does literature shape or reflect society?** Arthur Miller had a specific, critical agenda in mind in writing *The Crucible*—to show the damage that can result from widespread suspicion, paranoia, and repression in a society. What kind of picture of the sixteenth-century Puritan society of Salem does Miller convey in Act I of *The Crucible*? Develop your answer in an essay supported by details from Act I of the play.

The Crucible, *Act I*, by Arthur Miller
Selection Test B

Critical Reading *Identify the letter of the choice that best completes the statement or answers the question.*

____ 1. What is Reverend Parris upset about at the opening of Act I of *The Crucible*?
  A. rumors of witchcraft circulating in the community
  B. Abigail's dismissal from the Proctor household
  C. his daughter's condition and the possible connection to her inappropriate activities in the woods
  D. Tituba's influence over the children

____ 2. From the comments of Parris in *The Crucible, Act I*, his concern for his daughter seems primarily based on his
  A. anxiety about his reputation.
  B. fear for the fate of her soul.
  C. great love for his only child.
  D. terror of the Devil.
  e. concern prejudice against Tituba

____ 3. In *The Crucible, Act I*, how does Reverend Parris's belief in the supernatural affect his response to his daughter's illness?
  A. He refuses to send for a doctor.
  B. He professes his faith that God will heal her.
  C. He seeks help from Reverend Hale.
  D. He believes Abigail's assertion that Betty was not bewitched.

____ 4. What can be inferred from Act I of *The Crucible* about the attitude of Puritans toward their slaves?
  A. They saw their slaves as equals in God's sight.
  B. They saw their slaves as being only a step removed from paganism.
  C. They feared and mistrusted their slaves.
  D. They treated their slaves as valued members of the household.

____ 5. In *The Crucible, Act I* Thomas Putnam's attitude toward Reverend Parris is one of
  A. mistrust.
  B. respect.
  C. pity.
  D. contempt.
  e. neutrality

____ 6. This passage is from the background information at the opening of *The Crucible Act I*. For what detail that comes out later in Act I does this information prepare you?

  Long-held hatreds of neighbors could now be openly expressed, and vengeance taken, despite the Bible's charitable injunctions. Land-lust which had been expressed before by constant bickering over boundaries and deeds, could now be elevated to the arena of morality . . .

  A. Putnam arguing with Proctor about a piece of land to which both men lay claim
  B. Reverend Parris complaining about his salary
  C. Abigail's reluctance to tell the truth about what happened in the woods
  D. Abigail's dismissal from service in the Proctor household

_____ 7. How does Mrs. Putnam justify sending Ruth to Tituba in the first act of *The Crucible*?
A. Tituba promised to revive Mrs. Putnam's dead children.
B. Mrs. Putnam didn't think a little foolish "conjuring" would do any harm.
C. Mrs. Putnam thought it might help Ruth, who seemed to be ailing.
D. Mrs. Putnam feels she deserves to know why she has had to endure the deaths of seven children.

_____ 8. Mrs. Putnam's comments in *The Crucible*, Act I, suggest that her primary motivation in hunting for witches is
A. anger at having lost her children.
B. compassion for the two sick girls.
C. curiosity about the mysterious events in the woods.
D. resentment of Reverend Parris.

_____ 9. Which phrase in Act I of *The Crucible* best describes Abigail Williams's character?
A. impulsive and thoughtless
B. naive and timid
C. proud and manipulative
D. affectionate and vulnerable

_____ 10. From the scene in the first act of *The Crucible* in which the girls are alone, what can be inferred as the basis of Abigail's influence over the other girls?
A. her beauty and cleverly crafted purity
B. her social position as the minister's niece
C. her charm and magnetic persuasiveness
D. her use of her early experiences to terrorize them

_____ 11. Which word best describes John Proctor's words and actions in Act I of *The Crucible*?
A. compassionate
B. devout
C. independent
D. shrewd

_____ 12. Consider Tituba's state of mind when she began naming names in the first act of *The Crucible*. What can you infer about her motivation?
A. She was afraid of Reverend Hale and thought naming names would save her from punishment.
B. She actually saw Goody Good and Goody Osburn in the forest and wanted to tell the truth.
C. She was confused and was talking about a dream she once had.
D. She didn't like the women she named, and she hoped they'd be punished.

_____ 13. Given this piece of information from the stage directions in *The Crucible*, what can readers conclude about Tituba's behavior at the end of Act I?

She enters as one does who can no longer bear to be barred from the sight of her beloved, but she is also very frightened because her slave sense has warned her that, as always, trouble in this house eventually lands on her back.

A. Tituba is so fond of Betty that she'll try anything to help her.
B. Tituba is actually in love with Reverend Parris and confesses to keep him out of trouble.
C. Tituba's "slave sense" is what got her and the girls into trouble in the first place.
D. She is so sure that trouble will befall her that she plays along with Hale as he pushes her for information.

Vocabulary and Grammar

___ 14. In *The Crucible, Act I,* Abigail has an "endless capacity for dissembling," which means
A. she is a destructive person.
B. she is very quick to get at the heart of a matter.
C. she frequently conceals her true motives from those around her.
D. she is able to keep track of the different stories she tells to different people.

___ 15. If someone had just filed a lawsuit for slander, you could reasonably assume that he had been subjected to
A. calumny
B. inculcation
C. propitiation
D. dissembling

Essay

16. What kind of man is Reverend Parris? What does Miller reveal about him, both through background information and dialogue in *The Crucible*? How do Parris's nature and background affect his response to issues and situations in Act I? Answer these questions in an essay, and cite examples of Parris's actions and the motivations behind them.

17. The root of the conflict in Act I is Reverend Parris's discovery of Tituba and the girls in the woods on the night before the action in *The Crucible* begins. In an essay, trace the pieces of information that are revealed about the scene in the woods. Who did what and who saw what? How and when are pieces of information revealed to the reader and for what reasons? Finally, explain why you think Miller reveals all information about the activities in the woods through dialogue, not through background information. How and why is his method effective?

18. Miller provides extensive background information about the community of Salem as well as about its residents in the first act of *The Crucible*. What is the community like? What are the inhabitants like? How do they interact with one another? What are their beliefs? Explain how the atmosphere of Salem and the nature of its residents lend themselves to the situation that develops in Act I. How does the information Miller provides add meaning to the reading of the play? Answer these questions in an essay.

19. **Thinking About the Essential Question: How does literature shape or reflect society?** Arthur Miller had a specific, critical agenda in mind in writing *The Crucible*—to show the damage that can result from widespread suspicion, paranoia, and repression in a society. What kind of picture of the sixteenth-century Puritan society of Salem does Miller convey in Act I of *The Crucible*? Develop your answer in an essay supported by details from Act I of the play.

Vocabulary Warm-up Word Lists

Study these words from the selection. Then, complete the activities.

Word List A

calamity [kuh LAM uh tee] *n.* disaster
The loss of their house in a fire was a <u>calamity</u>.

compensate [KAHM pen sayt] *v.* to make up for
The insurance company offered to <u>compensate</u> Ronda for her loss.

deceit [dee SEET] *n.* lying; deception
Spies make <u>deceit</u> a way of life.

falter [FOL tuhr] *v.* to hesitate
Artie did not <u>falter</u> but scored almost as soon as he was put in the game.

indignant [in DIG nuhnt] *adj.* angry; outraged
Because they were so rude to us at the party, we felt highly <u>indignant</u>.

magistrate [MAJ is trayt] *n.* official judge
In the ancient Roman Republic, a consul was the highest-ranking <u>magistrate</u>.

resentful [ree ZENT fuhl] *adj.* offended; displeased
Paula has some irritating qualities, but try not to feel too <u>resentful</u> of her.

sarcasm [SAHR kazm] *n.* taunting or cutting remarks
<u>Sarcasm</u> can cause much damage because it hurts other people's feelings.

Word List B

begrudge [bee GRUJ] *v.* to feel ill will toward another person
We do not <u>begrudge</u> them their victory; after all, they were the best team.

civilly [SIV uhl ee] *adv.* politely
Although Mr. Bly had a reputation for being rude, he treated us <u>civilly</u>.

evasively [ee VAY siv lee] *adv.* in a tricky way; not straightforwardly
Tim answered us so <u>evasively</u> that we felt sure he was hiding something.

flailing [FLAYL ing] *v.* waving awkwardly
When the lifeguard saw Anita <u>flailing</u> in the surf, he ran to help her.

flinch [FLINCH] *v.* to shrink back; recoil
The sudden loud noise of a backfire made us <u>flinch</u>.

ineptly [in EPT lee] *adv.* awkwardly; incapably; in a clumsy fashion
The new waiter said he had experience, but he handled the dishes <u>ineptly</u>.

weighty [WAYT ee] *adj.* important; solemn
Only the most <u>weighty</u> cases reach the Supreme Court.

wily [WY lee] *adj.* cunning; ingenious
In Native American lore, the figure of Coyote is famous for his <u>wily</u> tricks.

The Crucible, *Act II* by Arthur Miller
Vocabulary Warm-up Exercises

Exercise A *Fill in the blanks, using each word from Word List A only once.*

Many people nowadays seem critical or even [1] _____ about the trend in

America towards a lawsuit-happy society. These days, it does not take a disaster or a(n)

[2] _____ to trigger a lawsuit. On the contrary, even the slightest mistake

or misfortune can lead to a formal action before a judge or [3] _____.

Often a jury is urged to [4] _____ the complaining party for damages.

In such cases, the witnesses may seem angry or [5] _____. Some-

times, however, this appearance of outrage is really part of an overall strategy of

[6] _____. Lawyers often urge their clients not to hesitate or

[7] _____ in presenting the most dramatic picture possible of their plight.

Some commentators on this legal picture have resorted to [8] _____,

pointing out that the only people who seem certain to gain much from these disputes

are the lawyers themselves!

Exercise B *Decide whether each statement below is true or false. Circle T or F, and explain
your answer.*

1. If you felt you deserved a prize, you might *begrudge* its award to someone else.
   T / F _____

2. Enemies insulting each other at the top of their voice are behaving *civilly*.
   T / F _____

3. When you answer a question *evasively*, you are speaking in a straightforward fashion.
   T / F _____

4. Someone *flailing* in the surf is a candidate for rescue by a lifeguard.
   T / F _____

5. Those who *flinch* before a challenge can be said to meet it enthusiastically.
   T / F _____

6. Employees who perform their job *ineptly* are likely to be promoted.
   T / F _____

7. A *weighty* decision deserves much research and consideration beforehand.
   T / F _____

8. A *wily* character should not be trusted.
   T / F _____

The Crucible, *Act II* by Arthur Miller
Reading Warm-up A

Read the following passage. Pay special attention to the underlined words. Then, read it again, and complete the activities. Use a separate sheet of paper for your written answers.

Before Casey won the tennis match, she had no idea that winning something could create so much distress. Her opponent, Belinda, had accused her of calling her serves out when they were in, a level of <u>deceit</u> that Casey would never have stooped to. By now everyone at tennis camp had heard the rumor that Casey was a cheater, a <u>calamity</u> for her reputation as an honest player. Everywhere she went, people greeted her with sneers, called her "The Champ" in voices full of <u>sarcasm</u>.

"You're a better player than everyone here," said her friend Amy, hoping to comfort her. "Belinda is just <u>resentful</u> because she knows she can't beat you fairly."

Casey just shut herself up in her room, though, <u>indignant</u> over how unfairly she was being treated. She also knew that Amy was right: She was the best player, certainly much better than Belinda.

She wished she could think of some way to prove her innocence, but the matches had no referees, no <u>magistrates</u> to appeal to for the right decision. The players would always call their own matches, based on the honor system, and when it came to being honest, Casey would never <u>falter</u>. After all, what would be the point of cheating, when the goal of tennis camp was to improve as a player? Though fiercely competitive, Casey had always tried to <u>compensate</u> by giving her opponents the benefit of the doubt on any close call.

The answer came to her that night as she lay awake in bed: She would challenge Belinda to a rematch. In fact, she would give Belinda a five-point advantage into the match. Whether she won or lost, she would at least clear her name, though she had a feeling she would win.

1. Underline the words in this and the previous sentence that give a clue to the meaning of <u>deceit</u>. Use the word *deceit* in an original sentence.

2. Circle the words in this sentence that give a clue to the meaning of <u>calamity</u>. Is a *calamity* greater or smaller than a setback?

3. Underline the words that give a clue to the meaning of <u>sarcasm</u>. How would a remark full of *sarcasm* sound?

4. Circle the words that offer a clue to the meaning of <u>resentful</u> here. What are two antonyms for the word *resentful*?

5. Underline the words in this sentence that hint at the meaning of <u>indignant</u>. What are two synonyms for *indignant*?

6. Circle the words in this sentence that offer clues to the meaning of <u>magistrates</u>.

7. Underline the words in this and the next sentence that give a clue to the meaning of <u>falter</u>. What are two synonyms for *falter*?

8. Circle the words in this sentence that give a clue to the meaning of <u>compensate</u>. Use the word *compensate* in an original sentence.

The Crucible, *Act II* by Arthur Miller
Reading Warm-up B

Read the following passage. Pay special attention to the underlined words. Then, read it again, and complete the activities. Use a separate sheet of paper for your written answers.

Soon after World War II, two plays swiftly established Arthur Miller as a major new talent in the American theater. The first was *All My Sons* (1947), a drama about a prosperous businessman with a <u>weighty</u> secret that amounts to a burden on his conscience. As the head of an airplane-parts company, Keller has approved the decision to ship out defective equipment. The defective parts led to the deaths of many wartime pilots. Confronted by authorities later, he refuses to <u>flinch</u> or confess to his crime. Instead, he <u>evasively</u> covers up the truth, insisting that he had no part in the matter. Keller's <u>wily</u> strategy fails in the end, however. He is unmasked as a man in whom morality has yielded to greed and ambition for his family.

Miller's second important play of this period was *Death of a Salesman* (1949). Few people today would <u>begrudge</u> this drama the status of an American classic. The play is the story of an aging salesman, Willy Loman, who is <u>flailing</u> in anguish to reconcile his dreams of material success with the reality of failure in his life. Willy has cherished an image of himself as a mover and shaker in his profession. The play, however, shows that he has performed <u>ineptly</u>—a sad victim of his own pretensions and his distortion of the American dream. In the end, we recognize the main character as more of a victim than a hero. After the play's opening night, critics reacted not only <u>civilly</u> but enthusiastically with their reviews, hailing Miller as a sensation, and later that year, the playwright won the Pulitzer Prize for Drama.

1. Underline the words that give a clue to the meaning of <u>weighty</u>. Write a sentence using the word ***weighty***.

2. Circle the words in this sentence that give a clue to the meaning of <u>flinch</u>. What are two synonyms for ***flinch***?

3. Underline the words in this and the previous sentence that hint at the meaning of <u>evasively</u>. Use a word meaning the opposite of ***evasively*** in a sentence.

4. Underline the words in this sentence and the next sentence that give a clue to the meaning of <u>wily</u>. What are two synonyms for ***wily***?

5. Circle the words in this sentence that give a clue to the meaning of <u>begrudge</u>. What do you feel when you do the opposite of ***begrudge***?

6. Underline the words in this sentence that hint at the meaning of <u>flailing</u>.

7. Circle the words that hint at the meaning of <u>ineptly</u>. Use a word meaning the opposite of ***ineptly*** in a sentence.

8. Circle the words in this sentence that hint at the meaning of the word <u>civilly</u>. What is a synonym for ***civilly***? What is an antonym for this word?

The Crucible, *Act II,* by Arthur Miller
Literary Analysis: Allusion

An **allusion** is a reference to some well-known thing or idea. In our society, for example, people often allude to sports phenomena: "This project is the Super Bowl for us." Common allusions often take their reference from the surrounding society, so it's little wonder that the Salem Puritans in *The Crucible* make **Biblical allusions** as knowledgeably and as frequently as we allude to sports

DIRECTIONS: *Use a dictionary or other reference work to explain the italicized allusion in each of the following items.*

1. At the beginning of Act II, a kind of *cold war* exists between John and Elizabeth because of past events.

   _____

   _____

2. Although an honest and strong man, John Proctor has an *Achilles heel*—his relationship to Abigail.

   _____

   _____

3. Something between a *siren* and a *harpy,* Abigail proves to be Proctor's undoing.

   _____

   _____

4. Reverend Hale brings an *ivory-tower* approach to his examination that ill fits the world he finds.

   _____

   _____

5. With the sword of Damocles above his head, Proctor flusters and cannot remember the Ten Commandments.

   _____

   _____

6. When Abigail walks through the courtroom, the crowd *parts like the Red Sea.*

   _____

   _____

Name _____ Date _____

The Crucible, *Act II*, by Arthur Miller
Reading Strategy: Make and Confirm Predictions

As you read a complicated drama such as *The Crucible,* you can use your **background knowledge** to help you **make predictions** about what will happen next in the story. Your background knowledge about life in seventeenth-century New England, along with what you have already observed in the first act of the play, plus your understanding of human nature in general, can help you form predictions about future events in the story. Pay attention to the author's hints about what might be coming up. You can **confirm your predictions** as you read and at the end of the play.

DIRECTIONS: *Before and during your reading of Act II, make predictions about future events in The Crucible in the chart below. Then explain what background knowledge made you think each event might happen. If you can confirm or disprove a prediction by the end of Act II, do so in the third column. You may come back when you have finished reading the entire play to confirm or disprove your other predictions.*

Prediction	Background Knowledge	Confirm or Disprove
1.		
2.		
3.		
4.		
5.		

The Crucible, *Act II,* by Arthur Miller
Vocabulary Builder

Using the Suffix *-ology*

The most common meaning of the suffix *-ology* is "the science or study of." The suffix derives from a Greek word meaning "reason" or "word."

A. DIRECTIONS: *Use a dictionary to discover and define the root of each of the following words. Then write the meaning of the root of each, and explain how the suffix -ology combines with the meaning of the root to make the word.*

1. sociology _____
2. ontology _____
3. entomology _____
4. zoology _____

Using the Word List

ameliorate   avidly   base   deference   pallor   theology

B. DIRECTIONS: *Choose the word or phrase most nearly similar in meaning to the Word List word. Circle the letter of your choice.*

1. pallor:
   A. ease
   B. majesty
   C. paleness
   D. sitting room

2. ameliorate:
   A. nourish
   B. improve
   C. criticize
   D. plot

3. avidly:
   A. rapidly
   B. loftily
   C. eagerly
   D. coolly

4. base:
   A. degraded
   B. faded
   C. safe
   D. planned

5. deference:
   A. distinction
   B. citation
   C. delay
   D. respect

6. theology:
   A. study of legal issues
   B. study of religious philosophy
   C. study of life forms
   D. study of ancient books

Name _____ Date _____

Support for Writing: Persuasive Letter

DIRECTIONS: *You will be writing a persuasive letter in which one character from the play tries to persuade another character to take a different course of action. To help you with your prewriting, review the first two acts of* The Crucible *and choose the character and position you will represent in your persuasive letter. In the chart below, record facts, examples, and personal experiences that can be used to support the course of action you want the reader of your letter to take. Remember that you are writing from the point of view of a character in the play.*

Character and position you will represent:

Evidence to Support Your Position

Facts	Examples	Personal Experience
1.		
2.		
3.		

The Crucible, *Act II,* by Arthur Miller
Enrichment: Film Adaptations

In 1957, Frenchman Raymond Rouleau directed a reasonably successful film version of Arthur Miller's play *The Crucible*. In 1996, American director Nicholas Hytner released his own version starring Daniel Day-Lewis as Proctor and Winona Ryder as Abigail.

With any film adaptation, special considerations have to be made about how to recast a story that was originally meant to be acted out on a stationary, limited stage. Arthur Miller himself worked on the screenplay for Hytner's 1996 production. As he developed the screenplay, Miller had to think in terms of filming on location, multiple and mobile cameras, and elaborate and authentic props and settings.

DIRECTIONS: *Suppose that you are developing your own film adaptation of Act II of* The Crucible. *How will you have to alter the act (if at all) to make it appropriate for modern filming? What additional stage directions will be required? Consider these issues as you answer the following questions.*

1. What is the setting of Act II? Thoroughly describe how the setting will look in your movie. Consider atmosphere, furnishings, lighting, and general dimensions in your response.

   _____

   _____

   _____

   _____

2. What has John Proctor been doing all day? As though you were coaching an actor in rehearsal, describe in detail Proctor's clothing and appearance as well as his manner of moving after a hard day's work.

   _____

   _____

   _____

   _____

3. Mr. Hale is a man of learning; he is different from the Salemites. How will his appearance and mannerisms reflect that difference? Write detailed stage directions for the actor who plays Hale in the scene in which he first enters the Proctors' home.

   _____

   _____

   _____

   _____

Name _____ Date _____

The Crucible, *Act II* by Arthur Miller
Open-Book Test

Short Answer *Write your responses to the questions in this section on the lines provided.*

1. As the Proctors converse in the opening scene of Act II of *The Crucible,* how would you characaterize their relationship? Cite evidence from the play to support your answer.

   _____

   _____

   _____

2. In the early part of Act II of *The Crucible,* Elizabeth tells Proctor that Mary Warren has been to court and speaks of Abigail, the chief accuser, as a saint. Knowing that Mary works for the Proctors, and that Abigail bears a grudge against Proctor, what prediction can you make about the impact of Mary's attitude on her employers?

   _____

   _____

   _____

3. Early in Act II of *The Crucible,* Elizabeth insists that John should go to Salem to testify to the falseness of the witchcraft charges. What does this show about what kind of woman she is?

   _____

   _____

   _____

4. In Act II of *The Crucible,* Hale has been called to Salem to help in determining whether the Devil is taking hold of the community. As Act II progresses, he begins to show signs of inner conflict about his initial assumptions about this issue. Use the graphic organizer to trace Hale's role and his evolving views of the witchcraft scare in Salem.

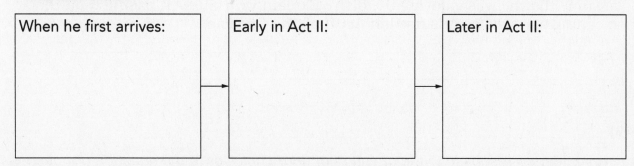

When he first arrives:	Early in Act II:	Later in Act II:

5. In Act II of *The Crucible,* John Proctor initially shows some reluctance to go to Salem to expose the falseness of Abigail's charges of witchcraft. His reluctance is due to an inner conflict over what longstanding issue?

   _____

   _____

   _____

6. When Mary returns to the Proctors' residence in Act II of *The Crucible*, why does she present a doll (poppet) to Elizabeth?

_____

_____

_____

7. In Act II of *The Crucible*, when Hale appears at the Proctors' door, he is described as "different now—drawn a little, and there is a quality of deference, even of guilt, about his manner now." What inner conflict accounts for this change?

_____

_____

_____

8. When Hale quizzes Proctor on the Ten Commandments in Act II of *The Crucible*, Proctor has trouble remembering one of them. Which one does he forget, and why?

_____

_____

_____

9. In Act II of *The Crucible*, when Hale hears that Rebecca Nurse has been charged, he is troubled. Read his allusion below to the story that the Devil was once an angel. What does he intend to point out by making this allusion?

   an hour before the Devil fell, God thought him beautiful in Heaven.

_____

_____

_____

10. If you noticed that your dinner companion was eating his meal avidly, would you assume that he was enjoying the dish? Explain your answer, basing it on the meaning of *avidly* as it is used in Act II of *The Crucible*.

_____

_____

_____

Essay

Write an extended response to the question of your choice or to the question or questions your teacher assigns you.

11. Early in *The Crucible*, Mary Warren seems like a timid and unimportant character. What does Mary learn throughout the first two acts that shows her a way to acquire more power and importance in the community? How does she use this knowledge? Explain Mary's changing role in an essay that cites details from the play.

12. Write an essay in which you explain the influence of Abigail Williams on the events of Act II of *The Crucible.* Does she actually appear in the act? How does her character affect the action and dialogue of the other characters? Consider Abigail's motivations for her actions and their impact on other characters.

13. In an essay, analyze the state of life in Salem at the end of Act II of *The Crucible.* Are most people in the community happy or unhappy? As the witchcraft trial proceeds, are standards of justice in the community rising or falling? What effect is the religious fervor surrounding the trials having on the moral life of the community? Cite evidence from Act II to support your response.

14. **Thinking About the Essential Question: How does literature shape or reflect society?** In *The Crucible*, Miller portrayed the religious hysteria of seventeenth -century Salem as being comparable to the anti-Communist fervor that spurred the divisive investigations of Senator Joseph McCarthy in the early 1950s in the United States. To emphasize the irrational, rigid nature of this fervor, Miller uses religious allusions throughout Act II. In an essay, give examples of at least two of these allusions, and explain how they deepen the reader's understanding of the elements of Puritan society that contributed to the hysteria over witchcraft.

Oral Response

15. Go back to question 6, 8, or 9 or to the question your teacher assigns to you. Take a few minutes to expand your answer and prepare an oral response. Find additional details in Act II of *The Crucible* that support your points. If necessary, make notes to guide your oral response.

The Crucible, *Act II*, by Arthur Miller
Selection Test A

Critical Reading *Identify the letter of the choice that best answers the question.*

____ 1. At the beginning of *The Crucible, Act II*, what is the relationship between the Proctors?

    A. difficult

    B. trusting

    C. comfortable

    D. affectionate

____ 2. In *The Crucible, Act II*, what does John Proctor mean when he says to Elizabeth that no matter what he does, "an everlasting funeral marches around" her heart?

    A. He fears she wishes he were dead.

    B. She is always sad, whatever he does.

    C. He wants to move and she doesn't.

    D. She goes to too many funerals.

____ 3. In *The Crucible, Act II*, what does Mary mean to suggest when she says that the crowd parted for Abigail like the Red Sea parted for the people of Israel?

    A. She compares Abigail's power to the power of Moses.

    B. She compares Abigail's power to the power of witches.

    C. She compares Abigail's power to the power of a queen.

    D. She compares Abigail's power to the size of the Red Sea.

____ 4. In *The Crucible, Act II*, what do these stage directions: *with a smile, to keep her dignity*, reveal about Elizabeth's character?

    A. She is always cheerful and dignified.

    B. She thinks it is undignified to show anger.

    C. She smiles all of the time.

    D. She is tired of trying to be dignified.

____ 5. What is John suggesting about Mary Warren when he says "It's strange work for a Christian girl to hang old women" in *The Crucible, Act II*?

    A. Mary is getting to be powerful.

    B. Mary is religious.

    C. Mary is leaving the church.

    D. Mary is dangerous.

___ 6. In *The Crucible, Act II*, Hale is in shock when the beloved Rebecca Nurse is accused. What does he mean when he alludes to the Devil, saying that: "an hour before the Devil fell, God thought him beautiful in Heaven"?

    A. Beauty and goodness are not the same.

    B. God's will is not for humans to know.

    C. Evil can masquerade as Good.

    D. God's opinions are unimportant.

___ 7. What do you learn about John's character in *The Crucible, Act II*, based on the stage directions that read "[*he*] *is striving against his disgust with HALE and with himself for even answering*"?

    A. He has the answers but hides them.

    B. He is often in conflict with himself.

    C. His feelings for Hale are scornful.

    D. He does not have the answers he needs.

___ 8. What is the "poppet" that is used in *The Crucible*?

    A. It is a toy made for children.

    B. It is a tool of witchcraft.

    C. It is a gift from woman to woman.

    D. It is evidence that one is religious.

___ 9. In *The Crucible, Act II*, Hale appears at the Proctors' door and is described as "*different now—drawn a little, and there is a quality . . . even of guilt, about his manner now.*" What do these stage directions allow you to predict about Hale's future actions?

    A. He will be completely comfortable with all of his actions.

    B. He will continue to respect the Proctors but will still believe they are guilty.

    C. He will become exhausted by his work and will want to quit.

    D. He will be increasingly disturbed by what he has seen in court.

___ 10. Why does Proctor think Abigail accuses his wife of witchcraft in *The Crucible, Act II*?

    A. to show Salem how much power she has

    B. to make John pay for rejecting her

    C. to punish Elizabeth for firing her

    D. to distract attention from her own sins

Vocabulary and Grammar

____ 11. Which word best replaces *pallor* in this sentence: "The *pallor* of her face suggested that she was frightened"?

A. smile

B. eagerness

C. excitement

D. paleness

____ 12. A volume on the subject of *theology* would most likely be concerned with interpreting which of the following books?

A. the Bible

B. an engineering manual

C. a collection of recipes

D. a history of early settlements in New England

____ 13. Which of the following words is CLOSEST in meaning to *deference*?

A. foresight

B. punishment

C. respect

D. similarity

____ 14. Which of the following words is most nearly OPPOSITE in meaning to *avidly*?

A. skillfully

B. enjoyably

C. indifferently

D. peacefully

Essay

15. When John Proctor tries to keep his wife Elizabeth from being dragged off to court in act II of *The Crucible*, Reverend Hale says, "The court is just," as if he is saying it is not his problem and that someone else will decide her fate. Do you think Hale should have taken on more responsibility? In a brief essay, describe what you believe to be the right path for Hale.

16. In *The Crucible*, Mary Warren seems like a quiet and powerless character at first. What does Mary learn in Act I, and now in Act II, that shows her a way to achieve more power? How does she use this knowledge? Write a brief essay to answer these questions.

17. **Thinking About the Essential Question: How does literature shape or reflect society?** In *The Crucible*, Miller portrayed the religious hysteria of seventeenth -century Salem as being comparable to the anti-Communist fervor that spurred the divisive investigations of Senator Joseph McCarthy in the early 1950s in the United States. To emphasize the irrational, rigid nature of this fervor, Miller uses religious allusions throughout Act II. In an essay, give examples of at least two of these allusions, and explain how they deepen the reader's understanding of the elements of Puritan society that contributed to the hysteria over witchcraft.

The Crucible, *Act II*, by Arthur Miller
Selection Test B

Critical Reading *Identify the letter of the choice that best completes the statement or answers the question.*

____ 1. What is the setting of Act II of *The Crucible*?
A. the following day at the home of John and Elizabeth Proctor
B. Reverend Parris's home, about a week after the accusations of witchcraft have begun
C. the Proctors' home, eight days after the girls have begun to accuse people
D. the Salem meeting house, just before Abigail's trial

____ 2. Based on the relationship between John and Elizabeth Proctor portrayed at the beginning of Act II of *The Crucible*, you can reasonably predict that, as the witch hysteria deepens, they will
A. turn on each other.
B. turn on their friends.
C. support each other.
D. lose faith in God.

____ 3. Which of the following sentences best describes the relationship between John and Elizabeth Proctor at the opening of Act II?
A. They are warm and affectionate.
B. They seem not to care about each other.
C. They seem ill at ease together.
D. They are hostile and bitter toward each other.

____ 4. When Elizabeth says to Proctor in the second act of *The Crucible*, "The magistrate sits in your heart that judges you," she means that Proctor
A. carries the knowledge of his own guilt.
B. is too quick to judge himself.
C. should speak more openly about his thoughts.
D. knows that she loves him and forgives him.

____ 5. Proctor's comment to Mary Warren in Act II of *The Crucible*, "It's strange work for a Christian girl to hang old women," implies that he thinks Mary's behavior is
A. cruel.
B. hypocritical.
C. cowardly.
D. rash.

____ 6. Which of the following words best characterizes Mary Warren in *The Crucible, Act II*?
A. pious
B. jealous
C. gullible
D. vicious

_____ 7. What is Mary's motive in giving the "poppet" to Elizabeth in the second act of *The Crucible*?
A. She wants to make friends with Elizabeth.
B. She wants Elizabeth to see her as an innocent girl.
C. She wants to plant evidence of witchcraft in Elizabeth's house.
D. She wants to make peace with Elizabeth after disobeying her.

_____ 8. In the second act of *The Crucible* when Mary says that the crowd parted for Abigail like the sea for Israel, she makes
A. a comparison to politics.
B. an allusion to the Bible.
C. eventual trouble for Abigail.
D. a bigoted joke.

_____ 9. When Hale appears at the Proctors' door in Act II of *The Crucible*, he is described as "different now—drawn a little, and there is a quality of deference, even of guilt, about his manner now." What accounts for this change?
A. He has seen events go beyond his expectations in Salem.
B. He no longer believes in witchcraft but must proceed.
C. He feels guilty that he has also felt desire for Abigail.
D. He fears that even he may be at risk.

_____ 10. Hale's interview with Proctor in *The Crucible*, *Act II* reveals Hale to be
A. blinded by power.
B. troubled but rigid.
C. kind but foolish.
D. tolerant and open.

_____ 11. Why does Proctor forget the commandment forbidding adultery in the second act of *The Crucible*?
A. He has a guilty conscience.
B. He has never properly learned the commandments.
C. He believes that it is an unjust commandment.
D. He is afraid of revealing his own sin.

_____ 12. In *The Crucible*, *Act II* Rebecca Nurse is charged, and Hale is troubled. What does he intend to point out by this allusion to the story that the Devil was once an angel?
    an hour before the Devil fell, God thought him beautiful in Heaven.

A. that people sometimes change as they get older
B. that even beauty is no indicator of goodness
C. the impossibility of determining God's will
D. the powerful skills of deception the Devil has

_____ 13. In the second act of *The Crucible*, Proctor calls Hale "Pontius Pilate." Proctor's intention is to
A. imply that Hale shares pagan beliefs.
B. charge Hale with manufacturing evidence.
C. send Hale to the Bible for study and thought.
D. accuse Hale of doing injustice by doing nothing.

_____ **14.** In Act II of *The Crucible* Proctor believes that Abigail accuses Elizabeth of witchcraft because
   A. Elizabeth treated Abigail harshly.
   B. Abigail wants to punish Proctor for rejecting her.
   C. Abigail fears that Elizabeth will denounce her for seducing Proctor.
   D. Abigail wants to distract attention from the episode in the woods.

Vocabulary

_____ **15.** If one does something *avidly*, one does it
   A. eagerly.
   B. shamefully.
   C. quickly.
   D. reluctantly.

_____ **16.** If one shows *deference*, one shows
   A. ignorance.
   B. disregard.
   C. respect.
   D. knowledge.

_____ **17.** Which of the following would most likely want to *ameliorate* conditions of injustice and inequality?
   A. a dictator
   B. a warrior
   C. an electrical engineer
   D. a social reformer

_____ **18.** Which of the following is the likeliest explanation for a case of extreme *pallor*?
   A. too much exercise
   B. a love of outdoor sports
   C. an aversion to sunlight
   D. overindulgence in food

Essay

19. Abigail Williams does not appear in Act II of *The Crucible*, but she has cast a long shadow from Act I, and her importance in Act II is powerful. Write an essay in which you tell about the significance of Abigail Williams in Act II, explaining her effect on characters and actions in this part of the play.

20. In Act II, Mary Warren gives Elizabeth Proctor a doll, a "poppet," which she says is a present. The shifts in blame surrounding the doll become a major factor in the actions of Act II. How does Miller use this token to create drama in *The Crucible*? Write an essay that explains the role of the poppet in the plot. Include how it is viewed, the plot developments surrounding it, and what characters do and don't know about the real responsibility for it.

21. One pivotal character in Act II has an apparently weak character as a human being. What motivates Mary Warren throughout this part of *The Crucible*? What does she want? How is it that she becomes such a focal point? Write an essay in which you assess the nature of Mary Warren as she appears in Act II, and explain how her character illustrates some of the play's concerns. Use examples from the play to support your ideas.

22. **Thinking About the Essential Question: How does literature shape or reflect society?** In Act II of *The Crucible*, Miller uses religious allusions to portray different elements of Puritan society. What is the overall effect these allusions? Which characters use religious allusions, and for what purpose? In an essay, give examples of at least two of these allusions, and explain how they deepen the reader's understanding of this society.

Study these words from the selection. Then, complete the activities.

Word List A

anonymity [a nuh NIM uh tee] *n.* condition of being nameless; obscurity
   The official said she would be quoted only on condition of <u>anonymity</u>.

baffled [BAF uhld] *v.* puzzled; mystified
   Sue's behavior <u>baffled</u> us; we could see no reason or motive for it.

disruption [dis RUP shuhn] *n.* disturbance
   An accident in the tunnel led to a major <u>disruption</u> of the traffic flow.

dutiful [DYOO ti fuhl] *adj.* obedient; conscientious
   Polly had a <u>dutiful</u> attitude toward her parents, never violating their wishes.

extravagance [eks TRAV uh guhns] *n.* lavish show or expenditure
   Living his life with <u>extravagance</u>, he soon faced the prospect of bankruptcy.

perjury [PUR juhr ee] *n.* lying under oath
   If you are convicted of <u>perjury</u>, you could be fined and imprisoned.

prodigious [pruh DIJ uhs] *adj.* very large; remarkable
   We were able to reach the mountaintop only with <u>prodigious</u> effort.

random [RAN duhm] *adj.* by chance; haphazard
   That poll was taken on a <u>random</u> basis, with respondents chosen by chance.

Word List B

apprehensively [ap ree HEN siv lee] *adv.* fearfully
   Carla lived <u>apprehensively</u>, as she always worried about her health.

befuddled [bee FUHD uhld] *v.* confused
   In his tennis matches, Ben often <u>befuddled</u> his opponents with drop shots.

connivance [kuh NYV uhns] *n.* cooperation in a wrongful activity
   The <u>connivance</u> of several employees helped the criminals rob the bank.

lurks [LERKS] *v.* stays hidden; exists unobserved
   Walking at night, Otis always fears that a mugger <u>lurks</u> in every corner.

placidly [PLA sid lee] *adv.* peacefully
   After drinking a bowl of milk, the cat <u>placidly</u> lay down by the fireside.

ploys [PLOYS] *n.* tricks; strategies
   Renzo learned new <u>ploys</u> that would improve his chess game.

qualm [KWAHLM] *n.* sudden feeling of doubt; twinge of conscience
   Chet hadn't the slightest <u>qualm</u> in asking his boss for a raise.

remorseless [ree MORS luhs] *adj.* pitiless; merciless
   The cat seemed <u>remorseless</u> in its stalking of the small bird in the shrubbery.

The Crucible, *Act III* by Arthur Miller
Vocabulary Warm-up Exercises

Exercise A *Fill in the blanks, using each word from Word List A only once.*

When she first arrived here from her native India, Ronu was [1] _____—
totally confused—by the [2] _____ and grandeur of the holiday decorations
at the shopping mall. As a junior reporter for the local newspaper, Ronu carried out
[3] _____ and conscientious interviews with some of the merchants at the
mall. A few participated only on condition of [4] _____, asking Ronu not to
publish their names. From her informants, Ronu discovered that holiday time resulted in a
significant [5] _____ of many merchants' normal routine. Merchants told her
that special holiday decorations cost them [6] _____ amounts of money. The
decorative style for any particular year seemed to be completely [7] _____,
following no consistent pattern. "I would commit [8] _____ if I told you that
all this is unnecessary," one merchant said, "but it certainly is a big cost for an uncertain
result."

Exercise B *Revise each sentence so that the underlined vocabulary word is logical. Be sure to
keep the vocabulary word in your revision.*

Example: Paul looked around <u>apprehensively</u>, for he was confident about the team's
success.
Paul looked around <u>apprehensively</u>, for he was doubtful about the team's success.

1. The lecture was so clear and easy to understand that it completely <u>befuddled</u> us.

   _____

2. The thief was working alone, and his <u>connivance</u> with several conspirators was plain.

   _____

3. The pack of hyenas <u>lurks</u> in plain view, and the prey can hardly fail to see them.

   _____

4. Thelma accepted the news <u>placidly</u>, breaking into a torrent of tears.

   _____

5. We later discovered that the salesperson's <u>ploys</u> were full of integrity.

   _____

6. If you feel a <u>qualm</u> beforehand, it is perfectly all right to take that action.

   _____

7. The <u>remorseless</u> villain felt guilt and regret for his crimes.

   _____

The Crucible, *Act III* by Arthur Miller
Reading Warm-up A

Read the following passage. Pay special attention to the underlined words. Then, read it again, and complete the activities. Use a separate sheet of paper for your written answers.

The excessive <u>extravagance</u> of Senator Joseph McCarthy's Senate investigations of the early 1950s captured headlines. However, an equally important group was active in the House of Representatives at the same time. This was the House Un-American Activities Committee (HUAC). In 1947, this committee started to devote <u>prodigious</u> amounts of energy and effort to uncover communist influences in the Hollywood motion picture industry.

At first, 41 so-called "friendly" witnesses testified voluntarily. These people may have been puzzled or <u>baffled</u> by the committee's questions. Possibly they feared a black mark or a <u>disruption</u> of their careers if they did not adopt an obliging, <u>dutiful</u> attitude toward the lawmakers. In any case, they gave the committee some names of people who, they said, belonged to left-wing organizations or were known to have left-wing views.

When called to testify, some of these witnesses agreed to cooperate by naming others. Others, however, invoked the Fifth Amendment's protection against self-incrimination and refused to give evidence. These witnesses faced a cruel choice. If they denied membership in a suspicious group that they had belonged to, they could be charged with <u>perjury</u>. If they admitted membership, they would have been forced to name other members, like those accused of witchcraft in Miller's *The Crucible*. In the end, many of the "Hollywood Ten," as this group was called, went to jail.

Eventually, over 300 writers, actors, directors, and technicians were placed on a blacklist drawn up by the Hollywood film studios. These people were either denied employment or had to work in <u>anonymity</u>, receiving no credit by name. Perhaps the most frightening part of this persecution was its <u>random</u> character. Disaster could strike a person anytime, and for almost any reason.

1. Underline the word that gives a clue to the meaning of <u>extravagance</u>. Use a word meaning the opposite of *extravagance* in a sentence of your own.

2. Circle the words in this sentence that give a clue to the meaning of <u>prodigious</u>. What are two synonyms of *prodigious*?

3. Underline the word in this sentence that gives a clue to the meaning of <u>baffled</u>. What is an antonym for *baffled*?

4. Underline the words that hint at the meaning of <u>disruption</u>. What is a synonym for this word?

5. Circle the word in this sentence that offers a clue to the meaning of <u>dutiful</u>. Write a sentence about someone acting in a *dutiful* fashion.

6. Underline the words in this sentence that hint at the meaning of <u>perjury</u>. What should you do to avoid being charged with *perjury*?

7. Underline the words in this sentence that hint at the meaning of <u>anonymity</u>.

8. Underline the words in the next sentence that give a clue to the meaning of <u>random</u>. What is a synonym for *random*?

Name _____ Date _____

Read the following passage. Pay special attention to the underlined words. Then, read it again, and complete the activities. Use a separate sheet of paper for your written answers.

During the 1600s, the labor force in the American colonies consisted largely of indentured servants. In this system, would-be emigrants from England to the New World sold themselves to an agent or ship's captain. The contract, called an "indenture," would then be sold to a buyer in the colonies. In return for the cost of the ocean passage, and also for food, clothing, and shelter, the servant would be obliged to work for a period of four to seven years.

Some indentured servants, no doubt, quietly and placidly expected that such strategies or ploys would successfully establish them in a land of opportunity. When these servants arrived in their new surroundings, however, they may have looked around them apprehensively. The realities of indentured servitude may have easily confused or befuddled them. Perhaps they had been misled, the victims of connivance between purchasers and agents. In any case, their work as household servants or farmhands was hard, the hours were long, and masters were often cruel and remorseless. Although indentured servitude has falsely been likened to apprenticeship, a more accurate comparison lurks beneath the surface: The system quite closely resembled slavery. Runaway servants were ruthlessly pursued. Masters who caught them did not suffer a qualm of conscience in extending the servant's term of service by several years. Indentured servants who misbehaved could be whipped. During the time of a person's indenture, he or she was considered as the master's personal property, and contracts could be inherited or sold. While under contract, an indentured servant was barred from marrying or having children.

1. Underline the word in this sentence that hints at the meaning of underlined placidly. What is an antonym for *placidly*?

2. Circle the words in this sentence that hint at the meaning of underlined ploys. What are two *ploys* a salesperson might use to make a sale?

3. Underline the words in this and the next sentence that hint at the meaning of underlined apprehensively. Use *apprehensively* in an original sentence.

4. Underline the words in this sentence that hint at the meaning of underlined befuddled. Write a sentence telling how a *befuddled* person might feel.

5. Circle the words in this sentence that hint at the meaning of underlined connivance. Are the connotations of this word positive or negative?

6. Circle the word in this sentence that gives a good clue to the meaning of underlined remorseless. What is an antonym for *remorseless*?

7. Underline the words in this sentence that hint at the meaning of underlined lurks. What is a synonym for *lurks*?

8. Underline the words in this sentence that hint at the meaning of underlined qualm.

Name _____ Date _____

The Crucible, *Act III*, by Arthur Miller
Literary Analysis: Dramatic and Verbal Irony

In real life, things are often different from what they seem. When this occurs—both in life and in literature—it is called **irony.** Writers and playwrights make use of two forms of irony to surprise and entertain their readers and viewers.

In **dramatic irony,** the characters think one thing to be true, but the audience knows something else to be true. This creates interest and tension in a story or play. In **verbal irony,** words seem to say one thing but mean something quite different.

DIRECTIONS: *Explain the verbal or dramatic irony that exists in the following passages.*

1. Upon hearing Proctor's and Mary's statements, Danforth is shaken by the idea that Abigail and the girls could be frauds. Danforth challenges Proctor with this: "Now, Mr. Proctor, before I decide whether I shall hear you or not, it is my duty to tell you this. We burn a hot fire here; it melts down all concealment."

   _____

   _____

   _____

2. Parris, to save his own reputation, is eager to support Abigail's claims and the court's decisions. He accuses several people of making attacks upon the court. Hale's response is this: "Is every defense an attack upon the court? Can no one—?"

   _____

   _____

   _____

3. Proctor reminds Mary of a biblical story about the angel Raphael and a boy named Tobias. In the story, the boy frees a woman from the devil and cures his father of blindness.

   _____

   _____

   _____

4. Proctor is informed that Elizabeth has said she is pregnant. Proctor says he knows nothing of it but states that his wife does not lie. Later, when questioned about her husband's fidelity, Elizabeth lies, thinking she is protecting her husband and his reputation.

   _____

   _____

   _____

Name _____ Date _____

Reading Strategy: Evaluate Arguments

Evaluate arguments in the court scene in Act III by determining if the evidence used to support the accusation is believable and logical. Watch for **logical fallacies,** which are ideas or arguments that appear logical even though they are based on completely incorrect assumptions. For example, Judge Danforth explains his reasoning for believing the accusations of witchcraft. Though his thoughts seem logical, all of them are based on a mistaken premise.

DIRECTIONS: *Fill in the chart to help you evaluate the arguments of each character in the trial scene.*

Character	Argument	Logical?	Believable Evidence?
1. Judge Danforth			
2. John Proctor			
3. Reverend Parris			
4. Reverend Hale			
5. Giles Corey			

Name _____ Date _____

Vocabulary Builder

Using Legal Terms

Scenes that take place in courtrooms are usually full of special words and phrases that have particular meaning for the judges, lawyers, and others present. This is true of Act III of *The Crucible.*

A. DIRECTIONS: *Find out what the following words mean. Then use each in a sentence about the action in Act III.*

1. affidavit _____

2. deposition _____

3. prosecutor _____

4. warrant _____

Using the Word List

anonymity   contentious   deposition   effrontery   imperceptible   incredulously

B. DIRECTIONS: *Choose the word or phrase that is most nearly* opposite *in meaning to the Word List word. Circle the letter of your choice.*

1. anonymity:
   A. obscurity
   B. fame
   C. solitude
   D. recklessness

2. contentious:
   A. competitive
   B. agreeable
   C. inclusive
   D. smoldering

3. deposition:
   A. shifting
   B. trial
   C. putting in place
   D. informal chat

4. effrontery:
   A. decoration
   B. rearward
   C. politeness
   D. lying

5. imperceptible:
   A. obvious
   B. untouchable
   C. understandable
   D. off track

6. incredulously:
   A. contemptuously
   B. dismissively
   C. skeptically
   D. trustfully

The Crucible, *Act III,* by Arthur Miller
Support for Writing: "Friend of the Court" Brief

DIRECTIONS: *You will be writing an Amicus Curiae—or "Friend of the Court"—brief, as if you are a respected member of a neighboring community who is advising the Salem court. To help you with your prewriting, fill in the chart below by stating your position and recording detailed supporting evidence and counterarguments.*

My position regarding the Salem witch trials is:

Evidence that supports my position:	1. 2. 3.
Arguments that might be made against my position:	1. 2. 3.
How I will defend my position:	1. 2. 3.

Name _____ Date _____

The Crucible, *Act III,* by Arthur Miller
Enrichment: Career as a Lawyer

Act III of *The Crucible* gives us Miller's interpretation of how the American colonists may have felt toward court proceedings, judges, and legal matters in general. Then, just as now, courtrooms were places where people were morally obligated to tell the truth. Judges were powerful people who commanded the respect of those around them. There were also procedures to follow, such as the lawful way to make an arrest or to present evidence.

In modern America, the legal system establishes rules that affect personal, social, and business activities, and provides a way to resolve disputes.

Lawyers make up the largest portion of those who pursue legal careers. Most lawyers choose to specialize in a certain kind of practice. Real estate lawyers, for example, draw up legal documents that have to do with the buying and selling of land and buildings. Probate lawyers help clients draw up wills, deeds of trust, and other documents connected with the distribution of an estate. Corporate lawyers advise large companies of their rights, obligations, and privileges under corporate law. And securities and exchange lawyers oversee the activities of individuals and corporations that trade in corporate securities and stock.

A lawyer may become a judge either through election or appointment. Judges listen to case presentations, accept or reject evidence, and settle disputes between lawyers. They also instruct juries and decide on punishments for persons found guilty of crimes.

Behind the scenes, supporting the work of the lawyers and judges, are thousands of trained legal assistants, called paralegals. They assist lawyers with interviewing witnesses, conducting legal research, drafting documents, and so on. In addition legal researchers and editors prepare thousands of legal publications in the United States every year. Organizing those legal publications are law librarians who staff both private and public law libraries.

DIRECTIONS: *Use the information on this page to draw conclusions about the pursuit of a legal career.*

1. What workplace skills do you think would be most useful to a person who wants to be a legal assistant?

   _____

   _____

2. In addition to a law degree, what other skills or interests would aid a securities and exchange lawyer in his or her job?

   _____

   _____

3. What personal qualities and workplace skills do you think a judge should have?

   _____

   _____

4. Of the legal areas mentioned on this page, which field or specialty is the most appealing to you? Why?

   _____

   _____

Name _____ Date _____

The Crucible, *Act III* by Arthur Miller
Open-Book Test

Short Answer *Write your responses to the questions in this section on the lines provided.*

1. *The Crucible* is a complex play with numerous characters who bring conflicting motives to the witch hunt that envelops Salem. It can often be helpful in understanding such a play to list the main characters and sort them out by their motives in relation to the main plot developments, in this case the witch trials. Use the following chart to classify some of the main characters' attitudes toward the witch hunt at the beginning of Act III of *The Crucible* by placing a check mark for each character in the appropriate column: For the Witch Hunt, Against the Witch Hunt, or Undecided. In each case, briefly explain your classification of the character.

Character	For the Witch Hunt	Against the Witch Hunt	Undecided	Explanation
Thomas Putnam				
John Proctor				
Mary Warren				
Reverend Hale				
Abigail Williams				
Giles Cory				
Danforth				

2. What can the audience conclude about the intentions of the court from Judge Hathorne's questioning of Martha Corey at the beginning of Act III of *The Crucible*? Explain why this examination is an example of dramatic irony.

_____

_____

_____

_____

3. In Act III of *The Crucible*, Francis Nurse attempts to convince the judges that the girls who have claimed to be possessed by witches are frauds. Hathorne's response is, "This is contempt, sir, contempt!" Hathorne's response is an example of what kind of irony? Briefly explain your answer.

_____

_____

4. In Act III of *The Crucible*, what is Proctor's main motive for bringing Mary Warren to court?

_____

_____

_____

5. What role does Parris play in the proceedings in Act III of *The Crucible*? What kinds of arguments and statements does he typically make to try to discredit the testimony of those who oppose him? Cite at least one example to support your answer.

_____

_____

_____

_____

_____

6. In Act III of *The Crucible*, Danforth mentions a rumor that Elizabeth Proctor is pregnant and uses this as a basis for giving her at least a year's reprieve from execution. What does this offer show about Danforth's character? What does Proctor's refusal of the offer show about his motives in presenting counterevidence to the court?

_____

_____

_____

_____

7. In Act III of *The Crucible*, Proctor presents to Danforth a testament from ninety-one citizens attesting to the good character of Rebecca Nurse and Elizabeth Proctor. How would you evaluate Danforth's response that all ninety-one should be arrested for "examination"? What is he trying to achieve with this response?

_____

_____

_____

_____

8. Throughout Act III of *The Crucible*, Hale shows himself to be a man struggling over the increasingly obvious travesties of the court's prosecutions. Explain what Hale means when he declares, "I dare not take a life without there be a proof so immaculate that no slightest qualm of conscience may doubt it."

_____

_____

_____

9. Near the end of Act III of *The Crucible*, after Proctor has confessed his adultery with Abigail and Mary has been intimidated into disowning her testimony on Elizabeth's behalf, Proctor tells Danforth, "God damns our kind especially, and we will burn, we will burn together." What does Proctor mean by this statement?

_____

_____

10. If you explained to your teacher why you failed to do your homework assignment, and your teacher looked at you incredulously, is it likely that the teacher has believed your explanation? Why or why not? Base your answer on the meaning of *incredulously* as it is used in Act III of *The Crucible*.

_____

_____

Essay

Write an extended response to the question of your choice or to the question or questions your teacher assigns you.

11. In Act III of *The Crucible*, there are changes in the behavior and attitudes of Reverend Hale and Mary Warren. In an essay, discuss these changes and the impact they have on events in Salem and on other characters in the play.

12. Reverend Hale's character continues to evolve throughout Act III of *The Crucible*. In an essay, analyze Hale's role in Act III. Is he more of a friend of those who have been accused or a friend of the court? How does his behavior in Act III compare to his behavior in the previous two acts? Support your answer with details from the play.

13. In Act III of *The Crucible*, John Danforth emerges as the most powerful and influential figure in the play. In an essay, analyze the character of John Danforth. What kind of man is he? Is there any evidence that he has any reservations about the proceedings? If so, why doesn't he stop the whole process? Support your answer with details from the play.

14. **Thinking About the Essential Question: How does literature shape or reflect society?** In the Bible worshiped by the Puritans of seventeenth-century Salem, one of the Ten Commandments reads, "Thou shalt not lie." Yet the intensely religious community of Salem is caught up in a web of lies and false accusations as the witchcraft hysteria overtakes the town. What does Act III of The Crucible reveal about the value the citizens of Salem place on truth-telling, and what does their view of this matter says about the kind of religion they practice? Develop your answer in an essay supported by details from the text.

Oral Response

15. Go back to question 4, 5, or 6 or to the question your teacher assigns to you. Take a few minutes to expand your answer and prepare an oral response. Find additional details in Act III of *The Crucible* that support your points. If necessary, make notes to guide your oral response.

Name _____ Date _____

The Crucible, *Act III*, by Arthur Miller
Selection Test A

Critical Reading *Identify the letter of the choice that best answers the question.*

_____ 1. As *The Crucible, Act III* begins, what categories do Martha and Hathorne represent?
  A. Christians and non-Christians
  B. liars and people who do not lie
  C. accusers and those who are accused
  D. witches and non-witches

_____ 2. Why does John Proctor bring Mary Warren to court in *The Crucible, Act III*?
  A. to prove he does not believe in witches
  B. to prove the court is not a just court
  C. to save Elizabeth from judgment
  D. to show that Parris is a fraud

_____ 3. How does Proctor behave toward Danforth during his questioning in *The Crucible, Act III*?
  A. joyfully
  B. meanly
  C. lovingly
  D. respectfully

_____ 4. Which of these characters in *The Crucible, Act III* unknowingly does harm by cooperating in an unjust process?
  A. Ezekiel Cheever   C. John Proctor
  B. Mary Warren   D. Reverend Parris

_____ 5. Why is Giles Corey's refusal to name names important in *The Crucible, Act III*?
  A. It shows him to be someone guilty of non-cooperation.
  B. It shows that he is the one who acts honorably, not the court.
  C. It shows that he does not have as much knowledge as he thought.
  D. It shows that the court has asked him a question too difficult to answer.

_____ 6. Why does John Proctor say to Frances Nurse in *The Crucible, Act III* that he wishes she had some "evil" in her so that she could "know" him?
  A. He wishes she were not so good, because she makes him look bad.
  B. He wishes she were evil so that she would be arrested.
  C. He wishes he had never met her, because she hates him.
  D. He wishes she were enough like him so she understood him.

____ 7. Why is Elizabeth's denial that John is lustful an example of dramatic irony in *The Crucible, Act III*?

A. She says it to protect John but ends up condemning him.

B. She says it to keep herself from being embarrassed in public.

C. She says it because she does not know he has been unfaithful.

D. She says it to prove that Abigail is unimportant to John.

____ 8. In *The Crucible, Act III*, why does Mary Warren change her testimony and join Abigail and the other girls?

A. She is tormented by Danforth's questions and accusations.

B. She is frightened when Abigail pretends to be attacked by Mary's spirit.

C. She is disgusted by Proctor's admission of his relationship with Abigail.

D. She is afraid that Abigail will no longer be her friend.

____ 9. Why is the use of the phrase "out of her infinite charity" to describe Abigail an example of dramatic irony in *The Crucible, Act III*?

A. The audience is unaware of Abigail's true character.

B. The audience is completely aware of Abigail's true character.

C. The audience realizes that Abigail has become a better person.

D. The audience expects Abigail to accuse Mary of witchcraft.

____ 10. Based on the evidence presented through Act III of *The Crucible*, which of the following best characterizes the claim that Abigail and the Reverend Parris are the two most villainous characters in the play?

A. There is not enough evidence to decide this claim one way or another.

B. The evidence clearly points instead to Proctor and Hale as the true villains.

C. The claim is false, because Abigail and the Reverend Parris are actually sincerely concerned for the welfare of others.

D. Based on the evidence presented, the claim is sound.

Vocabulary

____ 11. Which word best replaces *contentious* in this sentence: "The *contentious* witness was told to stop disagreeing with the judge"?

A. respectful

B. frightening

C. argumentative

D. pale

_____ 12. Which of the following words is most nearly OPPOSITE in meaning to
        incredulously?
        A. trustfully
        B. spitefully
        C. primarily
        D. legally

_____ 13. In which of the following settings would you most likely encounter a *deposition*?
        A. church
        B. stadium
        C. courtroom
        D. laboratory

_____ 14. Which word is CLOSEST in meaning to *effrontery*?
        A. intelligence
        B. rudeness
        C. seriousness
        D. buffoonery

Essay

15. In the third act of *The Crucible*, Abigail and the other girls persuade Danforth that
    they see the Devil and other evil spirits. Is Abigail like the other girls? How are they
    like her, and how are they different from her? Write a brief essay to answer these
    questions.

16. In Act III of *The Crucible*, Danforth first tells the girls that the Bible condemns a
    witch to death and a liar to hell. Then he asks them to tell the truth about whether
    they have either practiced witchcraft or lied about practicing witchcraft. In a brief
    essay, explain why Danforth has made it impossible for the girls to tell the truth
    about what they have done.

17. **Thinking About the Essential Question: How does literature shape or reflect
    society?** In the Bible worshiped by the Puritans of seventeenth-century Salem,
    one of the Ten Commandments reads, "Thou shalt not lie." Yet the intensely
    religious community of Salem is caught up in a web of lies and false accusations
    as the witchcraft hysteria overtakes the town. What does Act III of The Crucible
    reveal about the value the citizens of Salem place on truth-telling, and what does
    their view of this matter says about the kind of religion they practice? Develop
    your answer in an essay supported by details from the text.

The Crucible, *Act III*, by Arthur Miller
Selection Test B

Critical Reading *Identify the letter of the choice that best completes the statement or answers the question.*

_____ 1. What can the audience infer from Judge Hathorne's questioning of Martha Corey at the beginning of Act III of *The Crucible*?
   A. The court is determined to uncover the truth at any cost.
   B. Martha Corey's love of reading is the source of the accusations against her.
   C. The court presumes that anyone accused of witchcraft is guilty.
   D. Even the most respected citizens have come under suspicion.

_____ 2. In the third act of *The Crucible*, Francis Nurse tells the judges that the girls are frauds. Hathorne's response is, "This is contempt, sir, contempt!" What is this an example of?
   A. verbal irony
   B. dramatic irony
   C. sarcasm
   D. foreshadowing

_____ 3. What is Proctor's main purpose in bringing Mary Warren to court in the third act of *The Crucible*?
   A. to strengthen her character
   B. to discredit Reverend Parris
   C. to save his wife from condemnation
   D. to demonstrate the illegality of the court's proceedings

_____ 4. During the presentation of the evidence in Act III of *The Crucible*, Proctor's behavior toward Danforth can best be described as
   A. crafty.   C. evasive.
   B. defiant.   D. respectful.

_____ 5. Which character represents the tactic of making personal attacks on the integrity of witnesses in the third act of *The Crucible*?
   A. Herrick   C. Hathorne
   B. Danforth   D. Parris

_____ 6. As the action of the third act of *The Crucible* proceeds, the allusion to the story of Raphael and Tobias becomes ironic because
   A. the developments contradict the message of the story.
   B. the story is revealed to be false.
   C. the developments show that the characters have misunderstood the story.
   D. certain characters twist the meaning of the story to suit their own purposes.

_____ 7. Which type of character is represented by Ezekiel Cheever in *The Crucible*, Act III?
   A. the witness who uses the investigation as an instrument of personal vengeance
   B. the witness who suffers for his refusal to incriminate others
   C. the naive witness who harms others by cooperating in an unjust process
   D. the public figure who misuses the power of office

_____ **8.** In *The Crucible*, Act III, why is Parris's charge of conspiracy effective?
   A. It gives a plausible explanation for the divisions in the parish.
   B. It appeals to Danforth's fears of subversion.
   C. It feeds Danforth's sense of his own importance.
   D. It plays on Danforth's personal antagonism to ward Giles Corey and Francis Nurse.

_____ **9.** What motivates Hale's attempt to intervene on behalf of Proctor in the third act of *The Crucible*?
   A. Hale's admiration for the Proctors
   B. Hale's commitment to the truth
   C. Hale's questioning of Danforth's integrity
   D. Hale's dislike of Parris

_____ **10.** What development causes Mary Warren to recant her confession and rejoin Abigail and the other girls in Act III of *The Crucible*?
   A. John Proctor's confession of his relationship with Abigail
   B. Judge Danforth's persistent questions
   C. the confusion about Elizabeth Proctor's "poppets"
   D. Abigail's pretending to be attacked by Mary's spirit

_____ **11.** Why is the phrase "out of her infinite charity" in the following passage from the third act of *The Crucible* an example of verbal irony?

   MARY WARREN, *screaming at him*: No, I love God; I go your way no more. I love God, I bless God. *Sobbing, she rushes to* ABIGAIL. Abby, Abby I'll never hurt you more! *They all watch, as* ABIGAIL, *out of her infinite charity, reaches out and draws the sobbing* MARY *to her, and then looks up to* DANFORTH.

   A. It contradicts the audience's knowledge about Abigail's true nature.
   B. It presents a piece of information of which the audience is not aware.
   C. It emphasizes Abigail's ability to be forgiving under stress.
   D. It reveals Abigail's weakening condition.

_____ **12.** What does Proctor mean when he tells Danforth, "God damns our kind especially, and we will burn, we will burn together" in *The Crucible*, Act III?
   A. We who commit wrongs knowingly are the most guilty of all.
   B. The whole community will suffer damnation for the injustices being committed here.
   C. Danforth will suffer damnation if he condemns Proctor to death.
   D. Although women are accused of witchcraft, men are greater sinners.

_____ **13.** Which of the following pairs of categories would be the least useful way of classifying the characters in Act III of *The Crucible*?
   A. Christians and non-Christians
   B. accusers and accused
   C. believers in witchcraft and nonbelievers in witchcraft
   D. liars and truth tellers

___ 14. What character in *The Crucible*, Act III, does *not* fit into one of these categories: accuser, accused, court official?
   A. John Proctor
   B. Mary Warren
   C. Reverend Hale
   D. Giles Corey

Vocabulary

___ 15. A *contentious* person is someone who is prone to
   A. helpfulness
   B. disagreements
   C. laziness
   D. accidents

___ 16. Which of the following is most nearly OPPOSITE in meaning to *imperceptible*?
   A. noticeable
   B. unbreakable
   C. stubborn
   D. permanent

___ 17. Which of the following would be most typical of an author who craves *anonymity*?
   A. He appears frequently on television talk shows.
   B. His picture appears on the back cover of his books.
   C. He delivers numerous public lectures throughout the year.
   D. He writes under a pseudonym.

Essay

18. In an essay, identify at least three ironic statements or events in Act III of *The Crucible*. For each, describe the situation and explain why the statement or event is ironic. How does it represent something different from what readers or audience members expect or know to be true?

19. In an essay, describe Reverend Hale's role in Act III of *The Crucible*. What advice does he give to other characters, and under what circumstances? How is Hale's role different from that of all the other characters? Knowing what you know about Hale from Acts I and II, do you think his behavior is in keeping with his *previous* behavior, or contradictory to it? Explain your answer.

20. Judge Danforth is clearly a powerful and influential figure in Act III of *The Crucible*. What sort of man is he? What does he truly think of the proceedings? What does it mean when the stage directions say that he is rapidly calculating this, when told that Mary Warren admits she never saw spirits? What does it mean when Danforth acknowledges "with deep misgivings" that Mary's confession "goes to the heart of the whole situation"? What evidence is there that Danforth has at least a few thoughts about the folly of the proceedings? Why doesn't he stop the whole process? Answer these questions in an essay.

21. **Thinking About the Essential Question: How does literature shape or reflect society?** In the Bible worshiped by the Puritans of seventeenth-century Salem, one of the Ten Commandments reads, "Thou shalt not lie." Yet the intensely religious community of Salem is caught up in a web of lies and false accusations as the witchcraft hysteria overtakes the town. What does Act III of *The Crucible* reveal about the value the citizens of Salem place on truth-telling, and what does their view of this matter says about the kind of religion they practice? Develop your answer in an essay supported by details from the text.

Vocabulary Warm-up Word Lists

Study these words from the selection. Then, complete the activities.

Word List A

adamant [AD uh muhnt] *adj.* unyielding; unrelenting
  We tried to persuade Eric not to sail in gusty weather, but he was <u>adamant</u>.

bellow [BEL oh] *v.* to roar or cry out loudly
  We heard several cows <u>bellow</u> as they returned from pasture.

contention [kuhn TEN shuhn] *n.* dispute; argument; rivalry
  There is much <u>contention</u> around school about who should run for office.

embodiment [em BAHD ee muhnt] *n.* concrete expression of an idea or quality
  On the basketball court, Teresa is the <u>embodiment</u> of agility and grace.

mute [MYOOT] *adj.* silent
  When the enemy questioned the prisoners about the troops, they were <u>mute</u>.

nudges [NUJ uhz] *v.* pokes gently
  If Patrick wants the dog to get up, he <u>nudges</u> it slightly with his foot.

reprieve [ree PREEV] *n.* temporary relief; postponement of a punishment
  The judge refused to grant the defendant any <u>reprieve</u> from the prison term.

righteous [RYT chuhs] *adj.* just; upright; virtuous
  Judges must be <u>righteous</u> in order to retain their good standing in the courts.

Word List B

beguile [bee GYL] *v.* to trick
  We tried to <u>beguile</u> the cat to come indoors by shaking the box of cat food.

conciliatory [kahn SIL ee uh tohr ee] *adj.* eager for peace or reconciliation
  We would like to reconcile with Steve, so please be <u>conciliatory</u>.

disputation [dis pyoo TAY shuhn] *n.* disagreement; argument
  I had hoped for a calm, quiet evening, but Sally seemed bent on <u>disputation</u>.

gaunt [GAWNT] *adj.* thin and bony
  After a two-week hiking trip, they looked extremely thin, almost <u>gaunt</u>.

inaudibly [in AWD uh blee] *adv.* silently; in a way that cannot be heard
  Sarah and Luke whispered almost <u>inaudibly</u>.

penitence [PEN i tens] *n.* sorrow for sin, wrong, or misdoing
  In the Middle Ages, some people went on pilgrimages as <u>penitence</u>.

retaliation [ree tal ee AY shuhn] *n.* returning wrong for wrong; revenge
  Mike was hurt by Joe's remark, but he did not indulge in <u>retaliation</u>.

stench [STENCH] *n.* foul smell
  The dead fish had been on the dock for days, and the <u>stench</u> was unpleasant.

The Crucible, *Act IV* by Arthur Miller
Vocabulary Warm-up Exercises

Exercise A *Fill in the blanks, using each word from Word List A only once.*

My friend Hal is the incarnation or [1] _____ of the aggressive, successful

high school debater. Hal is never happier than when two rival teams are in

[2] _____ for a trophy or championship. At a crucial debate, he will sit

quietly behind his desk, remaining [3] _____ as his opponents make their

arguments. Then Hal [4] _____ his partner lightly on the arm. His team-

mate agrees that they will not give the opposition any [5] _____. When

Hal rises to deliver his speech, he inevitably seems [6] _____, full of good

will and common sense. As he drives home his points, however, it would be fair to

describe him as [7] _____ and unwilling to accept any concessions from

the other side. Starting out in a low but persuasive voice, it is not unusual for Hal to

[8] _____ his final point in the conclusion of his speech. Whatever you

think of Hal's tactics, it's clear he is a successful debater: He had won seven champion-

ship trophies.

Exercise B *Decide whether each statement below is true or false. Circle T or F, and explain your answer.*

1. If you suspect that people *beguile* you, you become wary of a trick.
   T / F _____

2. Someone in a *conciliatory* mood refuses the chance for a reconciliation.
   T / F _____

3. A *disputation* among various parties involves discord and disagreement.
   T / F _____

4. Someone who looks *gaunt* may not have been getting sufficient food and sleep.
   T / F _____

5. A person who speaks *inaudibly* can be heard by everyone in a large auditorium.
   T / F _____

6. *Penitence* for wrongdoing requires sincere regret.
   T / F _____

7. To take *retaliation* on others is a form of revenge.
   T / F _____

8. Most people find a *stench* appealing.
   T / F _____

The Crucible, *Act IV* by Arthur Miller
Reading Warm-up A

Read the following passage. Pay special attention to the underlined words. Then, read it again, and complete the activities. Use a separate sheet of paper for your written answers.

No one understood why Maggie was making such a big deal about the girls' volleyball team. They never drew much of an audience and usually had to struggle to find enough players. The boys' basketball team had just gotten new sweat suits, uniforms, and matching shoes, while the volleyball team had to make do with ragged old jerseys from ten years ago. Maggie was <u>adamant</u> that the girls' teams should receive equal treatment.

She spoke up in the middle of the school assembly, full of <u>righteous</u> conviction. The other students were so puzzled by her words that they remained <u>mute</u> at first; the auditorium was silent when she finished speaking. Then, a few boys began to giggle and <u>nudged</u> each other on the arm, making fun of Maggie's seriousness. To them, she seemed like the <u>embodiment</u> of jealousy, a silly person who liked to complain.

"I think you make a valid point," said the principal, Mr. Beale. He then explained, however, that a private donor, Slocum Heating and Oil, had donated the new shoes and uniforms for the boys' team. For many people in the auditorium, including the girls, this seemed to clinch the argument, but Maggie would give them no <u>reprieve</u>. Her <u>contention</u> was that private donations had no place in a public school. Then she argued that if the school was going to accept such a donation, it was the school's responsibility to see that the girls' teams received equal support.

"Sit down and be quiet!" yelled a boy in the back row. Then a few more boys began to <u>bellow</u> in the same way. Maggie's face turned red with anger and embarrassment, but she would not sit down. Eventually, she got Mr. Beale to promise that the volleyball team would get new uniforms.

1. Underline the words in this sentence and in the first sentence of the paragraph that give a clue to the meaning of <u>adamant</u>. Use the word *adamant* in a sentence.

2. Circle the words that give a clue to the meaning of <u>righteous</u>. What are two synonyms for *righteous*?

3. Underline the clue to the meaning of <u>mute</u>. Use a word meaning the opposite of *mute* in a sentence.

4. Circle the words that offer a clue to the meaning of <u>nudged</u> here. What is a synonym for *nudged*?

5. Circle the words that offer clues to the meaning of the word <u>embodiment</u>. Use this word in sentence.

6. Underline the words in this and the next sentence that give a clue to the meaning of <u>reprieve</u>. What are two synonyms for *reprieve*?

7. Circle the clues to the meaning of <u>contention</u> in this sentence. Use the word *contention* in a sentence.

8. Underline the words in this and the previous sentence that hint at the meaning of <u>bellow</u>. What is an antonym for *bellow*?

The Crucible, *Act IV* by Arthur Miller
Reading Warm-up B

Read the following passage. Pay special attention to the underlined words. Then, read it again, and complete the activities. Use a separate sheet of paper for your written answers.

In 1996, more than 40 years after *The Crucible* was first performed, the director Nicholas Hytner made the first English-language motion picture version of Miller's play. The film starred Daniel Day-Lewis as John Proctor, Joan Allen as Elizabeth, Winona Ryder as Abigail Williams, and Paul Scofield as Judge Danforth. Arthur Miller wrote the screenplay.

There was little disagreement or <u>disputation</u> among the critics, who warmly praised the film version. Winona Ryder was singled out for her interpretation of Abigail as a character of complex motivations. On one level, Abigail acts out of <u>retaliation</u> against John and Elizabeth, wishing to revenge herself for John's rejection. Abigail can thus <u>beguile</u> the court into accusing Elizabeth of witchcraft. On another level, however, Ryder interprets Abigail as appalled when events spin out of control. Late in the film, Abigail's eyes <u>inaudibly</u> express her horror. She does not, of course, become openly more <u>conciliatory</u> or retract her accusations; it is too late for that. However, her <u>gaunt</u> and almost haunted expression hint at a certain degree of regret, or even <u>penitence</u>, for her actions.

One of Arthur Miller's universal themes in *The Crucible* is the challenge to the individual of retaining self-respect when society seems bent on destroying it. This is the reason for John Proctor's most important decision in the play. For Proctor, the soiling of his reputation would amount to an everlasting foul odor, or <u>stench</u>, surrounding his name. This is why he refuses to sign the false confession that Danforth extracts from him. It is another virtue of the film version that this theme comes through loud and clear, thanks to Daniel Day-Lewis's excellent performance.

1. Underline the words that give a clue to the meaning of <u>disputation</u>. Write a sentence of your own using the word *disputation*.

2. Circle the words in this sentence that give a clue to the meaning of <u>retaliation</u>. What is an antonym for *retaliation*?

3. What are two synonyms for <u>beguile</u>?

4. Underline the words in this sentence that give a clue to the meaning of <u>inaudibly</u>. Use a word meaning the opposite of *inaudibly* in a sentence of your own.

5. Circle the words in this sentence that give a clue to the meaning of the word <u>conciliatory</u>. Use a word meaning the opposite of *conciliatory* in a sentence of your own.

6. Underline the words in this sentence that offer a clue to the meaning of <u>gaunt</u>. What are two synonyms for *gaunt*?

7. Circle the word in this sentence that hints at the meaning of <u>penitence</u>. Use the word *penitence* in an original sentence.

8. Circle the words in this sentence that hint at the meaning of the word <u>stench</u>.

Name _____ Date _____

The Crucible, *Act IV,* by Arthur Miller
Literary Analysis: Tragedy and Allegory

Tragedy is a dramatic form in which the main character—the **tragic hero**—is involved in a struggle that ends in disaster. The hero is usually a well-respected person whose downfall comes as a result of fate or a **tragic flaw.** The audience or readers feel sorry for the main character, who usually learns something profound and displays honor or nobility at the end.

An **allegory** is a story with more than one layer of meaning: a literal meaning and one or more symbolic meanings. The characters, setting, and themes in an allegory are symbols of ideas and qualities that exist outside the story.

A. DIRECTIONS: *Refer to Act IV of* The Crucible *as you answer the following questions.*

1. Who is the tragic hero of *The Crucible?* How do you know?

    _____

    _____

2. What is this character's tragic flaw? How does it lead to his or her downfall?

    _____

    _____

3. What does the hero learn at the end of the play? How does this affect his or her actions?

    _____

    _____

B. DIRECTIONS: *On the lines below, write a paragraph explaining how* The Crucible *is an allegory. Identify both its literal meaning and its symbolic meaning. Then evaluate the effectiveness of the play as an allegory and explain your assessment.*

_____

_____

_____

_____

_____

_____

_____

_____

_____

_____

_____

Name _____ Date _____

Reading Strategy: Evaluate the Influences of the Historical Period

The philosophical, political, religious, ethical, and social influences of the historical period portrayed in *The Crucible* shape the characters, setting, actions, and message of the play. Though some elements of the story could take place any time and in any place, many aspects of the play are completely dependent on the time period for their meaning.

DIRECTIONS: *Refer to Act IV to fill in the graphic organizer. In each circle, identify and briefly evaluate the influences of the historical period in the categories specified.*

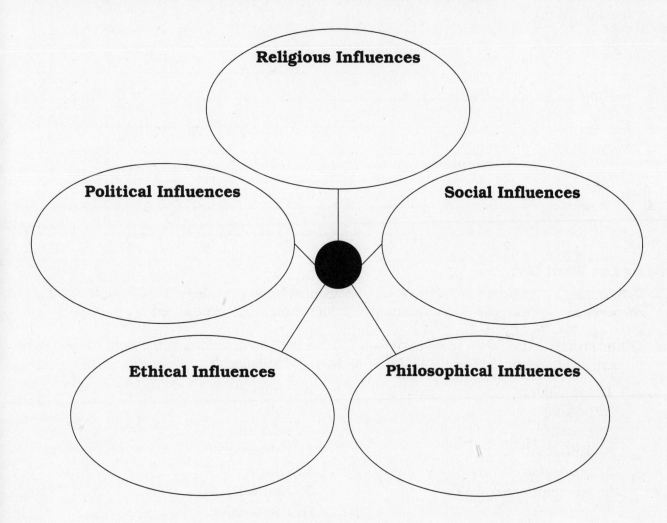

The Crucible, *Act IV,* by Arthur Miller
Vocabulary Builder

Using Words From Myths

Myths are fictional stories that account for natural phenomena or explain actions of gods. As English was developing, many writers and speakers were familiar with classical learning, including mythology. Thus, English includes names and stories from the myths of various cultures, and many words originate in these ancient tales.

A. DIRECTIONS: *Use a dictionary or other resource to explain the mythological origins of the following words.*

1. echo _____

   _____

2. volcano _____

   _____

3. Wednesday _____

   _____

4. museum _____

   _____

Using the Word List

adamant	beguile	cleave	conciliatory	mercy
penitence	principle	retaliation	salvation	tantalized

B. DIRECTIONS: *Match each word in the left column with its definition in the right column. Write the letter of the definition on the line next to the word it defines.*

___ 1. conciliatory   **A.** tempted

___ 2. beguile   **B.** belief

___ 3. cleave   **C.** resolute

___ 4. tantalized   **D.** deliverence

___ 5. retaliation   **E.** charm

___ 6. adamant   **F.** reprisal

___ 7. principle   **G.** compassion

___ 8. penitence   **H.** appeasing

___ 9. salvation   **I.** regret

___10. mercy   **J.** cling

The Crucible, *Act IV,* by Arthur Miller
Grammar and Style: Sentence Fragments and Run-Ons

Sentence fragments are incomplete sentences that may lack either a subject or a verb. Fragments are therefore parts of sentences incorrectly punctuated as though they were complete. A **run-on** is two or more complete sentences that are not properly joined or separated. To correct fragments and run-ons, follow these steps:

1. Decide if a problematic sentence is a fragment or a run-on.

2. If it is a fragment, add information to make a complete thought or combine the fragment with another sentence.

3. If it is a run-on, split it into two sentences. You might also add a comma or a conjunction to make it a correct single sentence.

A. PRACTICE: *On the space before each number, identify each of the following problematic sentences as a fragment or a run-on.*

_____ 1. Tried to get the prisoners to confess.

_____ 2. Proctor was not guilty he was willing to confess to save his life he wanted to be with his wife and children.

_____ 3. Although he spoke his confession willingly.

_____ 4. Rebecca Nurse bravely willing to die rather than confess to being a witch.

_____ 5. Proctor changed his mind he could not write his confession down and lose his honesty.

B. Writing Application: *On the lines below, revise each sentence in Practice A so that it is no longer a fragment or a run-on.*

1. _____
   _____

2. _____
   _____

3. _____
   _____

4. _____
   _____

5. _____
   _____

Name _____ Date _____

The Crucible, *Act IV,* by Arthur Miller
Support for Writing: Literary Criticism

DIRECTIONS: *You will write an essay in which you interpret* The Crucible's *main themes by exploring how the events, characters, and messages presented in the play both reflect the play's historical context then transcend that context to become universal. For your prewriting, review the play and generate a list of themes you think are important. Fill in the diagram below to record the themes and your interpretation of them.*

Theme

1.

2.

3.

Historical Meaning

1.

2.

3.

Universal Meaning

1.

2.

3.

The Crucible, *Act IV,* by Arthur Miller
Enrichment: Research

Time after time in the workplace, those who are well prepared with thorough documentation succeed. In *The Crucible,* Giles Corey succeeds in many of his legal dealings by doing his own research. Indeed, some of the credibility of the play comes from the fact that Miller had done enough research to seem authoritative on the events of 1692.

Today, knowing how to research is a valuable skill. Here are a few strategies:

1. **Define your topic.** What, exactly, do you want to know? Miller did not want to know about the Salem trials—he wanted to know about the people in them.

2. **Identify likely sources.** After you know what you're looking for, ask yourself where you would be most likely to find it. Information professionals try to organize data and information in the simplest, most logical way. Use the same idea to find what you need.

3. **Limit your search.** After defining a topic and identifying sources, further narrow the search. Internet and online information systems often help you refine your search through keywords.

4. **Pursue references.** You may not always find what you're looking for, but you may find a reference to the source that has exactly what you want. Bibliographies can also be a source.

5. **Follow your curiosity.** You know what you want, and if you've defined a topic and narrowed your search, trust your curiosity. Within reason, follow your instinct.

6. **Take careful, detailed notes.** Nothing is more frustrating than finding exactly what you want but failing to keep a good record of it. You also need to be able to document your work.

7. **Ask.** In almost any place you're seeking information, someone is available who knows how to find it. They'll be glad to show you how and where to look.

DIRECTIONS: *Show how the preceding principles of research might have been used by Arthur Miller in preparing to write* The Crucible.

1. _____

   _____

2. _____

   _____

3. _____

   _____

4. _____

   _____

5. _____

   _____

6. _____

   _____

7. _____

   _____

Name _____ Date _____

The Crucible, *Act IV* by Arthur Miller
Open-Book Test

Short Answer *Write your responses to the questions in this section on the lines provided.*

1. Based on the conversation involving Tituba, Sarah Good, and Herrick at the beginning of Act IV of *The Crucible*, what obsession of the day is weighing heavily on these characters?

   _____

   _____

2. In Act IV of *The Crucible*, Cheever comments on the "many cows wanderin' the highroads, now their masters are in jail and much disagreement who they will belong to now." What does the report of wandering cows symbolize about the effects of the witch trails on the society of Salem?

   _____

   _____

   _____

3. In Act IV of *The Crucible*, Parris complains to Danforth about the disappearance of Abigail and her apparent theft of his savings, as well as about the signs of growing discontent in the community over the wave of executions. Why does Danforth respond to him with contempt?

   _____

   _____

   _____

   _____

4. In Act IV of *The Crucible*, what does Danforth's determination to proceed immediately with the executions symbolize about the nature of the legal system? Explain your answer.

   _____

   _____

   _____

   _____

5. In Act IV of *The Crucible*, there are reports that the people of Andover have refused to cooperate with the witchcraft court there. What can the reader infer about the citizens of Andover from these reports?

   _____

   _____

   _____

6. In Act IV of *The Crucible*, it is evident that Elizabeth Proctor has changed during her imprisonment. How has she changed? Explain your answer, citing details from the text to support your answer.

_____

_____

_____

_____

7. In *The Crucible*, the line between religious and governmental authority is easily blurred and sometimes nonexistent. How is the relationship between church and state different in the present-day United States from the way it was at the time of *The Crucible*?

_____

_____

_____

8. In Act IV of *The Crucible*, John Proctor anguishes over having his signed confession made public. In what respect is Proctor's determination to preserve his good name, and his resulting tragic downfall, an echo of the McCarthy era of the 1950s?

_____

_____

_____

_____

9. One definition of the word *crucible* is "a severe test." Use the chart below to identify the key way in which each of the listed characters is tested by the events of *The Crucible*. Then, in the right-hand column, indicate whether that character passed or failed the "test."

Character	Test	Passed or Failed
Reverend Parris		
Reverend Hale		
Judge Danforth		
Elizabeth Proctor		
John Proctor		

10. If, after an argument with a friend, you wrote him a conciliatory note, would you be attempting to resolve the conflict? Why or why not? Base your answer on the meaning of *conciliatory* as it is used in Act IV of *The Crucible*.

_____

_____

_____

Essay

Write an extended response to the question of your choice or to the question or questions your teacher assigns you.

11. At the beginning of Act IV of *The Crucible,* it is discovered that Abigail has stolen money and run away with one of the other girls. Based on what you know of her from the play, why do you think she ran away? Develop your thoughts in an essay supported by details from the play.

12. In Act IV of *The Crucible,* John Proctor reluctantly expresses a willingness to admit to wrongdoing to save himself and his wife, but he will not accuse others. In an essay, explain why you think he takes this position and whether you agree with him. Support your answer with details from the play.

13. In Act IV of *The Crucible,* Reverend Hale pleads with Elizabeth Proctor to persuade John to confess and save his life. He argues that life is more precious than standing on a principle. Elizabeth answers, "I think that be the Devil's argument." What do you think she means by this comment? Develop your thoughts in an essay supported by details from the text.

14. **Thinking About the Essential Question: How does literature shape or reflect society?** A classic theme of literature in general—and of *The Crucible* in particular—is the conflict that can arise between a person's individual ideals and principles on the one hand and the expectations of society on the other. In an essay, discuss this theme as it applies to two major characters in *The Crucible.* Support your answer with details from the play.

Oral Response

15. Go back to question 1, 2, or 3 or to the question your teacher assigns to you. Take a few minutes to expand your answer and prepare an oral response. Find additional details in Act IV of *The Crucible* that support your points. If necessary, make notes to guide your oral response.

The Crucible, *Act IV,* by Arthur Miller
Selection Test A

Critical Reading *Identify the letter of the choice that best answers the question.*

____ 1. What is the setting of *The Crucible,* Act IV?
   A. the Proctors' home
   B. the Salem jail
   C. the woods outside of town
   D. the judge's chambers

____ 2. Which situation in *The Crucible, Act IV* symbolizes the message that unjust use of the law destroys communities?
   A. Cows have no farmers to care for them.
   B. Abigail and Mercy disappear from sight.
   C. Tituba plans to visit Barbados.
   D. Hale wishes for Rebecca's confession.

____ 3. Why does Danforth treat Parris with contempt in *The Crucible, Act IV*?
   A. He thinks Parris is committed to mercy.
   B. He thinks Parris a fool to believe Abigail.
   C. He thinks Parris cares only for himself.
   D. He thinks Parris wants only to get rich.

____ 4. In *The Crucible, Act IV,* Danforth plans to execute prisoners quickly. What theme is the author suggesting about the use of law that might also be applied to today's world?
   A. Justice is served by quick sentencing.
   B. Judges must act quickly in all cases.
   C. The law is not always just.
   D. Laws are made to be broken.

____ 5. In *The Crucible, Act IV,* what can the reader infer from the situation in Andover, where people have refused to cooperate with the witchcraft court?
   A. Andover is a community without law.
   B. Andover is fighting the hysteria.
   C. All Andover's witches have fled.
   D. Danforth will have to go to Andover.

_____ 6. Which event provides the moment of climax in *The Crucible*, Act IV?
   A. Abigail's disappearance from Salem
   B. Elizabeth's appearance in John's cell
   C. John's refusal to sign the confession
   D. Parris's plea to Elizabeth

_____ 7. In *The Crucible*, Act IV, John's destruction of the confession conveys what key message?
   A. Individuals are stronger than courts.
   B. Forgiveness is found even in courtrooms.
   C. One's honor cannot be signed away.
   D. Justice can be assured with documents.

_____ 8. How does the result of Proctor's refusal to sign away his honor in *The Crucible*, Act IV, compare to the result of people's refusal to testify during the McCarthy era of the 1950s?
   A. Fear of imprisonment made many people keep silent.
   B. People's lives were destroyed when they refused to testify.
   C. The Salem accusers were found to be Communists.
   D. People who testified against others in the 1950s were heroes.

_____ 9. Danforth's behavior in *The Crucible*, Act IV, exemplifies which of these truths?
   A. Justice is served by the legal process.
   B. Judges always rule for the good of all.
   C. Confession is good for the soul.
   D. The powerful act to preserve power.

_____ 10. How does Elizabeth show that she understands John at the end of *The Crucible*, Act IV?
   A. She does not plead to be present at his execution.
   B. She knows honor is more important to him than his life.
   C. She demands that he confess so that they may both live.
   D. She asks that he forgive her for her lack of trust.

Vocabulary and Grammar

_____ 11. A *conciliatory* person is one who tries to avoid
   A. air travel
   B. rich foods
   C. parties
   D. disagreements

___ **12.** Which word is CLOSEST in meaning to *retaliation*?
  A. injustice
  B. hysteria
  C. revenge
  D. forgiveness

___ **13.** Which word is most nearly OPPOSITE in meaning to *adamant*?
  A. harsh
  B. flexible
  C. unoriginal
  D. impatient

___ **14.** Which word best replaces *beguile* in this sentence: "The slick, lavish advertisement seeks to *beguile* the reader into believing that he or she simply must have a new car"?
  A. threaten
  B. tire
  C. charm
  D. inform

___ **15.** Which of the following is a sentence fragment?
  A. Stop the music.
  B. Just in case you were wondering, of course.
  C. I have no idea.
  D. Isn't it amazing?

Essay

16. In Act IV of *The Crucible*, John Proctor is at first willing to say he admits to wrongdoing, but he will not accuse others. Why do you think he takes this position, and do you agree with his action? In a brief essay, give your opinion.

17. In *The Crucible*, Act IV, Reverend Hale pleads with Elizabeth Proctor to persuade John to confess and save his life. He says that life is more precious than standing on a principle. Elizabeth's answer to Hale is, "I think that be the Devil's argument." What do you think she means by this comment? Write a brief essay to answer the question.

18. Thinking About the Essential Question: How does literature shape or reflect society? A classic theme of literature in general—and of *The Crucible* in particular—is the conflict that can arise between a person's individual ideals and principles on the one hand and the expectations of society on the other. In an essay, discuss this theme as it applies to two major characters in *The Crucible*. Support your answer with details from the play.

The Crucible, *Act IV,* by Arthur Miller
Selection Test B

Critical Reading *Identify the letter of the choice that best completes the statement or answers the question.*

_____ 1. The setting of *The Crucible,* Act IV, is
   A. Parris's house, where the investigation began.
   B. the Salem jail, the autumn after the trial.
   C. the prison in Andover, just before the Proctors' child is due.
   D. Danforth's chambers in Boston, where he hears final appeals.

_____ 2. What can the audience infer from the brief scene involving Tituba, Sarah Good, and Herrick that opens *The Crucible,* Act IV?
   A. Tituba and Sarah Good are about to be executed for witchcraft.
   B. Tituba and Sarah Good have come to believe the accusations against them.
   C. Herrick is drinking in order to dull his anguish at the injustices being done.
   D. Herrick has come to believe in the visions described by Tituba and Sarah Good.

_____ 3. In Act IV of *The Crucible,* Parris hopes that Rebecca Nurse and John Proctor will confess because he believes that
   A. confession will save their souls from damnation.
   B. sparing their lives will prevent public rebellion.
   C. their confessions will confirm the justice of all the trials and executions.
   D. their confessions will strengthen the faith of doubting parishioners.

_____ 4. What idea about the law is conveyed by Danforth's determination to proceed with the executions immediately in the fourth act of *The Crucible*?
   A. Judges tend to be corrupted by the power of their office.
   B. To delay doing justice is to commit injustice.
   C. Laws made by human beings cannot be reconciled with divine law.
   D. Injustice may be committed in the name of the law.

_____ 5. What is ironic about calling the confessions of witchcraft "coming to God" in *The Crucible,* Act IV?
   A. The confessions are made publicly, not in prayer.
   B. The confessions are lies and therefore sins against God.
   C. The confessions confirm that sins against God have been committed.
   D. Confession saves the confessor from death, thereby postponing the confessor's "coming to God."

_____ 6. By Act IV of *The Crucible,* what lesson has Elizabeth Proctor learned during her three months' imprisonment?
   A. that all people carry the seeds of evil within themselves
   B. that human beings cannot be held responsible for their actions
   C. that one should not judge human frailty too harshly
   D. that there are no meaningful standards of right and wrong

____ 7. In *The Crucible, Act IV* when Proctor refuses to condemn others to save himself, his behavior contrasts most strongly with the behavior of
   A. Parris.
   B. Hathorne.
   C. Danforth.
   D. Corey.

____ 8. The climax in Act IV of *The Crucible* occurs when
   A. Parris reveals that Abigail Williams has disappeared.
   B. Elizabeth Proctor is brought into the cell.
   C. Proctor decides to confess to witchcraft.
   D. Proctor refuses to sign the confession.

____ 9. Proctor's decision to tear up the confession conveys which important message about life in *The Crucible, Act IV*?
   A. Personal honor determines the worth of one's self.
   B. Government authority can be resisted single-handedly.
   C. Forgiveness can be extended to the guilty as well as the innocent.
   D. The variability of justice is an evil in itself.

____ 10. In *The Crucible, Act IV* Proctor's determination to preserve his good name speaks to the McCarthy era of the 1950's in that
   A. fear of persecution caused many to keep silent.
   B. laws were passed to prevent this kind of persecution.
   C. the Salem authorities act like communists.
   D. reputations were ruined by irresponsible accusations.

____ 11. Danforth's behavior in act IV of *The Crucible*, conveys the message that
   A. good and evil must finally be determined by law.
   B. those in power tend to act in the interest of preserving power.
   C. the absence of evidence renders authority powerless.
   D. legal systems cannot take personal character into account.

____ 12. In act IV of *The Crucible*, as Proctor is taken off to execution, Parris urges Elizabeth to go to her husband in order to
   A. comfort him in his final moments.
   B. try once more to persuade him to confess.
   C. show that she believes the death sentence is just.
   D. make a last appeal to the mercy of the judges.

____ 13. Which truth of life in colonial Salem in *The Crucible, Act IV* is applicable today?
   A. Superstitions of colonial America are no longer an issue.
   B. Belief in the supernatural is *ipso facto* dangerous.
   C. Government is overly concerned with religious issues.
   D. Fear and suspicion can lead to perversions of justice.

Vocabulary and Grammar

___ **14.** Someone who is *adamant* is
A. condemned.
B. regretful.
C. numb.
D. stubborn.

___ **15.** Someone who is *conciliatory* is a(n)
A. advisor.   C. peacemaker.
B. opponent.   D. scholar.

___ **16.** If you were *tantalized* by the chocolate cake on the dessert cart, you would find it
A. distasteful   C. unusual
B. tempting   D. unhealthful

___ **17.** Which of the following would most likely be thinking about *retaliation*?
A. the leader of a country that had just been attacked by its neighbor
B. someone who had just received an invitation to a party
C. an employee who had just been given a raise
D. the student committee that is planning this year's final assembly

___ **18.** Which of the following is a run-on sentence?
A. Even though she dislikes most sports, she does enjoy tennis on occasion.
B. Spicy foods appeal to my palate, but they often disagree with my stomach.
C. The pace of life in New York City is intense, I prefer a smaller town.
D. There is no excuse for ignoring the problem of pollution, in my opinion.

Essay

19. In Act IV of *The Crucible*, we learn that Abigail has stolen money and run away, but we do not hear exactly why. Write an essay in which you assess her motives for running away, based on what you know of her from the play. Use examples from the play to support your answer.

20. The word *crucible* means "a container for melting or purifying metals" and "a severe test." Why are both meanings appropriate for *The Crucible*? Write an essay explaining how characters are both reduced to their essences and tested. Use examples from the play to support your ideas.

21. Trials for sorcery, heresy, and witchcraft had been going on for centuries in Europe. Inquisitions had occurred since the Middle Ages, and the judicial methods used were not far different from those in *The Crucible*. Why do you think Miller might have chosen the Salem witch trials of 1692? How does this setting serve his dramatic and thematic goals? Write an essay explaining why Salem, Massachusetts, is an appropriate setting for the themes of *The Crucible*.

22. Thinking About the Essential Question: How does literature shape or reflect society? A classic theme of literature in general—and of *The Crucible* in particular—is the conflict that can arise between a person's individual ideals and principles on the one hand and the expectations of society on the other. In an essay, discuss this theme as it applies to two major characters in *The Crucible*. Support your answer with details from the play.

Name _____ Date _____

The Crucible by Arthur Miller
from **Good Night and Good Luck** by George Clooney and Grant Heslov
Comparing Political Drama Past and Present

The two selections in this pairing are examples of political drama, or drama that has an openly political topic and purpose. Whereas Arthur Miller's play focuses on the Salem witch trials of the seventeenth century, its underlying message concerns the McCarthy era of the twentieth century, which is also the focus of *Good Night and Good Luck*.

Directions: *Complete the following chart by explaining how each selection reflects the features of political drama.*

Features of political drama	*The Crucible*	*Good Night and Good Luck*
Reflects the author's political opinion		
Characterizes a politician or describes a series of political events		
Questions inequities and injustices of contemporary society		
Examines a political issue from the past or present or uses past events to comment on current problems		

Name _____ Date _____

The Crucible by Arthur Miller
from **Good Night and Good Luck** by George Clooney and Grant Heslov
Vocabulary Builder

A. DIRECTIONS: *Revise each sentence so that the underlined vocabulary word is used logically. Be sure not to change the vocabulary word.*

Example: We greeted the <u>insurmountable</u> task with joy.
We greeted the <u>insurmountable</u> task with dread.

1. Sylvia's <u>vulnerability</u> to accusations of incompetence made her an excellent candidate for president. _____
_____

2. Because Justin decided to <u>disregard</u> the ringing of his cell phone, he was on the phone all day. _____
_____

3. Maureen <u>acknowledges</u> the applause of the audience by leaving the stage immediately.
_____

4. The <u>statute</u> explained the punishment that the criminal would suffer. _____
_____

Using the Word List

acknowledges   disregard   statute   vulnerability

B. DIRECTIONS: *Write a complete sentence to answer each question. For each item, use a word from the Word List to replace each underlined word without changing its meaning.*

1. How might you help a friend whose <u>exposure</u> to food temptations has caused health problems? _____
_____

2. What might happen to someone who tended to <u>ignore</u> symptoms of illness? _____
_____

3. If a judge <u>recognizes</u> the validity of certain pieces of evidence, how should the jury respond?
_____

4. What is the <u>law</u> regarding dogs and leashes in your neighborhood? _____
_____

The Crucible by Arthur Miller
from **Good Night and Good Luck** by George Clooney and Grant Heslov
Support for Writing

Directions: *Use these charts to organize your thoughts for your compare-and-contrast essay.*

Characters from *The Crucible*	Actions That Represent Author's Political Opinion	Language That Represents Author's Political Opinion

Characters from *Good Night . . .*	Actions That Represent Authors' Political Opinion	Language That Represents Author's Political Opinion

Arthur Miller, **"The Crucible"**/George Clooney & Grant Heslov,
"Good Night and Good Luck"
Selection Test

MULTIPLE CHOICE *Choose the letter of the response that best answers each question.*

_____ 1. Both *The Crucible* and *Good Night and Good Luck* may be regarded as political dramas because they

    A. question inequities and injustices of society.

    B. contains a large number of characters.

    C. deal with election campaigns.

    D. present an intense conflict.

_____ 2. In *The Crucible*, Arthur Miller's political drama focuses on which of the following?

    A. the voyages of Christopher Columbus

    B. the Salem witch trials

    C. the American Revolution

    D. the Civil War

_____ 3. Which character in *The Crucible* represents the authority of the state?

    A. Reverend Samuel Parris

    B. John Proctor

    C. Governor Danforth

    D. Abigail Williams

_____ 4. Underneath the surface action of the play, the themes and conflicts in *The Crucible* are also linked to which of the following?

    A. the aggression of Adolf Hitler during the 1930s

    B. Senator Joseph R. McCarthy's anti-communist witch hunts of the 1950s

    C. the development of the space program during the 1960s

    D. the need for reform in U.S. immigration policy

_____ 5. In *The Crucible*, which of the following represents the most serious injustice?

    A. the fact that people who are accused are expected to admit their guilt before anything is proved against them

    B. the fact that people must live in a civil society controlled by the church

    C. the fact that courts as we know them today did not exist at the time of the play's events

    D. the fact that people are subjected to cruel and unusual punishments

_____ 6. In *Good Night and Good Luck*, which character most clearly represents the opinions of the authors of the screenplay?

    A. Fred Friendly

    B. Milton Berle

    C. Senator Joseph R. McCarrthy

    D. Edward R. Murrow

_____ 7. In *Good Night and Good Luck*, which of these serves as the background for the dramatization of conflicting points of view?

A. a dinner party

B. a newspaper Op-Ed page

C. a TV quiz show

D. a TV news magazine

_____ 8. In *Good Night and Good Luck*, what is the most likely reason that CBS invited Senator Joseph R. McCarthy to present a reply to a critical report about him broadcast previously by the network?

A. CBS felt it had made some mistakes in the report.

B. Congress and the courts ruled that McCarthy was entitled to reply.

C. CBS did not want to give McCarthy the chance to charge that the network was being unfair.

D. Edward R. Murrow hoped that McCarthy would change his ways.

_____ 9. In *Good Night and Good Luck*, which of the following best describes Senator McCarthy's reply to the CBS report?

A. a list of honors and awards that McCarthy has won

B. a personal attack on Edward R. Murrow consisting of a list of unproven accusations

C. a vivid, fearsome description of the Communist threat

D. a condemnation of TV news programs

_____ 10. What was most likely the authors' purpose in writing the screenplay *Good Night and Good Luck*?

A. to examine a political issue and convey the authors' opinion on it

B. to show the limitations of TV news

C. to question the accuracy of people on both sides of a debate

D. to entertain the audience

ESSAY

11. In a brief essay, discuss the term "witch hunt" as it applies to both *The Crucible* and *Good Night and Good Luck*. What is a witch hunt? In what sense does the plot of both works revolve around a witch hunt? What position do the authors of these works take on the crisis that a witch hunt poses? What personal qualities of character are required at such times of crisis? In your essay, be sure to illustrate your main ideas with specific references to the texts.

Writing Workshop—Unit 5
Persuasion: Persuasive Essay

Prewriting: Gathering Details

Use the T-chart below to help you organize the arguments for and against your viewpoint.

Your Essay Topic: _____

Evidence for your viewpoint	Evidence against your viewpoint

Drafting: Organizing the Essay

Use the chart below to effectively organize the arguments of your persuasive essay.

Interesting introduction	
Your second-strongest argument	
Other less strong arguments	
Present and refute opposing ideas	
Your strongest argument	
Catchy conclusion	

Writing Workshop—Unit 5
Persuasive Essay: Developing Your Style

Using Parallelism

Parallel structure is the repeated use of similar ideas in a similar grammatical form. In a persuasive essay, parallelism enhances the power of your language. Parallel expressions help you emphasize your arguments and create a compelling rhythm.

Not Parallel	Philadelphia is famous for *the First Continental Congress, housing the Liberty Bell,* and *publishing the nation's first newspaper.*
Parallel	Philadelphia is famous for *hosting the First Continental Congress, housing the Liberty Bell,* and *publishing the nation's first newspaper.*

Identifying Faulty Parallelism

A. DIRECTIONS: *For each item, circle the word or phrase that is not parallel with the others in the series.*

1. Cell phones provide fun, keeping you safe in an emergency, and convenience.

2. To avoid disturbing the people around you, turn off your cell phone in libraries, when you're going to the movies, and in school.

3. Don't embarrass yourself and others in public by talking too loud, discussing personal issues, or you shouldn't have an argument either.

4. Luxury cell-phone features include cameras, searching the Internet, and e-mail service.

Fixing Faulty Parallelism

B. DIRECTIONS: *Rewrite each sentence so that it uses parallel structures to present a series of ideas.*

1. Until recently, most people saved paper photos in shoeboxes, photo albums, or they bought frames for them.

   _____

2. Today, digital cameras are changing the way people take photos, how they are saved, and share them.

   _____

3. Digital cameras require no film, you have instant pictures, and allow easy sharing.

   _____

4. Digital photos are a good way for a group of people to share memories of a family celebration, a school program, or when you're on the same sports team.

   _____

   _____

Name _____ Date _____

Communications Workshop—Unit 5
Analyze and Evaluate Entertainment Media

Choose an example of visual entertainment media—a movie, TV show, or Internet clip. Use this form to help you examine how the selection shapes content and viewer response.

What is the name of the selection? _____

What type of entertainment medium does it represent?
_____

What cultural values does it express or imply? _____
_____

How are various groups of people represented? _____
_____

Which of the following techniques help shape content and response?

—*Special Effects:* _____
_____

—*Editing:* _____
_____

—*Camera angles:* _____
_____

—*Reaction shots:* _____
_____

—*Sequencing:* _____
_____

—*Music:* _____
_____

How does the genre (film, television, Internet video) affect the techniques used to create this selection? _____
_____

How does the genre affect viewer response? _____
_____

13. What would the chief conflict in a political drama most likely involve?
    A. a matter of public interest
    B. a dispute among friends
    C. an actual incident from history
    D. a king or other leader

14. What is a static character?
    A. a character who changes and develops during a story
    B. a character who tells a story rather than acts in it
    C. a character who does not reveal many sides
    D. a character who does not change or develop in a story

15. Read the poetic lines. What do the dash and line break after *cold* indicate to someone reading the lines aloud?

    The day dawned, bright,
    clear,
    cold—
    and alive.

    A. pause slightly after *cold*
    B. pick up speed after *cold*
    C. add emphasis to the word *cold*
    D. read the words *and alive* in a whisper

16. Which of the following most likely contains a detail of the setting of a story?
    A. He wore an elegant Victorian suit.
    B. Fog filled the street.
    C. The piano chords sounded mournful.
    D. She spun in the pale blue light.

Read this selection from a drama. Then, answer the questions that follow.

A backstage dressing room. A dresser is covered with perfume and makeup. On the wall is a large heart-shaped mirror. On either side of the mirror are photographs of KATE HARRISON. HARRISON, *a glamorous blonde, sits in front of the dresser, wearing a robe. Behind her stands* PEG PEACHUM, *a middle-aged woman, dressed in plain shirt and slacks, pinning up Kate's hair. She has hairpins in her mouth.*

KATE: [*in a fake British accent, sweeping her arms*] Oh, I feel good tonight, really I do. I can just see our reviews in tomorrow's paper—"Kate Harrison Gives Performance of the Century in New Play." [*Suddenly worried, she turns to* PEG] What do you think, hmmm?

PEG: [*mumbling through the hairpins*] Yes, Miss Harrison.

KATE: [*Suddenly angry.*] What are you doing? My hair looks terrible! [*It doesn't.*]

PEG: [*Wearily.*] It looks fine, Miss Harrison. You always look fine. Really.

KATE: [*Narrowing her eyes.*] Well, I don't care what you say—and look! I've got a spot on my makeup! You're going to ruin everything tonight! I know I'm going to be terrible tonight!

PEG: [*Unconsciously, then catching herself.*] Yes, Miss Harrison—I mean, of course not, Miss Harrison.

Unit 5 Resources: Prosperity and Protest

17. From the dialogue and stage directions, what can you conclude about the character of Kate Harrison?
    A. She is a talented actress whom audiences love.
    B. She is a poor actress who worries because she is unable to learn her lines.
    C. She is a vain, attractive actress, subject to mood swings.
    D. She is a quiet, shy actress who comes to life onstage.

18. How is the written description of the dressing room organized?
    A. chronologically
    B. in order of importance
    C. spatially
    D. in comparison-contrast order

19. What is the advantage of the type of organization used to describe the dressing room?
    A. It allows you to see the dressing room, moving back from the wall.
    B. It builds up to the most vivid, important, and interesting information.
    C. It shows how the room has changed over time.
    D. It shows the differences between Harrison's part of the room and Peachum's.

20. What do you predict will happen next in the drama?
    A. Peg will hug Kate to reassure her.
    B. Kate will find another reason to pick on Peg.
    C. Peg will tie Kate up, put on her costume, and become a star.
    D. Kate will take a breath and apologize for being rude to Peg.

21. What exposition is presented in this portion of the drama?
    A. Kate Harrison is in the middle of a successful performance of a play.
    B. Peg Peachum has worked backstage in the theater for years but wants to go onstage.
    C. Peg Peachum plans to destroy Kate Harrison's performance by making her look bad.
    D. Peg Peachum is helping the vain, insecure Kate Harrison dress for a play's opening night.

22. Which of the following is involved in the conflict in this scene?
    A. the reviewers and Kate Harrison
    B. Kate Harrison's sense of duty and her desire to go onstage
    C. Kate Harrison's vanity and her insecurity
    D. Kate Harrison's and Peg Peachum's powerful egos

23. Which of the following is evidence from the drama that would support an argument about the volatility of Kate's character?
    A. Kate's opening statement, combined with her anger toward Peg
    B. Kate's concern about her appearance, combined with her anger toward Peg
    C. Peg's keeping the hairpins in her mouth, combined with her answers to Kate
    D. Kate's anger at Peg, combined with Peg's answers to Kate

Answer the following questions.

24. Imagine that you forget to invite a close friend to a party. Your friend tells someone else that you two have stopped being close friends. The other person tells you, and you apologize to your friend. Which statement is true?
    A. The other person's intervention is the *effect* of your intentional cruelty to your friend.
    B. Your friend's hurt feelings have *caused* you to not invite her.
    C. Your friend's impression that your friendship is over is the *effect* of your apology.
    D. The other person's intervention *causes* your apology.

25. Which of the following is one way to evaluate the influence of a historical period on a work of fiction?
    A. observe the details that indicate that it is set in an earlier historical period
    B. observe the exploration of timeless themes
    C. observe the contrast between the author's apparent values and our own
    D. observe the use of unconventional characters, such inhabitants of other planets

Vocabulary

26. Based on your understanding of the Latin prefix *extra-*, choose the definition of *extraordinary*.
    A. extremely ordinary
    B. out of the ordinary
    C. within the range of ordinary or normal
    D. ordinary in a negative way

27. The Latin word part *super-* means "above." Which of the following is the best definition of *superlative*?
    A. very late   C. the best
    B. very easy   D. the first

28. Based on your understanding of the root *-vert-*, choose the meaning of *divert*.
    A. to turn something away   C. to be different
    B. untrue   D. to lead to the downfall of

29. Based on your understanding of the root *-grat-*, choose the meaning of *gratitude*.
    A. state of being thankful   C. sense of freedom
    B. state of being healthy   D. an agreeable personality

30. The Greek root *-anthropo-* means "human being." Which of the following is the best definition of the word *anthropology*?
    A. the creation of human life   C. the understanding of ocean life
    B. the study of human cultures   D. the teaching of life skills

31. Which word from Greek mythology best describes someone who is very vain?
    A. tantalizing
    B. titanic
    C. narcissistic
    D. hyacinth

Grammar

32. In which of the following sentences are the verb tenses correct?
    A. When I moved to a warm climate, I expect to see new animals.
    B. When I had moved to a warm climate, I will have expected to see new animals.
    C. When I moved to a warm climate, I expected to see new animals.
    D. When I move to a warm climate, I have expected to see new animals.

33. Which sentence choice revises the voice in this sentence from passive to active?

    Many places were visited on our vacation, and many memorable sights were seen.

    A. Many memorable sights were seen on our vacation, and we visited many places.
    B. We visited many places on our vacation and saw many memorable sights.
    C. Because we visited many places on our vacation, memorable sights were seen.
    D. On our vacation, many places were visited and memorable sights were seen.

34. Which of the following is a sentence fragment?
    A. I hope you can ride to the city with me.
    B. As though you remembered my name.
    C. Now I need to add a footnote to my paper.
    D. It's been a difficult promise to keep.

ESSAY

35. Think of an issue at school or in your community that you feel strongly about. It might be the use of school uniforms, the menu in the school cafeteria, zoning regulations in your neighborhood, community leash laws for pets, etc. Write a persuasive essay for or against the issue you choose. Be sure to include facts, details, examples, and reasons that will help you persuade your readers to your point of view.

36. Write an essay that analyzes the view of life as expressed by the speaker of a poem you have read. In your essay, explain how the speaker's words, images, figures of speech, emotions, and ideas help the reader understand the speaker's values and attitudes toward life.

37. Write a short play for presentation on the radio. Either adapt a story you have read or invent a situation and characters of your own. Keep in mind that every play should develop a conflict or problem that is worked out through the interaction of two or more characters. Include directions for sound effects, along with dialogue, to develop your characters and advance the action.

Name _____ Date _____

Vocabulary in Context

1. The photographer used an equipment bag to carry her_____.
   - A. apparatus
   - B. fragment
   - C. proprietor
   - D. streetcar

2. Because a highway was built through their farm, my uncle's family members were_____.
   - A. global
   - B. passionate
   - C. triangular
   - D. uprooted

3. Lars had an accident on the way to his meeting, so he missed his_____.
   - A. chairmanship
   - B. delta
   - C. exhilaration
   - D. rendezvous

4. To attract hungry shoppers to his restaurant, Brad built it in the_____district.
   - A. commercial
   - B. historic
   - C. maximum
   - D. secondary

5. The president asked the country to support the army during_____.
   - A. bedroll
   - B. generosity
   - C. translation
   - D. wartime

6. For warmth, Trung wears pants of thick, ribbed_____.
   - A. aftershave
   - B. corduroy
   - C. crepe
   - D. rite

7. At the end of the workday, Rafael's suit was wrinkled and his tie was_____.
   - A. accessible
   - B. askew
   - C. mutual
   - D. offshore

8. To avoid the crash ahead of her, the driver had to quickly_____.
   A. boycott
   B. diminish
   C. guffaw
   D. swerve

9. I am tired of hearing dripping water, so please turn off the_____tightly.
   A. ledger
   B. sampan
   C. scaffolding
   D. spigot

10. The children's nurse calms her patients with her_____manner.
    A. fictional
    B. pathetic
    C. placid
    D. sultry

11. The sound of constant hammering is_____Janis.
    A. anticipating
    B. irritating
    C. refreshing
    D. swiveling

12. Fallen branches and muddy litter were everywhere in the_____of the storm.
    A. aftermath
    B. deceit
    C. morality
    D. solace

13. Mia really liked the polite, thoughtful man because of his_____.
    A. cowardice
    B. elixir
    C. gospel
    D. sensitivity

14. After taking the oath of office, the president gave a speech at his_____.
    A. antithesis
    B. conspiracy
    C. inauguration
    D. oppression

15. When touring other nations, the queen meets with the British_____to each country.
   A. ambassador
   B. clergyman
   C. martyr
   D. orator

16. If you base your answer on evidence and reasons, it will be_____.
   A. faulty
   B. immoral
   C. logical
   D. prior

17. The description had so many details that it was able to_____images.
   A. analyze
   B. evoke
   C. lessen
   D. recoil

18. The boastful politician was not aware of how_____he sounded.
   A. depressed
   B. intricate
   C. pompous
   D. precise

19. The artist stored her best drawings in a(n)_____.
   A. aspect
   B. portfolio
   C. taboo
   D. verdict

20. You should consider how two things are alike to make an effective_____.
   A. analogy
   B. intersection
   C. installment
   D. pneumonia

Name _____ Date _____

Diagnostic Tests and Vocabulary in Context
Use and Interpretation

The Diagnostic Tests and Vocabulary in Context were developed to assist teachers in making the most appropriate assignment of *Prentice Hall Literature* program selections to students. The purpose of these assessments is to indicate the degree of difficulty that students are likely to have in reading/comprehending the selections presented in the *following* unit of instruction. Tests are provided at six separate times in each in each grade level—a *Diagnostic Test* (to be used prior to beginning the year's instruction) and a *Vocabulary in Context,* the final segment of the Benchmark Test appearing at the end of each of the first five units of instruction. Note that the tests are intended for use not as summative assessments for the prior unit, but as guidance for assigning literature selections in the upcoming unit of instruction.

The structure of all Diagnostic Tests and Vocabulary in Context in this series is the same. All test items are four-option, multiple-choice items. The format is established to assess a student's ability to construct sufficient meaning from the context sentence to choose the only provided word that fits both the semantics (meaning) and syntax (structure) of the context sentence. All words in the context sentences are chosen to be "below-level" words that students reading at this grade level should know. All answer choices fit *either* the meaning or structure of the context sentence, but only the correct choice fits *both* semantics and syntax. All answer choices—both correct answers and incorrect options—are key words chosen from specifically taught words that will occur in the subsequent unit of program instruction. This careful restriction of the assessed words permits a sound diagnosis of students' current reading achievement and prediction of the most appropriate level of readings to assign in the upcoming unit of instruction.

The assessment of vocabulary in context skill has consistently been shown in reading research studies to correlate very highly with "reading comprehension." This is not surprising as the format essentially assesses comprehension, albeit in sentence-length "chunks." Decades of research demonstrate that vocabulary assessment provides a strong, reliable prediction of comprehension achievement—the purpose of these tests. Further, because this format demands very little testing time, these diagnoses can be made efficiently, permitting teachers to move forward with critical instructional tasks rather than devoting excessive time to assessment.

It is important to stress that while the Diagnostic and Vocabulary in Context were carefully developed and will yield sound assignment decisions, they were designed to *reinforce*, not supplant, teacher judgment as to the most appropriate instructional placement for individual students. Teacher judgment should always prevail in making placement—or indeed other important instructional—decisions concerning students.

Diagnostic Tests and Vocabulary in Context
Branching Suggestions

These tests are designed to provide maximum flexibility for teachers. Your *Unit Resources* books contain the 40-question **Diagnostic Test** and 20-question **Vocabulary in Context** tests. At *PHLitOnline,* you can access the Diagnostic Test and complete 40-question Vocabulary in Context tests. Procedures for administering the tests are described below. Choose the procedure based on the time you wish to devote to the activity and your comfort with the assignment decisions relative to the individual students. Remember that your judgment of a student's reading level should always take precedence over the results of a single written test.

Feel free to use different procedures at different times of the year. For example, for early units, you may wish to be more confident in the assignments you make—thus, using the "two-stage" process below. Later, you may choose the quicker diagnosis, confirming the results with your observations of the students' performance built up throughout the year.

The **Diagnostic Test** is composed of a single 40-item assessment. Based on the results of this assessment, make the following assignment of students to the reading selections in Unit 1:

Diagnostic Test Score	Selection to Use
If the student's score is 0–25	more accessible
If the student's score is 26–40	more challenging

Outlined below are the three basic options for administering **Vocabulary in Context** and basing selection assignments on the results of these assessments.

1. For a one-stage, quicker diagnosis using the *20-item* test in the *Unit Resources:*

Vocabulary in Context Test Score	Selection to Use
If the student's score is 0–13	more accessible
If the student's score is 14–20	more challenging

2. If you wish to confirm your assignment decisions with a *two-stage* diagnosis:

Stage 1: Administer the 20-item test in the *Unit Resources*	
Vocabulary in Context Test Score	**Selection to Use**
If the student's score is 0–9	more accessible
If the student's score is 10–15	(Go to Stage 2.)
If the student's score is 16–20	more challenging

Stage 2: Administer items 21–40 from *PHLitOnline*	
Vocabulary in Context Test Score	**Selection to Use**
If the student's score is 0–12	more accessible
If the student's score is 13–20	more challenging

3. If you base your assignment decisions on the full 40-item **Vocabulary in Context** from *PHLitOnline:*

Vocabulary in Context Test Score	Selection to Use
If the student's score is 0–25	more accessible
If the student's score is 26–40	more challenging

Unit 5 Resources: Prosperity and Protest

Grade 11—Benchmark Test 9
Interpretation Guide

Skill Objective	Test Items	Number Correct	Reading Kit
Literary Analysis			
Implied Theme	1, 14		pp. 260, 261
Diction	15		pp. 250, 251
Grotesque Character	4		pp. 122, 123
Plot	7, 8		pp. 180, 181
Epiphany	5, 16		pp. 92, 93
Foreshadowing	6		pp. 116, 117
Parallelism	18		pp. 168, 169
Parody and Pun	24, 25		pp. 172, 173
Sound Devices	13, 23		pp. 238, 239
Figurative Language	2, 20, 22		pp. 114, 115
Repetition	21, 26		pp. 224, 225
Reading Skill			
Analyzing Political Assumptions	19		pp. 16, 17
Visualizing	3		pp. 266, 267
Drawing Conclusions From Details	12		pp. 84, 85
Summarize	9		pp. 252, 253
Use Background Knowledge to Make Predictions	10		pp. 264, 265
Read Aloud	17		pp. 204, 205
Interpret Connotation	11		pp. 140, 141
Vocabulary			
Latin Roots: *-sol-, -litera-, -rig-*	28, 29, 30		pp. 306, 307
Words from Other Languages	27		pp. 340, 341
Writing			
Comparison-and-Contrast Essay	31	Use rubric	pp. 424, 425
Character Analysis	32	Use rubric	pp. 422, 423
Creative Writing: Poetry	33	Use rubric	pp. 426, 427

Grade 11—Benchmark Test 10 Interpretation Guide

Skill Objective	Test Items	Number Correct	Reading Kit
Literary Analysis			
Style, Diction, and Voice	1, 3		pp. 250, 251
Rhetorical Devices	2, 4, 5		pp. 222, 223
Setting	16		pp. 232, 233
Symbol	11		pp. 254, 255
Eulogy and Mood	7, 9		pp. 158, 159
Plot	21		pp. 180, 181
Conflict and Resolution	13, 22		pp. 62, 63
Biblical Allusions	6		pp. 44, 45
Static and Dynamic Characters (Direct and Indirect Characterization)	14		pp. 246, 247
Tragedy and Allegory	12		pp. 4, 5
Dramatic Irony	10		pp. 144, 145
Reading Skill			
Reading Poetry According to Punctuation	15		pp. 204, 205
Cause and Effect	24		pp. 48, 49
Analyze Patterns of Organization	19		pp. 12, 13
Main Idea and Supporting Details	8		pp. 126, 127
Reading/Identifying Text Structure	17		pp. 258, 259
Evaluate Cultural and Ethical Influences of a Historical Period	25		pp. 100, 101
Making Predictions	20		pp. 152, 153
Evaluate Arguments	23		pp. 98, 99
Vocabulary			
Latin Roots: -extra-, -super-, -vert-, -grat-	26, 27, 28, 29		pp. 296, 297, 322, 323, 324, 325
Greek Word Part -ology	30, 31		pp. 276, 277
Grammar			
Sentence Fragments	34		pp. 392, 393
Participial Phrases	32		pp. 376, 377
Varying Sentence Structure	33		pp. 410, 411
Writing			
Persuasive Essay	35	Use rubric	pp. 440, 441
Creative Writing: Radio Play	36	Use rubric	pp. 428, 429
Character Analysis	37	Use rubric	pp. 422, 423

ANSWERS

Name and Terms to Know, p. 2

Sample Answers

A. 1. The Cold War was the largely bloodless struggle between the Soviet Union and the West

2. The Silent Generation were Americans of the 1950s, who were exhausted by the sacrifice and conflict of previous decades and preferred to live quiet lives, raise their families, and enjoy being consumers.

3. The Soviet Union's 1957 launching of Sputnik, the first artificial satellite to orbit the earth, marked the beginning of the Space Age.

4. *The Crucible* was a play by Arthur Miller that shed light on the 1950s by examining a fearful incident in colonial history.

5. John Hersey was a journalist and historian whose book *Hiroshima* was a realistic World War II account.

6. Martin Luther King, Jr., was the civil rights leader who helped America recognize that the American Dream still needed work and who was assassinated in 1968.

B. 1. The 1950s prized a quiet life of normality and conformity; the 1960s celebrated rebellion and individuality. The 1950s was an Age of Anxiety in which many were fearful of communist nuclear attack; the late 1960s saw an Age of Aquarius in which many spoke of universal peace and love.

2. Suburban life encouraged both conformity and isolation. The suburbs thrived as people prospered in the 1950s and left cities for homes with yards.

3. The Civil Rights movement made Americans more aware of the need for racial equality and helped African Americans gain more opportunities.

Essential Question: How did literature shape or reflect society? p. 3

Sample Answers

A. 1. a. In the 1950s, America and the Soviet Union were involved in the so-called Cold War, which grew "hot" in Korea and Vietnam.

b. Possibilities include the civil rights struggle, the women's movement, and the protest against the Vietnam War

2. a. The Age of Anxiety was a period after World War II when Americans seemed unable to stop thinking about terrible things that could or might happen, such as nuclear war or q Communist takeover.

b. The Age of Aquarius was an alternative to the Age of Anxiety that saw an era of peace and love.

3. a. Ironic writers included Joseph Heller and Kurt Vonnegut Jr.

b. Writers wrote to promote racial and women's equality, expose injustice, and to protest conformity and ills of postwar society.

c. Pop-culture favorites included Broadway musicals; TV sitcoms, westerns, and science fiction; and the Beatles.

B. 1. exploring new experiences

2. take up yoga

3. she makes them believe that good is possible

Essential Question: What makes American literature American? p. 4

Sample Answers

A. 1. a. They questioned what constituted the American Dream and whether success was worth the steep price it often involved.

b. Rebels of the 1960s protested their own society and culture.

c. It prompted literature of the era to explore the African American experience and struggle for racial equality.

2. a. Some writers served as witness to history, reporting on the horrors of warfare and political and social tensions.

b. Some writers withdrew from mainstream society, rebelled against it, and supported efforts aimed at changing it.

c. Some writers spoke for those participating in the civil rights, women's, and other social movements.

3. a. Arthur Miller shed light on the 1950s by examining a fearful incident in colonial history; Robert Hayden looked to Frederick Douglass's struggle for freedom in the Civil War era to inspire the civil rights movement of the 1960s.

b. Robert Lowell, Elizabeth Bishop, and Richard Wilbur produced poems in traditional forms, and Carson McCullers and Flannery O'Connor produced works in the Southern Gothic tradition.

c. William Carlos Williams, Wallace Stevens, and Ernest Hemingway continued to produce major Modernist works.

B. 1. to visit Europe on a family vacation

2. get a makeover

3. his lack of interest in their latest projects, robots

Essential Question: What is the relationship between place and literature? p. 5

Sample Answers

A. 1. a. Writers include Randall Jarrell, Norman Mailer, and John Hersey.

b. It did not echo the despair of literature that emerged from World War I and instead, despite its pain, seemed to hold out the possibility of meaningful courage and heroism.

2. a. Saul Bellow, Bernard Malamud, J.D. Salinger, James Agee, Philip Roth, Arthur Miller, and Lorraine Hansberry

b. It appeared as a symbol of modern American life

3. a. seemingly easier access to the American Dream

b. Many writers recognized that for some Americans, the dream could turn into a nightmare. These writers included John Cheever and John Updike.

B. 1. we talk about politics

2. an organized movement to preserve other landmarks

3. suburban houses are relatively close together and tend to be near shopping malls, and people in the suburbs often commute into nearby cities.

Following-Through Activities, p. 6

A. Students should complete the chart with concepts appropriate to the period and groups associated with these concepts.

B. Students should complete the chart with answers that will help them to research a form of spoken literature.

from Hiroshima by John Hersey
"The Death of the Ball Turret Gunner" by Randall Jarrell

Vocabulary Warm-up Exercises, p. 8

A. 1. proprietor

2. residential

3. commuting

4. rendezvous

5. reluctantly

6. conjunction

7. commercial

8. obsessed

B. Sample Answers

1. Faithful to her diet, Janice began a period of abstinence from cheese and ice cream.

2. Our reports were supposed to be comprised of five sections, so I was careful to include them all.

3. As sales continued to decline, the company's revenues dwindled.

4. We obeyed the order to evacuate our house and moved out before the storm hit.

5. The noise was incessant, making it difficult to concentrate on my homework.

6. To bury a bone, the dog was burrowing in the ground.

7. From his handsome, expensive suit of clothes, we could tell that he was extremely prosperous.

8. A basketball player showing restraint will be careful not to foul the opponents.

Reading Warm-up A, p. 9

Sample Answers

1. (scientists) (military leaders); *combination, union*

2. (where people lived); houses, apartment buildings

3. of a small business, store he owned; *owner*

4. traveling; To commute, people might use cars, trains, subways, or buses.

5. They had reservations; The opposite of *reluctantly* is *enthusiastically* or *willingly.*

6. (buying and selling); My father worked for a department store, part of a large *commercial* enterprise.

7. the first to do so [produce such a weapon]; tv show, Star Trek, sports, etc.

8. where scientists, engineers, and military leaders met; planned in advance

Reading Warm-up B, p. 10

Sample Answers

1. from the burning building; *leave, abandon, withdraw*

2. (ruined buildings, smoke, and panicked people running); *included, contained*

3. kept repeatedly exploding; The opposite of *incessant* is *occasional* or *rare.*

4. its successful shops and popular restaurants; *needy, poor*

5. (diminishing); The heat *increased* so we drew back from the fire.

6. (its efforts to demolish the city); *self-control, moderation*

7. beneath; *excavating, digging out*

8. late-night pizza; *indulgence*

Literary Analysis: Implied Theme, p. 11

1. a. objective—uses third-person point of view to report factually on the events experienced by Mr. Tanimoto; b. This excerpt shows how war disrupts the lives of its victims. It also emphasizes the feelings and humanity of people seen only as "the enemy" or as casualties of war.

2. a. objective—uses third-person point of view to report factually on the catastrophic effect of the atomic blast on the tin factory; b. This excerpt shows the destructive nature of war and how human knowledge, as represented by the books, can be destructive. Human knowledge is responsible for creating the terrifying weapon of mass destruction.

3. a. subjective—the poet uses poetic language ("loosed from its dream of life") and first-person narration to convey the subjective emotional experience of the ball turret gunner's reactions to being under enemy attack; b. This excerpt reveals the cruel and frightening nature of war through the eyes of a gunner perched below a World War II bomber. It emphasizes how death during war is treated with indifference—as if the soldiers fighting are merely killing machines.

Reading Strategy: Analyze Political Assumptions, p. 12

Suggested Responses

from *Hiroshima*—details: Students should include information such as Hersey's specific details, the ordinary day-to-day activities of the people, flashbacks, the settings of people's daily routines, the air raid warnings, and so forth; assumptions: students should note that Hersey's examples all point to the horrifying, destructive impact of war, especially on civilians, and that such details shows that Hersey is opposed to war in general and probably does not feel that the military advantages of dropping the bomb on Hiroshima were worth the price in innocent human suffering.

"The Death of the Ball Turret Gunner"—details: "from mother's sleep I fell into the State"—a fall from innocence and love into impersonal terror; "hunched in its belly till my wet fur froze"—picture of animal-like terror; "black flak and nightmare fighters"—the horror of facing death in battle; "they washed me out of the turret with a hose"—the impersonal nature of warfare; assumptions: war—any war— is an impersonal, hellish, terrifying nightmare with no redeeming qualities

Vocabulary Builder, p.13

A. 1. barricade
2. reconnaissance
3. khaki
4. blitz
5. coup

B. 1. A; 2. C; 3. A; 4. B; 5. C

Enrichment: Ethics of Warfare, p. 15

Suggested Responses

1. Students might say that people are entitled to human dignity. When people are involved in war, anger or other emotions are likely to impair their judgment. They might begin to see their adversaries as inhuman or unworthy of respect. That is why people need rules during such a highly emotional time.

2. Students should be able to support their opinions with concrete reasoning. Students might say that reading *Hiroshima* would help people to understand the effects of such a terrifying weapon. Reading about individual people and families might prompt people to have more compassion.

Open-Book Test, p. 16

Short Answer

1. The mood of the city is uneasy because of repeated reports of a possible air raid. This mood is apparent in Hersey's accounts of people leaving the city, taking their belongings to safety, and feeling unusual fatigue because of the stress of this threat and the measures needed to deal with it.
   Difficulty: *Average*   **Objective:** *Interpretation*

2. The distance shows how extensive the explosion's destruction was. It spread more than two miles from the center as it killed people and crushed buildings.
   Difficulty: *Challenging*   **Objective:** *Interpretation*

3. The implied theme is that whether one lives or dies in a war is a matter of chance.
   Difficulty: *Average*   **Objective:** *Literary Analysis*

4. Sample answer: Hersey is saying that in World War II in particular and in modern warfare in general, the civilians often bear as much of the brunt of battle and destruction as those in the military do.
   Difficulty: *Average*   **Objective:** *Reading Strategy*

5. Hersey's prolonged stay in East Asia made the bombing seem more personal to him, more immediate, especially after he had seen the effects of the destruction up close. He probably ended up with a more ambivalent view of the bombing than the typical American had.
   Difficulty: *Challenging*   **Objective:** *Reading Strategy*

6. Sample answer: Students' graphic organizers should include information such as Hersey's specific details, the ordinary day-to-day activities of the people, flashbacks, the settings of people's daily routines, the air raid warnings, and so forth. They can draw inferences that the bomb destroyed the lives of many ordinary people in a senseless manner. The implied theme is that the horrors of modern warfare reach everywhere into the civilian community, destroying the lives of innocent people.
   Difficulty: *Average*   **Objective:** *Literary Analysis*

7. Hersey wrote Hiroshima because he wanted to, because *volition* means "an act of using the will."
   Difficulty: *Average*   **Objective:** *Vocabulary*

8. The gunner is hit by enemy fire and dies in his position in the ball turret.
   Difficulty: *Easy*   **Objective:** *Interpretation*

9. Sample answer: The choice of the aircraft gunner implies that Jarrell's theme focuses on the the fact that death is everywhere in war.
   Difficulty: *Challenging*   **Objective:** *Literary Analysis*

10. The implied theme is that the treatment of soldiers during war is callous and impersonal, even in death.
    Difficulty: *Average*   **Objective:** *Literary Analysis*

Essay

11. Students might note that by using this technique, Hersey wants to show the horror of the blast as concretely as possible, as it affected the lives of many different people going about their daily routines. He also wants to show that no matter where a person was in Hiroshima that day, his or her life was turned upside down by the blast, if he or she survived.
    Difficulty: *Easy*   **Objective:** *Essay*

12. Sample answer: Hersey is opposed to warfare in general and the bombing of Hiroshima in particular. His images of people living in constant fear, waiting for some kind of attack, and his images of the destruction caused by the bomb and its impact on survivors reveal this attitude. He includes detailed descriptions because often during times of war, people's concrete, individual humanity is forgotten. He wants readers to see that people killed by the dropping of the bomb were not just casualties of war, but were living, breathing people with families, fears, and personalities.
    Difficulty: *Average*   **Objective:** *Essay*

13. Students might note that *Hiroshima* focuses on war's impact on civilians. Hersey highlights the tragedy of the effect of this bombing in particular, and war in general,

on the lives of ordinary people. "The Death of the Ball Turret Gunner" focuses on a lonely gunner who is experiencing his last moments of life aboard his plane. The last line of the poem, in which the gunner's body is being washed out of the turret, is particularly effective in expressing Jarrell's negative attitude toward the inhumanity and violence of war. Both poems share this concern and are critical of the dehumanizing effects of war on both civilians and soldiers.

Difficulty: *Challenging*   **Objective:** *Essay*

14. Students might note that the excerpt from *Hiroshima* shows the devastating effects of modern warfare on innocent civilians, far from the battlefield. In this case, the victims are people going about their everyday business in Hiroshima on the morning a U.S. plane dropped an atomic bomb on the city. With his detailed portraits of lives lost and upended by this monstrous force of modern technology, Hersey seeks not only to portray the reality of war but also to influence the reader to question whether such suffering of innocents can possibly be worth any cause that seeks to justify it. Likewise, students might note that the poem "The Death of the Ball Turret Gunner" seeks to shape the reader's perception of war by showing that it is not a noble and heroic adventure but rather a machinelike, impersonal factory of death, in which soldiers become mere cogs in a war machine and are cleaned out like so much waste matter if they are killed: "When I died they washed me out of the turret with a hose."

Difficulty: *Average*   **Objective:** *Essay*

Oral Response

15. Oral responses should be clear, well organized, and well supported by appropriate examples from the selections.

Difficulty: *Average*   **Objective:** *Oral Interpretation*

Essay

13. Students' essays should suggest that the writer wants to communicate the horror of the blast as well as the effect it had on specific individuals. He also wants to show that no matter where a person was in Hiroshima that day, he or she was affected by the blast.

Difficulty: *Easy*

Objective: *Essay*

14. Students should imagine themselves in the position of the ball turret gunner. They should use vivid, descriptive language to portray the gunner's external surroundings and inner thoughts and feelings.

Difficulty: *Easy*

Objective: *Essay*

15. Students might note that the excerpt from *Hiroshima* shows the devastating effects of modern warfare on innocent civilians, far from the battlefield. In this case, the victims are people going about their everyday business in Hiroshima on the morning a U.S. plane dropped an atomic bomb on the city. With his detailed portraits of lives lost and upended by this monstrous force of modern technology, Hersey seeks not only to portray the reality of war but also to influence the reader to question whether such suffering of innocents can possibly be worth any cause that seeks to justify it. Likewise, students might note that the poem "The Death of the Ball Turret Gunner" seeks to shape the reader's perception of war by showing that it is not a noble and heroic adventure but rather a machinelike, impersonal factory of death, in which soldiers become mere cogs in a war machine and are cleaned out like so much waste matter if they are killed: "When I died they washed me out of the turret with a hose."

Difficulty: *Easy*

Objective: *Essay*

Selection Test A, p. 19

Critical Reading

1. ANS: B	DIF: Easy	OBJ: Comprehension
2. ANS: A	DIF: Easy	OBJ: Literary Analysis
3. ANS: C	DIF: Easy	OBJ: Interpretation
4. ANS: B	DIF: Easy	OBJ: Comprehension
5. ANS: C	DIF: Easy	OBJ: Literary Analysis
6. ANS: A	DIF: Easy	OBJ: Literary Analysis
7. ANS: C	DIF: Easy	OBJ: Reading Strategy
8. ANS: B	DIF: Easy	OBJ: Reading Strategy
9. ANS: A	DIF: Easy	OBJ: Interpretation
10. ANS: A	DIF: Easy	OBJ: Comprehension

Vocabulary

11. ANS: B	DIF: Easy	OBJ: Vocabulary
12. ANS: A	DIF: Average	OBJ: Vocabulary

Selection Test B, p. 22

Critical Reading

1. ANS: B	DIF: Average	OBJ: Comprehension
2. ANS: B	DIF: Average	OBJ: Interpretation
3. ANS: C	DIF: Challenging	OBJ: Literary Analysis
4. ANS: B	DIF: Average	OBJ: Literary Analysis
5. ANS: B	DIF: Easy	OBJ: Comprehension
6. ANS: B	DIF: Challenging	OBJ: Interpretation
7. ANS: B	DIF: Average	OBJ: Literary Analysis
8. ANS: B	DIF: Average	OBJ: Reading Strategy
9. ANS: B	DIF: Challenging	OBJ: Interpretation
10. ANS: A	DIF: Easy	OBJ: Comprehension
11. ANS: C	DIF: Average	OBJ: Interpretation
12. ANS: B	DIF: Challenging	OBJ: Literary Analysis
13. ANS: C	DIF: Average	OBJ: Interpretation

Vocabulary

14. ANS: D   DIF: Average   OBJ: Vocabulary
15. ANS: B   DIF: Challenging   OBJ: Vocabulary

Essay

16. Students should understand that the line reveals the inhumanity that the poet associates with war. The line presents an image of death being treated quite casually and indifferently, and soldiers being treated as though they were objects rather than human beings. The line expresses the theme that war breeds cold and cruel behavior.

    Difficulty: *Easy*

    Objective: *Essay*

17. Students should understand that John Hersey has a negative attitude toward war and the bombing of Hiroshima. His images of people living in constant fear—waiting for some kind of attack—and his images of the destruction caused by the bomb and its impact on survivors reveal this attitude. He includes detailed descriptions because often during times of war, humanity is pushed aside. He wants readers to see that people killed by the dropping of the bomb were not just casualties of war, but were living, breathing people with families, fears, and personalities.

    Difficulty: *Average*

    Objective: *Essay*

18. Students should say that *Hiroshima* focuses on the effects of war on civilians. Hersey tries to emphasize the tragedy of the bombing, which killed many innocent people. His piece is critical of the war and the ways in which the lives of everyday people were affected. "The Death of the Ball Turret Gunner" focuses on a lonely gunner who is experiencing his last moments of life aboard his plane. The last line of the poem, in which the gunner's body is being washed out of the turret, is particularly effective in expressing Jarrell's negative attitude toward the cruelty and violence of war. Both pieces are critical of the attitudes and behaviors associated with war.

    Difficulty: *Challenging*

    Objective: *Essay*

19. Students might note that the excerpt from *Hiroshima* shows the devastating effects of modern warfare on innocent civilians, far from the battlefield. In this case, the victims are people going about their everyday business in Hiroshima on the morning a U.S. plane dropped an atomic bomb on the city. With his detailed portraits of lives lost and upended by this monstrous force of modern technology, Hersey seeks not only to portray the reality of war but also to influence the reader to question whether such suffering of innocents can possibly be worth any cause that seeks to justify it. Likewise, students might note that the poem "The Death of the Ball Turret Gunner" seeks to shape the reader's perception of war by showing that it is not a noble and heroic adventure but rather a machinelike, impersonal factory of death, in which soldiers become mere cogs in a war machine and are cleaned out like so much waste matter if they are killed: "When I died they washed me out of the turret with a hose."

    Difficulty: *Average*

    Objective: *Essay*

Editorial: "Backing the Attack"
Editorial Cartoon: "The Battle of the Easy Chair"
Advertisement Poster: "Junk Rally"
Primary Sources Worksheet, p. 25

Sample Answers

Thesis

Editorial: The war is very costly, but if everyone buys war bonds, we can pay for it.

Editorial Cartoon: This is no time to be complacent—everyone must be actively involved in the war effort.

Poster: Junk metal is a valuable commodity that can be used to make weapons and other equipment.

Facts and Figures

Editorial: The editorial uses many facts and figures related to the cost of the war.

Editorial Cartoon: No facts and figures—just a suggestion that the war will not be won quickly

Poster: Facts related to the upcoming junk rally, such as time, place, and purpose

Visual Elements

Editorial: None, except for different type faces to set off newspaper title and the quotation by Roosevelt

Editorial Cartoon: The entire cartoon is a visual element.

Poster: Includes visual elements of illustrations, boxed text, and varying type faces

Humor

Editorial: No humor

Editorial Cartoon: Humorous depiction of complacent gentleman

Poster: Humor in the visual of the iron hitting the man in the head

Quotations

Editorial: Quotation by Roosevelt

Editorial Cartoon: No quotations

Poster: No quotations

Catchy phrases

Editorial: No catchy phrases

Editorial Cartoon: The buttons on the gentleman's suit jacket have catchy phrases.

Poster: "Let's Jolt them with Junk from Winchester."

Appeal to Emotion

Editorial: Mentioning that small bond purchases would "outfit a sailor" or "buy a parachute"

Editorial Cartoon: The valet's worried look

Poster: Suggesting that donating scrap metal helps the war effort

Appeal to Logic

Editorial: Presenting the costs of the war as inducement to buy war bonds

Editorial Cartoon: None. This is an emotional appeal.

Poster: More emotional than logical

Vocabulary Builder, p. 26

A. Sample Answers

1. Yes, it is likely that you offended someone with your loose and inappropriate behavior.

2. No, a lazy person would avoid any serious task or challenge because it would take too much effort.

3. A team of five would do a better job of canvassing a neighborhood because they could talk to more people in a shorter amount of time than one person could.

4. A collective sigh by one hundred people would take about the same amount of time as the sigh of one person because the hundred people would all sigh together.

5. My weekly expenditures include lunch money, bus fare, and DVD rentals.

6. Estimates are not precise predictions of what a house would sell for; they just give a general idea.

7. A company's receipts represent its income.

8. A civilian is not likely to be wearing a military uniform (unless it's for a costume party) because a civilian does not belong to the military.

B. 1. B; 2. B; 3. D; 4. A

Selection Test, p. 27

Critical Reading

1. ANS: A	DIF: Average	OBJ: Literary Analysis
2. ANS: B	DIF: Average	OBJ: Literary Analysis
3. ANS: B	DIF: Challenging	OBJ: Literary Analysis
4. ANS: D	DIF: Average	OBJ: Literary Analysis
5. ANS: C	DIF: Easy	OBJ: Literary Analysis
6. ANS: B	DIF: Easy	OBJ: Reading Strategy
7. ANS: C	DIF: Average	OBJ: Literary Analysis
8. ANS: C	DIF: Average	OBJ: Literary Analysis
9. ANS: C	DIF: Easy	OBJ: Literary Analysis
10. ANS: A	DIF: Average	OBJ: Literary Analysis

"The Life You Save May Be Your Own"
by Flannery O'Connor

Vocabulary Warm-up Exercises, p. 30

A. 1. amble
2. gaunt
3. ominous
4. engulf
5. desolate
6. listed
7. uprooted
8. emphasize

B. Sample Answers

1. People are generally worried if they discover they are afflicted by a disease.

2. He was so depressed that he decided to go to bed early.

3. Russia covers a large expanse on the map of Europe and Asia.

4. The mechanism of a wristwatch is usually concealed inside the timepiece.

5. If you are morose, you usually feel downhearted and depressed.

6. When you feel oppressed by your employer, you may want to protest working conditions.

7. A person with a ravenous hunger cannot usually be satisfied with a small bite to eat.

8. The weather was so uncomfortably sultry that we decided to leave the beach early.

Reading Warm-up A, p. 31

Sample Answers

1. lonely . . . settings in the remote countryside; They lived in a *desolate* region, which was isolated and had little vegetation.

2. (swallowing them up); *swallow, overwhelm*

3. walks at a leisurely . . . Instead, the characters skulk, rush, lurch . . .; I try not to *rush* through a test.

4. *threatening; promising*

5. (. . . desperate-looking from anxiety and sleepless nights); After suffering through many crises, he looked pale and *gaunt.*

6. *stress, underline; minimize, pass over*

7. crazily to one side; The damaged ship *listed* heavily to starboard.

8. and transplanted them; *dug up*

Reading Warm-up B, p. 32

Sample Answers

1. tired . . . because she had to be at work waiting tables . . .; *dejected, downhearted*

2. (dim lighting); *sunny, glad, high-spirited*

3. Vin would never let her eat anything . . . with hunger, her stomach growling; After hiking through the woods for ten hours straight with no food, we felt *ravenous.*

4. under a heating lamp . . . with a big orange light bulb; the heating device is relatively primitive.

5. (with Parkinson's disease); badly affected

6. (along the . . . vinyl counter); she ran the rag along the whole counter, because *expanse* means "wide area."
7. <u>August heat</u>; Cool fall weather is *energizing*.
8. <u>the ugly, rasping sound</u>; *liberated*

Literary Analysis: Grotesque Characters, p. 33

Sample Responses

1. The woman is obsessed with her daughter and thinks the girl is a valuable prize. She would do anything to assure that her daughter is never parted from her.
2. Mr. Shiftlet is obsessed with the idea that cars are too expensive and that no pride of workmanship goes into them. Because of this obsession, he can be expected to be proud of any car he might have; he would take good care of it.
3. Mr. Shiftlet thinks the rest of the world is rotten, and he fails to see the rottenness in himself. A man like Mr. Shiftlet is likely to take advantage of other people, thinking he deserves any advantage he can get.

Reading Strategy: Draw Conclusions from Details, p. 34

Sample Responses

1. The man will turn out to be someone to fear.
2. She will convince Mr. Shiftlet to marry her daughter.
3. They will / will not get married.
4. Mr. Shiftlet is going to get money out of Mrs. Crater, though he wants it for other purposes than Lucynell.
5. Mr. Shiftlet is uncomfortable with the marriage and may take action to end it.
6. He is leaving Lucynell to move on by himself.

Vocabulary Builder, p. 35

A. Sample Responses

1. Mr. Shiftlet was a solitary figure as he made his way toward the house.
2. After their departure, Mrs. Crater was the sole occupant of the farm.
3. Mrs. Crater was solely responsible for Lucynell.
4. Mrs. Crater and Lucynell lived in solitude on their isolated farm.

B. Sample Responses

1. The shed *listed* as if it were perched on a hill, even though the ground was perfectly flat.
2. The *desolate* setting could do nothing but cause despair in the characters and in the readers.
3. Her disappointment caused her to be *morose* for days until she regained her spirits.
4. The *ravenous* children kept coming back for more helpings of stew.
5. The dark clouds in the distance were an *ominous* sight.

Enrichment: Human Resources Interview, p. 37

A. Sample Responses

Skills and Knowledge

1. What specific carpentry experience have you had?
2. Do you build things from scratch? Do you do repair work?
3. How did you acquire your skills?

Personality

1. How would you describe your ability to get along with people?
2. How would you handle the situation if a client refused to pay you for work you had already completed?
3. What three words best describe you?

B. Suggested Responses

Students' contributions to the memo should be evaluative without being judgmental. Comments about personality should address job-related issues, not personal preference. Job training may take the form of an apprenticeship, a seminar, or a class. Job opportunities must be limited to carpentry work, but students may suggest other work connected with the construction industry.

Open-Book Test, p. 38

Short Answer

1. He is interested in their car.
   Difficulty: *Average*   **Objective:** *Reading Strategy*
2. Both are opportunists who are trying to use each other to get what they want—the old woman a husband for her daughter, Shiftlet the car for himself.
   Difficulty: *Challenging*   **Objective:** *Literary Analysis*
3. Each character is physically handicapped in some respect. Mrs. Crater is missing all her teeth, Lucynell is deaf, and Shiftlet is missing an arm.
   Difficulty: *Easy*   **Objective:** *Literary Analysis*
4. The reader can conclude that he is probably dishonest and is trying to deceive Mrs. Carter by trying, rather too hard, to appear honest.
   Difficulty: *Average*   **Objective:** *Reading Strategy*
5. Sample answer: Traits: fast-talking, manipulative behavior; physical disability and the manner in which he deals with it; his exaggerated interest in the younger Lucynell; his obsession with the car; his cynical approach to life.

   Mr. Shiftlet is a grotesque character because of his physical disability and because he is extremely immoral and deceitful.
   Difficulty: *Challenging*   **Objective:** *Literary Analysis*
6. The old woman is obsessed with marrying off her daughter and will do or say anything to make it happen, no matter how corrupt (offering money) or dishonest (lying about her age or exaggerating her virtues). The extremes make her a grotesque character.
   Difficulty: *Average*   **Objective:** *Literary Analysis*

7. As soon as he agrees to marry her, his concerns turn quickly and exclusively to obtaining a sum of money from the old woman.

    Difficulty: *Easy* **Objective:** *Interpretation*

8. The statement is odd and ironic because nearly everything he does or says is corrupt or immoral.

    Difficulty: *Average* **Objective:** *Interpretation*

9. The hitchhiker's words and emotions are honest, which is surprising in view of the constant dishonesty and hypocrisy that has come from the other characters in the story.

    Difficulty: *Challenging* **Objective:** *Interpretation*

10. Yes, an ominous weather forecast would be one that promised more snow and therefore increased the possibility of an avalanche, because ominous means "threatening; sinister."

    Difficulty: *Average* **Objective:** *Vocabulary*

Essay

11. Students might suggest that if Mrs. Crater had been less grotesque, less obsessed with marrying off her daughter, she might have been more sensitive to Shiftlet's evil intentions. If Shiftlet had been less grotesque, he might have been more concerned about helping Mrs. Crater and her daughter without any ulterior motives. Students may feel that any shift toward more "normal" traits would have changed the outcome of the story completely, because the outcome is a direct result of the grotesque aspects of the characters.

    Difficulty: *Easy* **Objective:** *Essay*

12. Students might note that Shiftlet's reaction is odd because, as an immoral, cynical man, he would not be expected to show any sign of conscience or moral sensitivity, or to have any sort of religious beliefs that would lead him to pray. Moreover, the content of the prayer is surprising, since it shows his awareness of his own lack of morals in having dumped Lucynell in a diner without letting people know who she is or where she lives. The "slime" is his own rottenness. Students might suggest that his slight stirring of conscience is overwhelmed by his basically evil nature.

    Difficulty: *Average* **Objective:** *Essay*

13. Some students may point to her grotesque appearance; others, to her desolate surroundings: a dreary, run-down country residence. Students should also recognize that the old woman's obsession with marrying off her daughter and her belief that the daughter would be a "prize" for a husband, contribute to Mrs. Crater's grotesqueness. Also, her desperateness to marry off Lucynell blinds her to Shiftlet's immorality and deepens her own, since she is willing to sell off her daughter to Shiftlet.

    Difficulty: *Challenging* **Objective:** *Essay*

14. Students should note that the setting of "The Life You Save May Be Your Own" contributes to the sense of Gothic eccentricity that is expressed through the three main characters: Mrs. Crater, Lucynell, and Mr. Shiftlet. This broken-down old farm, this "desolate spot" that is seemingly in the middle of nowhere, seems to be on some planet other than the one inhabited by the thriving cities and suburbs of the 1950s United States— and therefore an environment in which these strange misfits are more likely to appear: the cynical old woman who is "the size of a cedar fence post"; the "crooked," one-armed Shiftlet with his cruel schemes; and the pathetic, innocent, barely literate Lucynell. Students might suggest that the odd fate and fortunes of these characters prompt the reader to think about departures not only from standard kinds of external places, but also from standard internal ways of being human—that there are grotesque secrets of the human heart that lie hidden on the hidden side roads of human experience, far from the well-paved main streets of everyday life.

    Difficulty: *Average* **Objective:** *Essay*

Oral Response

15. Oral responses should be clear, well organized, and well supported by appropriate examples from the selections.

    Difficulty: *Average* **Objective:** *Oral Interpretation*

Selection Test A, p. 41

Critical Reading

1. ANS: A	DIF: Easy	OBJ: Literary Analysis
2. ANS: C	DIF: Easy	OBJ: Interpretation
3. ANS: B	DIF: Easy	OBJ: Literary Analysis
4. ANS: D	DIF: Easy	OBJ: Comprehension
5. ANS: D	DIF: Easy	OBJ: Comprehension
6. ANS: C	DIF: Easy	OBJ: Reading Strategy
7. ANS: B	DIF: Easy	OBJ: Literary Analysis
8. ANS: D	DIF: Easy	OBJ: Reading Strategy
9. ANS: C	DIF: Easy	OBJ: Comprehension
10. ANS: C	DIF: Easy	OBJ: Literary Analysis

Vocabulary

11. ANS: B	DIF: Easy	OBJ: Vocabulary
12. ANS: A	DIF: Average	OBJ: Vocabulary
13. ANS: A	DIF: Easy	OBJ: Vocabulary
14. ANS: C	DIF: Challenging	OBJ: Vocabulary
15. ANS: D	DIF: Average	OBJ: Vocabulary

Essay

16. Students' essays should discuss one or more of the following: Mrs. Crater does not notice that Mr. Shiftlet rarely answers her questions directly. Second, she fails

to notice that he cares only about the car, no matter what else she discusses with him. She also fails to notice how depressed he acts at the wedding.

Difficulty: *Easy*

Objective: *Essay*

17. Students' essays should reflect that it is odd for Mr. Shiftlet to pray, since he is not a moral person. The "slime" is largely his own rottenness. He has abandoned Lucynell without letting people know who she is or where she lives.

Difficulty: *Easy*

Objective: *Essay*

18. Students should note that the setting of "The Life You Save May Be Your Own" contributes to the sense of Gothic eccentricity that is expressed through the three main characters: Mrs. Crater, Lucynell, and Mr. Shiftlet. This broken-down old farm, this "desolate spot" that is seemingly in the middle of nowhere, seems to be on some planet other than the one inhabited by the thriving cities and suburbs of the 1950s United States—and therefore an environment in which these strange misfits are more likely to appear: the cynical old woman who is "the size of a cedar fence post"; the "crooked," one-armed Shiftlet with his cruel schemes; and the pathetic, innocent, barely literate Lucynell. Students might suggest that the odd fate and fortunes of these characters prompt the reader to think about departures not only from standard kinds of external places, but also from standard internal ways of being human—that there are grotesque secrets of the human heart that lie hidden on the hidden side roads of human experience, far from the well-paved main streets of everyday life.

Difficulty: *Easy*

Objective: *Essay*

Selection Test B, p. 44

Critical Reading

1. ANS: D	DIF: Average	OBJ: Comprehension
2. ANS: B	DIF: Average	OBJ: Interpretation
3. ANS: C	DIF: Challenging	OBJ: Interpretation
4. ANS: A	DIF: Challenging	OBJ: Interpretation
5. ANS: A	DIF: Easy	OBJ: Comprehension
6. ANS: C	DIF: Average	OBJ: Interpretation
7. ANS: C	DIF: Average	OBJ: Reading Strategy
8. ANS: A	DIF: Easy	OBJ: Reading Strategy
9. ANS: D	DIF: Easy	OBJ: Literary Analysis
10. ANS: B	DIF: Average	OBJ: Literary Analysis
11. ANS: C	DIF: Challenging	OBJ: Literary Analysis
12. ANS: D	DIF: Average	OBJ: Interpretation
13. ANS: A	DIF: Average	OBJ: Reading Strategy
14. ANS: A	DIF: Challenging	OBJ: Interpretation
15. ANS: A	DIF: Average	OBJ: Interpretation

Vocabulary

16. ANS: B	DIF: Average	OBJ: Vocabulary
17. ANS: C	DIF: Easy	OBJ: Vocabulary
18. ANS: A	DIF: Easy	OBJ: Vocabulary
19. ANS: C	DIF: Average	OBJ: Grammar

Essay

20. Students should recognize that the only detail about the woman's physical appearance—the absence of teeth—creates a grotesque effect. The old woman lives in a desolate spot, though readers are not given any information as to exactly why or how it is desolate. This undesirable, slightly bizarre setting contributes to the woman's grotesque profile. Students must recognize that the woman is obsessed with her daughter—she believes that young Lucynell would be a "prize" for a husband. We are also told she is "ravenous for a son-in-law." This is really all we know about the old woman. She assumes that anyone who would marry Lucynell would stay at the farm because she, herself, cannot imagine being parted from Lucynell. That Mr. Shiftlet gains the old woman's trust so easily is a sign that the old woman's obsession has affected her judgment.

Difficulty: *Easy*

Objective: *Essay*

21. Students may choose any three symbols. The "crooked cross" is a reference to the Christian image of Christ being crucified on a cross. The symbolic nature of this reference is ironic. Shiftlet is anything but similar to the traditional concept of Christ. The human heart that doctors have cut out of a man's chest is a symbol for Shiftlet himself, who, it turns out, has no heart. Shiftlet spies the car's bumper almost immediately upon arriving at the farm. The car represents to him freedom and mobility. It may also symbolize his youth. He speculates that it's a 1928 or 1929 model, and we are told it has been sitting there for fifteen years, so it would be from a time when Shiftlet was young and innocent and still had his arm. The hitchhiker is a symbol for the truth. He speaks what he thinks is the truth, though it may be ugly. What he speaks is what Shiftlet claims to abhor. But what Shiftlet speaks is not the truth.

Difficulty: *Challenging*

Objective: *Essay*

22. Students should note that the setting of "The Life You Save May Be Your Own" contributes to the sense of Gothic eccentricity that is expressed through the three main characters: Mrs. Crater, Lucynell, and Mr. Shiftlet. This broken-down old farm, this "desolate spot" that is seemingly in the middle of nowhere, seems to be on some planet other than the one inhabited by the thriving cities and suburbs of the 1950s United States—and therefore an environment in which these strange misfits are more likely to appear: the cynical old woman who is "the size of a cedar fence post"; the "crooked," one-armed Shiftlet with his cruel schemes; and the pathetic, innocent, barely literate Lucynell. Students might suggest that the odd fate and fortunes of these characters prompt the reader to think about departures not only from standard kinds of external places, but

also from standard internal ways of being human—that there are grotesque secrets of the human heart that lie hidden on the hidden side roads of human experience, far from the well-paved main streets of everyday life.

Difficulty: *Average*

Objective: *Essay*

"The First Seven Years" by Bernard Malamud

Vocabulary Warm-up Exercises, p. 48

A.
1. anticipating
2. irritating
3. diminished
4. dissatisfied
5. inquired
6. probe
7. inscribed
8. grotesquely

B. Sample Answers
1. F; A *devious* person is deceptive, so you should probably mistrust his or her advice.
2. F; Someone with *diligence* would typically be careful and focused.
3. T; If a person drove *haphazardly*, his or her driving would be unpredictable and dangerous.
4. T; *Illiterate* means "unable to read or write."
5. T; There is no easy explanation for the behavior of people who act *inexplicably*.
6. T; An *insight* is typically a constructive, valuable perception or interpretation.
7. T; Glasses help many *nearsighted* people to drive.
8. F; Performers who are *temperamental* typically display selfish, quirky behavior.

Reading Warm-up A, p. 49

Sample Answers
1. her date with a boy named John; We are keenly *anticipating* the start of the World Series next month.
2. (like an exaggerated cartoon); *Outlandishly* is a synonym for *grotesquely*.
3. had started high; *Increased* is an antonym for *diminished*.
4. (business card), (the words); Words can be *inscribed* in stone or on a ring.
5. (disappointed); I saw my score, and I was *satisfied*.
6. From his attitude to his way of speaking; *Pleasing* and *gratifying* are antonyms for *irritating*.
7. (question); At the front desk, I *inquired* about the entry fee for the museum.
8. She kept asking questions; *Investigate* is a synonym for *probe*.

Reading Warm-up B, p. 50

Sample Answers
1. casually; He backed out of the *driveway carefully*.
2. (understanding); Reading her essay gave me further *insight* into the author's theme in that short story.
3. uneducated; *educated, learned*
4. skill; *carelessness, laziness*
5. (Jacob keeps his part of the bargain, but Laban turns out to be . . . He deceptively substitutes Rachel's sister Leah at the last minute); The opposite of *devious* is *straightforward* or *honest*.
6. hard to understand; *reasonably, logically, predictably*
7. he does not understand
8. (unpredictable)

Literary Analysis: Plot and Epiphany, p. 51

Sample Responses
1. Not epiphany—Feld is remembering something that he has thought before.
2. Not epiphany—The wish is not a moment of insight that reveals something significant about life.
3. Not epiphany—Feld merely decides on an alternative plan of action.
4. Not epiphany—Feld has learned about something that is going on. He has a heart attack but no profound insights.
5. Epiphany—Feld suddenly understands that Sobel and Miriam have been cultivating a close relationship over the past five years. There has been much more going on between his daughter and his assistant than he had ever imagined.

Reading Strategy: Summarizing, p. 52

Sample responses: Miriam—**relationship:** Feld loves Miriam but does not understand her; **learns:** He sees that she will never marry Max but is in love with Sobel; Sobel—**relationship:** Feld admires Sobel as a worker but looks down on him as a person because he does not understand his love of books and ideas; **learns:** he realizes that because Sobel and Miriam share deep personal values, they will eventually marry. Max—**relationship:** Feld admires Max as an ambitious young man with a solid future; **learns:** Feld realizes that Max and Miriam have nothing in common and will not make a good match.

Vocabulary Builder, p. 53

A. Sample Responses
1. literate—able to read, or knowledgeable about written works
2. literature—written work; writings; printed matter

B. Sample Responses

1. Feld thinks Max has *diligence* because he sees him going to school every day. Miriam has chosen not to go to school.

2. They are *not illiterate* because they can both read.

3. An *unscrupulous* employee might steal, do poor work, or lie.

4. Feld felt he could *discern* qualities in Max that Miriam could not perceive.

5. It was a poor, rough place, and Feld did not want Miriam to be exposed to such things; the idea was *repugnant*.

Enrichment: Conflict Resolution, p. 55

Sample Responses

1. Sobel might begin the conversation with, "I'd like to talk to you about the shoe leather. Its quality doesn't seem to be as good as the kind we used before." Sobel should *not* say, "This leather you're buying is no good," which accuses Feld of doing something wrong or inadequate.

2. Students may apply these tips to a disagreement among family members, classmates, or club or team members. Students should not relate what happened to cause the disagreement. Instead, they should talk about what could or should have happened had participants worked to resolve the disagreement constructively.

Open-Book Test, p. 56

Short Answer

1. The key plot development that is foreshadowed in this paragraph is Feld's scheme to serve as a matchmaker between Max and his daughter.

   Difficulty: *Easy*   **Objective:** *Literary Analysis*

2. Sample answer: Feld consistently wants what is best for his daughter, particularly material things, and thinks her life should be "better"—financially more secure—than his. So he forces his own ideas of what her life should be like on her. Miriam has developed an independence that allows her to tolerate Feld's actions and comments. But she pursues her own goals and wishes, which focus on books and ideas rather than money.

   Difficulty: *Challenging*   **Objective:** *Reading Strategy*

3. The contrast in their values makes it clear that they are basically incompatible and thus foreshadows the unsuccessful outcome of their two dates.

   Difficulty: *Challenging*   **Objective:** *Literary Analysis*

4. Sobel is different because another assistant would not be likely to do such a good job for such low wages. Sobel's exceptional performance is motivated by his desire to be near Miriam.

   Difficulty: *Average*   **Objective:** *Interpretation*

5. Max's questions show that he is someone who is mainly interested in appearances (his first question is to ask to see a picture) and in predictable, "normal" behavior.

The questions also show that he is a very practical-minded man of conservative, average values.

   Difficulty: *Challenging*   **Objective:** *Interpretation*

6. Feld respects Sobel's hard work and honesty and has come to depend on him for the success of his business. But he does not view him as a suitable match for his daughter because of his limited ambitions and career prospects. Sobel seems to regard Feld as a dependable employer but values him mainly because Feld allows Sobel to be near Miriam.

   Difficulty: *Average*   **Objective:** *Reading Strategy*

7. Sample answers: Feld loves Miriam but does not understand her; realization: He sees that she will never marry Max but is in love with Sobel

   Feld admires Sobel as a worker but looks down on him as a person because he does not understand his love of books and ideas; **realization:** he realizes that because Sobel and Miriam share deep personal values, they will eventually marry.

   Feld admires Max as an ambitious young man with a solid future: **realization:** Feld realizes that Max and Miriam: have nothing in common and will not make a good match.

   Difficulty: *Challenging*   **Objective:** *Reading Strategy*

8. Knowing that Feld has relented about his relationship with Miriam, Sobel is working steadily toward the time when he can propose marriage to her.

   Difficulty: *Average*   **Objective:** *Interpretation*

9. Sample answer: Feld realizes that Sobel truly loves his daughter and would do anything for her. He accepts the reality that he cannot change Sobel's and Miriam's feelings or force Miriam to love someone who can provide her with a more promising financial future.

   Difficulty: *Average*   **Objective:** *Interpretation*

10. Yes, you would expect that the person would be doing a good job, because *diligence* means "constant, careful effort."

   Difficulty: *Average*   **Objective:** *Vocabulary*

Essay

11. Sample answer: Dear Father, I am surprised that you would think that I could be interested in Max, who only thinks about money and possessions. You know perfectly well that I value books and ideas above possessions. For that reason, Sobel, the man who shares my passion for books and ideas, is the man who comes closest to my idea of a good husband. He is kind, and, as you know, honest. I can assure you that I will be happier with him even if it means we have less money. Love, Miriam

   Difficulty: *Easy*   **Objective:** *Essay*

12. Students might note that Feld is insensitive to Miriam in not letting her make up her own mind about college, work, and love. He is insensitive to Max in assuming that

Miriam would be a good match for him. He is insensitive to Sobel, who has worked closely with him for years, in not recognizing that Sobel has romantic feelings for Miriam, and that he would be a good match for her.

Difficulty: *Average*   **Objective:** *Essay*

13. Sample answer: Feld and Max seem to share the idea that happiness in life is achieved mostly through material things and financial security. That is why Feld works so hard at his modest business, and why Max is such a hard-working student. Sobel, who lives mainly for books and ideas, has no use for material wealth. In this respect, he and Miriam have basically the same worldview, which is the main reason they care so deeply for each other. Feld and Max, with their focus on the material, clash with Sobel and Miriam, who focus on books and ideas.

Difficulty: *Challenging*   **Objective:** *Essay*

14. Students might suggest that Feld the shoemaker is someone who grew up poor and who therefore views America as a place where, above all, one should pursue the many opportunities to strive for a more ample and secure material life; this is why he pressures his daughter, Miriam, to take an interest in Max, the aspiring young accountant. Miriam, on the other hand, shows no interest in money-making or social ambition—she is attracted, rather, to the studious and idealistic Sobel, Feld's bookish and high-minded assistant, who cares more for ideas than money. The clash of values between Feld on the one hand and Miriam and Sobel on the other captures this classic American conflict between the life of the spirit and the temptations of the material world.

Difficulty: *Average*   **Objective:** *Essay*

Oral Response

15. Oral responses should be clear, well organized, and well supported by appropriate examples from the selections.

Difficulty: *Average*   **Objective:** *Oral Response*

Selection Test A, p. 59

Critical Reading

1. ANS: B	DIF: Easy	OBJ: Reading Strategy
2. ANS: C	DIF: Easy	OBJ: Comprehension
3. ANS: A	DIF: Easy	OBJ: Reading Strategy
4. ANS: B	DIF: Easy	OBJ: Interpretation
5. ANS: C	DIF: Easy	OBJ: Interpretation
6. ANS: D	DIF: Easy	OBJ: Interpretation
7. ANS: C	DIF: Easy	OBJ: Comprehension
8. ANS: B	DIF: Easy	OBJ: Literary Analysis
9. ANS: A	DIF: Easy	OBJ: Literary Analysis
10. ANS: C	DIF: Easy	OBJ: Literary Analysis

Vocabulary

| 11. ANS: C | DIF: Easy | OBJ: Vocabulary |
| 12. ANS: D | DIF: Easy | OBJ: Vocabulary |

| 13. ANS: B | DIF: Challenging | OBJ: Vocabulary |
| 14. ANS: C | DIF: Average | OBJ: Vocabulary |

Essay

15. Students should write a letter, such as the following: Dear Father, I am surprised that you would think I could be interested in Max, who thinks only of money and possessions. When I do think about marrying, I want to tell you that I am drawn to your employee, Mr. Sobel. He is kind, and I know that you find him trustworthy. Father, please let me make up my own mind about what I do with my life. Your loving daughter, Miriam

Difficulty: *Easy*

Objective: *Essay*

16. Students' essays should reflect one or more of these examples: Feld is insensitive to Miriam in not letting her make up her own mind about college, work, and love. He is insensitive to Max in assuming that Max and Miriam would be a good match. He is insensitive to Sobel, who has worked closely with him for five years, in not recognizing that Sobel has romantic feelings for Miriam.

Difficulty: *Easy*

Objective: *Essay*

17. Students might suggest that Feld the shoemaker is someone who grew up poor and who therefore views America as a place where, above all, one should pursue the many opportunities to strive for a more ample and secure material life; this is why he pressures his daughter, Miriam, to take an interest in Max, the aspiring young accountant. Miriam, on the other hand, shows no interest in money-making or social ambition— she is attracted, rather, to the studious and idealistic Sobel, Feld's bookish and high-minded assistant, who cares more for ideas than money. The clash of values between Feld on the one hand and Miriam and Sobel on the other captures this classic American conflict between the life of the spirit and the temptations of the material world.

Difficulty: *Easy*

Objective: *Essay*

Selection Test B, p. 62

Critical Reading

1. ANS: D	DIF: Average	OBJ: Reading Strategy
2. ANS: B	DIF: Challenging	OBJ: Interpretation
3. ANS: D	DIF: Easy	OBJ: Comprehension
4. ANS: B	DIF: Easy	OBJ: Interpretation
5. ANS: C	DIF: Easy	OBJ: Comprehension
6. ANS: B	DIF: Average	OBJ: Reading Strategy
7. ANS: D	DIF: Average	OBJ: Interpretation
8. ANS: A	DIF: Challenging	OBJ: Reading Strategy
9. ANS: A	DIF: Average	OBJ: Comprehension
10. ANS: B	DIF: Challenging	OBJ: Literary Analysis

11. ANS: C	DIF: Average	OBJ: Interpretation
12. ANS: D	DIF: Average	OBJ: Literary Analysis
13. ANS: C	DIF: Easy	OBJ: Interpretation
14. ANS: B	DIF: Average	OBJ: Comprehension
15. ANS: D	DIF: Challenging	OBJ: Interpretation

Vocabulary

| 16. ANS: C | DIF: Easy | OBJ: Vocabulary |
| 17. ANS: B | DIF: Challenging | OBJ: Vocabulary |

Essay

18. Students should note that Miriam's choice to take a job gives her some financial freedom as well as the freedom to continue to pursue her own interests, such as the books Sobel supplies to her. Her choice does give her independence, though some would say it is limited by the type of job she can get without any further education. Feld's plan for college would open up doors of knowledge and opportunity. Miriam is opening some of those doors on her own through her reading, it seems. As to Miriam's decision, students may side with Miriam or Feld but must explain their reasons. Those who support Miriam's decision may say it was the right decision for her simply because it was hers. Others may feel that she threw away an opportunity because her father was *offering* to send her to college, and it would be a good idea to go and see what it's all about.

Difficulty: *Easy*

Objective: *Essay*

19. Students should acknowledge that Feld is absorbed by thoughts of his daughter's future right at the beginning of the story. He admires the diligence of Max, whom he sees trudging to school regularly. He wishes his daughter had that same diligence and desire for education. Feld runs his business as best he can, given his health. He tries not to meddle too much in Miriam's business, though he can't resist asking questions. Feld does admit that his least hope for Miriam is that she marry an educated man. This admission on Feld's part helps build to his epiphany. The second step on the way to the epiphany is Feld's thought about why Sobel reads so much. Feld resists the notion that "reading to know" is acceptable and is all that Miriam really wants from an "education" as well. When Sobel finally blurts out his reason for working for Feld for so long, Feld is both stunned and unsurprised. He had known and rejected the idea. Seeing Sobel's sincerity and earnestness, Feld gives up his notions of a "better" material life for Miriam and settles for the life that he assumes she will choose with Sobel. He leaves in silence, but then walks with a "stronger stride." It seems he is relieved that the issue has been settled, and he is perhaps less disappointed than one might have thought.

Difficulty: *Average*

Objective: *Essay*

20. Students should recognize that Feld starts out thinking that education and the resultant material benefits are the only road to "a better life," or success and happiness. His views change, of course, as he sees that Sobel really loves Miriam, and he is saddened yet satisfied with the outcome of the whole situation. Sobel, who has fallen in love and sacrificed material gain just to be near Miriam, obviously has no use for material wealth. His riches come from the books he reads and shares with Miriam. Miriam accuses Max of being a materialist. It seems he is only interested in "things." This is in keeping with his relentless pursuit of his education. Max will not agree to call Miriam for a date until he verifies her age and sees a picture of her. He is not satisfied with her father's assurances about her positive qualities. Finally, Miriam appears at one level to pursue material comfort because she chooses a job over the deprivation of going to college. Where she really lives, though, is in her books. Max, in his pursuit of accountancy, values things, and this bores Miriam. She prefers to consider ideas and feelings—the ones she finds in her books and in Sobel. Students may agree with any one character's notions, or a combination of several.

Difficulty: *Challenging*

Objective: *Essay*

21. Students might suggest that Feld the shoemaker is someone who grew up poor and who therefore views America as a place where, above all, one should pursue the many opportunities to strive for a more ample and secure material life; this is why he pressures his daughter, Miriam, to take an interest in Max, the aspiring young accountant. Miriam, on the other hand, shows no interest in money-making or social ambition—she is attracted, rather, to the studious and idealistic Sobel, Feld's bookish and high-minded assistant, who cares more for ideas than money. The clash of values between Feld on the one hand and Miriam and Sobel on the other captures this classic American conflict between the life of the spirit and the temptations of the material world.

Difficulty: *Average*

Objective: *Essay*

"Constantly Risking Absurdity" by Lawrence Ferlinghetti

Vocabulary Warm-up Exercises, p. 66

A. 1. taut
2. death-defying
3. absurdity
4. existence
5. theatrics
6. balancing
7. acrobat
8. spreadeagled

B. Sample Answers

1. OK

2. He was such a underline{realist} that he never took part in wild schemes.

3. The performance lasted so long that it seemed underline{eternal}.

4. She was so strong and agile that she could perform fantastic underline{entrechats}.

5. The professor spoke with such underline{gravity} that everyone could tell the matter was serious.

6. OK

7. If you underline{perceive} something, you have a very good idea what it means.

8. The underline{audience} was so small that the play was sure to make very little money.

Reading Warm-up A, p. 67

Sample Answers

1. (performance, staged effects); I enjoyed the *theatrics* of the play more than the story.

2. tightrope walkers; *teetering, being unsteady* or *off-balance*

3. China; My cat gets in such crazy positions that I think she is an *acrobat*.

4. Yes, it is probably good for a clown to have a sense of underline{absurdity}; *craziness, ridiculousness*

5. (the high-wire act); A person who likes taking risks engages in *death-defying* behavior.

6. underline{stretched}; The cord was so *taut* that it was hard to untie the knot on the end.

7. A underline{spreadeagled} clown would be sprawled with his arms and legs outstretched; I was *spreadeagled* once when I fell down the stairs.

8. underline{rewarding}; life, way of life

Reading Warm-up B, p. 68

Sample Answers

1. underline{she would never be good enough to dance at the highest level}; *idealist*

2. (jumping); The fleeing suspect made a *leap* into the river.

3. underline{cross her legs in the air more rapidly}; Yes, it would be hard because you would have to be very strong to jump in the air and do those motions.

4. underline{her family and friends, and those of her fellow dancers}; I was in the *audience* for my school's talent show.

5. (went over the correct way to execute a single step so many times); *endless*

6. way of standing; Being at attention in the military has a special *stance*.

7. (seriousness); The *gravity* and importance of the situation made it important to make the right decision.

8. underline{his mood worsening}; *recognize, sense*

Literary Analysis: Extended Metaphor, p. 69

Sample Responses

Possible responses: "Constantly risking absurdity / and death"—taking great creative risks with language and meaning; "climbs on a high wire of his own making"—sets high standards and goals to be achieved in the art of poetry; "performing entrechats / and sleight of foot tricks"—takes bold leaps of the imagination and makes agile and subtle use of words; "And he / little charleychaplin man"—the poet is really a poor hapless soul in the face of his grand ambitions; "who may or may not catch / her eternal fair form"—there are no guarantees that the poet will achieve his/her goal of capturing beauty and truth in words.

Reading Strategy: Visualize or Picture the Action, p. 70

Possible Responses

1. In picturing that image, I think about the high standards and ambitions that the poet sets for him/herself.

2. I visualize both great physical power of the kind needed to perform jumps such as entrechats and the very fine finesse skills needed to perform fancy footwork ("sleight-of-foot tricks"); these skills translate into the poet's ability to write poems that take bold leaps of the imagination and make very nimble and fine use of words.

3. I picture a mass of people who are hungry for amazement and spectacle—in the case of poetry, to be amazed by the spectacle of truth and beauty as created by the poet's words.

4. I visualize a modest, hapless, nervous person who is afraid of his own shadow. Students' responses will vary, depending on how much they know about or have seen of Charley Chaplin's films. Accept any response that seems well grounded in the language of the image.

Vocabulary Builder, p. 71

A. Sample Responses

1. No, she was not agreeing, because absurdity means "senselessness" or "silliness."

2. Yes, she was paying the movie a compliment, because taut means "tight" or "tense," which means that it was a well-plotted movie.

3. No, his program would not contain any unreasonable demands because *realist* means "one who is practical or unidealistic."

B. 1. b; 2. c; 3. a

Open-Book Test, p. 74

Short Answer

1. He compares the poet to a high-wire acrobat in a circus.
   Difficulty: *Easy*   **Objective:** *Literary Analysis*

2. Sample answer: "Constantly risking absurdity / and death" = taking great creative risks with language and meaning

   "climbs on a high wire of his own making" = sets high standards and goals to be achieved in the art of poetry

Unit 5 Resources: Prosperity and Protest
© Pearson Education, Inc. All rights reserved.
330

"performing entrechats / and sleight-of-foot tricks" =
takes bold leaps of the imagination and makes agile and
subtle use of words

"And he / little charleychaplin man" = the poet is really
a poor hapless soul in the face of his grand ambitions

"who may or may not catch / her eternal fair form" =
there are no guarantees that the poet will achieve his/
her goal of capturing beauty and truth in words.

Difficulty: *Challenging*   **Objective:** *Literary Analysis*

3. Students might suggest that in picturing that image
they think about the high standards and ambitions that
the poet sets for him/herself.

Difficulty: *Challenging*   **Objective:** *Reading Strategy*

4. Students will probably visualize both great physical
power of the kind needed to perform jumps such as
entrechats and the very fine coordination needed to
perform fancy footwork ("sleight-of-foot tricks"). These
skills translate into the poet's work as the ability to
write poems that take bold leaps of the imagination and
make very clever, able, and fine use of words.

Difficulty: *Average*   **Objective:** *Reading Strategy*

5. Ferlinghetti implies that the poet's work can advance
only by seeing things truly, for what they are. This idea
relates to the extended metaphor because the high-wire
artist must see precisely and truly to keep moving
forward on the wire.

Difficulty: *Average*   **Objective:** *Literary Analysis*

6. This image implies a mass of people who are hungry for
amazement and spectacle. In the case of poetry, the
audience wants to be amazed by the spectacle of truth
and beauty as created by the poet's words.

Difficulty: *Challenging*   **Objective:** *Reading Strategy*

7. Ferlinghetti capitalizes the first letter of *beauty* because
for him beauty is the highest ideal that can be attained
by the poet.

Difficulty: *Average*   **Objective:** *Interpretation*

8. Students will probably imagine a modest, hapless,
nervous person who is afraid of his own shadow. This
image does not seem consistent with the earlier images,
which seem to portray a bold, brave, skillful risk taker—a
figure more heroic than pathetic. Students' responses will
vary, depending on how much they know about or have
seen of Charley Chaplin's films. Accept any response that
seems well grounded in the language of the image.

Difficulty: *Easy*   **Objective:** *Reading Strategy*

9. Sample answer: the line "who may or may not catch /
her fair eternal form." In this line Ferlinghetti makes it
clear that the poet's daring attempt to snatch Beauty
out of the air is far from a sure thing and may end in
failure. Accept alternative lines as long as the students
explain their answers.

Difficulty: *Average*   **Objective:** *Interpretation*

10. No, that person would not be endorsing your proposal,
because *absurdity* means "nonsense; ridiculousness."

Difficulty: *Average*   **Objective:** *Vocabulary*

Essay

11. Some students might agree that writing poetry is risky
because the poet works hard to use language to capture
beauty and the highest truths about life. His objective is
to perceive "taut truth." This is such a great ambition
that if the poet fails, he risks looking pathetic and
ridiculous and absurd for even trying. Others might
argue that in real-world terms writing poetry is a
relatively safe task compared with jobs that are truly
physically dangerous, such as working as a policeman,
a firefighter, or as a test pilot.

Difficulty: *Easy*   **Objective:** *Essay*

12. Some students might argue that a poet is anything but
a realist, because a poet is concerned not with the hard
realities of everyday life but with playing with language
to capture higher ideals of truth and beauty. Others
might argue that it is just this pursuit of higher truths
that makes the poet not just a realist, but a super
realist. The poets wants to show the highest, most real
truths of life, not just to report and reflect common
perceptions about the world.

Difficulty: *Average*   **Objective:** *Essay*

13. Students might argue that it is doubtful that
Ferlinghetti believes that the poet literally risks physical
death when he or she writes a poem. He probably
believes that the poet is putting his life at stake in the
sense that he places his deepest convictions and beliefs
on the line to be accepted or rejected by the audience.
Therefore, the poet takes great risks with the kinds of
imaginative leaps ("entrechats") and combinations of
words ("sleight-of-foot tricks and other high theatrics")
that can either work or leave the poet falling flat on his/
her face. Students might suggest it is because the poet
invests so much of his/her creative energy in trying to
create something special with words that writing a poem
seems like putting one's life at stake, in a creative/
spiritual sense if not in a physical sense.

Difficulty: *Challenging*   **Objective:** *Essay*

14. According to "Constantly Risking Absurdity," the poet/
artist in this society must possess above all courage, for
he/she, in pursuing this art, constantly risks nothing
less than "absurdity and death"—by failing, risking at
least looking ridiculous and at worst failing to find a
deep or redeeming meaning in life, which is a kind of
death in life. Students might note that the stakes are so
high because this is a society in which poets/artists are
considered outsiders—the very act of pursuing an art
requires great reserves of skill and nerve of the kind
shown by the high-wire acrobat. The poem reflects a
society in which art and beauty are rare and marginal—
but for those reasons all the more precious and worth
striving for in a "death-defying leap" of creative
imagination.

Difficulty: *Average*   **Objective:** *Essay*

Oral Response

15. Oral responses should be clear, well organized, and well supported by appropriate examples from the selections.

Difficulty: *Average*   **Objective:** *Oral Interpretation*

Selection Test A, p. 77

Critical Reading

1. ANS: B	DIF: Easy	OBJ: Literary Analysis
2. ANS: C	DIF: Easy	OBJ: Interpretation
3. ANS: B	DIF: Easy	OBJ: Interpretation
4. ANS: B	DIF: Easy	OBJ: Literary Analysis
5. ANS: A	DIF: Easy	OBJ: Literary Analysis
6. ANS: I	DIF: Easy	OBJ: Reading Strategy
7. ANS: A	DIF: Easy	OBJ: Literary Analysis
8. ANS: B	DIF: Easy	OBJ: Literary Analysis
9. ANS: D	DIF: Easy	OBJ: Interpretation
10. ANS: A	DIF: Easy	OBJ: Interpretation
11. ANS: C	DIF: Easy	OBJ: Literary Analysis
12. ANS: B	DIF: Easy	OBJ: Literary Analysis
13. ANS: D	DIF: Easy	OBJ: Comprehension
14. ANS: A	DIF: Easy	OBJ: Interpretation
15. ANS: D	DIF: Easy	OBJ: Interpretation

Essay

16. Some students might agree that writing poetry is risky because the poet strains to use language to capture beauty and the highest truths about life—his objective is to perceive "taut truth." This is such a great ambition that if the poet fails, he risks looking pathetic and ridiculous—absurd—for even trying. Others might argue that in real-world terms writing poetry is a relatively safe undertaking compared with jobs that are truly physically dangerous, such as working as a policeman, a firefighter, or as a test pilot.

Difficulty: *Easy*

Objective: *Essay*

17. Some students might argue that a poet is anything but a realist, because a poet is concerned not with the hard realities of everyday life but with the rarefied pursuit of refining language to capture higher ideals of truth and beauty. Others might argue that it is just this pursuit of higher truths that makes the poet not just a realist, but a super realist—content not just to report and reflect common perceptions about the world, but only the highest—and hence most real—truths of life.

Difficulty: *Easy*

Objective: *Essay*

18. Students might argue that it is doubtful that Ferlinghetti believes that the poet literally risks physical death when he or she writes a poem. He probably believes that the poet is putting his life at stake in the sense that he places his deepest convictions and beliefs on the line to be accepted or rejected by the audience. In so doing, the poet takes great risks with the kinds of imaginative jumps ("entrechats") and magical combinations of words ("sleight-of-foot tricks and other high theatrics") that can either work or leave the poet falling flat on his/her face. It is because the poet invests so much of his/her energy and creative sweat in trying to create something splendid with words that writing a poem seems like putting one's very life at stake—in a creative/spiritual sense if not in a physical sense.

Difficulty: *Easy*

Objective: *Essay*

19. Students might argue that any number of performing-arts skills—acting, playing a musical instrument, dancing—involve practicing highly exacting skills and presenting them to an audience. They might note that all such endeavors involve a high degree of risk—the performer might make mistakes, or he or she might not win the approval of the audience. They might also note that the same degree of skill and risk is involved in athletic performance. Most students will argue that working at such skills is worth the risk of failure because of the satisfaction of expressing oneself through a creative, demanding activity.

Difficulty: *Easy*

Objective: *Essay*

Selection Test B, p. 80

Critical Reading

1. ANS: C	DIF: Easy	OBJ: Literary Analysis
2. ANS: D	DIF: Challenging	OBJ: Literary Analysis
3. ANS: A	DIF: Average	OBJ: Literary Analysis
4. ANS: D	DIF: Challenging	OBJ: Interpretation
5. ANS: C	DIF: Average	OBJ: Comprehension
6. ANS: A	DIF: Challenging	OBJ: Literary Analysis
7. ANS: A	DIF: Easy	OBJ: Interpretation
8. ANS: B	DIF: Average	OBJ: Interpretation
9. ANS: C	DIF: Challenging	OBJ: Interpretation
10. ANS: C	DIF: Challenging	OBJ: Reading Strategy
11. ANS: D	DIF: Average	OBJ: Comprehension
12. ANS: B	DIF: Average	OBJ: Literary Analysis
13. ANS: A	DIF: Average	OBJ: Reading Strategy
14. ANS: C	DIF: Average	OBJ: Comprehension
15. ANS: B	DIF: Challenging	OBJ: Interpretation

Essay

16. According to "Constantly Risking Absurdity," the poet/artist in this society must possess above all courage, for he/she, in pursuing this art, constantly risks nothing less than "absurdity and death"—by failing, risking at least looking ridiculous and at worst failing to find a deep or redeeming meaning in life, which is a kind of death in life. Students might note that the stakes are so high because this is a society in which poets/artists are

considered outsiders—the very act of pursuing an art requires great reserves of skill and nerve of the kind shown by the high-wire acrobat. The poem reflects a society in which art and beauty are rare and marginal—but for those reasons all the more precious and worth striving for in a "death-defying leap" of creative imagination.

Difficulty: *Average*   **Objective:** *Essay*

17. Most students will feel that the extended metaphor works; just as the circus performer puts his body on the line in his high-wire act, so the poet puts his heart and soul on the line in the act of trying to find just the right combination of words to say something beautifully and truly. Both risk a kind of humiliation if they fail—the high-wire artist by taking a tumble, and the poet by appearing ridiculous instead of profound in his use of language. They might note that the comparison works to the extent that both the high-wire performer and the poet apply highly polished skills of a very exacting sort before an expectant and demanding audience.

Difficulty: *Average*

Objective: *Essay*

18. Students might argue that although it is important for the poet to perceive and state the truth, doing so with a sense of beauty and grace is even more essential to the task of the poet. They might argue that truth can be stated in prose form, but it will not necessarily be beautiful. On the other hand, with the right combination of words and images, the poet can portray truth in a manner that is beautiful, and that this attempt to create beauty out of the materials of language is indeed the highest aspiration and achievement of the poet.

Difficulty: *Challenging*

Objective: *Essay*

19. According to "Constantly Risking Absurdity," the poet/artist in this society must possess above all courage, for he/she, in pursuing this art, constantly risks nothing less than "absurdity and death"—by failing, risking at least looking ridiculous and at worst failing to find a deep or redeeming meaning in life, which is a kind of death in life. Students might note that the stakes are so high because this is a society in which poets/artists are considered outsiders—the very act of pursuing an art requires great reserves of skill and nerve of the kind shown by the high-wire acrobat. The poem reflects a society in which art and beauty are rare and marginal—but for those reasons all the more precious and worth striving for in a "death-defying leap" of creative imagination.

Difficulty: *Average*   **Objective:** *Essay*

"Mirror" by Sylvia Plath and "Courage" by Anne Sexton

Vocabulary Warm-up Exercises, p. 84

A. 1. despair
2. unmisted

3. kinsman
4. acid
5. conclusion
6. wallowing
7. powdered
8. fondle

B. Sample Answers
1. F; *Flickers* implies weak or irregular shining.
2. T; If you have buried a treasure, you have covered it, which means it is *concealed*.
3. F; *Ordinary* and *uninspiring* are the opposite of *awesome*.
4. F; An *agitation* is a disturbance, not something calm and peaceful.
5. F; If you are *wringing* a towel, you are twisting or pressing it to remove liquid.
6. T; *Speckles* show up as a darker, contrasting color against a background, so the wall would contain at least two colors.
7. F; To *meditate* means to think and reflect deeply and at length.
8. T; *Spunk* and *daring* are synonyms for *courage*.

Reading Warm-up A, p. 85

Sample Answers
1. (deeply sad); *Joy* is an antonym for *despair*.
2. vinegar; Vinegar has a sharp, bitter, sour taste.
3. (outcome); Brina does her homework in Aunt Helen's living room instead of the dining room.
4. cousin; My *kinsman*, Austin, is my uncle.
5. dabbed with some sort of skin powder; After Bubbles the Clown applied her colorful make-up, she powdered it gently to help the bright shades of red, yellow, and blue remain in place longer.
6. (rolling back and forth); When the wind blew, her toy sailboat was wallowing in the waves of the lake.
7. the ears of a piglet; To *fondle* means to pet or caress affectionately.
8. (clear); An antonym for *unmisted* is *hazy*.

Reading Warm-up B, p. 86

Sample Answers
1. (remarkable); *Astonishing, breathtaking,* and *wonderful* are synonyms for *awesome*.
2. he manifests in order to overcome difficult obstacles and fine a way to safety; *Cowardice* is an antonym for *courage*.
3. (deep thoughts); A quiet, still, comfortable room could provide a good place to *meditate*.
4. a mental or visual disturbance; Loud, sudden noises outside the window can heighten my *agitation* when I am trying to do homework.
5. (covered up); *Exposed* and *revealed* are antonyms for *concealed*.

6. (twinkles); Fire *flickers*; so can a light bulb that is old or installed in a faulty lamp.

7. small dots; Hannah ordered peach ice cream flecked with *speckles* of real fruit.

8. squeeze...out; After the boat capsized, we were *wringing* out our clothes on the riverbank for a long time.

Literary Analysis: Figurative Language, p. 87
Sample Response:

Students might identify four of the following or any others they identify—accept any reasonable interpretation of the figures of speech: "The eye of a little god, four-cornered"—metaphor—the rectangular mirror has the truth-telling powers of a god; "Now I am a lake"—metaphor—the mirror reflects its surroundings as faithfully as a lake; " . . . and in me an old woman / Rises toward her day after day, like a terrible fish"—simile—the sight of her aging face is like a terrible monster from the deep; "the child's first step, as awesome as an earthquake"—simile—the child's first step is a momentous event; "Your courage was a small coal / that you kept swallowing"—metaphor—your courage was a difficult but necessary feat of survival; "love as simple as shaving soap"—simile—love is a simple, homespun, direct feeling; "each spring will be a sword you'll sharpen"—metaphor—in old age, each passing year will arm you with deeper wisdom and courage.

Reading Strategy: Interpreting the Connotations of Words, p. 88
Sample Responses

1. The mirror, as narrator of the poem, views itself as an infallible reflection of the world around it; as the poem progresses, we see that the all-powerful mirror seems threatening to the woman who sees in it her progress into old age—so the mirror can be said to "swallow" everything that looks into it because it devours any illusions that people might have as they look into it.

2. The mirror regards itself as an objective, almost merciless recorder of the world that surrounds it. So anything that would tend to hide certain visual realities in soft light—like candles or the moon—are not giving the full truth of what is to be seen and are therefore "liars" by the mirror's standards of cold, honest, total reflection of reality.

3. The poet states that despair can be a transfusion—something that gives you added strength—because we learn from suffering, and it can therefore make us wiser and stronger. Therefore, through the use of the word *transfusion*, the poet drives home the point that if we endure and overcome despair, then despair can strengthen rather than weaken us.

4. In this passage, the word *banner* connotes glory or pride. The use of the word emphasizes that the soldier acted courageously not for glory or ego but out of duty and conscience—so the courage is more noble because it aims to help others rather than to enhance one's own sense of grandeur or importance.

Vocabulary Builder, p. 89
Possible responses:

1. No, she would not think that you approached your topic with an open mind, because *preconceptions* means "ideas formed beforehand."

2. Yes, it is likely that he gave it an unfavorable review because *endured* means "held up under; withstood."

3. No, you would not be donating the blood, because *transfusion* means "the transferring of a life-giving substance from a source to a recipient," so you would be receiving the blood.

4. Yes, the movie had a powerful effect on her, because *transformed* means "altered; changed."

B. 1. A; 2. A; 3. C; 4. B;

Enrichment: Medals For Bravery in Battle, p. 91
Sample Response

Medal of Honor: to a soldier who distinguishes himself "...conspicuously by gallantry and intrepidity at the risk of his life above and beyond the call of duty while engaged in an action against an enemy of the United States..." (1862); Silver Star: for gallantry in action against an enemy of the United States not justifying a higher award (1932); Legion of Merit: Exceptionally meritorious conduct (1942); Distinguished Flying Cross: "Heroism or extraordinary achievement while participating in an aerial flight" (1926); Bronze Star: "Heroic or meritorious achievement or service" (1942); Purple Heart: "Being wounded or killed in any action against an enemy of the United States or as a result of an act of any such enemy or opposing armed forces" (1917).

Open-Book Test, p. 92
Short Answer

1. The "I" is the mirror.
   Difficulty: *Easy*   **Objective:** *Interpretation*

2. The poem reveals that the woman fears aging.
   Difficulty: *Average*   **Objective:** *Interpretation*

3. The metaphor is "The eye of a little god, four-cornered." This metaphor tells about the mirror and the woman. The rectangular (four-cornered) mirror has godlike powers of perception reflecting whatever appears in it with utter truth. The metaphor also applies to the woman because it is how she perceives the mirror.
   Difficulty: *Challenging*   **Objective:** *Literary Analysis*

4. This metaphor reinforces the notion of the mirror as a surface that reflects the appearances of the world.
   Difficulty: *Challenging*   **Objective:** *Literary Analysis*

5. The word *rewards* conveys the idea that the woman has made the mirror so important as a reflection of her identity, such a powerful force in her life, that the mirror can be "rewarded" by seeing the woman's emotional distress over the signs of aging that she sees in it.
   Difficulty: *Challenging*   **Objective:** *Reading Strategy*

6. These lines celebrate the spirit of modesty and generosity that underlies acts of courage.

Difficulty: *Average*   Objective: *Interpretation*

7. By using the word *fondle* in this context, Sexton emphasizes the importance of not undermining our courage by indulging in, growing comfortable with, or becoming attached to the sense of weakness that we all have to some degree.

Difficulty: *Average*   Objective: *Reading Strategy*

8. The metaphor is "each spring will be a sword you'll sharpen." It means that, in old age, each additional year that you are alive will bring you enhanced and deepened wisdom with which to do battle with the struggles of life and aging.

Difficulty: *Average*   Objective: *Literary Analysis*

9. Students should identify four of the following or any others they identify. Accept any reasonable interpretation of the figures of speech.

Sample answers: "The eye of a little god, four-cornered"—metaphor—the mirror has the truth-telling powers of a god; "Now I am a lake"—metaphor—the mirror reflects its surroundings as faithfully as a lake; ". . . and in me an old woman / Rises toward her day after day, like a terrible fish"—simile—the sight of her aging face is like a terrible monster from the deep; "the child's first step, as awesome as an earthquake"—simile—the child's first step is a momentous event; "Your courage was a small coal / that you kept swallowing"—metaphor—your courage was a difficult but necessary feat of survival; "love as simple as shaving soap"—simile—love is a simple, direct feeling; "each spring will be a sword you'll sharpen"—metaphor—in old age, each passing year will arm you with deeper wisdom and courage.

Difficulty: *Average*   Objective: *Literary Analysis*

10. Yes, it is likely that the rest of the review will be unfavorable, because *endured* means "held up under; withstood."

Difficulty: *Average*   Objective: *Vocabulary*

Essay

11. Students should clearly identify a kind of courage—from the poem or from their own experience—that they think is the most important. They should use clear reasoning and examples from the poem and/or their own experience to support their opinions.

Difficulty: *Easy*   Objective: *Essay*

12. Students might note that the mirror precisely portrays only the external appearance of what it reflects. This might be sufficient for inanimate objects, but it fails to capture the inner reality of a human being. Students might suggest the woman who looks into the mirror seems to identify her whole sense of being and worth with her physical appearance, and so she makes the mirror into a god that dictates who she is as she frets over her aging face. So the mirror does not tell the inner truth of this woman. It is her sense that how she looks determines who she is that gives the mirror its godlike power, not the mirror itself, which is only an inanimate object.

Difficulty: *Average*   Objective: *Essay*

13. Students might feel that "Mirror" is purely a picture of the personal pain and despair of an aging woman who thinks that her external appearance defines the whole of her being and so allows the mirror to dictate her sense of self-worth and identity. Others might note, however, that because the poem implies that it is the woman who gives this power to the mirror, she also has the power to take it away by redefining her identify in terms other than outward looks. Most students will probably feel that "Courage" is the more inspiring poem because it offers many more examples of people moving forward in the face of life's hurts and difficulties, such as standing up to parental abuse as "[drinking] their acid" or the aftermath of great despair as "picking scabs off your heart." Students might recognize that it is the positive notes that make up the inspiring part of the poem: for example, "love as simple as shaving soap," "[sorrow] woke to the wings of roses and was transformed."

Difficulty: *Challenging*   Objective: *Essay*

14. Students might suggest that, of the two poems, "Mirror" is the one in which private feelings are more clearly related to a social context: the narrator is obsessed with the way in which the mirror reflects her aging and the fear of losing her physical attractiveness—concerns that reflect modern society's tendency to judge people in general—and women in particular—by their external appearance. "Courage," on the other hand, deals with themes that seem to apply more to all societies at all times rather than to a particular social order: the need for courage in facing the trials and challenges of childhood, warfare, despair, and old age.

Difficulty: *Average*   Objective: *Essay*

Oral Response

15. Oral responses should be clear, well organized, and well supported by appropriate examples from the selections.

Difficulty: *Average*   Objective: *Oral Interpretation*

Selection Test A, p. 95

Critical Reading

1. ANS: B	DIF: Easy	OBJ: Interpretation
2. ANS: D	DIF: Easy	OBJ: Comprehension
3. ANS: D	DIF: Easy	OBJ: Interpretation
4. ANS: A	DIF: Easy	OBJ: Reading Strategy
5. ANS: B	DIF: Easy	OBJ: Literary Analysis
6. ANS: D	DIF: Easy	OBJ: Literary Analysis
7. ANS: B	DIF: Easy	OBJ: Literary Analysis
8. ANS: B	DIF: Easy	OBJ: Interpretation
9. ANS: A	DIF: Easy	OBJ: Literary Analysis
10. ANS: A	DIF: Easy	OBJ: Comprehension
11. ANS: D	DIF: Easy	OBJ: Interpretation

Essay

12. Students' essays might suggest that the woman does not want to see that she is aging. She turns to candles or the moon, which have softer light that smoothes out the wrinkles of age.

    Difficulty: *Easy*

    Objective: *Essay*

13. Students should be clear about the nature of the moment and why it required a special act of courage. They should explain why courage was important at that moment, and whether the act of courage was easily summoned or not. Their essays should use concrete descriptive details to help get their message across. Students should support their opinions with reasons and details.

    Difficulty: *Easy*

    Objective: *Essay*

14. Students might suggest that, of the two poems, "Mirror" is the one in which private feelings are more clearly related to a social context: the narrator is obsessed with the way in which the mirror reflects her aging and the fear of losing her physical attractiveness—concerns that reflect modern society's tendency to judge people in general—and women in particular—by their external appearance. "Courage," on the other hand, deals with themes that seem to apply more to all societies at all times rather than to a particular social order: the need for courage in facing the trials and challenges of childhood, warfare, despair, and old age.

    Difficulty: *Easy*

    Objective: *Essay*

Selection Test B, p. 98

Critical Reading

1. ANS: D	DIF: Easy	OBJ: Comprehension
2. ANS: C	DIF: Challenging	OBJ: Reading Strategy
3. ANS: A	DIF: Average	OBJ: Interpretation
4. ANS: D	DIF: Average	OBJ: Interpretation
5. ANS: D	DIF: Challenging	OBJ: Literary Analysis
6. ANS: C	DIF: Challenging	OBJ: Reading Strategy
7. ANS: D	DIF: Challenging	OBJ: Interpretation
8. ANS: B	DIF: Average	OBJ: Literary Analysis
9. ANS: B	DIF: Challenging	OBJ: Literary Analysis
10. ANS: C	DIF: Easy	OBJ: Comprehension
11. ANS: B	DIF: Challenging	OBJ: Interpretation
12. ANS: A	DIF: Average	OBJ: Reading Strategy
13. ANS: D	DIF: Average	OBJ: Literary Analysis
14. ANS: C	DIF: Easy	OBJ: Literary Analysis
15. ANS: A	DIF: Average	OBJ: Interpretation
16. ANS: D	DIF: Average	OBJ: Reading Strategy

Essay

17. Students should clearly identify a kind of courage—from the poem or from their own experience—that they think is the most important. They should use clear reasoning and examples from the poem and/or their own experience to support their opinion.

    Difficulty: *Easy*

    Objective: *Essay*

18. Students might note that the mirror precisely portrays only the external appearance of what it reflects—which might be sufficient for inanimate objects, but fails to capture the inner emotional and psychological reality of a human being. The woman who looks into the mirror evidently identifies her whole sense of being and worth with her physical appearance, and so she gives the mirror power to dictate who she is as she frets over her aging face. So the mirror does not tell the inner truth of this woman— it is her sense that she is how she looks that gives the mirror its power, not the mirror itself, which is only an inanimate object.

    Difficulty: *Average*

    Objective: *Essay*

19. Students might feel that "Mirror" is purely a picture of the personal pain and despair of an aging woman who thinks that her external appearance defines the whole of her being and so allows the mirror to dictate her sense of self-worth and identity. Others might note, however, that because the poem implies that it is the woman who gives this power to the mirror, she also has the power to take it away by redefining her identify in terms other than outward looks. Most students will probably feel that "Courage" is the more inspiring poem because it offers many more examples of people affirming life and moving forward in the face of life's most bruising hurts and difficulties, even though the portrayal of some of those problems is very blunt and unflinching, such as standing up to abuse as "[drinking] their acid" or the aftermath of great despair as "picking scabs off your heart." Students might recognize that it is the positive counternotes that make up the inspiring part of the poem: for example, "love as simple as shaving soap," "[sorrow] woke to the wings of the roses and was transformed."

    Difficulty: *Challenging*

    Objective: *Essay*

20. Students might suggest that, of the two poems, "Mirror" is the one in which private feelings are more clearly related to a social context: the narrator is obsessed with the way in which the mirror reflects her aging and the fear of losing her physical attractiveness—concerns that reflect modern society's tendency to judge people in general—and women in particular—by their external appearance. "Courage," on the other hand, deals with themes that seem to apply more to all societies at all times rather than to a particular social order: the need

for courage in facing the trials and challenges of childhood, warfare, despair, and old age.

Difficulty: *Average*
Objective: *Essay*

"Cuttings" and "Cuttings (later)" by Theodore Roethke

Vocabulary Warm-up Exercises, p. 102

A. 1. urge
2. delicate
3. loam
4. wrestle
5. nub
6. droop
7. tendrilous
8. grains

B. Sample Answers
1. F; People who are struggling are having a hard time.
2. F; Gentle nudges would not knock someone over.
3. F; Water would be seeping through small holes.
4. T; Tiny sprouts would be tender because they are so new.
5. T; Lopping off branches would make a tree look bare.
6. F; If you were weak, it would be hard to wrestle a heavy object up stairs.
7. F; If you have an urge to do something, you would think about it a lot.
8. T; Something with an intricate design would be very finely made.

Reading Warm-up A, p. 103

Sample Answers
1. (flowers); *coarse, rough*
2. impulse; I have an *urge* to eat French fries.
3. adding compost to the soil until it was a dark, rich; His lawn was green because his soil was rich *loam*.
4. on the end of a slender tree limb; The nub turned into a dark green leaf.
5. seeds; *rice, wheat*
6. (shoots); It was hard to *wrestle* the toy out of the plastic wrapper.
7. They grow quickly and thickly; Vines are described as *tendrilous* because they send out many tendrils to attach themselves to supports so that they can climb and grow.
8. Heat and lack of water cause a plant to *droop*; *sag, sink, hang, wilt*

Reading Warm-up B, p. 104

Sample Answers
1. native plants; A small child might need *coaxing* to try a new food.

2. No, a xeriscape design is rarely *intricate*; *simple, uncomplicated*
3. a great deal of organic mulch; Sprouts are tiny, new plants and they are delicate.
4. very small amounts of water; With less evaporation, there's more water for the plants' roots to drink.
5. (the plants' roots can take it up); It was fun to visit the *underground* cave.
6. (to provide them with adequate moisture); *working hard, toiling, laboring*
7. a tree branch; *cutting, chopping off*
8. pushes; *Nudges* means to give someone a very gentle shove.

Literary Analysis: Sound Devices, p. 105

Sample Response
1. This urge, wrestle, resurrection of dry sticks, . . .; alliteration—emphasizes the struggle to generate new life.
2. What saint strained so much, . . . ; alliteration and assonance—emphasizes the struggle and difficulty involved in generating new life.
3. I can hear, underground, that sucking and sobbing. . . .; alliteration—emphasizes the turbulent, emotionally wrenching process of generation and birth; also consonance, in the final *ng* consonant sound of *sucking* and *sobbing*.
4. When sprouts break out, . . . ; assonance—emphasizes the sudden, startling quality of the emergence of the sprouts; also consonance—the *t* sounds in *sprouts* and *out*.

Reading Strategy: Using Background Knowledge, p. 106

Sample Responses
1. Roethke's grandparents immigrated from Germany and settled in Saginaw, Michigan, where they made a living growing and selling plants.
2. Roethke's father and uncle went into the plant business, which they inherited from their parents. They did very well in the business, ending up with one of the largest commercial greenhouses in the state.
3. Roethke spent countless hours of his childhood in the greenhouse, where he learned a good deal about the art and science of gardening, especially making new plants from cuttings.
4. A cutting—also known as a slip—is a twig, branch, or leaf cut from a mature plant and placed in water or wet sand.
5. Diffusion occurs when water molecules move from areas of high concentration to areas of low concentration by passing through the walls of cells.
6. As more and more water enters the cells of the cutting, water pressure builds, which in turn causes the cutting to stand upright. Water pressure also stimulates cell

growth, and soon, under the proper conditions, the cutting will sprout new roots and leaves.

Vocabulary Builder, p. 107

Possible responses:

A. 1. No, the solution was not a simple one, because *intricate* means "complex."

2. No, the water was not leaking quickly, because *seeping* means "flowing slowly."

3. Yes, the movie was scary, because *quail* means "draw back in fear."

B. 1. C; 2. D; 3. B;

Enrichment: Family History, p. 109

Sample Response

Students should conduct interviews with available family members to collect the information that will allow them to answer the questions.

Open-Book Test, p. 110

Short Answer

1. Both poems focus on the processes of birth and growth and renewal.

   Difficulty: *Easy*   **Objective:** *Interpretation*

2. It is most useful to know that when he was growing up, his family owned several large commercial greenhouses where he learned a great deal about plant growth.

   Difficulty: *Easy*   **Objective:** *Reading Strategy*

3. This line is an example of consonance, the repetition of consonant sounds in stressed syllables—in this case, the l sounds at the end of the last three words of the line. It also contains alliteration, as in "small cells."

   Difficulty: *Average*   **Objective:** *Literary Analysis*

4. The alliteration in this line is the repeated *d* sound in *drowse* and *droop*. By emphasizing these two words with this repeated sound, Roethke conveys the heavy, sleepy, gradual process of growth that is the subject of the poem.

   Difficulty: *Challenging*   **Objective:** *Literary Analysis*

5. The alliteration is the repetition of the *n* sounds in *nub* and *nudges*. By relating and emphasizing these two words with alliteration, Roethke underscores the slowness and gradualness of the process of growth he is describing—a nub is a first tiny growth, and *nudges* evokes a slow, gradual movement.

   Difficulty: *Challenging*   **Objective:** *Literary Analysis*

6. The most important piece of background information for a reader is that a cutting or a slip, a twig, branch, or cut leaf from a mature plant can generate a new plant if placed in water or wet sand.

   Difficulty: *Average*   **Objective:** *Reading Strategy*

7. "Cuttings" describes the first, tentative, very slow and gradual signs of growth, for example with words like *nubs* and *nudge*. "Cuttings (later)," describes a

subsequent stage of growth that is more urgent and sudden, "when sprouts break out."

   Difficulty: *Average*   **Objective:** *Interpretation*

8. Sample answer: The sudden emergence of new life is a miraculous, moving thing.

   Difficulty: *Challenging*   **Objective:** *Interpretation*

9. 1. This urge, wrestle, resurrection of dry sticks, . . .; alliteration—emphasizes the struggle to generate new life.

   2. What saint strained so much, . . . ; alliteration and assonance—emphasizes the struggle and difficulty involved in generating new life

   3. I can hear, underground, that sucking and sobbing. . . .; alliteration—emphasizes the turbulent, emotionally wrenching process of generation and birth; also consonance, in the final ng consonant sound of *sucking* and *sobbing*.

   4. When sprouts break out, . . . ; assonance—emphasizes the sudden, startling quality of the emergence of the sprouts; also consonance—the *t* sounds in *sprouts* and *out*.

   Difficulty: *Average*   **Objective:** *Literary Analysis*

10. You would most likely be watching a horror film, because *quail* means "draw back in fear."

   Difficulty: *Average*   **Objective:** *Vocabulary*

Essay

11. Students should clearly identify one aspect of nature that they recall from a childhood experience. They should explain why that experience of nature left a strong impression on them and affected their outlook on life. Students' essays should be supported with vivid, concrete details and images.

   Difficulty: *Easy*   **Objective:** *Essay*

12. Students might note that while both "Cuttings" and "Cuttings (later)" focus on the miraculous, wondrous qualities of plant growth and renewal, "Cuttings" dwells more on the very gradual, slow stirrings of growth ("One nub of growth / Nudges a sand-crumb loose. . . ."), whereas "Cuttings (later)" emphasizes more turbulent and sudden lurches of growth: "wrestle . . . resurrection"; "saint strained"; "sucking and sobbing"; "sprouts break out." Students' should clearly express and explain their preference for the perspective of one of the two poems.

   Difficulty: *Average*   **Objective:** *Essay*

13. Students might note that the narrator "quail(s)" at the sight of the sprouts breaking out because new life, for plants as well as humans, is filled not only with promise but also with potential danger. Every new form of life—plant or human—is mortal and can easily die. Students might also note that humans grow emotionally and intellectually in much the same way that the plants do in the two poems. Sometimes they grow gradually and unnoticeably, from day to day, in the vein described in "Cuttings." But sometimes they grow through great leaps of determination and will as portrayed by the

words *urge, wrestle, strained,* and *break* out in "Cuttings (later)."

Difficulty: *Challenging* **Objective:** *Essay*

14. Students should use vivid language and concrete images in describing the childhood environment they have chosen to describe. They should also explain clearly how that environment has shaped their perceptions of—or outlook on—the world in much the same manner that Roethke's observations of plant growth as a child shaped his view of life and growth as expressed in the two poems in this section.

Difficulty: *Average* **Objective:** *Essay*

Oral Response

15. Oral responses should be clear, well organized, and well supported by appropriate examples from the selections.

Difficulty: *Average* **Objective:** *Oral Response*

Selection Test A, p. 113

Critical Reading

1. ANS: D	DIF: Easy	OBJ: Comprehension
2. ANS: A	DIF: Easy	OBJ: Literary Analysis
3. ANS: D	DIF: Easy	OBJ: Literary Analysis
4. ANS: C	DIF: Easy	OBJ: Reading Strategy
5. ANS: B	DIF: Easy	OBJ: Interpretation
6. ANS: D	DIF: Easy	OBJ: Interpretation
7. ANS: C	DIF: Easy	OBJ: Interpretation
8. ANS: B	DIF: Easy	OBJ: Literary Analysis
9. ANS: A	DIF: Easy	OBJ: Interpretation
10. ANS: C	DIF: Easy	OBJ: Literary Analysis
11. ANS: B	DIF: Easy	OBJ: Interpretation
12. ANS: D	DIF: Easy	OBJ: Comprehension
13. ANS: C	DIF: Easy	OBJ: Interpretation

Essay

14. Students should clearly identify a key experience from their lives and explain how it spurred them to a sudden spurt of emotional growth. They should support their answers with vivid examples and details.

Difficulty: *Easy*

Objective: *Essay*

15. Students should clearly identify an aspect of the plant or animal world that they find especially interesting— interesting enough to make them want to study it in enough detail to write a poem about it. They should support their answers with specific details and examples.

Difficulty: *Easy*

Objective: *Essay*

16. Students should use vivid language and concrete images in describing the childhood environment they have chosen to describe. They should also explain clearly how that environment has shaped their perceptions of—or outlook on—the world in much the

same manner that Roethke's observations of plant growth as a child shaped his view of life and growth as expressed in the two poems in this section.

Difficulty: *Easy*

Objective: *Essay*

Selection Test B, p. 116

Critical Reading

1. ANS: D	DIF: Easy	OBJ: Reading Strategy
2. ANS: A	DIF: Challenging	OBJ: Literary Analysis
3. ANS: A	DIF: Challenging	OBJ: Reading Strategy
4. ANS: B	DIF: Easy	OBJ: Literary Analysis
5. ANS: C	DIF: Average	OBJ: Literary Analysis
6. ANS: D	DIF: Average	OBJ: Literary Analysis
7. ANS: C	DIF: Challenging	OBJ: Interpretation
8. ANS: C	DIF: Average	OBJ: Reading Strategy
9. ANS: A	DIF: Easy	OBJ: Comprehension
10. ANS: B	DIF: Average	OBJ: Literary Analysis
11. ANS: D	DIF: Easy	OBJ: Comprehension
12. ANS: A	DIF: Average	OBJ: Interpretation
13. ANS: C	DIF: Easy	OBJ: Interpretation
14. ANS: A	DIF: Challenging	OBJ: Literary Analysis
15. ANS: C	DIF: Challenging	OBJ: Interpretation

Essay

16. Answers will vary. Students should identify a childhood experience that they remember clearly and that had a powerful influence on their subsequent view of life. They should support their answer with concrete, vivid examples.

Difficulty: *Easy*

Objective: *Essay*

17. Some students will identify closely with plants, noting that they go through the same cycles of birth, generation, decay, and death that humans experience. They might also note that plants and humans are part of the same overall phenomenon of life on Earth and share certain basic cell structures and metabolic processes. Others will note major distinctions between plants and humans—some will doubt that plants have emotions of any sort, and even more will note that plants lack the motor and perception capacities of higher animals and lack the reasoning powers of humans, so the possibility of identification can go only so far.

Difficulty: *Average*

Objective: *Essay*

18. Students might note that saints often achieve triumph and beatitude in the face of great trials and sufferings. Likewise, the plants striving to generate new life have been hacked apart—they are "lopped limbs" and so to that extent evoke the pain and suffering sometimes endured by some saintly figures. In addition, the plant's strenuous determination to generate new life in the face of such long odds evokes the saint's determination

to affirm the worth and holiness of existence in the face of evil and suffering. Students might note that the triumph of life and goodness in both cases can be considered something close to a miracle.

Difficulty: *Challenging*

Objective: *Essay*

19. Students should use vivid language and concrete images in describing the childhood environment they have chosen to describe. They should also explain clearly how that environment has shaped their perceptions of—or outlook on—the world in much the same manner that Roethke's observations of plant growth as a child shaped his view of life and growth as expressed in the two poems in this section.

Difficulty: *Average*

Objective: *Essay*

"The Explorer" by Gwendolyn Brooks and "Frederick Douglass" by Robert Hayden

Vocabulary Warm-up Exercises, p. 120

A. 1. alien
2. rhetoric
3. exiled
4. vague
5. fleshing
6. liberty

B. Sample Answers

1. F; A *frayed* jacket would typically be old and worn.
2. T; *Din* means loud noise.
3. T; An *instinct* is a natural tendency or reaction that requires no formal learning.
4. T; *Rhetoric* is eloquent, formal language that often contains little substance.
5. F; *Vague* instructions would be unclear and imprecise.
6. F; A *reflex* is an automatic response to a stimulus so it would not depend on forethought or planning.

Reading Warm-up A, p. 121

Sample Answers

1. (information about the date of his birth); A antonym for *vague* is *clear*, *certain*, or *definite*.
2. the details of Douglass' early life; *Fleshing* means figuring out the details about something, or filling out a story with missing information to make the story fuller.
3. (freedom); Reading books and magazines opens your mind up to new thoughts and ideas and to a desire for more learning; slaves were forbidden to learn, so reading would only make him hungry for the freedom to acquire more learning.
4. (empty flowery language); he could testify in detail to the horrific experience of slavery
5. (England and Ireland); During the Cold War, some people from Eastern Europe *exiled* themselves in the West.

6. (culture); An antonym for *alien* is *familiar*, *ordinary*, or *native*.

Reading Warm-up B, p. 122

Sample Answers

1. three staircases, and crystal chandeliers everywhere, even in the kitchen and bathrooms. The front exterior was decorated with a lacy, iron balcony, a tower with a pointed roof, and scarlet, climbing rosebushes. Above the front door, set into brick, was a carved, stone mural depicting ten figures dancing with spiraling, circling ribbons; A synonym for *gaudy* is *flashy*, *glaring*, or *loud*.
2. (circling); You might see leaves, seedpods, pieces of paper, or a tornado *spiraling* through the air.
3. worn and rundown, aged and tired; We knew it could be dangerous to touch the *frayed* end of an electrical cord.
4. (natural reaction); When I see a person frowning and crying, I know by *instinct* that this person is unhappy.
5. When they brought their families home for meals and celebrations; When the doctor tapped a rubber hammer against Jan's knee, her lower leg bounced slightly, due to a *reflex* action from her muscles.
6. (talk, laughter, jokes, and conversation); An antonym for *din* is *quiet* or *silence*.

Literary Analysis: Repetition and Parallelism, p. 123

Possible responses:

"The Explorer"

1. "Wee griefs, grand griefs"—both;
2. "There were no bourns. / There were no quiet rooms"—emphasize a message.

"Frederick Douglass"

1. "this beautiful / and terrible thing . . . / the beautiful, needful thing"—both
2. "when it is finally won; when it is more than the gaudy mumbo jumbo . . ."—emphasize a message.

Reading Strategy: Read the Poems Aloud, p. 124

Sample Responses

Students should choose any passage of the poem that is especially meaningful to them. In each case, students should identify the main technique in evidence in the passage—parallelism, repetition, or both—and then briefly summarize how reading the passage aloud enhanced the meaning of the poem for them. Sample responses:

"The Explorer"

Passage: "Somehow to find a still spot in the noise/ Was the frayed inner want, the winding, the frayed hope. . . ."; technique: repetition, parallelism; enhanced meaning: emphasizes the explorer's confusion and desperation.

"Frederick Douglass"

Passage: "visioning a world where none is lonely, none hunted, alien . . ."; technique: parallelism; enhanced meaning: reinforces nobility and splendor of Douglass's idealistic vision of life.

Vocabulary Builder, p. 125

Possible responses:

A. 1. a. physically worn or degraded; b. emotionally worn down or tested

2. a. showy or cheap in decor; b. pretentious in attitude.

B. 1. C; 2. A; 3. C

Enrichment: Poetry of Protest, p. 127

Sample Responses

1. The poem "The Explorer" shows that these environments can be filled with grief and unhealthy distractions. People treated as second-class citizens become frustrated and unhappy with themselves. When people are not supported or made to feel worthwhile for extended periods of time, they often lack the confidence to reach out and explore options. They stay in their safe environments, even if these are unpleasant.

2. The issue of slavery and the oppression of African Americans is addressed in "Frederick Douglass." Frederick Douglass was an important figure in the abolitionist movement. Hayden feels that people in modern society understand that freedom and liberty should be every person's rights, but they are not often sincere in upholding these rights. He upholds Douglass as an example of someone who fought sincerely and tenaciously for human rights and who still serves as an inspiring voice in that struggle.

Open-Book Test, p. 128

Short Answer

1. By repeating the word *frayed*, Brooks emphasizes that the person's wants and hopes are unfulfilled and perhaps a bit desperate.
   Difficulty: *Challenging*   **Objective:** *Literary Analysis*

2. The "still spot in the noise" represents peace of mind.
   Difficulty: *Easy*   **Objective:** *Interpretation*

3. The repetition of the word *somewhere* emphasizes that the subject does not know where "peace" and "hush" are to be found and thus feels lost and confused.
   Difficulty: *Average*   **Objective:** *Literary Analysis*

4. It is taking place inside the explorer's mind.
   Difficulty: *Average*   **Objective:** *Interpretation*

5. The parallel structure of the last two lines consists of the repetition of the phrase "There were no . . . ." By repeating this phrasing, Brooks emphasizes that there is no easy peace of mind to be found ("no quiet rooms") because of the endless variety of choices that life presents.
   Difficulty: *Challenging*   **Objective:** *Literary Analysis*

6. The effect is to build a sense of suspense and expectation about what will happen when freedom truly belongs to all people.
   Difficulty: *Average*   **Objective:** *Literary Analysis*

7. Reading the line aloud would help to bring out the line's rhythmic properties, especially the rhythm of the heartbeat conveyed in the words "diastole, systole."
   Difficulty: *Challenging*   **Objective:** *Reading Strategy*

8. You would emphasize vocally the repeated word *not*.
   Difficulty: *Easy*   **Objective:** *Reading Strategy*

9. Possible responses: a. "When it is finally ours," "when it belongs," "when it is finally won," "when it is won"—builds a sense of expectation and suspense about what will happen when freedom is won for all.
   b. "this man, this Douglass, this former slave, this Negro . . . this man . . . this man"—underscores the importance of the heritage of Frederick Douglass.
   c. "not with the statues rhetoric, not with legends and poems . . ."—emphasizes that Douglass's life is a living legacy to real people, not something frozen in statues and monuments.
   d. "the lives grown out of his life, the lives fleshing his dream"—emphasizes that Douglass's life continues to shape and inspire the lives of real people.
   Difficulty: *Average*   **Objective:** *Literary Analysis*

10. Yes, the architecture critic would be finding fault with the design of the lobby, because *gaudy* means "showy in a tasteless way."
    Difficulty: *Average*   **Objective:** *Vocabulary*

Essay

11. Students should choose a figure from history or from their own personal experience. They should be clear about exactly how and why this person has inspired them. Their answers should be based on clear reasoning and specific examples.
    Difficulty: *Easy*   **Objective:** *Essay*

12. Students should state clearly whether they agree with the poem's message or not, and then make a persuasive case for their opinion. Some students might argue that life's choices do at times seem endless—which friends you might make, where you might go to college, which town you might live in, what kind of career you might pursue. So complete peace of mind is hard to find because one might always wonder what would have happened had one pursued another course. Other students might argue that only the very fortunate have unlimited choices and that for some the range of choices is not so great, but that this very shortage of choices can disturb one's peace just as much as too many choices can.
    Difficulty: *Average*   **Objective:** *Essay*

13. Students might note that in "The Explorer," Brooks portrays the anxieties and fears that can arise from a wide array of choices in life. He implies that freedom is a path that leads to restless searching, not peace of mind ("He feared most of all the choices. . . ."). By contrast, students might suggest that Hayden, in "Frederick Douglass," portrays freedom as "beautiful." So he seems to cast it in a more favorable light than Brooks does.

They might note, however, that he also calls freedom this "terrible thing," also implying that there is a scary side to choice in life. Students should defend their preference for Brooks's or Hayden's portrait of freedom with specific examples from the poems.

Difficulty: *Challenging*   **Objective:** *Essay*

14. Students might argue that "The Explorer" is the poem that is more a reflection of society. It portrays a man confronted by a dizzying, disorienting multitude of life choices and possibilities—the kind of wide array of choices that often confronts people living in modern urban settings. The man dreams of a different way of life, but is more paralyzed than empowered by the freedom of choice presented to him. Students might suggest that "Frederick Douglass" also reflects society to some extent by emphasizing the lack of freedom that many people suffer in today's world. But the poem also seeks to shape society by holding up the example of Frederick Douglass as someone who devoted his life to fighting for his own freedom and the freedom of his people.

Difficulty: *Average*   **Objective:** *Essay*

Oral Response

15. Oral responses should be clear, well organized, and well supported by appropriate examples from the selections.

Difficulty: *Average*   **Objective:** *Oral Response*

Selection Test A, p. 131

Critical Reading

1. ANS: B	DIF: Easy	OBJ: Interpretation
2. ANS: B	DIF: Easy	OBJ: Comprehension
3. ANS: A	DIF: Average	OBJ: Literary Analysis
4. ANS: C	DIF: Easy	OBJ: Literary Analysis
5. ANS: B	DIF: Easy	OBJ: Reading Strategy
6. ANS: D	DIF: Easy	OBJ: Interpretation
7. ANS: C	DIF: Easy	OBJ: Interpretation
8. ANS: B	DIF: Easy	OBJ: Literary Analysis
9. ANS: C	DIF: Easy	OBJ: Literary Analysis
10. ANS: D	DIF: Easy	OBJ: Interpretation

Vocabulary

11. ANS: D	DIF: Easy	OBJ: Vocabulary
12. ANS: A	DIF: Easy	OBJ: Vocabulary
13. ANS: A	DIF: Challenging	OBJ: Vocabulary

Essay

14. Students might argue that normally having more choices is a good thing—it expands your sense of freedom and your sense of possibilities in life. Students might also note, however, that if a person is indecisive, having many choices can be frustrating—one will always be left wondering what might have happened if

one had made a different choice, especially if the choice that one made did not turn out as planned. With fewer choices, there might be fewer opportunities for regret and second-guessing oneself, and hence no need to fear choices as the explorer does.

Difficulty: *Easy*

Objective: *Essay*

15. Students might note that freedom is normally thought of as something beautiful—the ability to decide what one wants to do with one's life, who one wants to be, what political choices one thinks are best, where one wants to live, and so on. Freedom might be "terrible" in the sense that it imposes a responsibility—instead of having your life mapped out for you by someone else, you have to grapple with the decisions that will determine the course of your life. Such decisions are not always easy or simple—so freedom can sometimes seem as much a burden as a blessing.

Difficulty: *Easy*

Objective: *Essay*

16. Students might argue that "The Explorer" is the poem that is more a reflection of society. It portrays a man confronted by a dizzying, disorienting multitude of life choices and possibilities—the kind of wide array of choices that often confronts people living in modern urban settings. The man dreams of a different way of life, but is more paralyzed than empowered by the freedom of choice presented to him. Students might suggest that "Frederick Douglass" also reflects society to some extent by emphasizing the lack of freedom that many people suffer in today's world. But the poem also seeks to shape society by holding up the example of Frederick Douglass as someone who devoted his life to fighting for his own freedom and the freedom of his people.

Difficulty: *Easy*

Objective: *Essay*

Selection Test B, p. 134

Critical Reading

1. ANS: D	DIF: Easy	OBJ: Interpretation
2. ANS: A	DIF: Challenging	OBJ: Interpretation
3. ANS: C	DIF: Average	OBJ: Literary Analysis
4. ANS: B	DIF: Easy	OBJ: Literary Analysis
5. ANS: D	DIF: Average	OBJ: Literary Analysis
6. ANS: A	DIF: Average	OBJ: Interpretation
7. ANS: D	DIF: Challenging	OBJ: Interpretation
8. ANS: B	DIF: Average	OBJ: Comprehension
9. ANS: C	DIF: Easy	OBJ: Literary Analysis
10. ANS: C	DIF: Average	OBJ: Interpretation
11. ANS: A	DIF: Easy	OBJ: Comprehension
12. ANS: D	DIF: Average	OBJ: Interpretation
13. ANS: B	DIF: Easy	OBJ: Reading Strategy
14. ANS: C	DIF: Challenging	OBJ: Interpretation

Vocabulary

15. ANS: A   DIF: Easy   OBJ: Vocabulary
16. ANS: B   DIF: Average   OBJ: Vocabulary
17. ANS: D   DIF: Average   OBJ: Vocabulary

Essay

18. Students should choose a historical figure and explain why he or she is a source of inspiration, citing details about the person's life and achievements to support general statements about him or her.

19. Students might argue that normally having more choices is a good thing—it expands your sense of freedom and your sense of possibilities in life. Students might also note, however, that if a person is indecisive, having many choices can be frustrating—one will always be left wondering what might have happened if one had made a different choice, especially if the choice that one made did not turn out as planned. With fewer choices, there might be fewer opportunities for regret and second-guessing oneself, and hence no need to fear choices as the explorer does.

    Difficulty: *Easy*

    Objective: *Essay*

20. Students might note that freedom is normally thought of as something beautiful—the ability to decide what one wants to do with one's life, who one wants to be, what political choices one thinks are best, where one wants to live, and so on. Freedom might be "terrible" in the sense that it imposes a responsibility—instead of having your life mapped out for you by someone else, you have to grapple with the decisions that will determine the course of your life, so freedom can sometimes seem as much a burden as a blessing. Students should explain either view and cite details from either poem to support their ideas.

    Difficulty: *Easy*

    Objective: *Essay*

21. Students might argue that "The Explorer" is the poem that is more a reflection of society. It portrays a man confronted by a dizzying, disorienting multitude of life choices and possibilities—the kind of wide array of choices that often confronts people living in modern urban settings. The man dreams of a different way of life, but is more paralyzed than empowered by the freedom of choice presented to him. Students might suggest that "Frederick Douglass" also reflects society to some extent by emphasizing the lack of freedom that many people suffer in today's world. But the poem also seeks to shape society by holding up the example of Frederick Douglass as someone who devoted his life to fighting for his own freedom and the freedom of his people.

    Difficulty: *Average*

    Objective: *Essay*

MULTIPLE CHOICE

1. ANS: B
2. ANS: D
3. ANS: D
4. ANS: C
5. ANS: B
6. ANS: D
7. ANS: A
8. ANS: D
9. ANS: D
10. ANS: C
11. ANS: D
12. ANS: A
13. ANS: B
14. ANS: C
15. ANS: C
16. ANS: C
17. ANS: D
18. ANS: A
19. ANS: B
20. ANS: A
21. ANS: B
22. ANS: D
23. ANS: C
24. ANS: A
25. ANS: B
26. ANS: D
27. ANS: C
28. ANS: C
29. ANS: D
30. ANS: B

ESSAY

31. Students should choose two movies or television shows about war to compare and contrast. Essays should begin with a statement of general critical assessment of both works and a statement of the messages in the works. Essays should be organized with point-by-point comparisons and contrasts or by discussing first one work and then the other. Details from the works should support students' points.

32. Profiles should clearly state the character traits of a memorable character from literature, movies, or television. Students should indicate how each trait is illustrated in the work.

343

33. Poems should be on the topic of friendship and include an extended metaphor that compares the friendship to a concrete object or physical activity.

"One Art" and "Filling Station"
by Elizabeth Bishop

Vocabulary Warm-up Exercises, p. 144

A. 1. disaster
2. fluster
3. high-strung
4. master
5. realms
6. intent
7. disturbing
8. hirsute

B. Sample Answers

1. The weather was so warm and wet that the begonia was thriving.
2. The dusty and worn wickerwork furniture looked very old.
3. My new office is far vaster than the tiny cubicle I worked in before.
4. Most teachers don't care for students who make saucy comments in class.
5. When I was little, I loved to watch my grandmother decorate knickknacks with crochet.
6. In the summer, I love wearing peasant blouses decorated with embroidered flowers.
7. From his handsome and expensive suit of clothes, it was evident that he was extremely prosperous.
8. There is nothing so beautiful in the springtime as a field of marguerites.

Reading Warm-up A, p. 145

Sample Answers

1. goal; *aim, objective, purpose*
2. (trivial items)(if they aren't here); *state of bother, agitation*
3. kingdom; There are many *realms* that are ruled by kings or queens.
4. unsettling; *bothersome, upsetting, worrying*
5. (of disorganization); *fires, floods, earthquakes, hurricanes*
6. (system of organization); *geometry, golf,* etc.
7. peppermint candy; The dog was so *hirsute* that I couldn't see its eyes underneath its fur.
8. upset and agitated; *calm*

Reading Warm-up B, p. 146

Sample Answers

1. like giant parking lots or open fields; *smaller*
2. (witty); *respectful, polite*

3. that used goods are what people most commonly offer for sale; *Evident* means obvious or clear to see.
4. porch furniture; My uncle has some furniture that I think is *wickerwork*.
5. (arts of knitting); Yes, my aunt knows the art of *crochet*.
6. with lovely old-fashioned designs; Susan *embroidered* a tablecloth for us as a housewarming gift.
7. plants, tropical, furry-leafed; I like cactus plants.
8. (yellow and white) (cheery blooms); *daisies*

Literary Analysis: Diction, p. 147

Students might mention six of the following or other details from the poem: "dirty, oil-soaked monkey suit"; "greasy sons"; "cement porch"; "set of crushed and grease-impregnated wickerwork"; "a dirty dog, quite comfy"; "comic books provide the only note of color:; "big dim doily"; "taboret"; "big hirsute begonia"; "daisy stitch with marguerites"; "gray crochet"; "cans . . . that softly say: ESSO—SO—SO—SO."

Reading Strategy: Read According to Punctuation, p. 148

1. The exclamation point causes the reader to pause longer and to give greater emphasis to the line, which communicates the speaker's first and strongest overall impression of the filling station.
2. These lines from "Filling Station" express two sentences or complete ideas.
3. Commas indicate pauses, not full stops, so it is not a reasonable conclusion. Not every line in this stanza expresses a complete thought. The comma after "vaster" in the first line is merely a pause in a thought that ends with the period after "continent."
4. The fourth stanza of "One Art" expresses the most complete thoughts It contains four sentences, and hence four complete thoughts.

Vocabulary Builder, p. 149

A. Possible responses

1. extraterrestrial—beyond the confines of the earth
2. extrapolate—to go outside or beyond known data or knowledge to make an inference
3. extralegal—outside of or beyond the law or legality
4. extramarital—outside of marriage

B. 1. A; 2. A; 3. C; 4.B

Open-Book Test, p. 152

Short Answer

1. You would come to a full stop after the word *day* and after the word *spent* because each is followed by a period.
   Difficulty: *Easy*   **Objective:** *Reading Strategy*
2. Bishop changes from the declarative to the imperative because she wishes to involve the reader more directly.

She is encouraging the reader to act in a certain way with regard to loss, rather than just commenting on it, as she does in the first three lines.

Difficulty: *Average*   **Objective:** *Literary Analysis*

3. Each item is more significant and valuable than the preceding one.

Difficulty: *Average*   **Objective:** *Interpretation*

4. The exclamation "And look!" shows the poet's own increasing emotional intensity and prepares the reader for a shift to still more significant items to be lost.

Difficulty: *Average*   **Objective:** *Literary Analysis*

5. It is unique because it is addressed not to the reader but to the speaker/poet herself. It shows that the speaker must force herself to acknowledge, however reluctantly, that the loss of a beloved person is a disaster, even though she would like to pretend that it was not, as she has been doing throughout the rest of the poem.

Difficulty: *Challenging*   **Objective:** *Literary Analysis*

6. Bishop begins the poem with an exclamation to impress upon the reader her initial, overwhelming impression of the dirtiness of the place.

Difficulty: *Average*   **Objective:** *Literary Analysis*

7. The questions show that she is full of curiosity, especially about the private family life that takes place in the house on the grounds of the station.

Difficulty: *Easy*   **Objective:** *Literary Analysis*

8. The details associated with "somebody" are household tasks and details that show caring and give some beauty to the rough filling-station surroundings. All of these are characteristics of the loving touch of a woman. So the "somebody" who "loves us all" is probably the wife and mother of the men who labor at the filling station.

Difficulty: *Challenging*   **Objective:** *Interpretation*

9. Sample answers: "dirty, oil-soaked monkey suit"; "greasy sons"; "cement porch"; "set of crushed and grease-impregnated wickerwork"; "a dirty dog, quite comfy"; "comic books provide the only note of color"; "big dim doily"; "taboret"; "big hirsute begonia"; "daisy stitch with marguerites"; "gray crochet"; "cans . . . that softly say: ESSO—SO—SO—SO."

Difficulty: *Average*   **Objective:** *Literary Analysis*

10. No, the details would not be relevant to the topic, because *extraneous* means "unrelated or unconnected."

Difficulty: *Average*   **Objective:** *Vocabulary*

Essay

11. Students might suggest that the "somebody" is the wife and mother of the men who work at the filling station. Their descriptions of this "somebody"—whoever they imagine the person to be—should contain vivid, concrete details about her appearance, personality, and function in the life of the filling station.

Difficulty: *Easy*   **Objective:** *Essay*

12. Some students might prefer "One Art," with its reflections on the various forms of loss that people must confront in life and the ways in which they try to cope with it. Others might prefer the more concrete descriptions of "Filling Station." Students should explain their preference with clear reasoning and support it with details from the poems.

Difficulty: *Average*   **Objective:** *Essay*

13. Students might note that the speaker starts out by mentioning relatively trivial things people can lose—door keys, an hour wasted, and so on—which do seem easy to master. But then she includes larger kinds of losses—places you never got to travel to, a precious family heirloom, houses once lived in, and countries or continents where you have lived. Each time she increases the losses with the potential for greater emotional impact, her insistence that the loss is not a disaster seems less convincing. Finally, when she mentions a beloved person she has lost, she has to force herself to write the word *disaster*, because the loss is so difficult. By the end of the poem, we see that the emotional impact of losses can indeed be a disaster—especially in relation to people we have lost—and not so easy to master.

Difficulty: *Challenging*   **Objective:** *Essay*

14. Students might note that in "One Art," the art is learning how to cope with loss. In the poem, Bishop climbs the ladder of loss—going from small, insignificant things like door keys and watches to more significant items, such as places one has loved: house, "two rivers, a continent." They might suggest that the poet here emphasizes how attached we become to various places in our lives and how difficult it can be to move on and "lose" these places. "Filling Station" makes the same point—the importance of place—but in a completely different way: the poem evokes surprise and delight at finding a place—all the unexpected details of discovery about the filling station and the family that live there, the way in which it hints at revealing details of personal and emotional life that lurk on the surface of the everyday life of a common place.

Difficulty: *Average*   **Objective:** *Essay*

Oral Response

15. Oral responses should be clear, well organized, and well supported by appropriate examples from the selections.

Difficulty: *Average*   **Objective:** *Oral Interpretation*

Selection Test A, p. 155
Critical Reading

1. ANS: A	DIF: Easy	OBJ: Literary Analysis
2. ANS: D	DIF: Easy	OBJ: Interpretation
3. ANS: A	DIF: Easy	OBJ: Interpretation
4. ANS: A	DIF: Easy	OBJ: Literary Analysis
5. ANS: A	DIF: Easy	OBJ: Reading Strategy
6. ANS: C	DIF: Easy	OBJ: Reading Strategy

7. ANS: C	DIF: Easy	OBJ: Literary Analysis
8. ANS: A	DIF: Easy	OBJ: Interpretation
9. ANS: C	DIF: Easy	OBJ: Comprehension
10. ANS: B	DIF: Easy	OBJ: Literary Analysis
11. ANS: B	DIF: Easy	OBJ: Interpretation

Essay

12. Students should express clear opinions about why working from home makes home feel more or less like "home," and whether people feel more or less motivated to work in their own residence. Some might argue that setting aside a separate room as an office leaves the rest of the residence free of work associations; some might note that working on one's own, without the presence of a supervisor, requires extra self-discipline. They might also note that in the poem, it seems to be the job of "Somebody" to provide the little caring touches that make the filling station seem more like a home.

Difficulty: *Easy*

Objective: *Essay*

13. Students should clearly specify a loss they have suffered in their lives—whether of a material object or a place. They should then explain why that loss was easy to master or a disaster, and give reasons for their reaction. Their essays should be supported by specific examples based on their experience.

Difficulty: *Easy*

Objective: *Essay*

14. Answer will vary. Some students might suppose that the father and mother are very happy with the secure, predictable lives they have built up around their filling station. Some might suppose that one or the other might be restless and might be interested in pursuing some other kind of life. Encourage students to give free rein to their imaginations in portraying the lives of the people in the poem.

Difficulty: *Easy*

Objective: *Essay*

15. Students might note that in "One Art," the art is learning how to cope with loss. In the poem, Bishop climbs the ladder of loss—going from small, insignificant things like door keys and watches to more significant items, such as places one has loved: house, "two rivers, a continent." They might suggest that the poet here emphasizes how attached we become to various places in our lives and how difficult it can be to move on and "lose" these places. "Filling Station" makes the same point—the importance of place—but in a completely different way: the poem evokes surprise and delight of finding a place—all the unexpected details of discovery about the filling station and the family that live there, the way in which it hints at revealing details of personal and emotional life that lurk on the surface of the everyday life of a common place.

Difficulty: *Easy*

Objective: *Essay*

Selection Test B, p. 158

Critical Reading

1. ANS: B	DIF: Challenging	OBJ: Interpretation
2. ANS: C	DIF: Average	OBJ: Comprehension
3. ANS: C	DIF: Average	OBJ: Reading Strategy
4. ANS: A	DIF: Average	OBJ: Interpretation
5. ANS: C	DIF: Challenging	OBJ: Literary Analysis
6. ANS: C	DIF: Average	OBJ: Literary Analysis
7. ANS: D	DIF: Average	OBJ: Interpretation
8. ANS: A	DIF: Challenging	OBJ: Literary Analysis
9. ANS: D	DIF: Easy	OBJ: Comprehension
10. ANS: C	DIF: Average	OBJ: Literary Analysis
11. ANS: B	DIF: Challenging	OBJ: Interpretation
12. ANS: D	DIF: Esay	OBJ: Reading Strategy
13. ANS: C	DIF: Average	OBJ: Literary Analysis
14. ANS: B	DIF: Average	OBJ: Interpretation
15. ANS: B	DIF: Challenging	OBJ: Interpretation

Essay

16. Students might suggest that the people directly depicted in the poem—the father and his sons—do not consider their surroundings "dirty" because they are accustomed to being around the grit and smell of oil and gasoline—that's their working environment, and they are used to it. They might also suppose that the father and sons are proud of owning a business and are happy working and making an honest living in the way that they do. They might also note that the "somebody" of the poem—possibly the wife and mother of the family—makes their living and working environment that much more pleasant with little loving touches such as plants and doilies.

Difficulty: *Average*

Objective: *Essay*

17. Students might note that there is indeed a discernible and significant order to Bishop's list of losses in "One Art": she begins with relatively insignificant objects such as door keys or an hour badly spent and then progresses to weightier items, which she herself calls "losing farther": places, names, destinations you meant to travel to. Beyond these are houses and cities that carry major emotional associations for her, and beyond those even vaster places—both physically and emotionally—such as rivers and continents. Finally, she mentions a person she has lost, finally admitting, reluctantly and ironically in the last line, that losing on that scale is indeed a disaster, despite her earlier efforts to reassure the reader—and herself—that it is not.

Difficulty: *Challenging*

Objective: *Essay*

18. Students might suggest that imperatives—or imperatives given an urgent turn with an exclamation point—are appropriate in "One Art," because in that poem Bishop gives a good deal of advice about coping with loss, and the

imperative mood is a natural and common form in which to give advice or instruction. The irony that emerges by the end of the poem is that it turns out that she has been trying to convince herself—unsuccessfully—to believe that loss is easily mastered and not a disaster. Questions are the natural rhetorical device for a poem such as "Filling Station," in which the poet is filled with wonder about the circumstances of the lives of the people who live and work there. The question form is the best way to express the urgent sense of wonder and curiosity behind her observations of the filling station, the father, the sons, and the "somebody" that she imagines lurks in the background of their lives.

Difficulty: *Challenging*

Objective: *Essay*

19. Students might note that in "One Art," the art is learning how to cope with loss. In the poem, Bishop climbs the ladder of loss—going from small, insignificant things like door keys and watches to more significant items, such as places one has loved: house, "two rivers, a continent." They might suggest that the poet here emphasizes how attached we become to various places in our lives and how difficult it can be to move on and "lose" these places. "Filling Station" makes the same point—the importance of place—but in a completely different way: the poem evokes surprise and delight at finding a place—all the unexpected details of discovery about the filling station and the family that live there, the way in which it hints at revealing details of personal and emotional life that lurk on the surface of the everyday life of a common place.

Difficulty: *Average*

Objective: *Essay*

"The Rockpile" by James Baldwin

Vocabulary Warm-up Exercises, p. 162

A. 1. acquire
2. clambering
3. fidget
4. apprehension
5. jagged
6. confirmation
7. reckless
8. intimidated

B. Sample Answers
1. T; Since *benevolent* means "with good will," such a person might well be trusted.
2. F; *Decorously* implies propriety and appropriateness, so people will not be shocked.
3. F; Since *engrossed* means "absorbed," the viewer would probably not be bored.
4. F; An exasperated person would not be likely to respond with smiles or jokes, but with irritation.
5. T; Since *fascination* means "intense interest," this statement is true.

6. F; Since *intriguing* means "interesting" or "curious," a person would likely spend quite a bit of time on it.
7. T; Since *recoiled* means "pulled back," shrinking back would be a natural reaction.
8. F; A superficial, or shallow, acquaintance with a topic would not qualify someone to claim expertise.

Reading Warm-up A, p. 163
Sample Answers
1. how much work he had done; If you practice every day, you can acquire skill at the game of tennis.
2. (fearful); *Frightened* is a synonym for *intimidated*.
3. on top of each other; *Clambering* means "climbing awkwardly."
4. (the fearful way he was playing); *Confidence* and *assurance* are antonyms for *apprehension*.
5. (Brian dropped a pass thrown right to him); *Contradiction* is an antonym for *confirmation*.
6. sharp; *Rough* and *irregular* are synonyms for *jagged*.
7. (act nervously); Amy disliked sitting still and would often *fidget* in class.
8. he rushed over to tackle; diving for interceptions; *Cautious* is an antonym for *reckless*.

Reading Warm-up B, p. 164
Sample Answers
1. important and inspiring influences; Professor James had a benevolent nature and genuinely cared for all his students' welfare.
2. (able to explore); *Fascination* means "intense interest."
3. totally absorbed; *preoccupied*
4. quietly; *loudly, undignified*
5. (appealing and complex hero); The children were bored with the dull comedian.
6. in shock; *flinched*
7. (made the decision to forsake his homeland); He was probably frustrated with racial prejudice.
8. (more meaningful); *shallow*

Literary Analysis: Setting, p. 165
A. 1. A; 2. E; 3. C, E; 4. D, E; 5. E, G
B. 1. At the end of the street nearest their house was the bridge that spanned the San Francisco Bay.
2. John and Roy sat on the veranda and watched the busy street below.
3. Dozens of boys fought each other in the blinding blizzard.
4. One Tuesday, an hour after his father came home, Roy was wounded on the mountain and brought screaming inside.
5. They filled the air, too, with flying streamers, confetti, roses, hats, whatever could be picked up and thrown.

Reading Strategy: Identify Cause and Effect, p. 166

Possible Responses

1. EFFECT: Roy is spoiled.
   EFFECT: Elizabeth resents Gabriel.
2. CAUSE: Gabriel intimidates John.
   CAUSE: Elizabeth speaks for John.
3. EFFECT = CAUSE: Gabriel discovers Roy's injury.
   EFFECT = CAUSE: Gabriel blames John and Elizabeth.
   EFFECT = CAUSE: Elizabeth stands up to Gabriel.

Vocabulary Builder, p. 167

A. 1. Superior
   2. supercilious
   3. supersede
   4. supervisor
B. 1. B; 2. D; 3. C; 4. B; 5. C;

Grammar and Style: Avoiding Shifts in Verb Tense, p. 168

Sample Responses:

1. I will write a thank-you note to all the guests when I get home.
2. There were lots of exciting music acts at the concert I attended.
3. It is the duty of all citizens to help all those who are in need.
4. Last year's basketball team had a losing record despite the high hopes we had for it.
5. correct

Enrichment: Emergency Services, p. 170

Possible Responses

1. The number might be 9-1-1. If not, students should consult the community information section of the telephone book to find the number for their area.
2. Roy's family might have called 9-1-1, although the injury was not severe. If Richard had been reached in time, he would have been taken to a trauma center because his injury was severe and life-threatening.
3. In poor or small communities, emergency services might not be readily available.

Open-Book Test, p. 171

Short Answer

1. The setting is Harlem in the 1930s. Most of the story takes place in an apartment building that faces a busy street that features a rockpile.

   Difficulty: *Easy*   **Objective:** *Literary Analysis*
2. John and Roy look out longingly because to them the rockpile is a place of extraordinary doings, of freedom

and danger. It's far different from the kind of confinement and expectations imposed by their parents.

Difficulty: *Average*   **Objective:** *Literary Analysis*

3. The accidental drowning death symbolizes the dangers of the neighborhood, as is shown by her horror at the scene of his body being carried up the street.

   Difficulty: *Average*   **Objective:** *Literary Analysis*
4. Roy sees several of his friends walk by and wants to join them.

   Difficulty: *Easy*   **Objective:** *Reading Strategy*
5. Elizabeth is worried about the impending arrival home of her husband, Gabriel, from work, because she worries about how he will react to Roy's injury.

   Difficulty: *Average*   **Objective:** *Interpretation*
6. John is her child but not Gabriel's, so she fears that Gabriel will not treat him fairly.

   Difficulty: *Average*   **Objective:** *Reading Strategy*
7. Sample answer: John is supposed to be the man of the family when Gabriel is not home; he is quiet, shy, timid; he is afraid of the rockpile and the boys who play there; he is Elizabeth's favorite child; Gabriel and he get along well. Roy is the "bad boy" of the family; he is outgoing and a bit reckless; he wants very much to play at the rockpile and feels abused because he is not allowed; Elizabeth tolerates his behavior; he is Gabriel's favorite child. The boys are both caring and sensitive to their parents and each other, but Roy's outgoing, friendly personality sets him apart from John's quiet personality and causes significant differences in their behavior.

   Difficulty: *Challenging*   **Objective:** *Interpretation*
8. The argument is really about Elizabeth's and Gabriel's feelings about John and Roy. Gabriel accuses her of not caring for Roy, and threatens to beat John, whom he resents as a symbol of Elizabeth's "sinful" past. Elizabeth tells Gabriel that if he can't make Roy behave, Roy can't, and she implies that the cause of the accident is Gabriel's preferential and indulgent treatment of Roy, his biological son.

   Difficulty: *Challenging*   **Objective:** *Interpretation*
9. Upon seeing Elizabeth pick up Delilah, their daughter, he remembers that she is his wife and the mother of their children.

   Difficulty: *Easy*   **Objective:** *Reading Strategy*
10. No, you would not be easily distracted, because *engrossed* means "occupied wholly; absorbed."

    Difficulty: *Average*   **Objective:** *Vocabulary*

Essay

11. Sample answers: Gabriel is harder on John than on the other children; Elizabeth is forced to be more protective of John than the other children because of Gabriel's harshness; and John is usually afraid of Gabriel.

    Difficulty: *Easy*   **Objective:** *Essay*

12. Sample answer: A child getting hurt is often cause for tension because parents are always worried about their children's safety, and there might be a tendency to blame in such a situation, whether it makes sense or not. In this family's case, there are also deeper issues of resentment about Elizabeth's past and John's being the only child who is not Gabriel's biological child. This leads to accusations that Gabriel favors Roy over John. The issues of favoritism and unequal treatment are common in many families, even when all the children come from the same biological parents.

    Difficulty: *Average* **Objective:** *Essay*

13. Sample answer: The rockpile, a real physical threat in the neighborhood, symbolizes the evil and danger lurking in the characters' home. For instance, the rockpile symbolizes the danger that Gabriel poses to his family. Elizabeth tries to protect John from Gabriel's anger and blame. As he does with the rockpile, John avoids contact with a possible danger. On the other hand, Roy ignores his mother's warnings. He seems to believe that no real harm can come to him, either from the rockpile or from Gabriel.

    Difficulty: *Challenging* **Objective:** *Essay*

14. Students might note that early on in the story, Baldwin captures both the danger and fascination of the Harlem streets to the two young boys—John and Roy—when he states, "Each Saturday morning John and Roy sat on their fire escape and watched the forbidden street below" and refers to the "wickedness" of the bustling street scene and the boys' sense of wickedness for being fascinated by it. The rockpile especially represents a mysterious, dangerous, and exciting place that is beyond the control of parents. Students might suggest that the boys' differing attitudes toward the rockpile— the quiet, sensitive John is afraid of the pile, whereas the more assertive Roy seeks it out—help to illustrate the ways in which a social environment can shape and highlight personal characteristics and family dynamics.

    Difficulty: *Average* **Objective:** *Essay*

Oral Response

15. Oral responses should be clear, well organized, and well supported by appropriate examples from the selections.

Selection Test A, p. 174

Critical Reading

1. ANS: B	DIF: Easy	OBJ: Literary Analysis
2. ANS: C	DIF: Easy	OBJ: Comprehension
3. ANS: B	DIF: Easy	OBJ: Literary Analysis
4. ANS: D	DIF: Easy	OBJ: Interpretation
5. ANS: A	DIF: Easy	OBJ: Reading Strategy
6. ANS: A	DIF: Easy	OBJ: Interpretation
7. ANS: B	DIF: Easy	OBJ: Reading Strategy
8. ANS: A	DIF: Easy	OBJ: Comprehension
9. ANS: D	DIF: Easy	OBJ: Comprehension
10. ANS: B	DIF: Easy	OBJ: Interpretation

Vocabulary and Grammar

11. ANS: C	DIF: Easy	OBJ: Vocabulary
12. ANS: B	DIF: Easy	OBJ: Vocabulary
13. ANS: A	DIF: Easy	OBJ: Vocabulary
14. ANS: D	DIF: Easy	OBJ: Grammar

Essay

15. Students' essays should cite one or more of these effects: Gabriel is harder on John than on the other children; Elizabeth is forced to be more protective of John than the other children because of Gabriel's harshness; and John is usually afraid of Gabriel.

    Difficulty: *Easy*
    Objective: *Essay*

16. Students' essays should address the information that because Roy knows he is his father's favorite, he has no fear of going out to play on the rockpile. When Gabriel comes home, Roy takes advantage of his status to get protection from Gabriel at the expense of Elizabeth and John.

    Difficulty: *Easy*
    Objective: *Essay*

17. Students might note that early on in the story, Baldwin captures both the danger and fascination of the Harlem streets to the two young boys—John and Roy—when he states, "Each Saturday morning John and Roy sat on their fire escape and watched the forbidden street below" and refers to the "wickedness" of the bustling street scene and the boys' sense of wickedness for being fascinated by it. The rockpile especially represents a mysterious, dangerous, and exciting place that is beyond the control of parents. Students might suggest that the boys' differing attitudes toward the rockpile— the quiet, sensitive John is afraid of the pile, whereas the more assertive Roy seeks it out—help to illustrate the ways in which a social environment can shape and highlight personal characteristics and family dynamics.

    Difficulty: *Easy*
    Objective: *Essay*

Selection Test B, p. 177

Critical Reading

1. ANS: B	DIF: Average	OBJ: Comprehension
2. ANS: C	DIF: Easy	OBJ: Interpretation
3. ANS: B	DIF: Challenging	OBJ: Literary Analysis
4. ANS: B	DIF: Average	OBJ: Literary Analysis
5. ANS: D	DIF: Average	OBJ: Reading Strategy
6. ANS: A	DIF: Easy	OBJ: Reading Strategy
7. ANS: A	DIF: Average	OBJ: Interpretation
8. ANS: C	DIF: Average	OBJ: Interpretation
9. ANS: D	DIF: Easy	OBJ: Interpretation

10. ANS: B	DIF: Challenging	OBJ: Literary Analysis
11. ANS: D	DIF: Easy	OBJ: Comprehension
12. ANS: C	DIF: Average	OBJ: Reading Strategy
13. ANS: C	DIF: Challenging	OBJ: Interpretation
14. ANS: A	DIF: Challenging	OBJ: Interpretation

Vocabulary and Grammar

15. ANS: A	DIF: Easy	OBJ: Vocabulary
16. ANS: C	DIF: Average	OBJ: Vocabulary
17. ANS: D	DIF: Average	OBJ: Vocabulary
18. ANS: B	DIF: Average	OBJ: Grammar

Essay

19. Students should clearly identify a cause-and-effect relationship, such as the series of events that begins with Roy disobeying his mother and ends with his injury, the effects of Gabriel's favoring Roy, or the causes of Elizabeth's protectiveness of John. Students should draw logical conclusions about cause and effect. For instance, students might conclude that Elizabeth is protective of John because he is her first child, she feels guilty about her former "days in sin," or she identifies with John because Gabriel shuns her as he does John.

Difficulty: *Easy*

Objective: *Essay*

Students might suggest that the rockpile, a real physical threat in the neighborhood, symbolizes the evil and danger lurking in the characters' home. For instance, the rockpile symbolizes the danger that Gabriel poses to his family. Elizabeth tries to protect John from Gabriel's anger and blame; as he does with the rockpile, John avoids contact with a possible danger. On the other hand, Roy ignores his mother's warnings; he believes that no real harm can come to him, either from the rockpile or from Gabriel.

Difficulty: *Average*

Objective: *Essay*

21. Students should conclude that the dramatic tension in "The Rockpile" arises more from conflict among humans than between humans and nature. Students might explain that while the rockpile is a physical and natural threat, it serves only as a catalyst for the story's true tension—family conflict. For example, dramatic tension heightens as Elizabeth and John worry how Gabriel will react to Roy's injury. Tension increases as Gabriel's prejudice against John is revealed and Elizabeth confronts Gabriel.

Difficulty: *Challenging*

Objective: *Essay*

22. Students might note that early on in the story, Baldwin captures both the danger and fascination of the Harlem streets to the two young boys—John and Roy—when he states, "Each Saturday morning John and Roy sat on

their fire escape and watched the forbidden street below" and refers to the "wickedness" of the bustling street scene and the boys' sense of wickedness for being fascinated by it. The rockpile especially represents a mysterious, dangerous, and exciting place that is beyond the control of parents. Students might suggest that the boys' differing attitudes toward the rockpile—the quiet, sensitive John is afraid of the pile, whereas the more assertive Roy seeks it out—help to illustrate the ways in which a social environment can shape and highlight personal characteristics and family dynamics.

Difficulty: *Average*

Objective: *Essay*

"Life in His Language" by Toni Morrison

Vocabulary Warm-up Exercises, p. 181

A.
1. international
2. compatriots
3. intimacy
4. forbidden
5. unassailable
6. innocence
7. fathom
8. exposed

B. Sample Answers
1. F; If something is <u>astonishing</u> then no one expects it to happen.
2. F; If Rachael was a <u>rebel</u>, she would seldom or never follow the rules.
3. F; If he expressed himself with <u>clarity</u> then everyone would understand him.
4. T; If she was lost in <u>contemplation</u> then she might not hear him come in.
5. T; <u>Profound</u> feelings are deep and serious.
6. F; If you are <u>insistent</u> about doing something, then you care about it a lot.
7. F; If you engage in <u>hypocrisy</u>, you are probably dishonest about your beliefs.
8. T; If an actor has <u>inhabited</u> a role he is likely to give a great performance.

Reading Warm-up A, p. 182

Sample Answers
1. <u>schoolmates</u>; *classmates, fellow team members*
2. (novels); *local*
3. <u>simplicity</u>; *virtue, purity, blamelessness*
4. *certain*; winning the Pulitzer Prize
5. (controversial); because it deals with issues that make people uncomfortable
6. (truths); *showed, pointed out, uncovered*
7. <u>closeness between people</u>; my sister, my father, etc.
8. <u>cruelties</u>; *understand*

Reading Warm-up B, p. 183

Sample Answers

1. <u>the calm center of the complex world they occupied</u>; *lived in*
2. (unexpected); *expected, predictable, likely*
3. <u>deep thought</u>; considering something carefully
4. (outsider); Roscoe was such a *rebel* that he never followed the rules.
5. (his portrayal of the mind of a middle-class, conventional man living with the effects of racism); *understanding, clearness*
6. <u>dishonesty</u>; He constantly spouts *hypocrisy* instead of revealing his true opinions.
7. <u>he should deal only with racism</u>; My mother was *insistent* that I practice piano.
8. (deep); *shallow, superficial*

Literary Analysis: Eulogy and Mood, p. 184

Sample Responses

Students should recognize the basic mood of "Life in His Language" as celebratory, proud, and/or loving. They might cite examples from among the following or cite additional examples not listed here: "Well, the season was always Christmas with you there. . . ."; "You gave me a language to dwell in, a gift so perfect it seems my own invention. . . ."; "You made American English honest. . . ."; "you gave us undecorated truth"; "Yours was the courage to live life in and from its belly. . . ."; "Yours was a tenderness, a vulnerability, that asked everything, expected anything. . . ."; "This, then is no calamity. No. This is jubilee."

Reading Strategy: Analyze Syntax and Patterns of Organization, p. 185

1. Gift: "You gave me a language to dwell in, a gift so perfect it seems my own invention"; significance: Baldwin reshaped literary language to make it more honest and direct, more responsive to the feelings and concerns of African American readers and writers.
2. Gift: "The second gift was your courage. . . ."; significance: The courage that Baldwin showed in a variety of ways—moral, intellectual, political, artistic—set an example for an emerging generation of African American activists and writers who were struggling to find an identify and voice in a white-dominated society.
3. Gift: "your tenderness . . ."; significance: Baldwin's tenderness and generosity enabled him to share his gifts and insights with others in a way that inspired them to strive to be better people and artists.

Vocabulary Builder, p. 186

A.

1. False—the summation will come at the end of the lawyer's remarks, because *summation* means "summing up."

2. True—the executive will need to know about the consequences of every conceivable scenario, which means "situation."
3. True—an original essay will not rely on platitudes, which are "tired expressions."
4. False—The writer who appropriates from other authors is not careful about citing his sources, because *appropriate* means "to take or use something without permission."

B. 1. D; 2. C; 3. D; 4. D

Enrichment: African American Novelists, p. 188

Wright: September 4, 1908–November 28, 1960; *Uncle Tom's Children* (1938), *Native Son* (1940).

Ellison: March 1, 1913–April 16, 1994; *Invisible Man* (1952); *Juneteenth* (1999); National Book Award.

Baldwin: August 2, 1924–November 30, 1987; *Go Tell It on the Mountain* (1953), *Giovanni's Room* (1956); *Another Country* (1962); Eugene F. Saxon Memorial Award.

Hurston: January 7, 1891–January 28, 1960; *Their Eyes Were Watching God* (1937).

Morrison: February 18, 1931–; *Song of Solomon* (1977), *Tar Baby* (1981), *Beloved* (1987), *Jazz* (1992); Nobel Prize for Literature; Pulitzer Prize.

Walker: February 9, 1944 –; *The Color Purple* (1982); Pulitzer Prize, National Book Award.

Open-Book Test, p. 189

Short Answer

1. The use of the name "Jimmy" establishes a mood of familiarity and affection.
   Difficulty: *Easy*   **Objective:** *Literary Analysis*
2. Morrison states that Baldwin's life was so rich and complex that it cannot be easily or simply summed up, but instead demands careful thought and reflection.
   Difficulty: *Average*   **Objective:** *Comprehension*
3. The statement establishes a celebratory mood for the rest of the eulogy.
   Difficulty: *Average*   **Objective:** *Literary Analysis*
4. Baldwin's two most important achievements in transforming American English were (1) making it less pretentious and dishonest, more clear and truthful—"in place of soft, plump lies was lean, targeted power"; and (2) shaping it in ways that made it more receptive to and expressive of the unique rhythms, passions, and truths of the African American experience—"un-gated it for black people so that in your wake we could enter it . . ."
   Difficulty: *Challenging*   **Objective:** *Interpretation*
5. Morrison states that Baldwin's courage came from a combination of intelligence and feeling for his fellow humans, or, as she states it elsewhere, "mind and heart, intellect and passion."
   Difficulty: *Easy*   **Objective:** *Reading Strategy*
6. Baldwin's statement implies that history until now has been defined largely in terms of the accomplishments and activities of white people. However, this will no

longer be the case. The histories of people of color will become just as important.

Difficulty: *Challenging*   **Objective:** *Interpretation*

7. Baldwin's statement implies that the writer has an obligation, through his work and personal example, to work to make the world a better place, to fight for a more just, more compassionate world.

Difficulty: *Average*   **Objective:** *Interpretation*

8. Morrison feels that Baldwin's gift of tenderness was hard to accept because of the high standard of personal behavior it set. It made demands on her and others to be as good and as tender as he was.

Difficulty: *Challenging*   **Objective:** *Interpretation*

9. Students should recognize the basic mood of "Life in His Language" as celebratory.

Sample examples: "Well, the season was always Christmas with you there"; "You gave me a language to dwell in, a gift so perfect it seems my own invention"; "You made American English honest"; "you gave us undecorated truth"; "Yours was the courage to live life in and from its belly"; "Yours was a tenderness, a vulnerability, that asked everything, expected anything"; "This, then is no calamity. No. This is jubilee." Accept additional examples as long as they match the celebratory mood.

Difficulty: *Average*   **Objective:** *Literary Analysis*

10. Yes, she would be criticizing the speech for a lack of originality, because *platitudes* means "empty statements; tired expressions."

Difficulty: *Average*   **Objective:** *Vocabulary*

Essay

11. Most students will probably say that the essay inspired them to want to read more of Baldwin's works and to know more about his life, especially students with a special interest in the history and culture of African Americans. Some students might feel that Morrison did not make enough of a case to show how Baldwin's work would be relevant to today's society.

Difficulty: *Easy*   **Objective:** *Essay*

12. Students' choices should be someone from any of the arts, and students should be clear about what aspects of the artist's life and/or work has inspired their own life and/or work. Answers should be supported by specific examples.

Difficulty: *Average*   **Objective:** *Essay*

13. Some students might argue that if a writer expects to reach a large audience, he/she can and should in some way shape his/her writing to inspire others. Others might argue that the writer has only one obligation, to write well and truly, and whether or not his/her work inspires anyone to want to change the world is secondary to that.

Difficulty: *Challenging*   **Objective:** *Essay*

14. Students' essays should draw conclusions about Morrison's view of the role of writers and support those

conclusions with details from the selection. In discussing a writer's effects on individual lives, students may focus on the writer's effects on their writers, on readers, or both. In discussing a writer's effects on society as a whole, students should recognize Morrison's view that a writer can reveal and clarify social injustice and inspire others to fight that injustice.

Difficulty: *Average*

Objective: *Essay*

Oral Response

15. Oral responses should be clear, well organized, and well supported by appropriate examples from the selections.

Difficulty: *Average*   **Objective:** *Oral Interpretation*

Selection Test A, p. 192

Critical Reading

1. ANS: D	DIF: Easy		**OBJ:** Literary Analysis
2. ANS: B	DIF: Easy		**OBJ:** Comprehension
3. ANS: C	DIF: Easy		**OBJ:** Literary Analysis
4. ANS: B	DIF: Easy		**OBJ:** Literary Analysis
5. ANS: C	DIF: Easy		**OBJ:** Interpretation
6. ANS: D	DIF: Easy		**OBJ:** Literary Analysis
7. ANS: A	DIF: Easy		**OBJ:** Reading Strategy
8. ANS: C	DIF: Easy		**OBJ:** Interpretation
9. ANS: D	DIF: Easy		**OBJ:** Comprehension
10. ANS: D	DIF: Easy		**OBJ:** Interpretation
11. ANS: B	DIF: Easy		**OBJ:** Interpretation

Essay

12. Students should clearly identify a social or political issue that they feel strongly about and explain why they would want to speak out and act to resolve it. Students should use clear reasoning and specific examples in developing their essays.

Difficulty: *Easy*

Objective: *Essay*

13. Students should clearly identify a situation, event, or period of their life—or someone else's life—that required courage. They should explain how their or the other person's courage was critical in overcoming an obstacle or attaining a goal. Students should use specific details and examples in developing their answers.

Difficulty: *Easy*

Objective: *Essay*

14. Students' essays should draw conclusions about Morrison's view of the role of writers and support those conclusions with details from the selection. In discussing a writer's effects on individual lives, students may focus on the writer's effects on their writers, on readers, or both. In discussing a writer's effects on society as a whole, students should recognize Morrison's view that a

Unit 5 Resources: Prosperity and Protest

writer can reveal and clarify social injustice and inspire others to fight that injustice.

Difficulty: *Easy*

Objective: *Essay*

Selection Test B, p. 195

Critical Reading

1. ANS: C	DIF: Challenging	OBJ: Interpretation
2. ANS: C	DIF: Average	OBJ: Interpretation
3. ANS: A	DIF: Easy	OBJ: Reading Strategy
4. ANS: C	DIF: Average	OBJ: Interpretation
5. ANS: A	DIF: Average	OBJ: Literary Analysis
6. ANS: B	DIF: Average	OBJ: Interpretation
7. ANS: C	DIF: Challenging	OBJ: Interpretation
8. ANS: B	DIF: Challenging	OBJ: Interpretation
9. ANS: B	DIF: Average	OBJ: Comprehension
10. ANS: C	DIF: Average	OBJ: Interpretation
11. ANS: C	DIF: Easy	OBJ: Comprehension
12. ANS: D	DIF: Average	OBJ: Literary Analysis
13. ANS: A	DIF: Average	OBJ: Literary Analysis
14. ANS: C	DIF: Challenging	OBJ: Reading Strategy
15. ANS: D	DIF: Average	OBJ: Literary Analysis

Essay

16. Students should choose an eminent figure from history or a notable character from fiction. Their eulogies should be respectful but can range in tone from the somber to the celebratory. Students should emphasize the unique qualities and strength of the person they are writing about.

Difficulty: *Easy*

Objective: *Essay*

17. Students might note that the eulogy leaves an impression of James Baldwin as an enormously talented man who was able to reshape the ways in which people used and thought about language. They might also note that the eulogy creates the impression of a man who was at once thoughtful, courageous, generous, and tender. Students will probably express a wish that they could have known or been friends with a man of such great talent and conscience and generosity of spirit.

Difficulty: *Average*

Objective: *Essay*

18. Students should choose one of the gifts as being the most important and explain why they believe this to be the case. They should support their argument with clear logic and examples from the selection or from their general knowledge of people and social issues.

Difficulty: *Challenging*

Objective: *Essay*

19. Students' essays should draw conclusions about Morrison's view of the role of writers and support those conclusions with details from the selection. In discussing a

writer's effects on individual lives, students may focus on the writer's effects on their writers, on readers, or both. In discussing a writer's effects on society as a whole, students should recognize Morrison's view that a writer can reveal and clarify social injustice and inspire others to fight that injustice.

Difficulty: *Average*

Objective: *Essay*

"Inaugural Address" by John F. Kennedy
from "Letter From Birmingham City Jail"
by Martin Luther King, Jr.

Vocabulary Warm-up Exercises, p. 199

A. 1. attain
2. segregation
3. brutal
4. foe
5. renewal
6. loyalty
7. pledge
8. preserve

B. Sample Answers

1. When we had our first sight of the <u>adversary</u>, we were apprehensive.
2. His polite remarks were a sign of his <u>civility</u>.
3. Since Prof. Adams had influenced her so much, Mary's thesis <u>embodied</u> his philosophy.
4. We found it difficult to explain the <u>inexpressible</u> emotions that we experienced that day.
5. Teresa's conclusions were <u>precise</u>, and she had few problems in communicating them.
6. I was <u>profoundly</u> affected by the story and never forgot it.
7. The convincing <u>testimony</u> of the witness had a great effect on the jury.
8. The lively, energetic behavior of the dogs was proof of their <u>vitality</u>.

Reading Warm-up A, p. 200

Sample Answers

1. <u>as a result, Kennedy was not slow to . . . the admiration of journalists</u>; If you study hard, you will *attain* good grades in this course.
2. (were a time of challenge . . . was also an era of . . . , though); There was a *cancelation* of that subscription.
3. <u>faced a formidable . . . in the Cold War</u>; My *friend* gives me moral support.
4. *cruel; gentle*
5. (brutal injustices of racial . . .); In 1954, the Supreme Court held that *segregation* of public schools was unconstitutional.
6. <u>to a code of self-sacrifice and dedication</u>; *fidelity, devotion*

Unit 5 Resources: Prosperity and Protest

7. (he would usually . . . the dry, deadpan face of a skilled comedian); *maintain*
8. gave a witty . . . of his esteem; *guarantee*

Reading Warm-up B, p. 201

Sample Answers

1. affected the office of First Lady . . . left this position permanently changed; *lightly, superficially*
2. (a showcase for American . . . in the arts); *life force, power*
3. to American achievement and creativity; Her hours of careful study in biology were *testimony* to her interest in the subject.
4. an ideal of feminine beauty and a sense of style and fashion; The painting *embodied* the artist's feelings about nature.
5. (and charming good manners); I could not excuse the giggler's *rudeness*.
6. (opponent); ally
7. aided by experts . . . painstakingly researched; *exact, accurate*
8. *unable to be expressed*

Literary Analysis: Persuasion, p. 202

Students' responses might include the following examples:

Kennedy—parallel structure: "symbolizing an end, as well as a beginning—signifiying renewal, as well as change"—the parallel structure helps to persuade the reader of the significance of the occasion of his inauguration.

King: 'if you would observe their ugly and inhuman treatment . . .; if you would watch them push and curse . . .; if you would see the slap . . ."—the parallel structure helps to persuade the reader of the repeated instances of police brutality.

Antithesis: "the belief that the rights of man come not from the generosity of the state, but from the hand of God"—the antithesis drives home the contrast between the American view of rights as derived from God's merciful spirit as opposed to the communist doctrine in which the state is the source of all moral authority.

Kennedy—Anaphora: "Nor will it be finished in the first 1,000 days, nor in the life of this Administration, nor perhaps even in our lifetime on this planet"—the anaphora, by successively extending the time in which the task might be accomplished, persuades the reader of its magnitude and importance.

King: "Before the Pilgrims landed at Plymouth were here. Before the pen of Jefferson etched across the pages o history the majestic words of the Declaration of Independence, we were here"—the anaphora helps to persuade the reader of King's assertion that African Americans have been part of North America's history for as long as—or longer than—any other group.

Reading Strategy: Identify Main Idea and Supporting Details, p. 203

Sample Response

Selection: "Inaugural Address"

Main Idea: The task of defending freedom should be welcomed

Supporting Details: Kennedy refers to the opportunity that "few generations have been granted; he states "I do not believe that any of us would exchange places."

Selection: "Letter from Birmingham City Jail"

Main Idea: One day the South will recognize its real heroes.

'Supporting Details: braves actions by James Meredith and other ordinary people, Judeo-Christian values, democractic values of founders

Vocabulary Builder, p. 204

A. 1. averted
2. diverting
3. vertically
4. vertigo
5. convert

B. Sample Responses

1. They would want to join forces against their enemies.
2. The country might dispute the other country's border claims, might have a disagreement about trade policy, or might have a history of ethnic conflict with the other country.
3. You might want to get rid of a stain.
4. A philosopher is supposed to express deep thoughts.
5. He or she might not be used to a verbal attack.
6. Segregation went boldly against the nation's law.

Grammar and Style: Use Active, Not Passive, Voice, p. 205

A. 1. When the influence of Gandhi's philosophy on King *was posed* (P) by the questioner, the professor *affirmed* (A) that King *considered* (A) himself a disciple of Gandhi's philosophy of nonviolence.
2. Many presidents *have delivered* (A) forgettable or undistinguished inaugural addresses; Kennedy's address, by contrast, *is considered* (P) among the finest and most memorable by many historians.
3. *Ask* (A) not what your country *can do* (A) for you.
4. . . . we *were carrying* (A) our whole nation back to those great wells of democracy which *were dug* deep (P) by the Founding Fathers. . .

B. Possible responses

1. We will not finish all this in the first 100 days.
2. History has granted only a few generations the role of defending freedom in its hour of maximum danger.

3. Let us hope that we can lift the deep fog of misunderstanding from our fear-drenched communities.

4. Many communities throughout the country have honored Dr. Martin Luther King, Jr., by naming schools and streets after him.

Enrichment: Social Studies, p. 207

Sample Response

On April 4, 1968, while campaigning for the Democratic presidential nomination in Indianapolis, Robert F. Kennedy made a speech announcing the assassination of Martin Luther King, Jr. While Kennedy clearly mourned the loss of King, his main idea is to ask the American public for peace, understanding, and justice. He reminds Americans that his brother was killed by the same kind of senseless violence.

He believes that the country can best be moved forward through love, wisdom, compassion, and justice for both blacks and whites. With respect to "Letter from Birmingham City Jail," there is also an appeal for peace, understanding, and justice. However, the appeal comes in the form of a letter rather than a speech. Like King, Kennedy uses parallel structures in his speech to balance ideas and make them memorable: "What we need in the United States is not division; what we need in the United States is not hatred."

Open-Book Test, p. 208

Short Answer

1. The passage is an example of parallel structure because it repeats the same grammatical structure and phrasing (verb + "any") in three consecutive clauses.

   Difficulty: *Average*   **Objective:** *Literary Analysis*

2. Kennedy is using antithesis, the contrasting words "not" and "but." This device is effective in this context because it emphasizes the contrast between what Kennedy believes is *not* the source of human rights (the state) and what he believes is the source of human rights (the hand of God).

   Difficulty: *Challenging*   **Objective:** *Literary Analysis*

3. The element of antithesis is the opposing of "from" and "to." Its purpose is to emphasize the "word" and its intended audience.

   Difficulty: *Easy*   **Objective:** *Literary Analysis*

4. Kennedy means that those who seek power through violence are usually overthrown by violence.

   Difficulty: *Average*   **Objective:** *Interpretation*

5. In these paragraphs Kennedy is appealing to "both sides" in the Cold War to work together to solve common problems.

   Difficulty: *Challenging*   **Objective:** *Interpretation*

6. He is speaking about African Americans.

   Difficulty: *Easy*   **Objective:** *Comprehension*

7. King underscores the key argument that African Americans' history on this continent is as long and significant as that of any other group—perhaps more so.

   Difficulty: *Average*   **Objective:** *Literary Analysis*

8. His audience includes leading politicians, members of the clergy and "fellow citizens". He is hopeful because of America's history and sense of justice.

   Difficulty: *Challenging*   **Objective:** *Interpretation*

9. This passage reflects King's belief in a philosophy of nonviolent struggle against injustice. He is arguing that it would be inconsistent to use an immoral method, violence, to try to achieve a moral end, an end to racial segregation.

   Difficulty: *Challenging*   **Objective:** *Interpretation*

10. Yes, your teacher would be paying you a compliment, because *profundity* means "intellectual depth."

    Difficulty: *Average*   **Objective:** *Vocabulary*

Essay

11. Sample answer: Kennedy was promoting a message of citizens taking a more active role in helping their nation, either by participating more in government or by volunteering. This message is still relevant today, with citizens' organizations encouraging people to vote and many service organizations encouraging people to volunteer.

    Difficulty: *Easy*   **Objective:** *Essay*

12. Most students will consider this an effective, even powerful argument because King says that nothing else will ever be as brutal for African Americans as the history of slavery. He suggests that African Americans have the strength to endure a great deal of pain, given their history of oppression in the United States.

    Difficulty: *Average*   **Objective:** *Essay*

13. Students should point out that King bases his whole outlook, influenced by Gandhi, on the idea that violence in all its forms, used for whatever reason, is immoral. Therefore, violence applied as a means to achieve a worthy goal, such as desegregation, would be morally wrong. So, in King's view, the ends do not justify the means. The "pure" end, desegregation, should be reached in a moral way, not in a violent one.

    Difficulty: *Challenging*   **Objective:** *Essay*

14. Students should note that Kennedy delivered his inaugural address in the midst of the Cold War between the United States and the Communist-bloc nations, especially the Soviet Union. In that context, he emphasized both the great power of the United States and the need to use it wisely—"But let us never fear to negotiate." He also holds out the hope that a spirit of reason and dialogue can help the nations of the world find peaceful solutions to conflicts rather than risk nuclear destruction of the planet—"the dark powers of destruction." So Kennedy speaks of a powerful, rich country that is called upon to use its power and wealth wisely and judiciously. Students might note that King also appeals to the ideals of the American republic, but as an African American who has seen those ideals trampled by racism and oppression. He speaks with great feeling of "the majestic words of the Declaration of Independence," so he speaks as a patriot—but one who

sees American ideals more as a potential than as a
reality for his people.

Difficulty: *Average*   **Objective:** *Essay*

Oral Response

15. Oral responses should be clear, well organized, and well
supported by appropriate examples from the selections.

    Difficulty: *Average*   **Objective:** *Oral Response*

Selection Test A, p. 211

Critical Reading

1. ANS: D	DIF: Easy	OBJ: Literary Analysis
2. ANS: B	DIF: Easy	OBJ: Comprehension
3. ANS: C	DIF: Easy	OBJ: Interpretation
4. ANS: B	DIF: Easy	OBJ: Interpretation
5. ANS: C	DIF: Easy	OBJ: Reading Strategy
6. ANS: C	DIF: Easy	OBJ: Literary Analysis
7. ANS: B	DIF: Easy	OBJ: Interpretation
8. ANS: A	DIF: Easy	OBJ: Reading Strategy
9. ANS: A	DIF: Easy	OBJ: Literary Analysis
10. ANS: D	DIF: Easy	OBJ: Interpretation

Vocabulary and Grammar

11. ANS: C	DIF: Easy	OBJ: Vocabulary
12. ANS: C	DIF: Average	OBJ: Vocabulary
13. ANS: A	DIF: Average	OBJ: Vocabulary
14. ANS: D	DIF: Average	OBJ: Grammar

Essay

15. Students' essays should reflect that in 1963, Communism was considered a great threat to freedom. Students may suggest other times when people fought for
freedom, such as World Wars I and II, the Civil War, and
the Revolutionary War.

    Difficulty: *Easy*

    Objective: *Essay*

16. Students' essays should express their opinions. Students may say that his argument is powerful because
he says that nothing else will ever be as brutal for African Americans as the history of physical enslavement.
He suggests that African Americans have the strength to
endure a lot of pain.

    Difficulty: *Easy*

    Objective: *Essay*

17. Students should note that Kennedy delivered his
inaugural address in the midst of the Cold War between
the United States and the Communist-bloc nations,
especially the Soviet Union. In that context, he
emphasized both the great power of the United States
and the need to use it wisely—"But let us never fear to
negotiate." He also holds out the hope that a spirit of

reason and dialogue can help the nations of the world
find peaceful solutions to conflicts rather than risk
nuclear destruction of the planet—"the dark powers of
destruction." So Kennedy speaks of a powerful, rich
country that is called upon to use its power and wealth
wisely and judiciously. Students might note that King
also appeals to the ideals of the American republic, but
as an African American who has seen those ideals
trampled by racism and oppression. He speaks with
great feeling of "the majestic words of the Declaration of
Independence," so he speaks as a patriot—but one who
sees American ideals more as a potential than as a
reality for his people.

Difficulty: *Easy*

Objective: *Essay*

Selection Test B, p. 214

Critical Reading

1. ANS: B	DIF: Average	OBJ: Comprehension
2. ANS: A	DIF: Average	OBJ: Interpretation
3. ANS: D	DIF: Average	OBJ: Literary Analysis
4. ANS: C	DIF: Average	OBJ: Reading Strategy
5. ANS: A	DIF: Challenging	OBJ: Interpretation
6. ANS: A	DIF: Average	OBJ: Comprehension
7. ANS: C	DIF: Challenging	OBJ: Literary Analysis
8. ANS: D	DIF: Challenging	OBJ: Interpretation
9. ANS: B	DIF: Average	OBJ: Reading Strategy
10. ANS: D	DIF: Average	OBJ: Comprehension
11. ANS: A	DIF: Challenging	OBJ: Reading Strategy
12. ANS: C	DIF: Average	OBJ: Literary Analysis
13. ANS: A	DIF: Average	OBJ: Comprehension
14. ANS: C	DIF: Challenging	OBJ: Interpretation

Vocabulary and Grammar

15. ANS: A	DIF: Average	OBJ: Vocabulary
16. ANS: C	DIF: Easy	OBJ: Vocabulary
17. ANS: D	DIF: Challenging	OBJ: Vocabulary
18. ANS: C	DIF: Average	OBJ: Vocabulary
19. ANS: C	DIF: Average	OBJ: Grammar

Essay

20. Students should describe that Kennedy was promoting
a message of citizens taking a more active role in helping their nation, either by participating more in government or by volunteering. This message is still promoted
today by citizens' organizations that encourage people to
vote and many service organizations that encourage
volunteerism.

    Difficulty: *Average*

    Objective: *Essay*

21. Students should point to King's willingness to go to jail for his beliefs, his refusal to confront authority with violence, and his use of peaceful marches rather than confrontations. Students may or may not agree with King's view. They may point out ways African American leaders have either adhered to or distanced themselves from King's philosophy.

Difficulty: *Challenging*

Objective: *Essay*

22. Students should note that Kennedy delivered his inaugural address in the midst of the Cold War between the United States and the Communist-bloc nations, especially the Soviet Union. In that context, he emphasized both the great power of the United States and the need to use it wisely—"But let us never fear to negotiate." He also holds out the hope that a spirit of reason and dialogue can help the nations of the world find peaceful solutions to conflicts rather than risk nuclear destruction of the planet—"the dark powers of destruction." So Kennedy speaks of a powerful, rich country that is called upon to use its power and wealth wisely and judiciously. Students might note that King also appeals to the ideals of the American republic, but as an African American who has seen those ideals trampled by racism and oppression. He speaks with great feeling of "the majestic words of the Declaration of Independence," so he speaks as a patriot—but one who sees American ideals more as a potential than as a reality for his people.

Difficulty: *Average*

Objective: *Essay*

Contemporary Commentary

Arthur Miller on *The Crucible*, p. 217

1. The "correspondence" was between the Salem witch trials of 1692 and the anticommunist campaigns in American politics during the late 1940s and early 1950s.

2. He says that there must have been something marvelous in the spectacle of an entire village whose imagination was captured by a vision of something that didn't exist.

3. In both cases, the prosecutions alleged membership in a secret, disloyal group; in both cases, the honesty of a confession could be proved only by the willingness of the accused to name former confederates or associates.

4. People in many parts of the world have responded to the play's story because they think it resembles or echoes their own.

5. Answers will vary. Sample questions: What caused the sudden rise, and almost equally sudden death, of the Salem witch hunt? In the early 21st century, is it possible that anything similar could ever happen again in America, and if so, why?

Arthur Miller

Listening and Viewing, p. 218

Sample answers:

Segment 1: Arthur Miller's most famous works are *Death of a Salesman* and *The Crucible*. Students may answer that Arthur Miller wrote about tragic figures, morality, the plight of the common man, and the pressures of society, which were all relevant issues during the time of the Depression.

Segment 2: Senator Joseph McCarthy conducted Senate hearings to eliminate alleged communists from American public life. Students may answer that *The Crucible* tells the story of those accused of witchcraft and outcast from society, which can be compared to McCarthy's interrogating and blacklisting of accused communists in the 1950s.

Segment 3: According to Miller, dramas document and respond to history, much like newspapers do, without predicting what will come next. Students may answer that dramas written long ago are still relevant today because their themes and forms can be appealing and meaningful to new audiences.

Segment 4: Miller's plays portray power conflicts and social responsibility, and define man in terms of authority and freedom. Students may suggest that Miller was a great social commentator who wrote plays that documented history and are still widely read today.

The Crucible, *Act I*, by Arthur Miller

Vocabulary Warm-up Exercises, p. 220

A.
1. autocratic
2. villainous
3. somber
4. paradox
5. homage
6. faction
7. vindictive
8. hypocrisy

B. Sample Answers
1. That nation's government was unfair and unjust, so a state of <u>anarchy</u> prevailed.
2. They defied the law so <u>blatantly</u> that the police arrested them immediately.
3. Inez was shocked when she heard about Joseph's <u>defamation</u> of her.
4. Our decision was <u>drastic</u>, so we made a major change of course.
5. Because of his <u>parochial</u> mentality, he ignored different views.
6. When you act with <u>propriety</u>, most people are pleased and approving.
7. The team's loss <u>rankled</u> John, who had played his heart out as captain.

8. The squabble between the children over toys was a source of anxiety to their mother.

Reading Warm-up A, p. 221

Sample Answers

1. dictatorial; The United States government is *democratic*.
2. (complete loyalty and also their); *respect, praise*.
3. party or . . . opposed or criticized them; Among the senators, one *faction* opposed ratifying the peace treaty.
4. *vengeful; forgiving*
5. (had been victims of persecution . . . this sad, even . . . part of their history); Mike had a *somber* look on his face when he spoke about the auto accident.
6. or apparent contradiction; The Puritans wanted religious freedom, but they refused to tolerate dissent.
7. *evil; righteous, virtuous*
8. the clergy . . . emphasized narrowly legalistic concepts of morality but ignored the individual's capacity to choose ethical behavior; *pretense*

Reading Warm-up B, p. 222

Sample Answers

1. marked by disorder, even . . .; *order, calm*
2. (frequent quarrels or); small ones
3. narrow-minded; A *broad-minded* person sees more than one side of an issue.
4. thoroughgoing shift; *severe, extreme*
5. (turned openly and); I *secretly* wanted my own car.
6. (small farms were combined into much larger plantations . . . must surely have . . . the less prosperous colonists); *pleased, delighted*
7. leading life with elegant . . . and enjoying the privileges of an elite class; *decorum*
8. criticism of the planter slaveholders . . . would be severely punished as a slander; The magazine article was a *defamation* of the senator's career.

Arthur Miller: Author in Depth, p. 223

1932: graduated from high school
1947: *All My Sons* opened on Broadway
1949: won Pulitzer Prize for *Death of a Salesman*
1953: wrote *The Crucible*
1956: called to testify before the House Committee on Un-American Activities
1956: married Marilyn Monroe

Literary Analysis: Plot and Dramatic Exposition, p. 224

1. Miller reveals information about characters, their backgrounds, and 1690s Salem society.
2. Some of the information is critical to understanding the play, but it would be extremely difficult (if not impossible) to convey through dialogue and traditional stage directions alone.

3. The reader would have to work harder and make more assumptions in order to understand the characters and the setting. Readers might even have to look up historical information on their own in order to fully appreciate the story.
4. Most students will probably say that the rising action begins when the girls begin shouting out people's names to accuse them of being with the Devil.
5. Most students will probably say that Abigail's desire to protect herself from being exposed as an adulteress and trying to use dark magic to hurt Goody Proctor was the main conflict that started the girls' accusations. Others might say that the general sense of rising fear and the superstitious nature of the community prompted the accusation.
6. Answers will vary. Some might say that learning about Abigail's affair with Proctor is the most important information. Others might say the community's readiness to blame witchcraft for Betty's illness is the most important.

Reading Strategy: Dialogue and Stage Directions, p. 225

1. Parris believed he was being persecuted wherever he went (background information). As Parris tries to get information from Abigail, he mentions "enemies" and says they will drive him out if she does not tell him the truth (dialogue). Later, we are told that part of the community had supported a different candidate for Parris's position, but that Parris's supporters prevailed (background information about Thomas Putnam). Several characters are obviously eager to find witchcraft in Parris's house and, therefore, remove him from his post (dialogue).
2. She is an orphan (stage directions) who saw her parents killed by Indians (dialogue). She was a servant to the Proctors, but was dismissed (dialogue).
3. Abigail is "wide-eyed" and "absorbing his presence" when Proctor enters the room (stage directions), implying that she has strong romantic feelings for Proctor. They have been lovers and Abigail wishes they still were (dialogue). Proctor tries to deny any lingering attachment, though (dialogue).
4. Goody Putnam is a "twisted soul of forty-five, a death-ridden woman, haunted by dreams" (stage directions). She has a great deal of grief and pain because seven of her babies have died and she has only one living child (dialogue).
5. She is embarrassed and frightened (stage directions) because she is Proctor's servant (dialogue). She had been told not to leave the house. Now she has been caught at Parris's house disobeying instructions and having a conversation with Abigail that she hopes Proctor did not overhear (dialogue).

Vocabulary Builder, p. 226

A. 1. gratitude—the state of being thankful

2. gratuitous—something that is given to please, rather than in payment
B. 1. G; 2. B; 3. E; 4. C; 5. A; 6. D; 7. F

Support for Writing: Newspaper Article, p. 227
Sample Answers
Who: Betty, Mr. Parris, Abigail, Tituba, other girls from the town, the Putnams
What: Strange illness affects several girls
When: Spring of 1692
Where: Salem, Massachusetts
Why: Some young girls were dancing with the slave Tituba in an effort to raise spirits and lay curses on townspeople; people suspect witchcraft has caused Betty's stupor; people's fear and hysteria cause them to believe their neighbors are involved with witchcraft; some people want vengeance on their neighbors.
How: Young girls begin accusing townspeople of witchcraft.

Enrichment: Social Studies, p. 228
Possible Responses
1. The communist movement was a genuine challenge to the security of the Western world. Communist governments around the world made no secret of their hopes to expand, and the United States and the USSR were the two superpowers after the war. To many Americans communism represented an evil, atheistic, and ambitious world government in the making.
2. During both times, there was a climate of fear. Accusation meant the same as guilt. Those who were doing the accusing were not examined. Often the accused were forced into naming others to save themselves. People used faulty logic in their analyses of the situation.

Open-Book Test, p. 229
Short Answer
1. Betty has some sort of illness, but the doctor cannot figure out what it is. Abigail thinks she may be pretending. Tituba is afraid she will die.
   Difficulty: *Easy*   **Objective:** *Comprehension*
2. Abigail and Parris both know that the girls have been doing things like dancing in the forest that the community will associate with witchcraft.
   Difficulty: *Average*   **Objective:** *Comprehension*
3. Act I of *The Crucible* sets the stage for the play's examination of the town's growing hysteria over witchcraft. The girls' activities and Parris's suspicions become two of the key ingredients in fueling the town's gathering irrational fears about this issue.
   Difficulty: *Challenging*   **Objective:** *Literary Analysis*
4. The stage directions show that Thomas Putnam is a man who has suffered many insults, some imagined, some real, and his accumulated sense of grievance has made him mean and vindictive. John Proctor is a steady

man who has his faults, but he is basically decent and does not suffer fools gladly.
   Difficulty: *Average*   **Objective:** *Reading Strategy*
5. Abigail has worked as a servant for the Proctors. She has had an affair with John Proctor. She has been dismissed by Goody Proctor. The relationships between the characters is tense, with Abigail deeply jealous of Goody Proctor and full of wounded pride at John's rejection. For example: Proctor says, "Abby, you'll put it out of mind. I'll not be comin' for you more."
   Difficulty: *Average*   **Objective:** *Interpretation*
6. A major part of the drama of *The Crucible* is the portrayal of the town's gathering hysteria over witchcraft. Tituba's naming of names, motivated by a desire to satisfy Reverend Hale and thereby escape punishment, helps to reveal how the irrational fears about witches are triggered in the community.
   Difficulty: *Challenging*   **Objective:** *Literary Analysis*
7. Abigail is impatient, impulsive, and manipulative.
   Difficulty: *Average*   **Objective:** *Interpretation*
8. Abigail's influence over the other girls comes from her social position as the minister's niece.
   Difficulty: *Average*   **Objective:** *Interpretation*
9. Tituba is so sure that she will get into trouble that she plays along with Hale as he badgers her for the kind of "information" that he wants to hear.
   Difficulty: *Challenging*   **Objective:** *Reading Strategy*
10. The judge would be criticizing the witness, because *dissembling* means "disguising one's real nature or motives."
    Difficulty: *Average*   **Objective:** *Vocabulary*

Essay
11. Students should note that the girls were engaged in innocent dancing and frolicking in the woods, but that such joyful, sensual activities were considered completely unacceptable and subject to wild interpretation by the Puritan townspeople. The fascination with the girls' activities and the girls' fears about what might happen to them complicate perceptions of the event. Abigail and Parris, despite their original concerns about the unfairness of accusations of witchcraft, help to spread those very fears by their erratic behavior.
    Difficulty: *Easy*   **Objective:** *Essay*
12. Students might note that Miller paints a basically unfavorable portrait of Parris in Act I. We find that he was a former merchant accustomed to material comforts who complains about his small salary as a minister. Although he seems to take his duties as a minister seriously, he seems to feel persecuted wherever he goes. His concern about Betty's condition is as much about its effect on his own reputation as it is about the well-being of his daughter. He is concerned that accusations of

witchcraft could cause him to lose his post. A widower with no interest in or "talent with" children, he seems unable to understand the girls' playng in the woods for the innocent mischief that it was.

Difficulty: *Average* **Objective:** *Essay*

13. Students should note that the residents of Salem are narrow-minded, hard-working, strict, and interested in one another's business (perhaps too interested). Because the community is wedged between the sea and the forest, the residents have to work hard just to survive. Their success as a settlement is based on an ability to work hard toward a common good, a characteristic fueled largely by a belief in a strict, forbidding God who allows few pleasures in life. Neighbors who do not attend religious meetings are viewed with suspicion. Miller suggests that it is the very repressive, hard-working nature of life in Salem that leads to the outcry over witchcraft. Any hint of unusual or individualistic behavior is bound to spark suspicions. Without Miller's detailed background information about the community, its leading personalities, its social norms and its religious beliefs, the motivations of many of the characters would not be as understandable.

Difficulty: *Challenging* **Objective:** *Essay*

14. Students might note that Salem is portrayed as a gloomy place, where certain very strong, strict religious ideas dominate most people's thinking and tend to cause a conformist outlook on life—and terrible suspicion of anyone who strays—or seems to stray—from that outlook; for example, the community is so serious and joyless that Reverend Parris and the community as a whole tend to interpret the girls' carefree dance in the woods as some kind of witchcraft. It is in this harsh atmosphere that any expression of pleasure—such as the girls' dancing—or individuality can cause a harsh reaction, even hysteria.

Difficulty: *Average* **Objective:** *Essay*

Oral Response

15. Oral responses should be clear, well organized, and well supported by appropriate examples from the selections.

Difficulty: *Average* **Objective:** *Oral Interpretation*

Selection Test A, p. 232
Critical Reading

1. ANS: D	DIF: Easy	OBJ: Literary Analysis
2. ANS: C	DIF: Easy	OBJ: Reading Strategy
3. ANS: D	DIF: Easy	OBJ: Comprehension
4. ANS: B	DIF: Easy	OBJ: Interpretation
5. ANS: C	DIF: Easy	OBJ: Interpretation
6. ANS: C	DIF: Easy	OBJ: Interpretation
7. ANS: C	DIF: Easy	OBJ: Comprehension
8. ANS: B	DIF: Easy	OBJ: Interpretation
9. ANS: D	DIF: Easy	OBJ: Interpretation
10. ANS: B	DIF: Easy	OBJ: Interpretation

Vocabulary

11. ANS: B	DIF: Easy	OBJ: Vocabulary
12. ANS: D	DIF: Easy	OBJ: Vocabulary
13. ANS: C	DIF: Average	OBJ: Vocabulary
14. ANS: B	DIF: Challenging	OBJ: Vocabulary
15. ANS: A	DIF: Average	OBJ: Vocabulary

Essay

16. Students' essays should suggest that Abigail thinks that John's original attraction to her still exists. Students may suggest that her love for John and her wish to get revenge upon Elizabeth will motivate her actions.

Difficulty: *Easy*

Objective: *Essay*

17. Students' essays should suggest that the people of Salem believed in the Devil and feared the forest. In addition, the girls wanted to escape being punished for playing in the woods and their accusations achieved that aim. Also, none of them wanted to be left out of the excitement.

Difficulty: *Easy*

Objective: *Essay*

18. Students might note that Salem is portrayed as a gloomy place, where certain very strong, strict religious ideas dominate most people's thinking and tend to cause a conformist outlook on life—and terrible suspicion of anyone who strays—or seems to stray—from that outlook; for example, the community is so serious and joyless that Reverend Parris and the community as a whole tend to interpret the girls' carefree dance in the woods as some kind of witchcraft. It is in this harsh atmosphere that any expression of pleasure—such as the girls' dancing—or individuality can cause a harsh reaction, even hysteria.

Difficulty: *Easy*

Objective: *Essay*

Selection Test B, p. 235
Critical Reading

1. ANS: C	DIF: Easy	OBJ: Comprehension
2. ANS: A	DIF: Average	OBJ: Reading Strategy
3. ANS: C	DIF: Challenging	OBJ: Interpretation
4. ANS: B	DIF: Average	OBJ: Interpretation
5. ANS: D	DIF: Easy	OBJ: Interpretation
6. ANS: A	DIF: Average	OBJ: Literary Analysis
7. ANS: D	DIF: Average	OBJ: Comprehension
8. ANS: A	DIF: Average	OBJ: Reading Strategy
9. ANS: C	DIF: Challenging	OBJ: Interpretation
10. ANS: B	DIF: Average	OBJ: Interpretation
11. ANS: C	DIF: Easy	OBJ: Interpretation
12. ANS: A	DIF: Average	OBJ: Interpretation
13. ANS: D	DIF: Challenging	OBJ: Reading Strategy

Vocabulary

14. ANS: C   **DIF:** Easy   **OBJ:** Vocabulary

15. ANS: A   **DIF:** Average   **OBJ:** Vocabulary

Essay

16. Students should note that Miller indicates that there wasn't much good about Parris. He was formerly a merchant and apparently used to material wealth. He complains about his salary in an argument with Proctor and Putnam. He is apparently a devout minister who believes he is persecuted wherever he goes. This idea of persecution is obvious in discussions with both Abigail and Putnam. Parris worries that Betty's condition and the activities of the girls in the woods will be the undoing of him and will cause him to lose his post, his status, and so on. The confirmation of witchcraft, he tells Putnam, will "topple" him in the community. He is a widower who has no interest in or "talent with" children. This leads to Parris's inability to understand that the girls might have been up to utterly harmless mischief just because that's what children do.

Difficulty: *Easy*

Objective: *Essay*

17. Students should recognize that the first information about the woods comes in a conversation between Parris and Abigail. Parris discovered the girls "dancing like heathen in the forest." Abigail maintains they only danced. Parris speaks of witchcraft and conjuring; Abigail denies such charges. Then Parris says he saw Tituba waving her arms over a fire and screeching and that he saw someone naked. Later, Mrs. Putnam admits to having sent her Ruth to Tituba to conjure the spirits of her dead babies. Abigail offers that just Tituba and Ruth were conjuring. A conversation between Abigail, Mercy, and Mary reveals that Mercy was, indeed, naked. Finally, in the course of Mr. Hale's "inquisition," Abigail admits that Tituba called the Devil, and/or then Tituba made them drink chicken blood. Then, Tituba says that Abigail begged her to conjure. Tituba, under pressure, begins naming names. Abigail joins in, and finally Betty rises up and joins in as well. Miller's development of these details through dialogue, rather than through background information, allows meting it out a little at a time. This builds suspense in such a way that readers as well as characters are led to the crying out at the end of the act.

Difficulty: *Average*

Objective: *Essay*

18. Students should acknowledge that the Salemites are described as parochial, snobby, hard-working, devout, strict, and interested in one another's business. The community is wedged between the sea and the forest, and the residents have to work hard just to survive, much less to thrive. Their success as a settlement is credited to working together and establishing a junta to govern the settlement. They believe in a strict, forbidding God who allows few pleasures in life. Virtue comes through hard work and prayer. Hard judgments were made against neighbors who did not attend meetings or who frittered away their time at idle pursuits. Neighbors frequently brought suits against one another, which were settled by decision of a governing body. The play mentions one such instance between Proctor and Giles Corey. Miller suggests that the very hard-working, repressive nature of the Salemites' lives lent itself to the crying out. In such a society, there is little if any room for individuality. So how could individuals survive but by accusing others of being individuals? Miller's background information is nearly invaluable to a reader of the play in terms of adding meaning to the relationships among characters, to characters' actions and attitudes, and to the situation as a whole. Without the background information, many of the characters' motives, in particular, would not be apparent.

Difficulty: *Challenging*

Objective: *Essay*

19. Students might note that Salem is portrayed as a gloomy place, where certain very strong, strict religious ideas dominate most people's thinking and tend to cause a conformist outlook on life—and terrible suspicion of anyone who strays—or seems to stray—from that outlook; for example, the community is so serious and joyless that Reverend Parris and the community as a whole tend to interpret the girls' carefree dance in the woods as some kind of witchcraft. It is in this harsh atmosphere that any expression of pleasure—such as the girls' dancing—or individuality can cause a harsh reaction, even hysteria.

Difficulty: *Average*

Objective: *Essay*

The Crucible, *Act II,* by Arthur Miller

Vocabulary Warm-up Exercises, p. 239

A. 1. resentful
2. calamity
3. magistrate
4. compensate
5. indignant
6. deceit
7. falter
8. sarcasm

B. **Sample Answers**
1. T; If you believed you deserved the prize, you might feel ill will toward the winner.
2. F; *Civilly* means *politely.*
3. F; When you answer *evasively,* you are being the opposite of straightforward.
4. T; A person awkwardly waving around in the surf might need to be rescued.
5. F; To *flinch* means "to shrink back" or "recoil."
6. F; Promotion would be unlikely for incapable employees.
7. T; Since *weighty* means "important," this statement is true.

8. T; *Wily* means *cunning,* so a wily person might easily inspire mistrust.

Reading Warm-up A, p. 240

Sample Answers

1. winning something could create so much distress . . . had accused her of calling her serves out when they were in, a level of . . . that Casey would never have stooped to . . .; We suspected that he was not telling the truth and was guilty of *deceit.*
2. (everyone had heard the rumor that Casey was a cheater . . . for her reputation as an honest player); greater
3. people greeted her with sneers; bitter, ironic, mocking
4. (because she can't beat you fairly); *benevolent, gracious*
5. over how unfairly she was being treated; *angry, outraged*
6. (referees . . . to appeal to for the right decision)
7. (when it came to being honest, Casey would never . . . what would be the point of cheating . . .); *hesitate, pause*
8. (by giving her opponents the benefit of the doubt on any close call); The insurance company agreed to *compensate* Dana for her loss.

Reading Warm-up B, p. 241

Sample Answers

1. that amounts to a burden on his conscience; On the eve of their emigration, the family reconsidered their *weighty* decision.
2. (he refuses to . . . or confess to his crime); *shrink back, recoil*
3. . . . he refuses to flinch or confess to his crime . . . covers up the truth, insisting that he had no part in the matter; I described the accident *honestly.*
4. strategy fails in the end . . . he is unmasked; *ingenious, tricky, cunning*
5. (few people today . . . the status of an American classic); good will, approval
6. in anguish to reconcile his dreams of material success with the reality of failure in his life
7. (a sad victim of his own pretensions and his distortion of the American dream); She prepared *efficiently* for the party.
8. (not only . . . but enthusiastically); *politely; rudely*

Literary Analysis: Allusion, p. 242

Sample Responses

1. *Cold war* is an allusion to the relationship between the United States and the Soviet Union from the close of World War II to the early 1990s. A cold war is characterized by opposing philosophies and hostility, but lacks open combat.
2. An *Achilles heel* is a weak point in an otherwise strong defense. The mythical warrior Achilles, could not be harmed because he had been dipped as in infant in the

river Styx by his mother, but because her hand covered his heel and left it vulnerable; he died when struck there by an arrow.
3. A *Siren* is an alluring woman, so called because of the seductive nymphs who lured sailors to their doom in Greek and Roman mythology. A *harpy,* also mythical, was a vicious winged monster with the head and trunk of a woman and the tail and talons of a bird of prey.
4. An *ivory tower* is a remote place of contemplation, and the term is often applied to institutions of higher learning, such as universities.
5. According to Greek legend, a sword was suspended by a single hair above the head of courtier Damocles by the king of Syracuse to teach the courtier the perils of a ruler's life. A *sword of Damocles* is any impending danger.
6. In the Bible, God commanded Moses, the leader of the Jews, to part the Red Sea to enable the Jews to escape from the Egyptians into Canaan. So when the crowd opens up to allow Abigail and the other girls through, it is like Moses *parting the Red Sea.*

Reading Strategy: Make and Confirm Predictions, p. 243

Sample Responses

1. Prediction: The people accused by the girls will be executed. Background: Many people died during the Salem witch trials. Confirmation: The court has said it will execute any accused person who does not confess to being a witch; some have been sentenced to hang, but none have yet been executed by the end of Act II
2. Prediction: Goody Proctor will be arrested. Background: Abigail is jealous of Goody Proctor and wants her husband. Confirmation: Goody Proctor is arrested before the end of Act II.
3. Prediction: Hale will eventually believe Proctor's assertion that Abigail and the others are pretending. Background: Hale is a reasonable and intelligent man who clearly wants to do the right thing. Confirmation: At the end of Act II, Hale still has faith in the court and is hesitant to believe Proctor. So this prediction cannot be confirmed yet. (Hale does come to believe Proctor later in the play.)
4. Prediction: People in Salem will use the witch hysteria to take revenge on their neighbors for past conflicts. Background: Miller states in the background information at the beginning of the play that people would do this. Confirmation: In Act II, Walcott charges Martha Corey with witchcraft because a pig he bought from her died.
5. Prediction: Mary Warren will not testify against the other girls in court. Background: She is terrified and says she cannot. Confirmation: One cannot confirm by the end of Act II whether or not Mary Warren will testify against the other girls. (She does testify against them in Act III.)

Vocabulary Builder, p. 244

A. 1. The root *socio-* refers to society, so *Sociology* is the study of how societies work.

2. The root *onto-* refers to the state of being or existence, so *ontology* is the study or consideration of the nature of being or reality.

3. The root *entomo-* refers to insects, so *entomology* is the study of insects.

4. The root *zoo-* refers to animals, so *zoology* is the study of animals.

B. 1. C; 2. B; 3. C; 4. A; 5. D; 6. B

Support for Writing: Persuasive Letter, p. 245

Sample Responses

A student might choose to represent Proctor trying to convince Hale that Abigail and the other girls are pretending.

Facts from Acts I and II that support his position include Abigail telling him Betty's illness had nothing to do with witchcraft; the accusations against women who are clearly good and pious; and Abigail's jealousy of Proctor's wife.

Examples might include how Giles Corey's wife was accused in revenge for a pig Walcott killed out of neglect; Rebecca Nurse being arrested despite how clearly she is a good church-going woman; and Mrs. Proctor being arrested despite her ability to name all Ten Commandments and prove that she is a Christian woman.

Personal experiences include Proctor's witnessing Abigail's confession; his affair with her and knowledge of her jealousy of his wife; and his understanding of Abigail's low character.

Enrichment: Film Adaptations, p. 246

Suggested Response

1. Students will have to do some research to learn about authentic seventeenth-century housing and furniture. They should also glean details from Miller's stage directions: fireplace, stairs, "low, dark, and rather long living room." Aside from being primitive, though, will the home seem warm and cozy or stark and unfriendly? Will the firelight make a warm glow, or is the scene a dark place, barely lit by a few candles?

2. Students should note that Proctor has been out planting seeds in the far field, a constant process of bending and stooping. His clothes are that of a rough country person. His pants are well worn and dirty at the bottom from walking in the field all day. His shoes probably have heavy soles, perhaps with dirt still clinging to them. His movements are those of a strong man who is weary from the hardest kind of work there is, as well as from isolation and tension with his wife.

3. Students may envision Hale as a smaller man, with neater clothing and clean fingernails. Caution students about stereotyping this character. Hale is nervous upon his entry to the Proctor household, which makes his behavior hesitant and reluctant. Students' stage directions should indicate how Hale's movements

communicate his discomfort and his knowledge that he is different from these people.

Open-Book Test, p. 247

Short Answer

1. Their relationship is warm yet uneasy. When he kisses her, he comes away disappointed. At one point, a stage direction says, "It is as though she would speak but cannot . . . A sense of their separation arises."
   Difficulty: *Challenging* **Objective:** *Interpretation*

2. If Mary has been cooperating with Abigail, then it is likely that she will play some kind of role in getting one of the Proctors in trouble with the court on Abigail's behalf.
   Difficulty: *Average* **Objective:** *Reading Strategy*

3. Her urging John to go to Salem to argue against the witchcraft charges shows that she is a woman of courage, honesty and good character.
   Difficulty: *Challenging* **Objective:** *Interpretation*

4. Sample answer: Hale's mission is to determine whether or not there are witches in Salem; he sees potential signs of witchcraft when he first arrives in Act I; In Act II, he begins to suspect some of the accusations as having no basis in fact (especially when he sees that Abigail and Mary have probably tried to frame Elizabeth with the poppet), and he begins to suspect that a mass hysteria is spreading throughout the community.
   Difficulty: *Average* **Objective:** *Interpretation*

5. His reluctance is based on an inner conflict over his past adulterous affair with Abigail.
   Difficulty: *Average* **Objective:** *Literary Analysis*

6. She wants to plant evidence of witchcraft in Elizabeth's house.
   Difficulty: *Easy* **Objective:** *Interpretation*

7. He has seen events in Salem go beyond his expectations into a kind of hysteria, and he is no longer completely comfortable with the direction of the trials.
   Difficulty: *Average* **Objective:** *Literary Analysis*

8. Proctor has trouble remembering the commandment about adultery, probably because of his guilty conscience over his affair with Abigail.
   Difficulty: *Average* **Objective:** *Interpretation*

9. He intends to point out the Devil's powerful skills of deception.
   Difficulty: *Challenging* **Objective:** *Literary Analysis*

10. Yes, you would assume that he was enjoying his dish, because avidly means "eagerly."
    Difficulty: *Average* **Objective:** *Vocabulary*

Essay

11. Students might note that Mary Warren sees that Abigail gets a great deal of attention when she accuses people of being witches. In Act II, she helps set up a trap for Elizabeth Proctor. She lies when she is questioned,

which gains her more and more attention. Mary Warren has learned how to use dishonesty and hysteria to gain power.

Difficulty: *Easy*   Objective: *Essay*

12. Students should note: Abigail's strong influence over the other girls; her careless attitude toward what will happen to Tituba when she blames her; her animosity toward and jealousy of Elizabeth Proctor; her continuing obsession with John Proctor; and her rebellious, manipulative manner with Parris. Her testimony has had a powerful influence on the court proceedings, and her production of the doll and the faking of her own stabbing begin to convince Hale that claims against Abigail must be false. So, despite the fact that she does not appear in the act, she is still a major player because she influences the events that unfold in Act II.

Difficulty: *Average*   Objective: *Essay*

13. Students might note the increasing unhappiness of the community by the end of Act II as accusations and suspicions of witchcraft lead to a sense of general paranoia and suspicion, with neighbor turning against neighbor. They should note that as people become more and more caught up in this climate of fear and paranoia, they become more and more willing to engage in false testimony (Tituba, the girls), either to save themselves or to carry out personal vendettas. They also become more and more likely to believe unproven charges against innocent people (such as Elizabeth Proctor). So standards of justice are collapsing. In general, a religious fervor that claims to want to banish the influence of evil (the Devil) from the community is itself the cause of evil (lying, false accusations, irrational fears) in the community.

Difficulty: *Challenging*   Objective: *Essay*

14. Students might suggest that Miller's use of religious allusions is designed to show that people's tendency to fall prey to hysteria over witchcraft was based, in part, on an unthinking, blind loyalty to some beliefs and myths (for Miller, McCarthy's anti-Communist inquisition was a kind of crusade) rather than rational thinking. For example, early in the act, Elizabeth compares Abigail's new-found power over the townspeople: "Where she walks the crowd will part for her like the sea for Israel." This allusion shows how inclined the "crowd" of Salem was to blind conformity because of dogma. Later in the act, Hale declares that "the Devil is alive in Salem"—his way of pointing out how the virtue deep religious belief has somehow produced its opposite—the unreasoning evil of lies and false accusations. Finally, later in the act, Proctor shouts at Hale, "Pontius Pilate! God will not let you wash your hands of this!" With this biblical allusion Proctor accuses Hale of knowing involvement in the unjust persecution of Elizabeth—of bending to the same kind of injustice that led the crowd, when given a choice by Pilate, to choose to crucify Jesus.

Difficulty: *Average*   Objective: *Essay*

Oral Response

15. Oral responses should be clear, well organized, and well supported by appropriate examples from the selections.

Difficulty: *Average*   Objective: *Oral Interpretation*

Selection Test A, p. 250

Critical Reading

1. ANS: A	DIF: Easy	OBJ: Comprehension
2. ANS: B	DIF: Easy	OBJ: Interpretation
3. ANS: A	DIF: Easy	OBJ: Literary Analysis
4. ANS: B	DIF: Easy	OBJ: Interpretation
5. ANS: D	DIF: Easy	OBJ: Interpretation
6. ANS: C	DIF: Easy	OBJ: Literary Analysis
7. ANS: B	DIF: Easy	OBJ: Interpretation
8. ANS: B	DIF: Easy	OBJ: Comprehension
9. ANS: D	DIF: Challenging	OBJ: Reading Strategy
10. ANS: B	DIF: Easy	OBJ: Comprehension

Vocabulary

11. ANS: D	DIF: Easy	OBJ: Vocabulary
12. ANS: A	DIF: Challenging	OBJ: Vocabulary
13. ANS: C	DIF: Easy	OBJ: Vocabulary
14. ANS: C	DIF: Challenging	OBJ: Vocabulary

Essay

15. Students' essays should suggest an opinion. They may say Hale is refusing to take a stand and letting someone else do the dirty work. They may also say that no one could have stopped what was going on in Salem because people had become so hysterical.

Difficulty: *Easy*

Objective: *Essay*

16. Students' essays should reflect that Mary Warren sees that Abigail gets a great deal of attention when she accuses people of being witches. In Act II, she helps set up a trap for Elizabeth Proctor. She lies when she is questioned, which gains her more and more attention. Mary Warren has learned how to use dishonesty and hysteria to gain power.

Difficulty: *Easy*

Objective: *Essay*

17. Students might suggest that Miller's use of religious allusions is designed to show that people's tendency to fall prey to hysteria over witchcraft was based, in part, on an unthinking, blind loyalty to some beliefs and myths (for Miller, Senator McCarthy's anti-Communist inquisition was a kind of crusade) rather than rational thinking. For example, early in the act, Elizabeth compares Abigail's new-found power over the townspeople: "Where she walks the crowd will part for

her like the sea for Israel." This allusion shows how inclined the "crowd" of Salem was to blind conformity because of dogma. Later in the act, Hale declares that "the Devil is alive in Salem"—his way of pointing out how the virtue deep religious belief has somehow produced its opposite—the unreasoning evil of lies and false accusations. Finally, later in the act, Proctor shouts at Hale, "Pontius Pilate! God will not let you wash your hands of this!" With this biblical allusion Proctor accuses Hale of knowing involvement in the unjust persecution of Elizabeth—of bending to the same kind of injustice that led the crowd, when given a choice by Pilate, to choose to crucify Jesus.

Difficulty: *Easy*

Objective: *Essay*

Selection Test B, p. 253

Critical Reading

1. ANS: C	DIF: Easy	OBJ: Comprehension
2. ANS: C	DIF: Average	OBJ: Reading Strategy
3. ANS: A	DIF: Easy	OBJ: Interpretation
4. ANS: B	DIF: Average	OBJ: Interpretation
5. ANS: D	DIF: Average	OBJ: Interpretation
6. ANS: C	DIF: Easy	OBJ: Interpretation
7. ANS: B	DIF: Average	OBJ: Interpretation
8. ANS: B	DIF: Average	OBJ: Literary Analysis
9. ANS: B	DIF: Average	OBJ: Interpretation
10. ANS: A	DIF: Challenging	OBJ: Interpretation
11. ANS: D	DIF: Challenging	OBJ: Interpretation
12. ANS: D	DIF: Average	OBJ: Literary Analysis
13. ANS: D	DIF: Average	OBJ: Literary Analysis
14. ANS: B	DIF: Easy	OBJ: Interpretation

Vocabulary

15. ANS: A	DIF: Average	OBJ: Vocabulary
16. ANS: C	DIF: Easy	OBJ: Vocabulary
17. ANS: D	DIF: Average	OBJ: Vocabulary
18. ANS: C	DIF: Challenging	OBJ: Vocabulary

Essay

19. Responses should indicate that students understand these things about Abigail's effect on Act II: Her relationship with John Proctor has alienated Proctor from Elizabeth; his guilt over the relationship silences him about Abigail's character until too late; and she is sufficiently daring to attempt an overt move (the poppet plot) against Elizabeth. Although Abigail does not appear in Act II, her effects dominate it. The initial alienation between John and Elizabeth, which Miller dramatizes both in direction and dialogue, is a result of the relationship between Abigail and John, which she still desires and with which he still struggles. Abigail has begun in Act II to lead the testifiers and has won awe for

her performance, for "the crowd will part like the sea for Israel." She seizes on the doll to fabricate a false sorcery, and it is from guilt over his affair with her that John is reluctant to tell all he knows of her character. Although Mary finally admits she put the needle in, Abby has faked her own stabbing with a needle, and Hale has been sufficiently impressed with her performance to believe that claims against Abigail must be the result of witchcraft as well.

Difficulty: *Easy*

Objective: *Essay*

20. Responses should indicate that students recognize that in the climate of fear, even so trivial a thing as a doll is seized upon as evidence of witchcraft. Mary has given the doll to Elizabeth. Abigail fakes an attack of pain and somehow produces a needle like the one she knows is in the doll. When Cheever discovers the needle in the doll, he takes it as a form of witchcraft perpetrated against Abigail by Elizabeth. Mary, though, is forced to admit that she gave the doll to Elizabeth. Rather than dismissing it all then, Hale, because he believes that there must be a fire to go with so much smoke, reasons backward to conclude that the witchcraft is not the doll itself, but in someone's compelling Mary to make the doll, store the needle, and blame no one. Hale, the most educated man in the play, employs a false theological analysis to justify a conclusion already made, all hinging on a ludicrous homemade doll and the transparent plot of a jealous lover.

Difficulty: *Average*

Objective: *Essay*

21. Mary Warren is a weak person, striving for status, easily used by people more clever than she. Mary wants to seem important, and when she has a chance to do so by joining in with the accusers, her imagination takes flight. She makes up an account about Sarah Good's mumbling. She enjoys being an "official of the court," using it to rise above her status as a servant. She defends her actions to the Proctors, "striving for her authority," but when pressured, she collapses. Abigail easily uses her in her plot with the poppet. She is probably the most passive character in the play, and Hale's misinterpretation of her leads to disaster for the Proctors. Thus Miller illustrates that when fear and unreason substitute for logic, no amount of sanity may prevent horrible events from following.

Difficulty: *Challenging*

Objective: *Essay*

22. Students may cite a number of characters who use religious allusions in Act II of *The Crucible*. For example, early in the act, Elizabeth compares Abigail's new-found power over the townspeople: "Where she walks the crowd will part for her like the sea for Israel." Later in the act, Hale declares that "the Devil is alive in Salem." Finally, later in the act, Proctor shouts at Hale, "Pontius Pilate! God will not let you wash your hands of this!" Students should note that members of Puritan society would at once recognize and identify with these allusions. They embody power, fear, and a strong sense

of moral justice—students should examine each character's motive for evoking religious allusions and what them reveal about the characters.

Difficulty: *Average*
Objective: *Essay*

The Crucible, Act III, by Arthur Miller

Vocabulary Warm-up Exercises, p. 257

A.
1. baffled
2. extravagance
3. dutiful
4. anonymity
5. disruption
6. prodigious
7. random
8. perjury

B. Sample Answers
1. The lecture was so disorganized and confusing that it completely befuddled us.
2. The thief was not working alone, and his connivance with several conspirators was plain.
3. The pack of hyenas lurks behind bushes so that the prey cannot see them.
4. Thelma accepted the news placidly, shrugging her shoulders.
5. We later discovered that the salesperson's ploys were full of deceit.
6. If you feel a qualm beforehand, it may not be all right to take that action.
7. The remorseless villain felt no guilt or regret for his crimes.

Reading Warm-up A, p. 258

Sample Answers
1. excessive; He likes the *simplicity* of casual clothes.
2. (amounts of energy and effort); *remarkable, very large*
3. puzzled; *clear-headed*
4. a black mark; *disturbance, upset*
5. (obliging); Mark was extremely *dutiful* in his attention to his homework.
6. if they denied membership in a suspicious group that they had belonged to; tell the truth under oath
7. receiving no credit by name
8. strike a person anytime, and for almost any reason; *haphazard*

Reading Warm-up B, p. 259

Sample Answers
1. quietly; *loudly, turbulently*
2. (such strategies or); being deceptive about the total cost, misrepresenting the important features of the merchandise

3. may have looked around them . . . realities of indentured servitude; Jenna hadn't studied hard, so she worried *apprehensively* about how she would do on the exam.
4. easily confused or; John, totally *befuddled*, scratched his head thoughtfully and hoped the teacher would ask another student to answer the question.
5. (the victims of . . . between purchasers and agents); negative
6. (cruel); *compassionate*
7. beneath the surface; *hides*
8. did not suffer . . . of conscience

Literary Analysis: Dramatic and Verbal Irony, p. 260

Sample Responses
1. The phrase "it melts down all concealment" is ironic because the audience knows that all concealment is not being melted down—Abigail and the girls are "concealing" all sorts of things and apparently getting away with it.
2. Hale asks this question incredulously, and to the audience the *obvious* answer is "yes!" Thus far, every defense *has* been viewed as an attack upon the court.
3. The allusion to the story is ironic because Mary's actions turn out to be the opposite of Tobias's. Instead of freeing someone from the devil, Mary accuses someone of working *with* the devil. Instead of "giving someone sight," Mary "blinds" or fools people by her denial of the truth and her return to Abigail and the girls.
4. Elizabeth's lie is ironic because her husband has insisted that she does not lie. When she does lie, she believes she is saving her husband from the court. In fact, Proctor is condemned by her lie, not for lechery but for being a liar himself.

Reading Strategy: Evaluate Arguments, p. 261

Sample Responses
1. Danforth argues that people have nothing to fear if they are not witches, but he tells them they will be hanged if they do not confess to being witches once they are accused. This is not logical because they are condemned either way. His evidence is the children's testimony, and there is an absence of other witnesses, so the evidence is not supported.
2. Proctor argues that the girls are lying and none of the accused are in fact witches. His argument is logical because several of the accused can be proven to be good, church-going people who have never done anything bad. His evidence is Mary Warren's confession and his own confession of adultery, which gives Abigail motive; this is believable evidence, but ultimately not enough to convince the judge.
3. The Reverend Parris argues that Proctor, Corey, and Nurse have come to overthrow the court. His argument is not logical because it is based on his own fear of being exposed and punished if his niece's lie is proved. Parris

does not present evidence for his argument, but Cheever reveals that Proctor ripped up the warrant for his wife's arrest and cursed the court, and then Proctor refuses to drop the charge that the girls are lying, even though his wife will be safe until their child is born; these revelations almost convince Danforth that Parris is right.

4. Hale argues that there is sufficient doubt about the girls' truthfulness that the convictions of the accused cannot be upheld. His argument is logical. His evidence is that Mary Warren has confessed, that Proctor would not have revealed his lechery if he were not telling the truth, and that Rebecca is clearly a good woman, which are all believable reasons to cast doubt on the verdicts of the court.

5. Corey argues that Putnam made his daughter accuse a man of witchery in order to get his land. His argument is logical, but he does not have enough evidence to prove it. He says that because only Putnam could afford Jacobs's land, Putnam must have had him accused to get it. He will not give the name of the witness because he wants to protect the man from being punished.

Vocabulary Builder, p. 262

A. 1. Danforth requests that Corey provide an *affidavit*, or formal written statement, of his evidence.

2. Mary Warren's *deposition* was her formal written statement that she and the other girls were pretending all along and never saw townspeople with the Devil.

3. Danforth acted as both the judge and the *prosecutor* when he took the role of a lawyer trying to prove that the girls were telling the truth.

4. Cheever had a *warrant* for Goody Proctor's arrest, which was a document given to him by the court authorizing him to take her into custody.

B. 1. B; 2. B; 3. D; 4. C; 5. A; 6. D;

Support for Writing: "Friend of the Court" Brief p. 263

Sample Responses

A student might choose to take the position that there is sufficient doubt about the "proof" of witchcraft and the girls' truthfulness that the convictions cannot be upheld.

Evidence might include Mary Warren's confession; Francis Nurse's 91 signatures vouching for the accused woman's good character; the neighboring town's findings that there was no witchcraft; the faulty logic of the forced confessions versus being hanged; and so on.

Arguments against this position include the inability of the accused to prove their innocence; the girls' very believable performances; the belief that the innocent have nothing to fear; Mary Warren's reversal; and so on.

The student can defend his or her position by arguing that the court's position is illogical since it is based on a logical fallacy, and that it is impossible to prove witchcraft

beyond the shadow of a doubt since the court must rely on the testimony of supposed victims, who might be motivated by jealousy, greed, or vengeance.

Enrichment: Career As a Lawyer, p. 264

Sample Responses

1. ability to follow instructions, work independently *and* cooperatively, solve problems, and conduct research; attention to details; good interpersonal communication

2. a business background, as well as good mathematical skills and/or training

3. fair-mindedness, compassion, ability to take in and weigh information, excellent listening and communicating skills, thorough knowledge of laws and procedures, ability to remember details

4. Students should support their answers with reasons and details.

Open-Book Test, p. 265

Short Answer

1. Sample answer: Thomas Putnam, Abigail Williams and Danforth are all for the witch hunt—Putnam and Abigail for personal reasons, and Danforth because he feels it is his duty. John Proctor and Giles Cory are against it—they know that the girls are lying for various reasons. Mary Warren, at the beginning of the act, has been convinced to tell the truth, so she's against it. Reverend Hale, at the beginning of Act III, is vacillating, but turns against the proceedings by the end of Act III.

   Difficulty: *Average* **Objective:** *Literary Analysis*

2. The questioning shows that anyone accused of witchcraft is presumed to be guilty. The examination is an example of dramatic irony because, despite the court's pretensions to be just and fair, the audience knows that the proceedings are a charade in which the accused have no real rights and are treated unfairly.

   Difficulty: *Average* **Objective:** *Literary Analysis*

3. This is an example of dramatic irony, because there is a contradiction between what Hathorne is saying and what the audience knows to be true—that Francis Nurse is speaking the truth.

   Difficulty: *Average* **Objective:** *Literary Analysis*

4. Proctor's main motive for bringing Mary Warren to court is to have her testify to save his wife from execution.

   Difficulty: *Easy* **Objective:** *Literary Analysis*

5. Throughout Act III, Parris desperately tries to defend the legitimacy of the court and to discredit anyone who tries to bring evidence to clear the accused. His main form of argument is to personally attack anyone questioning the court's presumption of guilt. For example, when Proctor tries to present Mary's change of mind about her claims of having seen witches, Parris counters with an attack on Proctor's motives: "He's come to overthrow the court, your Honor!"

   Difficulty: *Challenging* **Objective:** *Reading Strategy*

6. The offer shows that Danforth is a cynical man who is trying to appeal to Proctor's sense of self-interest to get him to drop the presentation of counterevidence that might discredit the court and, with it, Danforth himself. Proctor's refusal shows that his motives in presenting counterevidence are principled, extending beyond his self-interest to the interests of all the unjustly accused.

Difficulty: *Average* **Objective:** *Literary Analysis*

7. Danforth is trying to intimidate the signers of the testament by making them subject to arrest and appearance in court. He is trying to do anything he can to suppress any challenges to the conclusions of the court.

Difficulty: *Average* **Objective:** *Reading Strategy*

8. Hale feels that there should be proof and is finding that the court's version of "proof" amounts to unfounded accusations, mostly based on the hysterical pretenses of the girls' testimony.

Difficulty: *Challenging* **Objective:** *Interpretation*

9. Proctor means that those, including himself and Danforth, who commit wrong knowingly are the most guilty of all and will be punished by God.

Difficulty: *Challenging* **Objective:** *Interpretation*

10. No, it is not likely that the teacher has believed the explanation, because incredulously means "skeptically."

Difficulty: *Average* **Objective:** *Vocabulary*

Essay

11. Students might note that the Reverend Hale begins Act III as a skeptic about the court proceedings. By the end of the act, based on what he has seen of the various witnesses, he has turned increasingly against the court. But his protests seem to have little impact and seem to bring little aid and comfort to the accused and their love ones. It might be called a case of too little too late. Mary begins the act with a willingness to disown her testimony about witchcraft, and her change of mind promises to bring some help to Elizabeth Proctor. By the end of the act, however, she falls back under the spell of Abigail and withdraws her earlier testimony. Her return to Abigail's fold has a devastating impact on the Proctors, insuring Elizabeth's death, and further fuels the witchcraft hysteria that is consuming Salem.

Difficulty: *Easy* **Objective:** *Essay*

12. During Act III, Hale evolves into more and more of a friend of those who are accused and into a critic of the court. There are several incidents where he speaks up for Giles Cory, Francis Nurse, John Proctor, and Mary Warren as reasonable, reliable people. At the same time, he counsels the husbands to calm down and follow the rules of the court. Hale even challenges Danforth on one occasion, suggesting that he must hear or accept evidence, even if it is contrary to the previous conclusions of the court. Students might note that in the earlier acts, Hale seems more inclined to be of service to the court and more inclined to believe the accusation of witchcraft. During Act III, he sees the girls for the frauds they are, sees the vindictive nature of the accusations, and denounces the court.

Difficulty: *Average* **Objective:** *Essay*

13. Students should note that Danforth appears at first to be a fair-minded man who follows the rules of the court. Nevertheless, he knows how powerful he is and is not beyond throwing his weight around to intimidate witnesses or potential critics of the court. When he is presented with evidence that contradicts previous accusations, he accepts the evidence reluctantly. Students might note the stage direction that shows him "calculating" after hearing about Mary's confession shows that he is weighing the consequences of her testimony on his own reputation. Students might note that if Mary's reversal of her previous testimony is accepted, Danforth will have been responsible for executing dozens of innocent people. He therefore has an interest in supporting Abigail and the girls' account of witchcraft in the community.

Difficulty: *Challenging* **Objective:** *Essay*

14. Students might note that refusing to lie and valuing truth-telling are matters of conscience that should be reinforced by the biblical commandment "Thou shalt not lie." But in the hysterical atmosphere of Salem, religion is used as a club against the truth and in favor of lies; Miller seems to be saying that the strict Puritanism of Salem does not practice what it preaches. For example, at the beginning of the act, the conscience-stricken Mary confesses that she has been lying about her and Abigail's and the other girls' involvement in witchcraft; but Abigail's seemingly religious hysteria frightens Mary into recanting her confession and going back to her previous lie. Thus, religious fervor in Salem becomes the tool of lying and the enemy of the truth. Hale's recognition of the injustice of the court proceedings, the product of reasoning and conscience that are at odds with the hysteria of Salem, proves to be too little too late—the power of lies has taken hold, thanks in part to people's tendency to believe authority—of the Court, of the Church—rather than the evidence of reason and conscience.

Difficulty: *Average* **Objective:** *Essay*

Oral Response

15. Oral responses should be clear, well organized, and well supported by appropriate examples from the selections.

Difficulty: *Average* **Objective:** *Oral Interpretation*

Selection Test A, p. 268

Critical Reading

1. ANS: C	**DIF:** Easy	**OBJ:** Comprehension
2. ANS: C	**DIF:** Easy	**OBJ:** Literary Analysis
3. ANS: D	**DIF:** Easy	**OBJ:** Comprehension
4. ANS: A	**DIF:** Easy	**OBJ:** Interpretation
5. ANS: B	**DIF:** Easy	**OBJ:** Interpretation
6. ANS: D	**DIF:** Easy	**OBJ:** Interpretation

7. ANS: A	DIF: Easy	OBJ: Literary Analysis
8. ANS: B	DIF: Easy	OBJ: Literary Analysis
9. ANS: B	DIF: Easy	OBJ: Literary Analysis
10. ANS: D	DIF: Challenging	OBJ: Reading Strategy

Vocabulary

11. ANS: C	DIF: Easy	OBJ: Vocabulary
12. ANS: A	DIF: Challenging	OBJ: Vocabulary
13. ANS: C	DIF: Challenging	OBJ: Vocabulary
14. ANS: B	DIF: Easy	OBJ: Vocabulary

Essay

15. Students' essays should express a point of view. Some students may say that all the girls use lies and fantasy to gain attention and power. Other students may say that Abigail is very different from the other girls because she is related to the powerful Reverend Parris. Abigail uses her female qualities to attract and defeat John Proctor.

Difficulty: *Easy*

Objective: *Essay*

16. Students' essays should suggest that Danforth has set up a situation in which no matter what the girls say, even if it is the truth, they are in trouble. They are either condemning themselves to death (witchcraft) or to hell (lying).

Difficulty: *Easy*

Objective: *Essay*

17. Students might note that refusing to lie and valuing truth-telling are matters of conscience that should be reinforced by the biblical commandment "Thou shalt not lie." But in the hysterical atmosphere of Salem, religion is used as a club against the truth and in favor of lies; Miller seems to be saying that the strict Puritanism of Salem does not practice what it preaches. For example, at the beginning of the act, the conscience-stricken Mary confesses that she has been lying about her and Abigail's and the other girls' involvement in witchcraft; but Abigail's seemingly religious hysteria frightens Mary into recanting her confession and going back to her previous lie. Thus, religious fervor in Salem becomes the tool of lying and the enemy of the truth. Hale's recognition of the injustice of the court proceedings, the product of reasoning and conscience that are at odds with the hysteria of Salem, proves to be too little too late—the power of lies has taken hold, thanks in part to people's tendency to believe authority—of the Court, of the Church—rather than the evidence of reason and conscience.

Difficulty: *Average*

Objective: *Essay*

Selection Test B, p. 271

Critical Reading

1. ANS: C	DIF: Average	OBJ: Interpretation

2. ANS: B	DIF: Average	OBJ: Literary Analysis
3. ANS: C	DIF: Easy	OBJ: Literary Analysis
4. ANS: D	DIF: Average	OBJ: Literary Analysis
5. ANS: D	DIF: Challenging	OBJ: Interpretation
6. ANS: A	DIF: Average	OBJ: Literary Analysis
7. ANS: C	DIF: Challenging	OBJ: Interpretation
8. ANS: B	DIF: Challenging	OBJ: Reading Strategy
9. ANS: B	DIF: Easy	OBJ: Literary Analysis
10. ANS: D	DIF: Average	OBJ: Comprehension
11. ANS: A	DIF: Average	OBJ: Literary Analysis
12. ANS: A	DIF: Challenging	OBJ: Interpretation
13. ANS: A	DIF: Easy	OBJ: Interpretation
14. ANS: C	DIF: Average	OBJ: Reading Strategy

Vocabulary

15. ANS: B	DIF: Challenging	OBJ: Vocabulary
16. ANS: A	DIF: Challenging	OBJ: Vocabulary
17. ANS: D	DIF: Average	OBJ: Vocabulary

Essay

18. Students may choose any number of examples from Act III. Their explanations should focus on how the statement or situation represents something contrary to readers' expectations or knowledge. Here are a few examples from Act III: (1) Elizabeth Proctor's lie is ironic because her husband has sworn that she does not lie. Further, she thinks she is *saving* her husband with the lie, when she ends up condemning him by it. (2) Abigail reaches out to comfort the hysterical Mary "out of her infinite charity," say the stage directions. This is ironic because Abigail, in her condemnation of dozens of neighbors, is anything but charitable. (3) Early in the act, Herrick and the judges threaten Francis Nurse, Giles Corey, and John Proctor that they will be condemned for lying in the court. This is ironic because they are the only ones who *are* telling the truth. Abigail and the girls are lying and are certainly not being condemned for it.

Difficulty: *Easy*

Objective: *Essay*

19. Students should be able to cite several incidents when Hale speaks up for Giles Corey, Francis Nurse, John Proctor, and Mary Warren as reasonable, reliable people. Hale feels strongly that the accused deserve to be defended, and that such defense is *not* an attack on the court, as Parris asserts. At the same time, he counsels the husbands to be calm and to follow the rules of the court, and not to be overwrought. Hale even challenges Danforth on at least one occasion, suggesting that he must hear or accept evidence, even if it is contrary to the direction in which the proceedings are going. Students may cite Hale's "differences" as follows: He is not a resident of Salem; he does not have any family members

involved in the trial; he does not have a long history of acquaintance with the Salemites; he approaches the whole situation from an intellectual viewpoint and, some might say, a more objective one than the Salemites'. Students should recall that in Act I, Hale is eager to provide his services, confident that if there is evidence of the Devil's work, it will be tangible and he will find it. In Act II, Hale arrives at the Proctor home to let them know that Elizabeth has been "mentioned" in court. He quizzes the Proctors some on their beliefs, trying to find out for himself whether there is any cause for suspicion. Though Hale still believes that the Devil exists as an active force in the world, his opinion of the situation in Salem alters during Act III. He sees the girls for the frauds they are, he sees the vindictive nature of the accusations, and he denounces the court. This is in keeping with his intellectual approach to the subject, which would require hard evidence for proof. He recognizes that there is no hard evidence for anything that has been charged.

Difficulty: *Average*

Objective: *Essay*

20. Students should acknowledge that Danforth appears on the surface to be fair-minded and certainly that he adheres to general rules of the court. At the same time, he is powerful and he knows it. He has a high profile; his importance has brought him all the way from Boston. He understands that people all over the colonies are hearing or will hear of the proceedings in Salem and his role in them. Students should note that when presented with evidence that is contradictory to the general direction of the accusations, he accepts the evidence with reluctance. The "calculating" stage direction implies that he is quickly figuring the possible consequences of Mary's confession *and how those consequences would reflect on him.* Similarly, when Danforth accepts Mary's deposition, he has misgivings because the whole situation could land on his shoulders. Evidence of Danforth's thoughts comes mostly from stage directions. He is variously described as "astonished," "horrified," and "dumbfounded" as new bits of information come to light. Students should be able to conclude that if Danforth accepts Mary's deposition and if Abigail and the girls are exposed as frauds, Danforth will have been responsible for putting to death dozens of innocent people. It is vital to Danforth's reputation as well as to his own peace of mind to continue to believe that Heaven *is* speaking through Abigail and the girls and that the community is being purged of its evil elements.

Difficulty: *Challenging*

Objective: *Essay*

21. Students might note that refusing to lie and valuing truth-telling are matters of conscience that should be reinforced by the biblical commandment "Thou shalt not lie." But in the hysterical atmosphere of Salem, religion is used as a club against the truth and in favor of lies; Miller seems to be saying that the strict Puritanism of Salem does not practice what it preaches. For example, at the beginning of the act, the conscience-stricken Mary confesses that she has been lying about her and Abigail's and the other girls' involvement in

witchcraft; but Abigail's seemingly religious hysteria frightens Mary into recanting her confession and going back to her previous lie. Thus, religious fervor in Salem becomes the tool of lying and the enemy of the truth. Hale's recognition of the injustice of the court proceedings, the product of reasoning and conscience that are at odds with the hysteria of Salem, proves to be too little too late—the power of lies has taken hold, thanks in part to people's tendency to believe authority—of the Court, of the Church—rather than the evidence of reason and conscience.

Difficulty: *Average*

Objective: *Essay*

The Crucible, *Act IV*, by Arthur Miller

Vocabulary Warm-up Exercises, p. 275

A. 1. embodiment
2. contention
3. mute
4. nudges
5. reprieve
6. righteous
7. adamant
8. bellow

B. **Sample Answers**
1. T; *Beguile* means "to trick."
2. F; A person in a *conciliatory* mood would be receptive to reconciliation.
3. T; *Disputation* would involve lack of agreement.
4. T; Lack of food and sleep might cause a thin and bony look.
5. F; This statement is inconsistent with the meaning of *inaudibly*.
6. T; *Penitence* implies sorrow or regret.
7. T; *Retaliation* involves revenge.
8. F; A *stench* is a foul odor.

Reading Warm-up A, p. 276

Sample Answers
1. Maggie was making such a big deal . . . that the girls' teams should receive equal treatment; The union representatives were *adamant* and would accept no compromise on the issue of a new contract.
2. (full of . . . conviction); *just, virtuous*
3. the auditorium silent when she finished speaking; She was *vocal* about the movie she wanted to see.
4. (each other on the arm); *poked gently*
5. (. . . of jealousy, a silly person who liked to complain); Christian is the *embodiment* of courtesy, maintaining polite composure even when he is under pressure.
6. seemed to clinch the argument, but Maggie would give them no . . . her contention was that . . . ; *relief, postponement*

7. (private donations had no place in a public school); The defense attorney's *contention* was that his client had acted in a state of diminished mental capacity.

8. . . . yelled a boy in the back row . . . a few more boys began to . . . in the same way; *murmur*

Reading Warm-up B, p. 277

Sample Answers

1. little disagreement or . . . among the critics, who warmly praised the film version; During the debate, Ted enjoyed his *disputation* with the opposing team.

2. (wishing to revenge herself for John's rejection); *forgiveness*

3. *trick, deceive*

4. Abigail's eyes . . . express her horror; His shouts showed that he was *audibly* angry.

5. (become openly more . . . or retract her accusations); We had to stop the dog's *aggressive* behavior.

6. and almost haunted expression; *thin, bony*

7. (regret); Billy certainly showed *penitence* when he was caught in a lie by his parents.

8. (foul odor)

Literary Analysis: Tragedy and Allegory, p. 278

A. 1. John Proctor is the tragic hero because he is involved in a struggle that ends in disaster, is well-respected in the community, and falls due to his pride and honor.

2. Proctor's tragic flaws are that he committed adultery and that he is too proud to confess to a crime he did not commit.

3. Proctor learns that he would rather die with honor by telling the truth than live a lie while others die with the implication of witchcraft attached to their names. If he confesses, he realizes that he makes them all look guilty by association.

B. *The Crucible* is an allegory because Miller uses one historical period and setting (seventeenth-century New England) to comment on another (1950s America). The play is an allegory for modern events. The Salem witch trials are an allegory for the anti-Communist hysteria of the 1950s "Red Scare." The comparison is effective because in both cases people could be accused with very little or no proof, and it was extremely difficult to defend oneself against the logical fallacies inherent in the accusations.

Reading Strategy: Evaluate the Influences of the Historical Period, p. 279

Sample Responses:

Religious: Puritanism made the people of Salem more likely to believe in the possibility of witchcraft and punish it very harshly.

Social: Greed for land, desire to prove their own virtue, jealousy and vengeance were all motives for townspeople to accuse others of being witches.

Philosophical: Puritans believed in the value of pure behavior to maintain order in their community and ensure the well-being of all.

Ethical: A strong belief in good and evil and the idea that the innocent have nothing to fear drove several of the characters' behavior throughout the play. Other characters based their ethics on logic and basic decency rather than biblical or civic laws.

Political: Residents of Salem adhered to strict religion-based laws that were meant to keep public order and protect the souls of the townspeople.

Vocabulary Builder, p. 280

A. 1. *Echo* is a nymph in Greek mythology who pined away for love of Narcissus until only her voice remained.

2. *Volcano* comes from the name of the Roman god Vulcan, the god of fire and metalworking.

3. *Wednesday* is named for the Norse god Woden, or Odin.

4. A *museum* is a place for study or art, so named for the Muses of Greek mythology, who inspired writers, artists, and scientists.

B. 1. H; 2. E; 3. J; 4. A; 5. F; 6. C; 7. B; 8. I; 9. D; 10. G

Grammar and Style: Sentence Fragments and Run-Ons, p. 281

A. 1. fragment
2. run-on
3. fragment
4. fragment
5. run-on

B. Sample Corrections:

1. Reverend Hale tried to get the prisoners to confess.

2. Proctor was not guilty, but he was willing to confess in order to save his life. He wanted to be with his wife and children.

3. Although he spoke his confession willingly, Proctor refused to write it down and sign it.

4. Rebecca Nurse was bravely willing to die rather than confess to being a witch.

5. Proctor changed his mind; he could not write his confession down and lose his honesty.

Support for Writing: Literary Criticism, p. 282

Sample Responses:

Theme:

1. A man can be a hero in spite of his flaws.

2. Courage, honesty, and personal integrity are valuable qualities that one should strive to demonstrate in one's life.

3. Judging others is wrong.

Historical Meaning:

1. There is a biblical basis for the idea of redemption after one has committed sins.
2. Some who faced accusations of witchcraft in Salem during the 1600s were hanged because they would not lie and say they were witches.
3. Those who were hanged were not really witches, and they were not evil; their neighbors should not have accused them, judged them, or punished them in this way.

Universal Meaning:

1. No one is perfect—everyone has flaws—but everyone also has it in him or her to be a hero.
2. In most cultures, courage, honesty, and integrity are valued and rewarded.
3. Throughout history, when one group of people begins judging another group unfairly, it generally does not end well.

Enrichment: Research, p. 283

Sample Responses

1. What were the people like in the Salem trials?
2. Who were the people? Start with general reference. Consult history texts. Next, examine land records, court proceedings, wills, church records, marriage records, death records, taxes, criminal records, and records of proceedings.
3. Select a few characters to focus on. See what can be learned about Parris, Proctor, Hale, Giles Corey, and Danforth.
4. Answer would depend on references found for item 3. See also item 7.
5. Is there any information about those executed? Are there sources outside Salem for Danforth and Hale? What happened to Abigail Williams?
6. Compile notes thoroughly before interpreting. Make a chart of relationships and a timeline.
7. Who are experts on this historical era whom I could interview? To what sources might they lead me?

Open-Book Test, p. 284

Short Answer

1. All three of the characters speak of the Devil and/or Hell.

   Difficulty: *Easy*   **Objective:** *Reading Strategy*

2. The wandering cows symbolize the chaos and disintegration of the social order of Salem that has resulted from the witch trials.

   Difficulty: *Average*   **Objective:** *Literary Analysis*

3. Danforth regards Parris as a selfish man, someone who is interested mainly in his own well-being and his own reputation. He sees that Parris is now wavering about the executions not because of any principle, but because there is evidence that there is dissatisfaction with the witch hunt in the town that could cost Parris his reputation and job.

   Difficulty: *Challenging*   **Objective:** *Interpretation*

4. Danforth's determination to proceed immediately with the executions symbolizes the imperfection of the machinery of the law. It shows that the legal system can sometimes enforce or perpetuate injustice.

   Difficulty: *Challenging*   **Objective:** *Literary Analysis*

5. The reader can infer that the citizens of Andover are resisting the kind of hysteria that has befallen Salem.

   Difficulty: *Easy*   **Objective:** *Interpretation*

6. She has become less harsh in her judgment of others. Her final comment of the play exemplifies this change.

   Difficulty: *Average*   **Objective:** *Interpretation*

7. Now the separation between church and state is much clearer and better defined than it was at the time of *The Crucible*. In fact, it is a basic part of the U.S. Constitution and legal system.

   Difficulty: *Average*   **Objective:** *Reading Strategy*

8. During the McCarthy and House Un-American Activities Committee investigations of the 1950s, reputations and lives were ruined by people who "named names" or confessed to irresponsible allegations just to save themselves.

   Difficulty: *Average*   **Objective:** *Literary Analysis*

9. Sample answers: Reverend Parris—whether he is true to the Christian ideals of his calling as a minister—fails (because he promotes a hysteria of lying and death, and proves more concerned about his own welfare than the welfare of others).

   Reverend Hale—whether he is true to the Christian ideals of his calling as a minister—passes (because he struggles with his conscience and comes down on the side of truth and justice to resist the hysteria of the witch trials).

   Judge Danforth—whether he is an impartial and fair judge and enforcer of the law—passes and fails (shows a minimal amount of respect for proper legal procedure, but proves more interested in swift justice than finding out the truth and attaining true justice).

   Elizabeth Proctor—whether she will value the truth over her personal well-being—passes (because she refuses to admit to being a witch to save herself and with good intentions lies at the end to try to help her husband).

   John Proctor—whether he will risk his life to uphold true Christian ideals—passes. (He refuses to admit to the false accusations against him; even though he wavers at the end, he triumphs by refusing to sign a public declaration, even though this act of conscience costs him his life.)

   Difficulty: *Average*   **Objective:** *Interpretation*

10. Yes, you would be trying to resolve the conflict, because *conciliatory* means "tending to soothe anger."

    Difficulty: *Average*   **Objective:** *Vocabulary*

Essay

11. Students might note that Abigail's stealing money and running away are consistent with what we learn about her from the very start, that she is capable of "endless dissembling" and willing to inflict misery and death on others in order to achieve vengeance and to get her way. With the failure of her plans to win over Proctor and with the people of the town slowly turning against the trials, she would eventually be exposed as a liar, so she takes the easy way out. She escapes responsibility for her actions, while others pay with their lives.

    Difficulty: *Easy*   **Objective:** *Essay*

12. Students should express an opinion supported with detail from the play. They may say that John Proctor becomes a hero in *The Crucible* when he refuses to implicate others and then also refuses to destroy his good name. Students may also say that he is ashamed of his actions earlier in the play and is trying to clear his conscience.

    Difficulty: *Average*   **Objective:** *Essay*

13. Students might suggest that Elizabeth realizes that Hale is making arguments he hopes will sway her to help save her husband's life. She realizes that in so doing she would be working on behalf of the Devil, because the only way John can save his life is to confess to something he did not do, or to lie.

    Difficulty: *Challenging*   **Objective:** *Essay*

14. Students might note that John refuses to implicate others despite the intense pressures from the court to do so. Students may also say that he is ashamed of his actions earlier in the play and is trying to make up for his earlier lack of moral courage. They might also note that Elizabeth resists pressure from Hale to try to persuade John to save his life by falsely confessing to the charges, for she realizes that standing for honor and conscience are too important to trade in at any price, even one's life. Students might also note that the Reverend Hale is torn between his loyalty to the court and official religious doctrine and his understanding that many of the witchcraft accusations are unjust and based on lies—a conflict between loyalty to church/community and individual conscience.

    Difficulty: *Average*   **Objective:** *Essay*

Oral Response

15. Oral responses should be clear, well organized, and well supported by appropriate examples from the selections.

Selection Test A, p. 287

Critical Reading

1. ANS: B	DIF: Easy	OBJ: Comprehension
2. ANS: A	DIF: Easy	OBJ: Literary Analysis
3. ANS: C	DIF: Easy	OBJ: Interpretation
4. ANS: C	DIF: Easy	OBJ: Reading Strategy
5. ANS: B	DIF: Easy	OBJ: Interpretation
6. ANS: C	DIF: Easy	OBJ: Interpretation

7. ANS: C	DIF: Easy	OBJ: Interpretation
8. ANS: B	DIF: Easy	OBJ: Literary Analysis
9. ANS: D	DIF: Easy	OBJ: Literary Analysis
10. ANS: B	DIF: Easy	OBJ: Interpretation

Vocabulary and Grammar

11. ANS: D	DIF: Average	OBJ: Vocabulary
12. ANS: C	DIF: Easy	OBJ: Vocabulary
13. ANS: B	DIF: Average	OBJ: Vocabulary
14. ANS: C	DIF: Chalenging	OBJ: Vocabulary
15. ANS: B	DIF: Average	OBJ: Grammar

Essay

16. Students should express an opinion. They may say that John Proctor becomes a hero in *The Crucible* when he refuses to implicate others and then also refuses to destroy his own good name. Students may also say that he is ashamed of his actions earlier in the play and is trying to clear his conscience.

    Difficulty: *Easy*

    Objective: *Essay*

17. Students' essays should suggest that Elizabeth realizes that Hale is making arguments he hopes will sway her to help save her husband's life. She realizes that in doing so she would be doing the Devil's work, because the only way John can save his life is to confess to something he did not do, or to lie.

    Difficulty: *Easy*

    Objective: *Essay*

18. Students might note that John refuses to implicate others despite the intense pressures from the court to do so. Students may also say that he is ashamed of his actions earlier in the play and is trying to make up for his earlier lack of moral courage. They might also note that Elizabeth resists pressure from Hale to try to persuade John to save his life by falsely confessing to the charges, for she realizes that standing for honor and conscience are too important to trade in at any price, even one's life. Students might also note that the Reverend Hale is torn between his loyalty to the court and official religious doctrine and his understanding that many of the witchcraft accusations are unjust and based on lies—a conflict between loyalty to church/community and individual conscience.

    Difficulty: *Easy*

    Objective: *Essay*

Selection Test B, p. 290

Critical Reading

1. ANS: B	DIF: Easy	OBJ: Comprehension
2. ANS: C	DIF: Average	OBJ: Interpretation
3. ANS: C	DIF: Challenging	OBJ: Interpretation
4. ANS: D	DIF: Easy	OBJ: Reading Strategy

5. ANS: B	DIF: Challenging	OBJ: Literary Analysis
6. ANS: C	DIF: Average	OBJ: Interpretation
7. ANS: A	DIF: Easy	OBJ: Interpretation
8. ANS: D	DIF: Average	OBJ: Interpretation
9. ANS: A	DIF: Challenging	OBJ: Interpretation
10. ANS: D	DIF: Average	OBJ: Literary Analysis
11. ANS: B	DIF: Average	OBJ: Literary Analysis
12. ANS: B	DIF: Average	OBJ: Comprehension
13. ANS: D	DIF: Challenging	OBJ: Reading Strategy

Vocabulary and Grammar

14. ANS: D	DIF: Easy	OBJ: Vocabulary
15. ANS: C	DIF: Challenging	OBJ: Vocabulary
16. ANS: B	DIF: Average	OBJ: Vocabulary
17. ANS: A	DIF: Challenging	OBJ: Vocabulary
18. ANS: C	DIF: Average	OBJ: Grammar

Essay

19. Student responses should indicate that they understand Abigail's action in running away as consistent with her character. She is introduced as capable of "endless dissembling" from the very beginning. She takes revenge on Proctor, whom she claims to love, and makes up lies that are fatal to Sarah, Tituba, and others. No strength of character is revealed here, so it is not surprising that she would steal. Additionally, her plans to win Proctor have gone awry. Finally shaken, Parris would reject her, and more and more people would eventually find out she lied. Her prospects for a future in Salem are not good, and it is reasonable she would take the easy way out. She will escape responsibility for her actions, while others will die, heightening the tragedy.

Difficulty: *Easy*

Objective: *Essay*

20. Student essays should reflect an understanding that the trials reveal the true nature of the various characters. Parris's weakness and smallness are exposed. Abigail steals from her uncle and runs away. Hale abandons his intellectual vanity, and his fundamental decency appears. Elizabeth learns to forgive. Giles Corey never gives in. Danforth's leadership is mere bureaucratic cowardice. Proctor's essential core remains unchanged, but he dies for his honesty. The heat of the experience reduces the complicated trappings of personality and circumstance to an essential test of character: The Proctors and Reverend Hale, though their lives are destroyed, are genuine. Danforth, Parris, Abigail, and others are essentially cowards. Other lives melt away.

Difficulty: *Average*

Objective: *Essay*

21. The central reason that Salem is an ideal setting for Miller's explorations in *The Crucible* is that it is an American setting. Miller's themes about justice, law, the role of religion in society, individual rights, and due process are fundamental issues in American life and history. The play begins in familiar territory, for we all know the story of the Pilgrims, but it goes beyond to explore the conflict between prevailing belief and civil liberties. The founding idea of the American nation is civil liberty, and the idea of freedom is part of the progression of colonial history. Miller also shows that America has not been free of some of the things it tries to escape, both in that time and this, and although the setting of the play predates the founding of the United States, the parallels point out that we have not fully succeeded in establishing the rule of reason and the protection of the individual.

Difficulty: *Challenging*

Objective: *Essay*

22. Students might note that John refuses to implicate others despite the intense pressures from the court to do so. Students may also say that he is ashamed of his actions earlier in the play and is trying to make up his her earlier lack of moral courage. They might also note that Elizabeth resists pressure from Hale to try to persuade John to save his life by falsely confessing to the charges, for she realizes that standing for honor and conscience are too important to trade in at any price, even one's life. Students might also note that the Reverend Hale is torn between his loyalty to the court and official religious doctrine and his understanding that many of the witchcraft accusations are unjust and based on lies—a conflict between loyalty to church/community and individual conscience.

Difficulty: *Average*   Objective: *Essay*

The Crucible by Arthur Miller
from **Good Night, and Good Luck** by George Clooney and Grant Heslov

Comparing Political Drama Past and Present, p. 293

Reflects the author's political opinion

The Crucible clearly shows that Miller disapproves of the methods of those in charge of the Salem witch trials.

Good Night, and Good Luck shows how the authors disapprove of Senator McCarthy's methods.

Characterizes a politician or describes a series of political events

The Crucible describes a series of political events.

Good Night, and Good Luck characterizes Senator McCarthy by showing what he said and what was said about him.

Questions inequities and injustices of contemporary society

By showing how unfair the trials were and how unreliable the witnesses, *The Crucible* exposes the inequities and injustices of the time.

Good Night, and Good Luck exposes the way Senator McCarthy lied and twisted the truth to make his victims appear guilty of treason.

Examines a political issue from the past or present or uses past events to comment on current problems

The Crucible examines a political issue from the past, using it to draw parallels to a then-current problem.

Good Night, and Good Luck examines a political issue from the recent past.

Vocabulary Builder, p. 294

A. 1. Sylvia's <u>vulnerability</u> to accusations of incompetence made her an unlikely candidate for president.

2. Because Justin decided to <u>disregard</u> the ringing of his cell phone, he was able to enjoy his vacation.

3. Maureen <u>acknowledges</u> the applause of the audience by taking a bow and then performing an encore.

4. The <u>statute</u> explained the law that the criminal had broken.

B. 1. I might help a friend whose vulnerability to food temptations has caused health problems by avoiding fast food places when we are together. _

2. Someone who tended to disregard symptoms of illness might get worse.

3. If a judge acknowledges the validity of certain pieces of evidence, the jury should consider that evidence.

4. The statute regarding dogs and leashes in my neighborhood is that dogs must be on leashes unless they are in their own yards or homes.

Selection Test, p. 296

Critical Reading

1. ANS: A	DIF: Average	OBJ: Literary Analysis
2. ANS: B	DIF: Easy	OBJ: Comprehension
3. ANS: C	DIF: Average	OBJ: Interpretation
4. ANS: B	DIF: Average	OBJ: Interpretation
5. ANS: A	DIF: Challenging	OBJ: Interpretation
6. ANS: D	DIF: Easy	OBJ: Interpretation
7. ANS: C	DIF: Average	OBJ: Interpretation
8. ANS: C	DIF: Challenging	OBJ: Interpretation
9. ANS: B	DIF: Average	OBJ: Interpretation
10. ANS: A	DIF: Average	OBJ: Interpretation

Essay

11. Answers will vary. Students' responses should point out that a witch hunt is an organized attempt to convict people of wrongdoing through a campaign of unfounded or unproven accusations. The plot of *The Crucible* focuses on the Salem witch trials, while that of *Good Night, and Good Luck* focuses on Senator Joseph R. McCarthy's smear campaign against alleged Communists in the United States. The authors take the position that such

witch hunts are dangerously irresponsible and jeopardize people's basic rights and freedoms. In order to oppose witch hunts at times of crisis, people need the qualities of integrity and courage, as demonstrated by John Proctor in *The Crucible* and Edward R. Murrow in *Good Night and Good Luck*.

Difficulty: *Average*

Objective: *Essay*

Writing Workshop

Job Portfolio and Résumé: Integrating Grammar Skills, p. 298

A. 1. active

2. active

3. passive

4. passive

B. 1. I teach fifth graders to use Internet search engines.

2. I write reviews of new computer games for a community newspaper.

3. I run the cash register, take orders, and clean tables, as needed, in my family's restaurant.

4. I answer the phone and take messages in the school office three periods each week.

Writing Workshop

Persuasive Essay: Developing Your Style, p. 299

A. 1. keeping you safe in an emergency

2. when you're going to the movies

3. you shouldn't have an argument either

4. searching the Internet

B. Sample Answers

1. Until recently, most people saved paper photos in shoeboxes, photo albums, or frames.

2. Today, digital cameras are changing the way people take, save, and share photos.

3. Digital cameras require no film, supply instant pictures, and allow easy sharing.

4. Digital photos are a good way for a group of people to share memories of a family celebration, a school program, or a team event in sports.

Vocabulary Workshop—Unit 5: Idioms, p. 301

A. Sample Answers

1. "put her best foot forward" = did the very best that she could

2. "hit a brick wall" = reached an impasse, were forced to stop

3. "from hand to mouth" = poor, with barely enough for survival

4. "like shooting fish in a barrel" = extremely easy, hard to miss

5. "threw a monkey wrench into" = disrupted, jammed, ruined

B. Sample Answers

1. Her election would be a breath of fresh air for the country.
2. After a rough week, they planned to blow off steam on Saturday.
3. The opponents went after each other tooth and nail.
4. You will succeed only if you put your nose to the grindstone.
5. His crime is so serious the judge wants to throw the book at him.

Benchmark Test 10, p. 303

MULTIPLE CHOICE

1. ANS: B
2. ANS: C
3. ANS: D
4. ANS: A
5. ANS: C
6. ANS: D
7. ANS: B
8. ANS: A
9. ANS: A
10. ANS: D
11. ANS: D
12. ANS: C
13. ANS: A
14. ANS: D
15. ANS: A
16. ANS: B
17. ANS: C
18. ANS: C
19. ANS: A
20. ANS: B
21. ANS: D
22. ANS: C
23. ANS: A
24. ANS: D
25. ANS: A
26. ANS: B
27. ANS: C
28. ANS: A
29. ANS: A
30. ANS: B
31. ANS: C
32. ANS: C
33. ANS: B
34. ANS: B

ESSAY

35. Essays should clearly and reasonably state a position and back it up with facts, details, reasons, and examples. All appeals should be fairly stated, and persuasive techniques should rely on facts rather than empty opinions or obvious emotions.
36. Students should choose and analyze a poem. The essay should include examples of words, images, figures of speech, emotion, and ideas that point to and develop a particular view of life that is held by the speaker of the poem.
37. Students' radio plays should use dialogue and stage directions for sound effects to develop a story. The characters' manner of speaking should be distinct. Non-verbal actions should be described in dialogue or expressed as appropriate sound effects.

Vocabulary in Context, p. 309

MULTIPLE CHOICE

1. ANS: A
2. ANS: D
3. ANS: D
4. ANS: A
5. ANS: D
6. ANS: B
7. ANS: B
8. ANS: D
9. ANS: D
10. ANS: C
11. ANS: B
12. ANS: A
13. ANS: D
14. ANS: C
15. ANS: A
16. ANS: C
17. ANS: B
18. ANS: C
19. ANS: B
20. ANS: A